MEMORIES

Anecdotes of a Modern-day Saint

VOLUME 3

MEMORIES

Anecdotes of a Modern-Day Saint

VOLUME 3

Transcriptions from video interviews
conducted and compiled
by Siddhanta das

Monsoon Media is a division of Illusion Television Productions, Inc.
CH Books is a division of Monsoon Media.

First printing 2005
Printed in the United States of America

Cover and book design by Yamaraja das

Published simultaneously in the United States of America and Canada by Monsoon Media.

ISBN 0-9773597-0-0

For more information, contact the Publisher:

MONSOON MEDIA
P. O. Box 1015, Culver City, CA 90232-3415, USA
www.monsoonmedia.org

Dedicated to

His Divine Grace
A. C. Bhaktivedanta Swami Prabhupada

I offer my respectful obeisances
unto His Divine Grace A.C. Bhaktivedanta Swami
Srila Prabhupada, who is very dear to Lord Krishna,
having taken shelter at His lotus feet.

Our respectful obeisances are unto you,
O spiritual master and servant of Sarasvati Goswami.
You are very kindly teaching the message
of Lord Chaitanya Mahaprabhu
to the western countries, which are filled
with impersonalism and voidism.

CONTENTS

FOREWORD

WITH THE PUBLICATION in video and print of *Memories: Remembrances of Srila Prabhupada,* Siddhanta has made a contribution of monumental and historical proportions to our understanding of Srila Prabhupada,the modern Gaudiya Vaisnava movement, and human religiosity in general. All too often, the contemporary followers of a great religious leader have failed to adequately record his or her life and teachings, resulting in long centuries of frequently futile debate and conflict among historians and religionists alike.

Thus Siddhanta's documentation in both video and print of the testimonies of Srila Prabhupada's disciples about their master provides an invaluable, irreplaceable, and unique treasure of information to all those who desire today, or seek in the future, an accurate, reliable, true picture of Srila Prabhupada, the Founder-Acarya of the International Society for Krishna Consciousness.

Siddhanta's patient, creative and professional work will surely be seen by future generations as one of our generation's greatest contributions to the human family. Thus it is with the soundest of reasons that I acknowledge here my deep personal gratitude to Siddhanta, congratulate him on his outstanding achievement, and urge all those seriously interested, for whatever reason, in Krishna, Srila Prabhupada, ISKCON, and spirituality itself, to stock the favorite shelves of their library with the singular treasures of the *Memories* series.

With best wishes,
Hridayananda das Goswami

PREFACE

MY FIRST CONTACT with the Hare Krishna movement came in the summer of 1969 when I saw its members chanting on the streets of Hollywood. My initial reaction to the shaven heads, saffron-colored robes, and seemingly strange activity was one of bewilderment and, to some degree, comic relief. It was not until a year later that I was able to appreciate the sound philosophy which stems from one of the world's oldest religious traditions, as explained in their *Back to Godhead* magazine. I soon realized that there was a tremendous wealth of knowledge and logic behind the activities of the International Society for Krishna Consciousness and that it was far from being a new "hippie" cult. In fact, the information contained in that first magazine concisely answered all the questions I ever had regarding life, its purpose, and more.

The next year in Dallas, Texas, it was my good fortune to actually come in personal contact with the author of that *Back to Godhead* magazine, the founder of the Hare Krishna movement, His Divine Grace A.C. Bhaktivedanta Swami Srila Prabhupada. I greeted him along with the other devotees at the airport and then followed the procession back to the temple, where Prabhupada gave a Sunday Feast lecture. What struck me most about that lecture more than anything was one question that was asked of him by a member of the audience. Srila Prabhupada had been stressing the importance of chanting the Hare Krishna *maha*-mantra: Hare Krishna Hare Krishna, Krishna Krishna Hare Hare, Hare Rama Hare Rama, Rama Rama Hare Hare, and the guest asked what Srila Prabhupada personally felt when he chanted this mantra. Without hesitation, Srila Prabhupada answered, "I feel no fear." Because his response was so immediate and filled with such conviction, I sensed that not only what he said was true, but I felt an urgency to try the same mantra-meditation process myself.

Over time, it became apparent to many who observed him firsthand that Srila Prabhupada was steadily situated in a higher state of consciousness, beyond anything that was part of our common experience. But that was not all. After a further study of the teachings in his books and observing his interactions with others, I realized that here was a person who was not materially motivated. He was not interested in mundane acquisition, exploitation, or adoration. He was also in complete control of his senses, the very foundation of all yoga practice. By his own example, he was a perfect teacher of the divine process of devotional service, or *bhakti-yoga*. And by means of his unconditional love and devotion, he was in touch with and connected to the Supreme Being. His mission appeared to be for all of our best interests by making me, and everyone else who cared to listen, spiritually happy by engaging our mind, body, and soul in serving God, Krishna. Srila Prabhupada taught that as a fish out of water cannot be happy out of its constitutional element, similarly, we as spiritual beings cannot be happy simply engaging in activities meant to satisfy our material senses.

Years later, after accepting Srila Prabhupada as a pure representative of God and having taken spiritual initiation from him in Denver, Colorado, I had the opportunity to be with him again. Previously I had been convinced on an intellectual level that Prabhupada was in direct contact with the Absolute Truth, but not until I offered flowers at his feet and looked at him as I offered my obeisances did I understand on an emotional level the depth of my guru. When Srila Prabhupada looked at me, he looked right through the external me, touching the internal me, the soul. I felt naked in front of him, feeling as though he could not only read my mind but my heart as well. It was the most humbling experience of my life.

That morning during Srila Prabhupada's daily walk, he was talking about *prasadam*, food offered to God before it is personally consumed. Prabhupada said *prasadam* is so spiritually potent that if a human being simply eats *prasadam* once, in his next life he will take birth in a family of devotees. He then stated that if an animal eats *prasadam,* in its next life it will immediately take birth in the human form of life, jumping over all other species of life that a soul would normally have to pass through before obtaining a human birth.

After this discussion, I was contemplating asking him about something that had been bothering me for some time. I had become affected by so many people I met when distributing Srila Prabhupada's books who would say that we as devotees should get jobs and not take from society by asking for donations. I said to Srila Prabhupada, "People think we are just trying to escape material life by joining this *sankirtan* movement." Srila Prabhupada turned to me, smiled, and asked, "A rich man, does he work? We are rich men. We don't work. Any rich man, he is not working. Is he escaping? He is engaging everyone in the factory, but he is not working. So is that escaping? We are rich men. We are Krishna's sons." He said the problems we have are eating, sleeping, and mating, and we can arrange for these things very easily. Prabhupada taught the philosophy of "Simple Living, High Thinking." One can till the ground anywhere and get some food. He said, "I keep some cows, and I have got land: my whole economic question is solved." He asked, "Why shall I make big, big arrangements for these things?" He continued, "You may do it, but why should you forget your real business? That is the defect, that you are so foolish that only for maintaining this body, you have forgotten your real business—self-realization." Prabhupada then said, "In the spiritual world there is no question of working. You get everything. So why not endeavor to go there?"

Prabhupada then looked around the beautiful park that we were walking in, surrounded by trees, lakes, and swans. He noted how there was no one else in the park and how we were the only ones who were taking advantage of the park and all its beauty. He said, "They worked so hard, yet they are sleeping. We are taking advantage." He then told the story of the mouse and the snake. The mouse builds a nice home for himself underground and lives comfortably. Then the snake comes and eats the mouse and lives comfortably in the home the mouse has built. He finished by telling me and the others that accompanied him on his morning walk that we can tell people that actually, "Yes, we are escaping this horrible condition of life—meat-eating, drinking, and intoxication. We are escaping these things, but not happiness."

In his kindness, Prabhupada dispelled my doubt about distributing books rather than living to fulfill the expectations of the public by having a 9-to-5 job. I had been affected by the negative feedback I received from the people I met, but Prabhupada, who was unaffected by them, reminded me that the point of life is self-realization, and our role in the *varnashram* scheme of things was to remind others about that fact.

Later on I realized that if I had this small glimpse of truth from being with Srila Prabhupada for such a brief period of time, there must be many more realizations from other devotees who had as much or more association with His Divine Grace. It was obvious that each devotee's encounter would be unique and would reveal other aspects of Srila Prabhupada's personality and boundless wisdom that were not necessarily contained in his books, which could help me and others in our daily lives. It is with that belief that I ventured out to acquire the stories contained in this book. These stories are not only informative but also entertaining in the way the devotees express themselves, seemingly going into a regression-type trance as they recall those times spent with Srila Prabhupada. From an historical standpoint, it seemed important to record these personal instructions thinking that if someone had been able to record the recollections of the disciples of Jesus Christ, that these memories would be meaningful today. So starting in 1991, the process of obtaining the oral histories of Srila Prabhupada's disciples began through videotaped sessions and subsequently transcribed to be presented in this book form.

There are no hard and fast rules in reading this collection of memories, as they are not recorded in any chronological order or by subject matter. The memories are simply a stream of consciousness by each devotee and therefore can be read in a nonlinear fashion. This book is meant to be, as Srila Prabhupada stated once about his books, readable in such a way that one can start in the middle and still derive sweetness, as biting into candy anywhere will result in the same sweet taste. As there were some 5,000 initiated disciples, this process has just begun, and we hope that there will be more volumes to come in the future.

We must thank Dinadayadri dasi for her hard work in the transcription process; Sri Kanta for the assembly of the Glossary; Visakha dasi for her tremendous work in refining the transcriptions; and Bhojadev das for his assistance with the Introduction. This publication would not be in its present form without the hard work and patience of two members of the *Back to Godhead* staff: Yamaraja das who formatted the book and also beautifully designed the cover, and Nagaraja das who contributed valuable assistance and suggestions. We want to acknowledge Ambarish das for his encouraging words and financial support in bringing Srila Prabhupada's message to the world. I also want to acknowledge my wife, Ajita devi, and daughters Kartika and Renukah for their emotional and spiritual support in this on-going project. We of course would be remiss not to give our heart-felt appreciation to all the devotees who shared their memories of Srila Prabhupada, and we pray that we have delivered their stories accurately.

Siddhanta das

INTRODUCTION

sadhu-sanga, sadhu-sanga—sarva-sastre kaya
lava-matra sadhu-sange sarva-siddhi haya

"The verdict of all revealed scriptures is that by even a moment's association with a pure devotee, one can attain all success." (Cc 22.54)

THIS BOOK OF ORAL HISTORIES is a word-for-word transcription of the video series *Memories of Srila Prabhupada,* which are interviews of those fortunate souls who had that all-important association with a pure devotee in the person of His Divine Grace A.C. Bhaktivedanta Swami Srila Prabhupada. The founder-*acharya* of the International Society for Krishna Consciousness, His Divine Grace has been well recognized by scholars, religionists, and lay persons alike, as one of the most prominent ambassadors of India's spiritual culture in modern times.

The recollections presented here are testimony to the transcendental character of Srila Prabhupada, whose purity, compassion, knowledge, humor, humility, strength, and determination seemed to be almost effortlessly exhibited on a daily basis. To get a complete picture of Krishna consciousness, it is essential to not only have the written teachings contained within Srila Prabhupada's books, but also how he acted in so many circumstances, so that we may follow in his footsteps, as he is a true *acharya*, one who teaches by example.

Many times Srila Prabhupada did mention that everything he wanted to tell us was in his books. Yet oral tradition is part of every society and culture, and we can only offer as a disclaimer that the interviews documented here have been accepted at face value, with the onus of veracity left to the integrity and memory of the interviewed party. On our part, we feel all of the accounts are genuine, as many of these events / interactions were witnessed by more than one person.

In his *Prabhupada Nectar* books, His Holiness Satsvarupa das Goswami has chronicled numerous anecdotes in which Srila Prabhupada's transcendental perspective is gloriously revealed through his interaction with his disciples and well-wishers. As mentioned in the Preface to *Prabhupada Nectar*, the glories and pastimes of the Lord's pure servants are seen to be as sweet and instructive as the Lord's own unlimited pastimes.

In the same mood of appreciation for Srila Prabhupada's transcendental glories and instructions, we hope this volume will be of some value for initiates and novices alike who are thirsting for new or revisited facets of the spiritual jewel that is Prabhupada-*sanga*. As the disciples in this book are guaranteed spiritual benefit from the direct contact they had with their spiritual master, it is our hope and prayer that anyone who hears or reads of this relationship with the pure devotee will also receive that same benediction for success in life.

TAPE 29

Jahnava dasi
Nischintya das
Tamal Krishna Goswami
Hridayananda Goswami

Jahnava: Of all Srila Prabhupada's qualities, the one that overwhelmed me was his inconceivable humility. His humility disarmed my illusion to the point that I could sincerely ask him a question. At first, when I raised my hand he ignored me. He waited until somebody else in the room raised their hand, and he answered their question. This happened three or four times and in my mind I was rephrasing my question. Then I asked my question. I closed my eyes and said, "Sri Bhaktivedanta Swami?" I said his name and for a moment I became disoriented. I couldn't even go on with the question. Srila Prabhupada very patiently waited for me. It was an intense moment because his glance and his mercy were upon me. I said, "How is it that the Absolute, which is at this point, for me, beyond human comprehension, how can it take this form of Krishna-Radha?" Prabhupada said, "It is His mercy." Then he said something astounding, a mystical thing that broke through my hippie misconceptions. Srila Prabhupada said, "The *Bhagavatam* says that if you want to understand God, His name, His quality, His paraphernalia, His form, it is not possible by your present senses. Your senses are so contaminated that it is not possible for you to understand God by speculation. Then? How it is possible? God reveals Himself to you by your service attitude. And that service attitude begins from your tongue. How? You chant Hare Krishna and taste Krishna *prasadam.* Two things.

"You cannot understand what is God, but God will reveal to you, 'Here I am.' Just as you cannot ask the sun, 'Please rise up I want to see you.' Oh, the sun is not your servant. But when the sun reveals himself to you, you see yourself, you see the sun, and you see the whole world nicely. You have to wait for that revelation."

Six months before this, after I'd fasted for days, I had climbed a mountain all night long and was sitting on the edge of a cliff meditating on *om*. My plan was that when the sun rose, I would merge with it and become one with the One. But the day was cloudy and when the sun rose I couldn't see it. The night before I had come to Krishna consciousness, I had prayed to a deity of Lord Shiva to please help me know the answer for everything, and then the next day I met Srila Prabhupada. How everything happened was wonderful.

Nischintya: I joined the Chicago temple just before Janmastami and Vyasa-puja in 1972. The devotees had just buzzed me up and we were all piling in a van to go to the big festival in New Vrindavan. You were a new devotee. You were ecstatic, Prabhupada's coming. When Srila Prabhupada pulled up in the car and got out, in every molecule of my body I could feel that I had been traveling all over the material universe—the higher planets, the middle planets, the lower planets—for millions and millions of lifetimes. It wasn't theoretical. I felt it. And there he was, the person who was my ticket out. My sojourn in the material world was over. I was in complete ecstasy. My hairs were standing on end and I was crying like anything. I can't even remember if I paid my obeisances. I was so stunned and bowled over by a great feeling of relief. All I had to do was follow Srila Prabhupada and everything would be taken care of.

Tamal Krishna Goswami: Srila Prabhupada and I were walking in Regents Park in London in October or November. It was quite cold and the walkway was icy. Prabhupada had a wool striped airline blanket wrapped around his waist on top of his *dhoti*. I'm sure Prabhupada didn't steal the blanket from the airline, but somebody had. As we were walking, Prabhupada would stop and with his stick he'd smack a puddle that had frozen. Then he'd walk on. When he came to the next one he'd smack it and it would shatter. I guess he was waiting for me to ask him why he was doing that, so I asked him and Prabhupada said, "Because this is not the natural condition of the water." He said, "Similarly, it is not our nature to be in illusion. We must break the back of the material energy." And he said, "To be in *maya* is not our natural condition." We kept walking and at one point he noticed a lake that was frozen except for the portion around the trees. He said, "The Goswamis knew this secret. That's why they lived under trees, because underneath a tree it is warm in the winter and cool in the summer." He said, "You can see that because around the tree the water is not frozen."

Hridayananda Goswami: When Prabhupada came to America from a foreign country, many times he would have a press conference and he would declare to the reporters, "These are American boys and girls. I have not imported them from India." It was important for Prabhupada to show that the people of each country were accepting Krishna consciousness. Similarly, one time a GBC representative sent Prabhupada a big glossy picture of a new castle that had been rented in Geneva, Switzerland, and outside the castle there were about thirty devotees in a group photograph. Prabhupada wrote back and said, "It is very nice, but I have one question. Are these local devotees or have you brought them from somewhere else?" Prabhupada was concerned that local people understand Krishna consciousness. For example, when Africa was just being opened and Prabhupada went to Nairobi, he gave a special lecture in which he urged the people in a third world country not to follow the false example of so-called developed countries. He requested them to pursue development according to Krishna consciousness.

So, in different countries Prabhupada presented something that was appropriate and meaningful to the people of that country. For example, in America, knowing that Americans would naturally be proud of having the most important country materially, Prabhupada simultaneously praised America and pointed out its flaw by saying, "You have so many achievements, but all these achievements are like zeroes. The fine roads, the buildings, the prosperity, they are material achievements but they're also zeroes. If you put the One of Krishna in front of the zeroes, then these achievements become real achievements." That was Srila Prabhupada's preaching for America.

Jahnava: After Srila Prabhupada's lecture, he went back to his apartment and we all got ready for bed. Thirty minutes later word got out that Srila Prabhupada had come back. We scrambled together, came into the temple room and sat there expectantly. Srila Prabhupada was grave. At first he didn't say anything. He played a tape of Vande 'ham with himself on the harmonium and said, "I have just received a telegram from India saying that His Holiness Keshava Maharaj, my *sannyasa* guru, is no more. He has entered Krishna's abode." Srila Prabhupada said that Keshava Maharaj was a Vaishnava, an ocean of mercy, and he said, "I am offering my respectful obeisances to him along with my disciples." As he talked, he remembered Keshava Maharaj, and a tear slowly came and hovered a little while. That tear was like the shining diamond of his separation from his *sannyasa* guru, it was such a beautiful tear. And at last it fell.

Srila Prabhupada had written a resolution of bereavement and asked everyone to sign it. One girl, Madhavi-lata, took it around. She wasn't going to let another guest and me sign but Srila Prabhupada said, "No, no, everyone here, they are all witnesses." Then I knew that Srila Prabhupada was accepting me as a part of something that was happening. It was a wonderful experience.

Nischintya: The *pujari* in Hawaii had put banana leaves, mounds of *tulasi* and flowers on the altar and when Srila Prabhupada began his lecture, he commented on how beautiful the Deities were and how the *pujari* had done a wonderful job. Prabhupada said, "You must decorate the Deities very nicely. By decorating the Deities, you are decorating your heart." Everyone was ecstatic. Then in a grave voice Prabhupada said, "If you neglect decorating the Deities, you will neglect decorating your heart. Then your heart will become black. And that is why so many have left." At that point, everybody got nervous.

Tamal Krishna Goswami: By 1970, active street *sankirtan*—chanting Hare Krishna on the streets and distributing *Back to Godhead* magazines—had been going on for a year or a year-and-a-half, and when we arrived in India in 1970, we applied the same formula. We chanted Hare Krishna on the streets. But some people ridiculed us and there were newspaper articles in the same mood. When Prabhupada heard this, and he heard that people were throwing coins at us, he told us to immediately stop doing daily street *kirtan* because people were taking it cheaply. Later things changed a little, but it was significant that Prabhupada was willing to completely adjust the fundamental strategy of street chanting if it didn't have the desired effect. A preacher has to be an expert judge of time, place and circumstance and know how to present Krishna consciousness in an effective way to the local population. One formula may be totally unsuitable in another place. One of Prabhupada's most outstanding qualities was how he knew which formula was suitable for which place. He wasn't a stereotyped thinker. He used to say, "Spiritual is not static, it's ecstatic." It was a pun on the words, "It's ecstatic." Prabhupada was always thinking of brilliant, unique ways to spread Krishna consciousness.

Hridayananda Goswami: When I was Prabhupada's secretary in Mayapur in February 1976, just before the annual meeting, Prabhupada told me several jokes. One was about an Indian servant of a British lord who had to leave his service, and who convinced a friend to take over for him. The friend protested, "I don't know English. How can I serve this British lord?" The servant said, "You only have to know three words: yes, no, and very good." He said, "If you know that, that's enough." So the friend took the job and one time there was something missing. The British lord confronted this servant and said, "Did you take this object?" He said, "Yes." So, "Will you give it back?" "No." So, "I'm going to call the police!" "Very good."

Jahnava: Once I was with Srila Prabhupada in his room for two hours. There were so many things that happened. Later, I went into tears and said, "Okay, I'm leaving ISKCON, I can't take it anymore. I can't become a pure devotee." Then Nara-Narayan and Jaya Gopal, said, "You're right! This is not an ascending process! You cannot do it, but Srila Prabhupada is so great that he can make a devotee even out of you!" That one glorification of Srila Prabhupada—thank you, Nara-Narayan and Jaya Gopal—has kept me all these years.

Nischintya: I arrived in Hawaii in March, around Gaur-purnima time, and Srila Prabhupada was coming in May. I immediately started to learn everything I could about Hawaii because Prabhupada would regularly ask devotees questions about the place he was visiting. I learned about Hawaii's history, the hotels, the beaches—you name it, I knew it. I thought that on a walk with Prabhupada one day I'd be able to answer any question he might ask about Hawaii.

So, on Waikiki Beach I was carefully walking in Srila Prabhupada's actual footsteps—they were leaving an impression in the sand and I was thinking, "You don't get an opportunity like this in millions of lifetimes." And I was also thinking, "Prabhupada's going to ask a question, I'm going to know the answer. I'm going to be the man." Suddenly Srila Prabhupada stopped, turned and looked right at me. He was very close. He pointed and said, "What is that?" I looked over, and I had no idea what it was. I was shaking. I felt about one inch tall. I was on the hellish planets and my entire life was ruined. And in the distance, I heard somebody say, "Prabhupada, that's a device that measures how far a person has walked." Prabhupada was still looking at me and he said, "So, they should make a device that tells how far death is, but that they cannot do." Then he turned around and kept walking. I recovered a little, my pride had been completely eliminated, and I was ecstatic thinking of Prabhupada's mystic power. He knew I'd learned all about Hawaii. I wanted him to ask a question, and I wanted to impress him. I understood that you don't show off to your spiritual master.

Besides his mystic power, I was also impressed with the philosophy and teachings Prabhupada gave, and his sense of humor. I had been chastised but it was humorous. And at the same time, he instructed all the devotees that you can't measure how far away death is.

Tamal Krishna Goswami: Prabhupada was speaking to some Indian people in his room in Vrindavan. He was upset because some of his god-brothers criticized his *sannyasi* disciples because they couldn't read Sanskrit. Prabhupada said, "Where does it say that one must be able to read Sanskrit to go back to Godhead? Where does it say that?" He was adamant. He said, "My disciples may be disqualified in so many ways, but they have one qualification; whatever I tell them to do, they do. They have full faith in what I say." I appreciated that point because in terms of etiquette, we certainly were not qualified. In fact, Prabhupada said, "I know they often make mistakes in terms of etiquette. But whatever I tell them to do, they do." Our good fortune was that we were following the Lord's pure devotee and despite all disqualifications, that one qualification surpassed every good qualification anyone else might have.

Jahnava: One night Srila Prabhupada called for us to come to his quarters at 26 Second Avenue. The new temple was a block or two down the street at 61 Second Avenue. We all knew the history and the privilege of seeing Srila Prabhupada at 26 Second Avenue, and Rukmini, Saradiya and I were on our way, but at the last minute, Saradiya said she couldn't come. She had to tend to the laundry or something. When Rukmini and I walked through Prabhupada's door, Srila Prabhupada said, "Where is Saradiya?" Then we understood that Srila Prabhupada was concerned for each of his daughters, where they were, how they were being engaged, how they were feeling. He wanted to know why she had stayed back.

Nischintya: Prabhupada said that the person dressing the Lord and the person cleaning the Lord's temple are equal in the eyes of the Lord. He said one shouldn't think that because he's dressing the Deity or because he's a manager, he's more important than the person who is washing the pots or cleaning the temple. Prabhupada said, "The dresser and the cleanser, they are the same. We are all serving Krishna, and Krishna sees every devotee's service equally."

Hridayananda Goswami: Prabhupada had an individual relationship with each person, and what was appropriate for one person may not be for another, depending on the special relationship each had with Prabhupada. Once we were walking on Venice Beach, and Prabhupada was trying to bring an intelligent young Indian boy to the Krishna consciousness movement. The boy came from a good Hindu background, and as Prabhupada was speaking, the boy occasionally quoted some Sanskrit from the *Bhagavad-gita* and Prabhupada praised and encouraged him, "Oh, that's very nice. You know that verse, very good." I thought, "This boy is getting so much mercy from Prabhupada by quoting *Gita* verses. I know *Gita* verses. I want to get some of this mercy myself." Of course, this boy was an outsider that Prabhupada was trying to cultivate. I was supposed to be Prabhupada's trusted son. But, as we were driving back, Prabhupada said something, and I said, "Oh, yes, Prabhupada, that reminds me of the *Bhagavad-gita* verse . . .", and I quoted the Sanskrit. Prabhupada turned around, gave me a look and said, "There are so many verses." That's the last time I ever tried that one.

Jahnava: Srila Prabhupada said, "I had no reason to leave Vrindavan to come here." We were wondering why Srila Prabhupada said that. It was almost as though something was going on that had displeased him. It was a heavy thing for him to say. Then he said, "And you have no reason to come here to see me, except Krishna." And he smiled beautifully. He went around the room looking at all of our eyes and said, "So, I want that each of you open a center. This Krishna consciousness must go all over the world." Rukmini asked, "Does that mean women too?" And Srila Prabhupada said, "Yes." Then he mentioned the person that I was named after, Jahnava Mata, and he said that she had been a great preacher in Krishna consciousness.

Tamal Krishna Goswami: By letter, I described a *pandal*, a large outdoor public program that we were arranging for ten days, and I asked Prabhupada, "Are you willing to come? If you are, we will advertise." Prabhupada was in Australia on his way back to India, and he sent me a telegram, "You preach if mass, I preach if class." That's all it said.

Nischintya: In Hawaii, Prabhupada told Sudama Maharaj that the devotees could maintain their health by going swimming every day in the ocean, and Sudama Maharaj thought that the devotees wouldn't just take a dip and come out, but they'd go swimming all day. Sudama Maharaj said, "Prabhupada, no, no, no!" So Prabhupada said, "Okay, but at least once a week they must go swimming." So, it was very pleasant and joyful in Hawaii. But Prabhupada regularly reminded us that even though we were in a heavenly place, we were still in the material world, and that we needed to pay attention to our service and not get distracted by heavenly pleasures.

Jahnava: Gargamuni told Srila Prabhupada, "We have just begun the Spiritual Sky incense business." Srila Prabhupada said to twelve-year-old Virabhadra, "So Virabhadra, you should work for Gargamuni. And Gargamuni, you should pay Virabhadra." We were all astounded—here's a little boy who's going to earn money. And the little boy was beaming, "I'm going to have money!" Even if it was five dollars, it was more than any *brahmacari* had at that time. So Srila Prabhupada reiterated it, saying, "So you'll work for Gargamuni. And Gargamuni, you'll pay something to Virabhadra." Then Srila Prabhupada said it a third time and he added, "And Virabhadra, you give the money to me." The look on Virabhadra's face made us all laugh.

I wanted to be a part of that kind of atmosphere, where everything's light, joyful, and intimate. I asked Srila Prabhupada, "Swamiji, when I chant Hare Krishna, can I pray for all living entities?" Srila Prabhupada said, "You? Do you know all living entities? No, you pray to Krishna, and let Krishna take care of all living entities."

Tamal Krishna Goswami: Prabhupada first gave Gayatri mantra in Boston, and then in September of 1968 he came to San Francisco and gave some of us Gayatri mantra. He taught us how to chant and gave out a sheet with the Gayatri mantras. Jayananda found it difficult to pronounce the mantras, so he decided to ask Srila Prabhupada about the pronunciation and he took me along with him. We sat in front of Srila Prabhupada and Prabhupada asked him to pronounce the mantras. As Jayananda tried, Prabhupada leaned back and roared with laughter. Prabhupada shook his head and said, "It's hopeless. But it doesn't matter. Because you are so sincere, Krishna will accept your chanting."

Nischintya: Paramahamsa Swami let me put the garland on Prabhupada and knowing that no one was assigned to do it, I made sure that I regularly garlanded Prabhupada. Nobody said anything to stop me.

Then a devotee told me an ecstatic story about how he ground sandalwood paste and added camphor to make it cooling and saffron to make it a nice orange color, and how he dabbed it on Srila Prabhupada's forehead. So I proudly thought, "I'm going to put the sandalwood paste on Prabhupada too." I diligently ground it up, made it the right consistency so it wouldn't drip and put in the right amount of camphor, but when I put it on Prabhupada, Prabhupada got a cross look on his face. I understood that it was supposed to be put on his temples more than his forehead. I was shaking, but somehow or other I got it on Prabhupada's temples. I paid my obeisances, and I was thinking again, "My pride has been squished, I am on the hellish planets," but as I got up I was in ecstasy because I had been chastised by my spiritual master. That was mercy too. Praise was mercy, and chastisement was mercy also. My pride had been curbed and I was in ecstasy that I had been chastised, although ordinarily I never become ecstatic if I'm chastised. So, it was instructive, and it was sweet.

Jahnava: Srila Prabhupada called Baradraj and me to his room to talk about painting for the *Krsna* book. Baradraj was already speaking to Srila Prabhupada when I came in. The minute that I came in, Srila Prabhupada turned to me and said, "So, at the end of his life, what was Einstein's conclusion?" Now, I'm not a scholar—I don't know anything—but the amazing thing is that I knew the answer to that question. I said, "That there is a higher consciousness. That the universal order implies a higher being." Srila Prabhupada said, "Yes," and then he continued speaking to Baradraj. Similarly, Srila Prabhupada asked Brahmatirtha the meaning of one verse out of the 700 verses of the *Bhagavad-gita*. And that verse was the only one that Brahmatirtha had memorized and he was able to quote it to Srila Prabhupada.

So, Srila Prabhupada began telling *Krsna* book stories we had never heard before. He said, "Lord Krishna, He was such a naughty boy. A naughty boy is an intelligent boy. I was naughty when I was a little boy, and so was Lord Krishna and so was Lord Chaitanya." He said, "Lord Krishna used to pass urine on the clean floor, and then He'd go *'ptoo'* on it," and Srila Prabhupada went like that. Of course, in the book it says, "spit" but Srila Prabhupada went *"ptoo."* Then Srila Prabhupada began telling us about the Universal Form, the universe contained within the mouth of Lord Krishna when Mother Yasoda asked Him to open His mouth. Srila Prabhupada described how, "There were oceans and seas, and there was air and fire and earth and water and the ten directions, north, south, east and west, mountains and . . ." for about five minutes. As he was speaking in this wonderfully charismatic way, Baradraj and I, unbeknownst to us, were gradually leaning forward, getting involved in the story. Then at one point, Srila Prabhupada said to Baradraj, "Now you paint that!" It was such a shock. It was a double shock because we were coming closer and closer and we weren't expecting Srila Prabhupada to suddenly say that, and it was also a shock to be asked to paint it. Baradraj almost lost his balance, and I fell backwards too. Months later, Baradraj was in Montreal struggling with how to paint this picture. He wrote to Srila Prabhupada and said, "Srila Prabhupada, in all due honesty, I cannot figure out how to put all those things in Krishna's mouth." Srila Prabhupada sent back a little sketch that showed a stick figure of Mother Yasoda standing up, a little stick figure of child Krishna sitting down with a balloon coming out of His mouth, and Prabhupada said, "That's how you do it." Then Baradraj made the beautiful painting that's in the original *Krsna* book of the universe in Krishna's mouth. That painting now hangs in the foyer of the Montreal temple.

Tamal Krishna Goswami: Krishna gives intelligence to His surrendered devotee, so by the grace of Krishna, Prabhupada knew everything because he knew Krishna. He knew, for example, when it was appropriate to quote a particular verse. Prabhupada's son, Vrindavan-candra, told me that during his *grihastha ashram,* Prabhupada studied the *Bhagavatam* for four hours every day and worshiped Radha-Krishna Deities. In the morning he would awaken the Deity, then offer *arati,* bathe the Deity, personally cook for the Deity and sew the Deity's clothing. He really took care of those Deities.

What we know of Srila Prabhupada, we know from after he came to America; we don't know everything that happened before that, and we certainly don't know how Krishna and he are related. Prabhupada was able to hear from Krishna everything he needed to know. Prabhupada's learning is a combination of both his studying and also Krishna's revelation to him.

Nischintya: Either because I was the *sankirtan* leader or because I had distributed more books than anybody else, I was going to get to bathe Srila Prabhupada's feet. Prabhupada's feet were swollen, and I could feel that Prabhupada had gone through so much. It wasn't like he was touring around the world enjoying. Prabhupada was giving his life so that we would have life in Krishna consciousness. When I was bathing his feet, I was in ecstasy and somebody behind me said, "Hurry up, hurry up!" Then I got nervous and hurried. After that, anytime anybody said anything, I was oblivious to whatever they said. I thought, "You will get this close to Prabhupada only once, twice, three times in your lifetime. Just get this mercy and forget what anybody says."

Once I had made the sandalwood paste and was ready to put it on Prabhupada when Tamal Krishna Goswami took it from me and put it on Prabhupada. I thought, "Who does he think he is? I made that paste." The next day I had a big *chadar* on and I hid the sandalwood paste and flower underneath it. Tamal looked all over for the sandalwood paste, and finally he gave up, offered Prabhupada a flower and paid his obeisances. Foom! My *chadar* went off and I put the sandalwood paste on Prabhupada. Prabhupada smiled. I think he knew what I did. We became transcendental rascals to get Prabhupada's mercy.

I was attached to that *chadar* because while we were in India at

Haridas Thakur's *bhajan-kutir*, Gurudas said, "Prabhupada needs something to sit on," and that *chadar* came off, "Here." Later Gurudas gave it back to me and I thought, "Prabhupada sat on this *chadar*." On that day, Prabhupada gave the lecture in an Indian language, and we had no clue as to what he was saying. But I sat at his feet, looked at his feet and at him talking, and thought, "I'm getting purified even though I don't understand anything he is saying." That was also very sweet. Usually in India I didn't get that close to Prabhupada. But that time, I was able to get close and do some personal service. In Hawaii, it was more intimate, you could get close, and you could pull tricks like hiding the sandalwood paste from Tamal Krishna Goswami to put it on Prabhupada yourself.

Hridayananda Goswami: On Vyasa-puja day in 1972 in New Vrindavan, we had a ceremony in a special pavilion, and the devotees had cooked a great feast and a very large cake for Srila Prabhupada. Somehow, word got around that the feast and the cake were *mahaprasadam*, that Prabhupada had tasted it, and there was a devotional feeding frenzy. The devotees were mad after *mahaprasadam* on Prabhupada's Vyasa-puja day.

After the Vyasa-puja ceremony, Prabhupada's car didn't show up to take him back to his house, which was a couple of miles through the hills. Somehow or other Krishna inspired me, like Rudolph the red-nosed reindeer, that this was my chance. I was a new *sannyasi* and I had a little yellow Volkswagen bug. I raced to my car, turned the ignition, came right in front of the stage where Prabhupada was, ran out, opened the door and said, "Srila Prabhupada, you can go now." And I drove Prabhupada back in my little car. One of the big leaders was absolutely infuriated by this, but Prabhupada got in the car and off we went. I can't imagine a more sublime experience on Prabhupada's Vyasa-puja day than driving him alone through the forest and the hills. As we pulled in to Prabhupada's house, that leader had somehow gotten there and he was cursing me in a way that Prabhupada couldn't see. I thought,

"Well, I got the mercy and Prabhupada didn't have to wait." We went into Prabhupada's house and Prabhupada said, "Where is the lunch?" Then he learned that the devotees mistakenly thought it was already *mahaprasadam*. On Prabhupada's birthday, his Vyasa-puja day, he had no lunch *prasadam*. Prabhupada's servant immediately said, "I'll go cook," and he began to cook. But Prabhupada was totally undisturbed. Not to say that he would never become angry. He was as soft as a rose and as hard as a thunderbolt like Lord Chaitanya Mahaprabhu Himself. But on that particular occasion, he was peaceful and happy. We talked for a while until his lunch was ready.

Nischintya: I was the *sankirtan* leader and I was supposed to keep the book room in order, but I'm a sloppy person. I knew where the books were, but there were empty boxes and other things around. It was messy. Then one day we heard that Prabhupada was inspecting the temple. I thought, "Oh, no!" and I ran to the book room. I stacked books up, busted boxes up, threw stuff in the trash, and then swept. I had just finished sweeping when Prabhupada came to the door and looked at me. I didn't pay my obeisances. I was frozen. Prabhupada asked, "What is it?" And Srutakirti said, "This is the book room, Srila Prabhupada." Then Prabhupada looked at me, and this time there was eye contact. I understood that Prabhupada knew that I had just cleaned that book room and that it was regularly messy, and that his book room should not be a mess. After that I resolved that the book room would always be clean and organized so that if Prabhupada was going on a walk, I'd be all right, I could walk with him and not have to run to the book room.

Jahnava: Bhagavan, Kirtanananda, Brahmananda and many other devotees came to the Boston airport in 1969. Brahmananda instructed us, "Previously, you jumped over chairs at the airport, but this is not good. We have to have some kind of protocol and etiquette in public. This is public relations." So, everybody was behaving nicely. Then after a long wait, we saw Srila Prabhupada's bead bag above some kind of Customs wall. Then Kirtanananda lost it. He was holding his danda, flying, and jumping, and all of us were flying and jumping. When Srila Prabhupada came out he was beaming. We all bowed down. There was a sea of us bowing down. Meanwhile, newspaper reporters with their cameras were looking at this sea of Americans in 1969 bowing down to this Indian *sannyasi*. Srila Prabhupada noted it and said, "The spiritual master is to be worshipped as God." You could've heard a pin drop in that part of the airport. "But, if the spiritual master thinks that he is God, then he is dog." Then he had them.

Tamal Krishna Goswami: One time Prabhupada gave me a *lugdoo*, a *lugloo* as Prabhupada called them. He asked me what my impression of it was, and when I tasted it I couldn't believe the taste. I said, "It's not of this world." Prabhupada said, "You're right. This is the same recipe that Mother Yasoda cooks for Krishna when He goes out to tend the cows, and Krishna likes them so much that He keeps extra in his pockets so that He can eat them throughout the day." When Prabhupada was speaking, it was clear to me that it *was* Mother Yasoda's recipe and Prabhupada knew it very well.

Nischintya: There's only one question you should ask the spiritual master, and that's "How may I serve you?" I thought I already knew how I was supposed to serve Prabhupada—by distributing his books, taking care of the temple, cleaning, cooking. But when I saw Ganesh worship on Gurukripa Swami's party in Chicago, I wanted to do Ganesh worship too. I told the *sankirtan* devotees in Hawaii, "They're collecting so much money there by doing Ganesh *puja*." The *sankirtan* devotees got into it but when the temple president found out, he told us to stop. We didn't listen. Then the GBC got involved. We said, "Oh, who's the GBC? He doesn't know anything. The *Swami* is doing it."

So, the first question I asked Srila Prabhupada was if I could do Ganesh *puja*. I didn't say anything about money. I said that *The Nectar of Devotion* mentions Ganesh worship. All the *sankirtan* devotees signed the letter and Prabhupada wrote back, "My dear sons, please accept my blessings." When we were sitting around reading it, we thought, "That's it. Our lives are perfect. Prabhupada has given us his blessings." Then Prabhupada wrote, "Krishna says just to worship Him, and you're proposing to worship a demigod. Why is this? Krishna says you're less intelligent if you do this." We wouldn't have taken that from anyone, but we were in ecstasy when Prabhupada told us that. Prabhupada went on to say, "But still if you are attached to worshipping Ganesh for huge amounts of laxmi" . . . and then penciled in—"to serve Krishna—then you please send me one hundred thousand dollars a month and not a single farthing less." That was a very nice instruction. We stopped our Ganesh *puja* and went on *sankirtan*. Nobody else could have told us that, but when Prabhupada told us we were in ecstasy.

Jahnava: Pariksit said, "Srila Prabhupada, should we attend classes?" At that time Baradraj was taking the devotee-artists to the Los Angeles County Art Museum where we were studying art and he was giving us sketching classes and so on. Srila Prabhupada said, "Yes." Pariksit said, "But I mean . . ." Srila Prabhupada said, "Yes, morning and evening classes." Pariksit interrupted him and said, "But I mean . . ." Srila Prabhupada interrupted him and said, "Morning and evening classes." Then Prabhupada said, "By your attending these classes, you will please the Lord within your heart and you will receive instructions from the Lord within."

Tamal Krishna Goswami: It was wonderful to watch Prabhupada record *bhajans*. He would play the harmonium, and I'd gently play the *kartals* and try to keep the rhythm because there was no *mridanga*. Then Prabhupada would put on headphones and, while listening to the recording with the harmonium and *kartals*, he'd play the *mridanga*. On a lot of the taped *bhajans*, Prabhupada is playing both the harmonium and the *mridanga*. Prabhupada was an expert musician. When the recording engineer heard the chanting that Prabhupada did on the "Happening" album, the first Hare Krishna album, he said that Prabhupada had perfect pitch. He was very impressed with Prabhupada's voice.

Nischintya: Prabhupada had a unique ability to chastise people or point out their folly or their lowness. The way he said it, you didn't take any offense, you felt, "Oh, okay." Once Prabhupada was walking in Hawaii, and he said that because the people there ate so many pigs they looked like pigs. Some Hawaiians heard Prabhupada say that and they wanted to talk to him about it. Prabhupada explained to them how they're a soul, how they're not their body but that there are different kinds of bodies and the bodies look different, and as he talked to them they became happy. They realized Prabhupada wasn't offensive. They were enveloped in Prabhupada's love and his spiritual instructions. We were thinking, "Only Prabhupada can do things like that. If we said anything like that, there would be a riot."

Hridayananda Goswami: A few months after I took *sannyasa*, I was staying underneath Prabhupada's quarters in Los Angeles in a small room without windows that was reserved for *sannyasis*. At that time, I was feeling discouraged and morose because I thought, "I'm not a very good devotee. How will I ever become a good devotee? How will I ever come to the proper standard of serving Prabhupada?"

Every afternoon Prabhupada would come down the stairs and walk along the little walkway in the back of the building to go to his garden. The day that I was feeling morose, Prabhupada, without saying a word, came by my room, opened my door, and came in. I immediately offered obeisances. Prabhupada looked around and then continued on his way. I understood that he was calling me, so I immediately got up and ran behind him without saying a word. We went to the garden, his servant went to do something else, and I sat alone with Prabhupada. In a very sweet, gentle way, Prabhupada began to preach to me. What was unique about this preaching was that he never said Krishna or God, but he kept saying, "the Father." He said, "What does a father want? He simply wants to see that you're happy, but you also have to serve the father." He preached for about fifteen minutes using the word "the Father." He lifted my spirits. It was very compassionate. It was very kind preaching. It completely entered my heart and lifted me out of the doldrums, and I became again very enthusiastic. Of course, Prabhupada was also the father.

I was practicing the principle of not trying to enjoy the guru, so I would stay in my room. And every afternoon for the next few days, on his way to the garden, Prabhupada would walk into my room, look around, then turn on his heel and walk out. And every day I would run behind him.

Nischintya: Both times he was in Hawaii, Prabhupada talked about surfers. He said, "You say surfer, I say sufferer." Every devotee who was a surfer told me Prabhupada looked right at him when he said it. I laughed at that because there were so many surfer devotees. But they all say that Prabhupada looked right at them when he said, "You say surfer, and I say sufferer."

Tamal Krishna Goswami: Once, just after we'd arrived in Calcutta, Prabhupada laughed at me. At the time I was a *grihastha*, and Srila Prabhupada's entourage were all *sannyasis* –Kirtanananda Swami, Madhudvisa Swami, Devananda Swami, Kartikeya Swami and Tamal Krishna das Adhikari. Prabhupada had just formed the GBC and I grabbed India—the zone where Prabhupada would be spending most of his time. I didn't know what the GBC was all about, but it was the right move because for eight months a year for the next four years, Prabhupada was in India. But I had to pay for it and I started paying as soon as we arrived in Calcutta.

Now, in America in those days, ISKCON was so small that it didn't matter how we kept our financial accounts. And anyway we were tax exempt. But when you keep accounts in India, you literally have to keep track of every *paisa*. So, Prabhupada had instituted the Life Membership Program and money started coming in. Someone had to keep the accounts, keep tabs on who the members were, issue receipts and print up membership books. Every time I tried to get someone to help, they said, "I'm a *sannyasi*. I play the harmonium." Nobody was supposed to do anything because they were *sannyasis*. I practically went mad. After about two weeks I went to Prabhupada and broke down. I said, "I can't take it anymore." He said, "What's wrong?" I said, "Nobody's helping me do anything. I have to do everything." To my surprise, Prabhupada started laughing at me. I was crying and he was laughing. He said, "Arjuna found himself in the same position. This is very good." I was hoping for sympathy and assistance but instead Prabhupada started laughing at me and telling me it was very good. So I stopped crying, and tried to figure out why it was very good. Prabhupada said, "We should pray for this situation. We should pray to be so constantly engaged in Krishna's service that *maya* cannot find any means to enter. This is very fortunate."

Once, Prabhupada told a story about an Indian train. Local trains in India are packed. In any third world country, you learn what the word "packed" means. So, you have a nice seat on a train and a skinny guy comes to sit next to you. You try to ignore him but you know he wants to sit down. There is no room, but he smiles at you, then plops down and wiggles around between you and the next person. You make some room. Suddenly he calls his little kid and gets his kid in, and you're moving towards the edge of the seat. Then he brings another kid and he gets three kids next to you. Next his fat wife comes and then you give up your seat. It all started because you had a little sympathy and let this guy sit down. In this way, Prabhupada said, if you allow maya even an inch to enter, she knows how to take over everything.

Jahnava: In Los Angeles in 1975, Srila Prabhupada made a tour of the community. We had just whitewashed the walls of the Art Department to make this dumpy-looking place look nice for Srila Prabhupada. There was a picture by Jayarama prominently displayed, but Srila Prabhupada sat down in the packed room and made no comment. Ramesvara said, "Srila Prabhupada, Jayarama did this beautiful painting of Radha and Krishna!" Srila Prabhupada made a facial expression of indifference. I contemplated that expression a lot. Srila Prabhupada knew us so well. It wasn't very long after that that Jayarama left the movement and started painting for the Scientologists. The symptoms of his leaving us were already in full swing.

Then Baradraj said, "Srila Prabhupada, when the artists and I go to the Mayapur festival, we would also like to go on a tour of India. We will take sketches in all the holy places to make our paintings more authentic." Srila Prabhupada said, "We are not archeologists," and he explained that as we advance in devotional service our inspiration comes from Paramatma. As I paint today, Srila Prabhupada's statement that we are not archeologists is one of my mantras.

Nischintya: The devotees used to have a farm on the big island. Prabhupada asked them, "What grows here easily?" They said, "Prabhupada, we can grow cauliflower and broccoli" and they started telling him all the things they could grow. Prabhupada said, "No, no. What grows without any work?" The devotees said, "Well, corn and guavas, Prabhupada." Prabhupada said, "Very good. We will have guava juice *prasadam* for breakfast, corn *chapatis* for lunch, business finished. The rest of the time chant Hare Krishna." I don't think the devotees thought they could do that.

Another time Prabhupada told the devotees that *dabs* were very healthy and that you could actually live on two *dabs* a day. I don't think anybody tried to do that either. But it was fun because Prabhupada made comments that were instructive and applied to being right there. When the geckos made their clicking sound

Prabhupada said, "When you hear this, you know the truth is being spoken." In Hawaii we got all kinds of goodies like that, little things that we thought were special to Hawaii and the devotees there.

Tamal Krishna Goswami: At his Vyasa-puja in London in 1977, I was enumerating a few of Prabhupada's outstanding accomplishments and at one point he said, "Yes, whatever I am doing now, I learned from my father when I was a child. Everything except one thing—book publishing—that I learned from my Guru Maharaj."

It was an interesting Vyasa-puja because Prabhupada was ill, so the Vyasa-puja glorification was my talk. Prabhupada had me speak. Somehow, on that day Krishna empowered me to speak for forty-five minutes about Prabhupada. Three times Prabhupada interrupted my lecture to insert that, "My Guru Maharaj ordered me to publish and distribute books." Three times. Everything else about the lecture was fine, but somehow he wanted three times more emphasis on book distribution. Very interesting.

Nischintya: Prabhupada finished the Fifth and Seventh Cantos of the *Srimad Bhagavatam* in Hawaii, and he started the Sixth and Eighth Cantos there. At the end of the Seventh Canto, he wrote, "Completed on the night of Vaisakhi Sukla Ekadasi, the tenth of May, 1976 in the temple of the Pancatattva, New Navadvipa (Honolulu) by the mercy of *sri-krsna-caitanya prabhu nityananda sri-advaita gadadhara srivasadi-gaura-bhakta-vrnda*. Thus we may happily chant *Hare Krsna, Hare Krsna, Krsna Krsna, Hare Hare/ Hare Rama, Hare Rama, Rama Rama, Hare Hare*."

In the beginning of the Eighth Canto, he writes about how he has faithfully tried to publish these books on the order of his spiritual master, Srila Bhaktisiddhanta Saraswati Thakur, and he asked all the devotees to help him continue to publish more and more volumes of *Srimad-Bhagavatam*. That was written in Hawaii, and we proudly thought, "Prabhupada translates here more than anywhere else in the world. Prabhupada loves coming to Hawaii."

Prabhupada would make us feel very special in Hawaii. I think he really did like Hawaii and the devotees reciprocated with that mood. We would do whatever we could to make it special for Prabhupada.

Jahnava: In Dallas in 1972, the Deities, Sri Sri Radha-Kalachandji, arrived the same day as Srila Prabhupada, and Srila Prabhupada wanted to install Them in two days. The Deities were covered with something sticky and little pieces of burlap and cloth were stuck to painted areas like Their eyes and so on. The head *pujari*, Ichhamati, was concerned because she knew that when we dressed the Deities in the future we would have some difficulty. So, we tried every solvent that we could think of. Nothing would get this sticky substance off. When we had tried everything, Ichhamati left me in charge of taking this stuff off. I'd already suggested paint remover, and we had thought about it a little bit. Finally, she left and I began to use paint remover. My great offense was that I was confident that I could take all the paint off the Deities and repaint them in two days time. I removed all the paint from the Deities and when the head *pujari* came back, she was in a state of shock. I said, "It's all right," but I understood I had done something in an unauthorized way. I did not know at that time that these Deities were already installed. I didn't know that they had been worshipped and that they were 500-year-old Deities, although this does not minimize my offense. Anyway, I was painting the Deities all night in Srila Prabhupada's quarters. And the next morning the Deity was totally wet. I was using a Japanese dryer but I could see that something was wrong, it was not going according to plan.

So, Satsvarupa Maharaj informed Srila Prabhupada of the situation on a morning walk. Srila Prabhupada stopped and said, "Pack my bags immediately. I am leaving this temple. You can do whatever you like with the Deities, but just don't consult me." Naturally, I went into a suicidal state. I was emotionally crying and devastated by my offense of having acted in an unauthorized way. Then the GBC, the head *pujari*, the temple president, everyone gathered for a meeting in Srila Prabhupada's room. Srila Prabhupada said, "Who has done this?" Everyone said, "Jahnava, Jahnava did it." Srila Prabhupada turned his glance to me and said, "Who told you to do this?" At that moment, I was choked with emotion. There was no question of speech coming out of my mouth. And at the same time, I remembered the *Srimad-Bhagavatam* where the bull does not blame anyone for his condition. I could have pointed my finger a few places but I didn't. I felt that I should not do this. And from within, I felt that Srila Prabhupada appreciated me not blaming someone else. Srila Prabhupada said, "Why did you do this?" And again, I was choked with emotion. I had been crying hysterically for two hours. Srila Prabhupada began to be disgusted with me, and he started turning his glance and his mercy away from me. I thought, "Krishna's kicking and His kissing is the same. I want it. I want whatever Srila Prabhupada has to give me. It's mine. This is my quota." So I choked it off. When Srila Prabhupada asked, "Why have you done this?" I said, "Nonsense, Srila Prabhupada." Srila Prabhupada said, "Suicidal nonsense."

Then he asked me, "So, what is to be done about it?" Now he'd changed his tone of voice a little bit and he seemed pleased. I felt a little let off the hook. I said, "I just called Baradraj in L.A. and explained that the paint is not drying, and he suggested I use . . ." Srila Prabhupada said, "Baradraj? Baradraj? I am your spiritual master, and I am sitting right in front of you! Why do you not ask me?"

The sound reverberations of that form of Srila Prabhupada as a servant of Lord Nrsinghadev are going out into the universe, still reverberating to this day. It took me about two or three years to calm down. It was a wonderful, cleansing process. Srila Prabhupada was disgusted with me, and he turned his glance away from me and said, "What is to be done about this?" Then Ichhamati said the same thing I did, but with humility. She said, "Srila Prabhupada, if we use an enamel paint, it can dry in six to eight hours. Would it be all right with you if we use that kind of paint?" Srila Prabhupada said, "Do it immediately."

Nischintya: Once Prabhupada was talking about the regulative principles, because the devotees in Hawaii were notorious for falling down. They used to call it a *sannyasi* graveyard. Prabhupada said that Hawaii was perfect for spiritual life and he said, "also for material life." Prabhupada would push home this point on a regular basis. Devotees were telling him that some people were chanting but not following the regulative principles. He said, "They may have to chant for 700 lifetimes before they can follow the regulative principles." I thought, "I don't want to do that. I better get serious."

As much as we were in ecstasy serving Srila Prabhupada, we were still very immature young people and there were always disagreements, fights, and craziness. When he got to a temple, Prabhupada would ask, "Is everything okay?" or "Is everything all right?" and when Prabhupada asked that, immediately our craziness dissipated. Even if we'd just been in a big fight or the temple commander was on our case, anything we'd been through, it was completely gone, and "Yeah, everything's all right, everything's okay." Prabhupada actually meant it. He was concerned and he wanted to know that we were all right. Prabhupada really cared about us. He loved us and he appreciated what we were doing for him. You could feel his love. And when he said, "Is everything all right?"—it was all all right.

Hridayananda Goswami: Late 1972, when ISKCON Press was in Brooklyn, Prabhupada came there. After he'd been there a few days, the artists showed Prabhupada their new paintings for Prabhupada to approve or make suggestions or request corrections or whatever. Prabhupada looked at all the paintings, and suddenly he felt something very deep within himself and he asked for us to play his own *bhajan* tape of "Jiv Jago." We brought in the tape player, he sat listening, and he was, in Vedic language, in *samadhi*. He closed his eyes and he was with Krishna in the spiritual world. It was so powerful that there was silence in the room. No one could say anything, no one could move and he didn't open his eyes until the tape was over. Then Jadurani said that she had one more painting to show Prabhupada, and she brought the painting in. Prabhupada was still in this very deep internal mood. He looked at the painting and said, "It is very good." Then he said, "Actually all of you are very good." At this point, he became very humble and was speaking very seriously. In other words, at that point, due to his love for Krishna, he could no longer pretend to be the *madhyama-adhikari* who was preaching. He was exhibiting his real position as a *paramahamsa.* He looked at all of us and very seriously and humbly said, "Actually all of you are very good. And in your association, even I am good. Otherwise I am very bad." Everyone was shocked and no one could say anything or hardly breathe. Then gradually one by one we offered our obeisances and left the room.

Tamal Krishna Goswami: Prabhupada wrote me in a letter, "Throughout my life I had so many opportunities for sense gratification, but Krishna always saved me. I never knew what is meat-eating, gambling, intoxication or illicit sex." He wrote, "There was never a moment when I was ever forgetful of Krishna." He actually wrote that in a letter to me. He said, "There was never a moment when I was ever forgetful of Krishna."

TAPE 30

P. L. Sethi
Daivishakti dasi
Hari das

P. L. Sethi: The temple work was to start. This is sea area. Every building has piling. Piling goes thirty feet to thirty-five feet below the ground. So I said to Guruji, "We must put piling in this land to build the temple." Guruji suddenly said, "No piling is required in our land." After that we called the soil specialist who tested the soil and they also reported that piling is required. Then we called another engineer who also said piling is required. He also discussed with Guruji. But Guruji said, "No. Piling is not required in our land." So Guruji said, "You can test the soil by using a boring machine." So I called one boring *wala*. When the boring went five feet, the boring tool could not be pulled out. So then Guruji said, "You dig the land." And we dug the land, and could see the sand and the stone melted up with very hard stone. Then I called that soil-testing engineer who said, "You can build an eight-story building here, no fear, no dangers."

When I took *darshan* of Radha-Rasabehari, Madhudvisa told me, "Just now Prabhupadaji came from America, so you can take *darshan* from him." So he took me to Prabhupada, and Prabhupada questioned me, "What are you working?" I told him, "Yes, Prabhu, I am getting up early in the morning, taking one cup of tea, go to the bathroom and then go to my business." And Prabhupadaji suddenly said, "What is the difference between you and a pig? He is also eating. He has his children just like you. But you are not chanting the *maha*-mantra or Krishna's name." So I said, "Prabhupada, I have not got such a relation to the *sat-sanga*, that I don't have a habit of this." Then Prabhupadaji suddenly called Madhudvisa and asked me, "Where you are staying?" I said that I am staying at Gorygon. So Prabhupadaji ordered to Madhudvisa that, "Every Sunday after *mangal arati*, all the devotees should go to the Sethi's house and do the *nagar sankirtan* there. He must get association with you and he will be a devotee." So for one year, all the devotees came to my house every Sunday and we would do *nagar sankirtan* there about ten miles or fifteen miles, and then back to my house. And then they would take a feast there. So by this way, I attached with ISKCON.

Daivishakti: I would always make sure, because Pishima trained me like this, to stay very quiet and distant from Srila Prabhupada so I wouldn't disturb him. Because so much of the time we would be in direct contact with Srila Prabhupada in his house, doing the cleaning, doing the cooking, bringing him so many things, making his medicines, so I learned to never disturb Prabhupada in any way. But I saw that a lot of the other devotees were able to act in a very open manner with Prabhupada and were always asking him questions. It looked like they were joking with him. So I started to think, "Well, these devotees, they're so much more advanced than me because they get to have a closer relationship with Prabhupada. And I'm such a fool never asking Prabhupada any questions, just doing my service and being very careful not to talk to Prabhupada. So maybe I should start being more friendly with Srila Prabhupada." So one evening I decided to try it out and I brought Prabhupada in some sweets, and he immediately saw my change of personality and stopped me right then and there. I knew that I had done the wrong thing, and Prabhupada also let me know immediately that I shouldn't change my mode of service. So the next evening, Prabhupada was sitting in his room with Bhagatji and another god-sister and Prabhupada started telling them that he liked my service because I was always silent and hardworking. So Bhagatji immediately came out after talking to Prabhupada and he repeated to me what Prabhupada had said, not knowing the plan of action I had tried the night before. So Prabhupada was letting me know through Bhagatji that he appreciated more the fact that I was silent and hardworking in my service instead of trying to become too artificially affectionate with him.

Hari: It was 1975. He asked me, "Now you have learned so many things, you should go around the world and preach." I said, "Yes, I'll go." So I tried to get my passport. On the passport application the father's name was required and I didn't know who my father was, so I didn't bother. So after a month Prabhupada asked, "You are still here? You should go and preach." I said, "I'm not getting my passport." He said, "Why you are not getting your passport?" I said, "They require my father's name." He said, "Bring that form." So Amrita was there for secretarial typing and she had the form. He told her, "Write my name A.C. Bhaktivedanta Swami Prabhupada as the father". He signed the application, sealed it and said, "Go get your passport." So I went to Mr. Sethi who arranged the passport in two days. On the third day I was on the flight to travel the world. Then I think Brahmananda or Bhagavan asked him, "Prabhupada, why did you put your name as his father?" He said, "Because I put my guru's name as my father in my passport." So I accepted. Ever since, I have all my documents with Prabhupada's name for the father, in my driver's license, passport, property, everything.

P. L. Sethi: I was sick sitting in this chair and Guruji said, "So many Gita *slokas* and why are you weeping? That is nothing. That is only that the soul is changing clothes. Just like the body changes, the soul is changing the body. That is nothing. Why you are weeping for that? But you cannot die by this disease because you have to work for the temple so much." So I said, "The doctor says that if I pull out the tubes from my neck and chest, I will die." And Guruji said, "Pull out the tubes and throw them out the window. I will show you, you will not die." So I pulled out the tubes and threw them out the window, and Guruji sat here about two hours and then said, "You have not died. You are alive. So you cannot die by this disease. The thing is you remember you have promised to Krishna some time ago. Remember that." So after some minutes I got that memory that when I came here to Bombay from Pakistan, I had no house to live in. I had no money to work. So I promised to Krishna that, "Krishna, if You kindly give me one house and one *lakh rupee*, then I will always chant Your name." And I said to Guruji, "Yes, I remember this promise I made to Krishna." And Guruji said, "He has given so many *lakhs* of *rupees*, so many houses, but you have not chanted to Krishna. So Krishna slapped me. "Now you go and build the building. You cannot go to the toilet? No, you take this *mala* and do the *japa* and you will be all right."

Daivishakti: Again, in 1974, maybe in August, after Janmastami, Prabhupada was again recovering from his sickness. And we used to cook for Prabhupada, and then after cooking for Prabhupada we would make something for his servants and secretaries to eat. There were three of them that we were cooking for at that time. I think it was Brahmananda Swami, Bhagavan, Srutakirti and maybe a few others. So we would bring that *prasadam* for them around to the front, and then a servant would come and drop off their plates and we'd have to wash them all out here in the garden because there was no water in the house then. We'd have to draw all the water from the front well. So I was still cleaning the kitchen up and the plates of the servants had been left outside of the kitchen. The devotees hadn't finished their *prasadam* that day, so there were some remnants on their plates. Prabhupada came into the kitchen to go to his bathroom and he saw these plates, and he called me and he said, "What is this?" And I saw the plates. Normally I would have taken them and washed them right away. I said, "Oh, that's a mistake, Prabhupada, I was supposed to clean them." And he looked quite displeased. So immediately Prabhupada walked through his house to the front room where his secretaries lived, and seeing that Prabhupada was displeased I picked up the plates and came the back way to show Brahmananda what Prabhupada had seen and how he wasn't happy about it. So simultaneously Prabhupada came from one door and I came from another door with the plates in my hands, and Prabhupada called me in and had me show them the plates with the *prasadam* on it. And he explained to them that no matter who you are, no matter whether you're GBC or anyone, once you touch the plate, whatever is on that plate you have to finish it because it's *prasadam*. You shouldn't leave any *prasadam* on the plate. So Brahmananda jokingly said, "But Prabhupada, I had burped. I thought that after you burped you couldn't finish it." Prabhupada then said, "You can take off first. If they've given you too much, before you start, you take off and that doesn't have to be completed. But whatever you have on your plate when you start, you have to finish that *prasadam*." So he was telling the topmost members of our society, the GBCs and personal secretaries, they had to finish their *prasadam*. Just like a father he was instructing them.

P. L. Sethi: One day Prabhupadaji was slightly sick and Tamal Krishna was standing at the gate so that no one could enter to Prabhupadaji's quarters. My wife and I went there to take *darshan* of Guruji. So I said to Tamal Krishna, "I want to take *darshan* of Guruji." Tamal Krishna said that nobody was allowed to take *darshan*. Prabhupadaji heard my voice inside and Prabhupadaji called, "Tamal Krishna, Sethi is there?" Tamal Krishna said, "Yes." "Yes, allow him to come here." When I went inside, Guruji said to me, "Mr. Sethi, go see the entire flat and how the devotees have furnished my quarters." So I went and saw the bed and carpets, and the kitchen and bathroom were all very well furnished. I came back and said, "Guruji, this is very well furnished." And Guruji suddenly said, “You should come here and stay. I am a *sannyasi*. I don’t want this decoration. I will go to another room.” How kind of Guruji. Such an elevated guru was being so kind to me. I am nothing, but he loved me so much. So you see the mercy of Guruji.

Hari: One day Prabhupada was alone in his room. Usually he was quiet but this day he was laughing and talking to himself. I went by his room and I said, “Prabhupada, what you are laughing at?” Prabhupada said, “The reason I was laughing was that I just remembered my past life.” Then I said, “Prabhupada, what was your past life?” Then he said, “I was a medical person and I had not committed any sin. I had a guru. One day I remember it was raining and I was serving my guru. I was fanning my Guru Maharaj and he could see in the rain that there was one snake and he made me go kill that snake.” Then he said, “Now I remember why my Guru Maharaj made me kill that snake; so I had to take birth again in this life to save so many snakes like you all.”

P. L. Sethi: Prabhupada was so merciful. I have seen that he is loving to everybody. He had so much love for the devotees. One Christian boy came to the temple, this Hare Krishna Land, and there was a tree of papita. He took some papita from the tree and as he was leaving, a devotee caught him and he brought that boy to Guruji and said, “This boy is stealing our papita.” And Guruji said, “What will he do with the papita?” The devotee said, “He will eat it.” Then Guruji said to the devotee, “If you will take that papita, what you will do?” He said, “I will also eat that papita.” “Then what is the difference? He will eat papita and you will eat papita.” From that day, this Christian boy’s parents became devotees. Prabhupada saw no difference between the devotee and the Christian. He is equal as a human being. “He will eat the papita and you will eat the papita, then what is the difference?” So Prabhupadaji said to that boy, “You want more? If you want more, take more.” So every time Guruji was always giving, saying that make more *prasadam*, more and more *prasadam*. If they will eat *prasadam*, they will chant Hare Krishna. Their mind will be purified if they take Krishna *prasadam* and they will become a devotee. So the main thing that Guruji wanted to teach everyone is that we are not different. Whether your skin is white, whether your skin is black, whether you are Hindu, whether you are Muslim, whether you are Christian, no difference. One thing in common in all of us is that we are the soul, we are the sons of Krishna and we want to return to Krishna. Simply chant Hare Krishna. No knowledge is required, no need for someone to be a professor, a spiritual master, a scientist, an engineer. Only simply you chant the *maha-*mantra and your situation will increase and you will be with Krishna.

Mrs. Nair came to my home with her lawyer and Guruji was sitting upstairs. Then Mrs. Nair told the lawyer, "You please sit here. First I will take time with Guruji to discuss the case we have put upon ISKCON and ISKCON put upon me. Then I will call you." And Mrs. Nair went upstairs and she sat about five minutes there. Five minutes, only five minutes. She was so impressed with Prabhupada that she came back and told the solicitor, "I surrender to Guruji. Please you can go. I will pay your fees. I will pay your fees, but you go. You can go." In the same day, we came to live in this house and Guruji said, "A *sannyasi* cannot live in a *grihastha* household, so I am going." So Guruji went to Chataya yath where Mahatma Gandhi stayed and was built by Sumati Morarji. Around 12:00 p.m., two or three devotees came to say that "Mrs. Nair went to Guruji and he is calling to you." So when I went there, Mrs. Nair was sitting outside the Chataya yath and she was weeping. So I went and she said, "You please ask Guruji to forgive me for the whole trouble that I have given to the ISKCON devotees." Then I went to Guruji, and Guruji said, "If the man who forgets his own path in the morning but he comes in the evening to his house properly, he has not forgotten the path because he came at last to his place." I went to Mrs. Nair and said, "Guruji forgives you." And Mrs. Nair was with the registrar who registered the documents. Guruji got up from his *asana,* and

Mrs. Nair put all the documents to this Hare Krishna Land at the feet of Guruji and said, "Please forgive me". Guruji said, "You will not get any trouble from today." Otherwise, she was always seeing in her dreams her husband's soul and could not sleep the whole night. But after that she became all right.

Daivishakti: When Prabhupada's house was first built and we first started using his kitchen, there were no windows or doors, it was just some pieces of wood covering up the holes. At night the animals used to come in, so we'd have to have everything very carefully covered. Even then they would get to the things. But one night Prabhupada had sent down some *kachoris* that he wanted saved. He wanted them kept for 24 hours because he wanted to try them the next night to see if they were still good. They were training up how the restaurant cooks should prepare the things. He wanted to see if these *kachoris* would last for selling purposes. So Navayogendra brought down the *kachoris* and I was busy making Prabhupada's night meal and he said, "Prabhupada wants you to save these and feed them to him tomorrow night." I said, "Just put them there on the shelf," and I immediately forgot about them. So the next night it was 8:30 and just at 8:30 I remembered, "Oh, the *kachoris*, they were on the shelf." So I went to get the *kachoris* and, sure enough, the only thing that was there were a few crumbs. Right then Navayogendra comes down and said, "Prabhupada wants to try the *kachoris*." I said, "Prabhu, the cat must have eaten them, they're not here." So he got scared, and he ran up and he told Prabhupada. He came running back down with his face all red. He said, "Prabhupada says that whoever says the cat has eaten them, they have eaten them." So I knew I hadn't eaten the *kachoris*, but Prabhupada was saying that I had eaten the *kachoris*. So I was in a real fix because my spiritual master, Srila Prabhupada was accusing me of something that I knew I hadn't done. So it was a big test in my spiritual life. I knew I hadn't done it and Prabhupada said I was doing it, so I realized with all the years of *sankirtan*, you had to just continue and not give up in your service even if there's some setback. Prabhupada said I took those *kachoris*. Well, I just as well might have eaten them because he wants to eat them and they're not here and it's my fault. So I realized, "Now, what is the real issue here? That Prabhupada wants some *kachoris*." So I had twenty minutes, it was twenty minutes until 9:00, and I remembered that in the restaurant as I was running by, they were grinding up some *urad dahl*. So I quickly ran over to the restaurant and I got their *urad dahl* and I whipped up some *kachoris*. And, at exactly 9:00, I brought up those *kachoris* to Prabhupada with his milk. And he ate those *kachoris*. He ate five in a row and he said, "These *kachoris* are better than the other ones, and I want you to cook them for me every night." So that was a big test of my Krishna consciousness, that even when there are setbacks, especially in the personal service of Prabhupada when you're so closely connected with him, you have to just continue in that service and there's always some way that Prabhupada gives you to rectify even if there's a mistake that you've committed.

P. L. Sethi: One day I was building one story on the old building for the devotees because there was nowhere for them to live. They were staying in Chataya yath. One day I was working very hard and cement and sand were on my clothes. I thought, "I will not go to Guruji in this position." But my mind said, "Why you are not going to Guruji? Go to Guruji. What is the problem? We're working near and there must be some cement and sand that will be on when I'm working like this." And I went to Guruji and all these sannyasis like Giriraj Swami and Sridhar Swami were sitting there. And Guruji said, "Mr. Sethi, you are building houses for my devotees and your house is being built in Krishnaloka." And I said, "I am a sinful man, Prabhupada. How I can go to Krishnaloka?" Then Guruji said, "This I will see. This is not your duty. I will see that you will go to Krishnaloka." You see how Krishna loves the devotee who serves the devotees. Guruji showed mercy upon that person who served the devotees that he allows him to enter Krishnaloka. What a big thing.

What mercy of Guruji to say that, "The person who serves my devotees, he will go to Krishnaloka." What a big thing, what a big philosophy.

TAPE 31

Nanda Kishor das
Guru Kripa das
Krishna Kanti das
Pavamana das
Vaikunthanatha das
Pariksit das
Madhavananda das
Havi das

Nanda Kishor: I first saw Prabhupada in the summer of '66 on a television show called *The Alan Burke Show*. Alan Burke was a thin, frustrated-old-poet type, who smoked and wore a goatee. He was an interviewer who, after about a fifteen-minute interview, would start insulting his subject, "You are a stupid this and that . . ." He seemed like somebody who never made it but his show was interesting. My mother and I would watch it together. One week Burke interviewed a *yogini* who talked about yoga and who appeared on the show along with some devotees who chanted the *maha*-mantra. The next week the same devotees came with Srila Prabhupada.

On this show, Alan Burke talked about cosmic consciousness and Prabhupada talked about yoga. I had no idea that yoga had anything to do with religion or the laws of God. Most of what Prabhupada said I could not understand. I was a spaced-out hippie and Prabhupada's accent was thick, but there were two things I remember. One was that Alan Burke did not insult Prabhupada like he did the usual guests, but he did have a criticism. He said, "Well, if this movement is spiritual, why do you have a car? How is that spiritual?" Prabhupada said, "If a car is used in Krishna consciousness, then it is a spiritual car." I said, "Wow! A spiritual car! That's incredible!" The second thing that struck me was the mantra. Prabhupada said, "*Hare Krishna Hare Krishna, Krishna Krishna Hare Hare, Hare Rama Hare Rama, Rama Rama Hare Hare,*" and I said, "Wow, that's far out!" It was the reaction of a hippy. It was more than a year later that I finally came to the movement.

Guru Kripa: I first met Srila Prabhupada in 1970 when he attended the Ratha-yatra in San Francisco. At least a hundred people greeted him in the airport and I was Bhakta Greg in the crowd. I was a new devotee, only three or four months in the temple.

When Srila Prabhupada came through the doors, we all bowed. It was like seeing the sun come from behind a cloud. Vishnujana prabhu was playing the drum and singing and when Prabhupada walked by him, Visnujana bowed down and Prabhupada patted him on the back. Then Prabhupada walked into the crowd and came directly to me. He put his arms around me and hugged me. I'd never met him but we knew each other. This wasn't our first meeting. Afterwards, people asked me, "Do you know him? Do you know him?" I said, "No, I don't remember him."

Krishna Kanti: I was working at a television station in Seattle when I started chanting Hare Krishna by listening to the Happening record album Srila Prabhupada had made in New York in 1966. Then I met Upendra and started visiting the Seattle temple because the devotees there were chanting Hare Krishna just like I was. Upendra told me, "You have to establish your relationship with your guru. You should write to him, and if you give him a donation for his Book Fund, that will please him." So I started writing short letters to Srila Prabhupada and sending him $50 or $100.

Then in the summer of 1969, I went to San Francisco for Rathayatra, and just before the festival I saw Srila Prabhupada for the first time. He was lecturing at the storefront temple in the Haight Ashbury district. At that time, Ratha-yatra was a one-chariot festival and I saw Prabhupada sitting gloriously on the *ratha* cart. It was a long festival that ended in the Family Dog Auditorium.

After that I had a little more time, so I drove Revatinandana and a few other devotees to Los Angeles. The second day I was in Los Angeles, the devotees said, "Since you're new, you can go on a walk with Srila Prabhupada." Almost everybody had lots of association with Srila Prabhupada. I'd had a shaved head for about seven days, I could barely tie my *dhoti*, and I was now going on a walk with Srila Prabhupada. I was about to meet him face to face. I was petrified. In all my looking and studying and trying to find spiritual life, I'd read about many encounters, Zen master encounters, and that's what I thought was about to happen. I was going to get grilled on the *Bhagavad-gita*, I was going to be asked questions and I was going to make a fool of myself.

The devotees took me to the house near the La Cienega Temple where Prabhupada was staying, and I waited for Srila Prabhupada, mortified. When Prabhupada came in and sat down, his servant said, "This is Bhakta Karl. He's the devotee from Seattle who has been giving donations for your Book Fund." Prabhupada looked at me, smiled, and thanked me. I was so put at ease. I felt, "Oh, I am in front of a real spiritual master. He is humble, he has no false ego, he's so full of love for Krishna that he's thanking a mere mortal person like me for giving a few dollars to his Book Fund." I knew at that moment that I was in the presence of a truly pure devotee. He had dispelled my fears and projected ideas.

Pavamana: My first contact with Hare Krishna was the song in the 1960's musical, *Hair*. In the last scene they dance around less than fully clothed and chant Hare Krishna. I used to listen to that album every day. Later, in 1985, I met a man in New York who said that he was present when Prabhupada was preaching to the playwright of *Hair* and Prabhupada told him to include the Hare Krishna mantra in his play. So that last song was there because Srila Prabhupada requested it.

Nanda Kishor: A lady said, "If there is a God, why are people starving?" Srila Prabhupada said, "Sometimes if a patient is sick, the doctor will prescribe that he does not eat." That was the answer. That's called eloquence.

Another time, during the question and answer period at 26 Second Avenue, a boy in the back of the room said to Prabhupada, "Somebody told me that people who chant Hare Krishna are crazy." Prabhupada said, "Not 'somebody.' Who somebody?" The boy said, "My doctor." Prabhupada said, "Oh, a medical man?" with the tone of saying, "garbage man." Prabhupada said, "What does a medical man know about spiritual science? But if he wants to understand, let him read our essay, 'Who is Crazy?'" Then Prabhupada ended the class with, "We are not dry philosophers. Now distribute *prasadam*." There were *gulabjamons* there. It was perfect drama.

Guru Kripa: I wrote to Prabhupada, "Personally, I don't think I can ever follow all these rules." At the time I was following them, but I was being sincere. "And, therefore, I have to make one request. I have read that there are three types of people who reach perfection: the *nitya-siddha*, the *kripa-siddha* and the *sadhana-siddha.* I cannot follow all these rules, so how I will ever become perfect? I request you to make me a *kripa-siddha*." Prabhupada said, "All right, Guru Kripa, I will give you." He can do as he likes, he is independent.

Vaikunthanatha: In 1972, when Prabhupada gave a series of lectures on *The Nectar of Devotion* for one month in Vrindavan, a thought was plaguing me. When I first joined, I'd been taught that the *parampara* system is like a chain, and if you're not initiated, if you're not linked up to this chain, then you can't go back to Godhead. I thought, "We're distributing so many books, but if the people who read them are not initiated, then they can't go back to Godhead." So, one day I followed Prabhupada from Rupa Goswami's *samadhi,* where he lectured, and just before Prabhupada stepped onto his courtyard, I said, "We're distributing so many books but if people aren't initiated, then they can't go back to Godhead." Prabhupada turned, looked at me right in the eyes and said, "Just by reading my books they are initiated." I thought, "That is an incredible example of compassion."

Pavamana: The first time I saw Srila Prabhupada in person, he was speaking in the compound of the Radha-Damodara temple in Vrindavan. On one side was Rupa Goswami's *samadhi*, and on the other, Rupa Goswami's *bhajan kutir* . As Prabhupada described it, this place is the center of the universe. Seeing Srila Prabhupada there, it struck me how listening to Srila Prabhupada's lectures and reading Prabhupada's books is the same as associating personally with Prabhupada. There isn't any difference. To be in Prabhupada's presence, all you need to do is open his book and it's as good as Srila Prabhupada sitting there. There is no difference.

Pariksit: In 1972, we had established ISKCON Press at Tiffany Place, near the Brooklyn temple. It was a little dangerous there—a couple of devotees had gotten beaten up—so we also established night guards. Once, when I was stuck on night guard duty over at Tiffany Place, Prabhupada had just arrived and everybody else was in the temple with him. It wasn't until seven or eight o'clock in the morning, when it was time for me to receive my *gayatri* mantra initiation, that I came to the temple. I went into Prabhupada's room. Prabhupada was about to give me my *gayatri* mantra when he looked at my hands and said, "Your fingernails should be short and clean, like mine." I had been neglecting my fingernails for a while. They were long and because I was involved in construction, they weren't clean. Ever since Prabhupada said that, however, I've kept my fingernails short and clean.

Madhavananda: In Calcutta in 1972, Srila Prabhupada was on a morning walk with a lot of *brahmacharis*. Some of the *brahmacharis* were complaining because women also lived at the Calcutta temple, at 3 Albert Road. The *brahmacharis* said, "Srila Prabhupada, sometimes the women don't put their saris over their heads," and "Why can't the women get a place outside, separate from the *brahmacharis*? Their presence is not conducive to our *brahmachari* life." Prabhupada was silent for the entire walk. Sometimes he stopped walking and then started again, but he didn't respond to the *brahmacharis*. We came up the stairs of 3 Albert Road, someone opened the door, and there was Yamuna and Palika and Shyamasundar's wife, Malati, and Kaushalya and Madri and other women who had stayed behind to wash the floor, cook for the Deities, bathe the Deities, dress the Deities, prepare Srila Prabhupada's *vyasasana* and the cushions for the guests. The women immediately offered their obeisances and said, "*Jaya,* Srila Prabhupada!" Prabhupada turned to all of us and said, "But, if you associate with *these* women, you will go back to Godhead."

Last night I told Srutakirti that story, and he brought my attention to page 250 in *My Glorious Master* by Bhurijan prabhu called, "Women, Widows and Success." It reads: "Srutakirti then rubbed mustard oil onto Prabhupada's back. I moved to face Prabhupada's front and was enjoying the sweet atmosphere that surrounded him. With his eyes closed, Prabhupada spoke. 'My god-brothers criticize me that I have allowed women to live in our temples. This is not done in India. Only *brahmacharis* can live. But I have become successful because I have made this adjustment.' Prabhupada opened his eyes and continued, 'although they criticize me, their Gaudiya Maths are empty. The only time they have people coming is during *parikram* in Mayapur for Gaur-purnima. And who is coming to *parikram*? Widows—women in white. But because I have made this adjustment, I was successful.' Srutakirti then moved to massage Srila Prabhupada's side and asked, 'Prabhupada how can we tell the difference between making an adjustment and changing a principle?' Prabhupada's eyes closed and Srutakirti continued to massage. After a few moments, Srila Prabhupada opened his eyes and said, 'That takes a little intelligence.'"

Guru Kripa: Prabhupada never talked to me. He only asked me questions I could not answer, like, "Why does the grass grow in the cracks on the sidewalk?" Or, when we were walking along the beach in Madras, and he saw a statue across the street of a man on a horse, he said, "Who is that man on the horse?" How would I know? His questions made me feel like a fool. *Murkha*, fool, one should always be a *murkha* in front of the guru. As soon as you think, "Now I've become friendly with the guru, now I know a little bit more," then you are finished. People sometimes think, "Now I will go somewhere else and I will get some higher instruction." No. Prabhupada will instruct you according to your surrender, according to what you are ready for. But if you think for a second that the guru doesn't know something, then you are finished. Srila Prabhupada strongly ingrained that idea in me. He made me feel like a fool.

When the devotees asked Prabhupada questions for the discussions on dialectic spiritualism, I snuck into the room every afternoon and listened. I would hear the champion of the world spar with these past "great" thinkers and watch him defeat them and present Krishna. It was great entertainment and it was life. Then I began to think, "How I can get in the inner circle with His Divine Grace?" And I understood, "I must do something to get his attention." I was going daily for preaching, but I had to do something more. Srila Prabhupada wasn't close with somebody because he liked the way they looked, dressed, or put on their *tilak*. It was the service attitude that endeared one to Srila Prabhupada. So, Yasodanandan and I went to

Bangalore in South India. We preached and learned Sanskrit mantras. We did many things. Then Prabhupada began to write to us.

Nanda Kishor: Prabhupada always dealt with everyone according to *desa-patra-kala*, the place, circumstance and time. He was a perfect artist in preaching because he dealt with each person individually. Different people could ask the same question, and Prabhupada would answer in a completely different way. For example, at Harvard, on May 6, in '69, the night before Prabhupada married Rukmini and Baradraj, Saradiya and Vaikunthanatha, and Jahnava and me, a Harvard scholar asked, "What does 'Krishna' mean?" and Prabhupada said, "Krishna is a proper noun. Don't you know that a proper noun cannot be translated? My name is Bhaktivedanta Swami. Can you give a translation for that?" He answered this question in what I call three waves, and the third wave was, "If you want to understand, we have so many books. You can read them."

Havi: In 1975, Srila Prabhupada came from Mexico to Caracas, Venezuela. In those years we had buses and we were distributing lots of books. When Prabhupada arrived, another devotee and I were asked to wash Prabhupada's feet. Our hearts were joyful. I jumped so high I almost touched the ceiling. Srila Prabhupada came, sat down, and a devotee told me, "Havi, go and wash his feet." But I was not trained in how to do it. I was in front of Srila Prabhupada along with the honey, milk, water, yogurt—but what was I supposed to do? I concluded that I should offer it from thick to thin.

Prabhupada had his socks on, and I waited for him to spread his legs, which he did. I took his socks off and I touched his feet, which were warm. I understood that the principle behind washing a saint's feet was that in traveling from one town to another, walking long distances, the host refreshes the holy man by bathing his feet with nice ingredients. So, although I was very nervous, I started to pour honey on Prabhupada's right foot while the devotees chanted *sri-*

guru-carana-padma. Then I poured the yogurt, then the milk, and with my fingers I started to massage his feet and toes. Behind me a devotee said, "Havi, what are you doing?" and Nitai kicked my behind to tell me that I was doing something wrong. I stopped and slowly lifted my head towards Prabhupada. Prabhupada smiled at me and nodded his head as if to say, "Don't listen to them. Go on." I went on with enthusiasm.

Tamoha was supposed to wash Prabhupada's other foot, so I called him. But Prabhupada said, "No, no, no. You." Then I did something childish. I showed off. I lifted Prabhupada's feet and he had to brace himself by putting his hands behind him. Anyway, after I washed both his feet, I had a big bowl with yogurt, honey, milk, and ghee. I thought, "Let me distribute it," and I started to sprinkle it on the devotees while they were chanting Nitai-Gaura *haribol.* After everybody was wet, what was I supposed to do with the rest? There was still a lot left and I wasn't going to throw it away. So I drank it.

Guru Kripa: Prabhupada instructed to me to collect money because I'd shown that I had an ability to do that. I thought I would collect some money and go on my way, but Srila Prabhupada told me, "You collect because the other leaders have local projects and do not give me money."

Prabhupada said there were two types of devotees, the second class ones who say, "I want to serve Krishna this way." To them Srila Prabhupada said, "Yes, do that." And the first-class devotees who say, "I am a fool, I don't know anything. Tell me." Prabhupada could instruct that type of devotee. Prabhupada knew how to do everything. He is the representative of the Supersoul. Once he said, "If I had eighteen good men, I could take over the world."

Our teaching is, *yasya deve para bhaktir yatha deve tatha gurau.* If one has unflinching faith in God and in *guru*, then the *guru* will reveal Krishna to that person. You must only be sincere and make the effort. So, Srila Prabhupada ordered me, "You collect money."

I argued with him daily in Vrindavan. Nicely, I objected, "Srila Prabhupada, the temple presidents don't want me in America. They shun me. The *brahmacharis* want to go with me because we're fired up, and it's natural to travel and see the world instead of sitting in one place. But the temple presidents don't want *sannyasis* coming." Prabhupada said, "You did well before. You should go again." I said, "Srila Prabhupada, you know we are collecting money eighteen hours a day." Srila Prabhupada said, "Eighteen hours a day? Our process is twenty-four hours." There was no getting around Prabhupada's order. Finally Prabhupada quoted the Sixth Chapter, Text One of *Bhagavad-gita, "Anasritah karma-phalam karyam karma karoti yah,"* that a *sannyasa* is one who works as he's obligated and is not attached to the result.

But a *Vaishnava sannyasi* is different. A *Vaishnava* generally takes *sannyasa* out of *bhava*, or love for Krishna. He has nothing to renounce. We already know the material world is all an illusion. It is all the Lord's play, so what we are renouncing? We are renouncing our illusion. What is *sannyasa*? Out of ecstasy it is taken for service. But if one is not mature, as we were not, it may last six months or a year. Yet, to expand this movement Srila Prabhupada gave many people *sannyasa* so we could do something for some time. That was for our good and the good of other conditioned souls. So, Prabhupada instructed us to get money to construct these temples. These temples should be there—that was Prabhupada's order—and by his grace they are still there. Therefore, the collection was divine and it was successful. It was not done with false ego or trying to get on the BBT charts as a great collector. It was done for the satisfaction of His Divine Grace. We did not have our names read in the temple every morning. Going out seven days a week was hard work, and all the devotees that assisted are eternally benefited.

Srila Prabhupada did not make a personality cult—he taught the science of how to see God. As we understand more of the science of *bhakti* we will see God, just as Srila Prabhupada did. It is not that he will see Krishna and we will not see Him. Sometimes people would ask Prabhupada, "Are you seeing Krishna?" And Srila Prabhupada would answer, "So if I am, what good is it doing you? Are you seeing Him? If I am eating and you are not eating, what good is it if you watch me eat?" So we have to eat, and he is offering us that. And if we do not get it, we are the big loser. We are faithless. If our faith increases we will see Krishna immediately. That is what Prabhupada is offering us. Gradually, we will see only the lotus feet of the *guru*, and nothing else. In this age there are only three things of any value: the holy name of the Lord, service to the *Vaishnavas* and the remnants of the *Vaishnava's* food. Srila Prabhupada has taught us and personally showed us how to be spiritually intelligent—how to get Krishna. Many people see many different things, but we see he has given that science to us.

Krishna Kanti: About 1974, Agnidev, some devotee musicians and I recorded the *Gopinatha* album. When Prabhupada came to L.A., Karandhar invited me to Prabhupada's room to play the record for him. I was excited. Prabhupada listened to the record and when it was over he said, "Yes, that was very nice." And he said, "What do you plan to do with this record?" Our idea was to try to use it on *sankirtan*, to distribute the record instead of incense.

Prabhupada heard this idea and thought for a minute. He closed his eyes, bobbed his head, and then said, "Well, that would be okay as long as it doesn't decrease the distribution of my books." Prabhupada squeezed two of his fingers tightly together and said, "As long as it doesn't decrease my book distribution by this much." I was sitting to the side and I understood what he meant right away but Karandhar said, "What did you say Prabhupada?" And Prabhupada repeated, "As long as it doesn't decrease my book distribution by even this much" as he again squeezed two of his fingers tightly together. We said, "Oh, yes, oh sure, Srila Prabhupada." After we left the room, Karandhar and I never dared bring up that subject again. Prabhupada had seen into the future—later we had trouble because the sale of record albums destroyed the purity of *sankirtan*.

Nanda Kishor: In the airport a skinny, stupid newsman interviewed Prabhupada. He said, "Swamiji, what difficulties do you encounter in your travels from place to place?" Prabhupada said, "I have no difficulties. *You* have difficulties." The newsman said, "Oh, yeah." Then, after Prabhupada had walked through the airport and stepped onto an escalator, the newsman asked him, "If your movement is so important, why do you have so few followers?" Prabhupada said, "Because we have four rules: no illicit sex, no intoxication, no meat eating, no gambling." The man said, "Oh, I see."

Vaikunthanatha: I was fortunate to be in the room with Prabhupada when the Archbishop of the Anglican Church came to see him. Prabhupada melted this archbishop and transformed that room into Vaikuntha. The next day the headline in the paper was, "We have nothing to fear from the Hare Krishnas."

Nanda Kishor: Janos Damburgs was an intellectual studying for his Ph.D. at McGill University, but from the time that he was thirteen he was looking for someone who could tell him about God. Once, at Dr. Mishra's *ashram* in upstate New York, Damburgs asked Dr. Mishra about God. Dr. Mishra said, "Don't worry, just meditate." Prabhupada was at the asrama then, and the next day at breakfast in the big breakfast hall when all the uptown yoga *ashram* visitors were sitting eating, Prabhupada went to Damburgs and said, "Would you like to go for a walk?" Damburgs was taken aback but said, "Yes." As they walked on the big campus, Prabhupada said, "This grass is so nice. Only Krishna could make a carpet like this." As they walked further, Prabhupada said, "You see that pond over there?" Damburgs said, "Yes." Prabhupada said, "There are millions and millions of living entities in that pond that we cannot perceive, but Krishna knows every one of them." A little later, Damburg looked at the *tilak* on Prabhupada's forehead and said, "What does that mark on your forehead stand for?" Prabhupada said, "It stands for victory." That was the beginning of Damburg's relationship with Prabhupada.

Later he became initiated as Janardana.

Guru Kripa: Once I deposited $108,000 dollars in the ISKCON India account (that was the way I gave Prabhupada money) and in Vrindavan I showed Prabhupada the receipt. At that time Prabhupada was walking on the construction site of the Krishna-Balaram Temple. I went to take a bath, came back and went up to him while he was still walking around. He immediately yelled at me, "Take that *dhoti* off!" It was the wrong color. "Never let me see you in that again!" he said.

On many occasions he would chastise me. One of the hardest things in management was to take the hit for other people. Once in Hawaii, Srila Prabhupada ordered us to hold a 24-hour *kirtan*. I organized it. We didn't have much of a crew but we started. Prabhupada's room was just above the temple room and that evening a devotee with a terrible voice was singing. He sounded like the cat out in the alley. Srila Prabhupada said, "Who is that?" I said, "It's the 24-hour *kirtan*." "What 24-hour *kirtan*?" I said, "Srila Prabhupada, you ordered a 24-hour *kirtan*." He said, "I didn't order any 24-hour *kirtan*." So we stopped it. He made it seem as if he didn't know anything about it. He was training us.

If you were in a big position, you would get big credit, and if you made a blunder, you would get severely chastised. Once in Japan, when we were having trouble with the police, I took the Deities out of the country. Srila Prabhupada said that he would close Mayapur before he closed Japan, and he practically didn't talk to me for three months. I rectified my mistake. Chastisement was his mercy.

Sometimes he would chastise for no reason. Once in Hawaii, he sent his servant at 12:30 a.m. to wake me. The servant said, "Srila Prabhupada wants to talk with you." So I went there, sat down, and Prabhupada excused the servant. We were sitting alone. I said, "Yes, Srila Prabhupada?" I thought I was doing well. I was sleeping five hours a day, getting up, serving, and organizing. Srila Prabhupada said, "What are you doing?" I said, "Taking rest." "Why?" "Because

I'm tired." "Why are you tired?" He said, "I am sitting here translating books. I have had only one-and-a-half hours sleep, that is enough. Why you cannot sit with me and translate?" I said, "Srila Prabhupada, you're a *parmahamsa*, I am a beginner." "Why you are not a *paramahamsa*?" I became frustrated and angry. What did I do? Usually you need a reason to get yelled at. Then I said, "I'm just a nonsense." He said, "Why are you a nonsense?" And I was trapped. My face turned flushed and blue, and I saw that now I've become angry with Prabhupada. What could I do? People thought it was easy to be around His Divine Grace. I laugh at that. I scoff. That time in Hawaii he got me in a corner and there was nothing left to do, so I started to cry. I was defeated. Then he hugged me, told me a story about Krishna from the *Krsna* book and said, "Now go take rest." He sent me to bed like a kid.

So in this way, if you could take it, he set the pattern for future relationships. Once I had to give some money for a devotee to go to Taiwan. I didn't like that devotee because he would not cooperate, so I refused. "No, Prabhupada, I won't give him any money." Srila Prabhupada said, "I will give him." I said, "Prabhupada, you're wasting your money on this man," and we discussed this. Finally I got angry, stood up and said, "I quit, I quit, I quit." Srila Prabhupada said, "I will also quit. Now sit down." Then after I cooled down, I said, "I'm sorry Srila Prabhupada that I got so excited." He said, "That is good you are enthusiastic." It was not a bowl of cherries to be around His Divine Grace. It was not easy. He was the *acharya* and he had to set the standard.

He was very grateful for the service you did, but you could not use that. In the beginning he used to thank me and say how nicely I was collecting money. But later on, I would deposit the money, a hundred thousand, two hundred thousand, and he never said a word. He'd just push the receipt aside without even a thank you. If you ever gave me two hundred thousand dollars, I would say something nice. But for Prabhupada it was service to Krishna, and we took it as that. There was no expectation of a reward. We were simply waiting for his mercy. We must have firm faith, and it must be as solid as the rock of Gibraltar or the Himalayan Mountains. Krishna is testing.

Someone may come with a little potency but he isn't even half a speck next to His Divine Grace, and his teachings are not the same, yet people think, "Oh, I will get it cheap over there." They don't want to pay the price, neither do they understand the price. It is not an easy thing. To understand *guru-tattva* is a difficult subject matter. When you understand *guru-tattva*, Krishna is guaranteed, but beginners switch from this guru to that because their faith is not solid. Srila Prabhupada has given everything a thousand times over. If you hear his tapes he's saying the same thing because we need to hear it. Nowhere else in the world you will see any guru getting daily *guru-puja*. With other gurus, *guru-puja* is held only once a year on their appearance day. And nowhere else will you hear the *Samsara* prayers sung at *mangal arati*. Why did Prabhupada stress worship of the *guru*? Because Westerners are headstrong. First we have to catch the importance of the guru's mercy. And by satisfying the guru, *yasya prasadad bhagavat-prasadah*, then we can satisfy Krishna. Then we can think of other things.

Nanda Kishor: The first time I came before Prabhupada, I was thinking, "Wow, I'm a great devotee." Brahmananda, the temple president of 26 Second Avenue, had made me think like that just to encourage me. So I thought, "Here I am bringing *prasadam* to Prabhupada, and he's going to say something to me like what Bhaktisiddhanta said to him, that, 'You should preach the message of Lord Chaitanya . . .'" Prabhupada took the *prasadam* I brought, but he did not even recognize my existence. He could do that. It was as if he said, "You think that you're a big devotee? This is how I deal with you." And if you were actually humble, he might pat you on the head. He always reciprocated appropriately.

Pariksit: We artists were painting pictures to illustrate the *Caitanya-*

caritamrta, and we had special opportunities to be with Prabhupada. Whenever he would come to New York, we would see him, he would comment on our paintings, and we would ask him questions about them. Since Jadurani was the oldest artist, she would ask the questions, and I was always in the background, afraid to speak up. But, when I moved to Los Angeles before the rest of the artists, I was the only person painting for Prabhupada's *Caitanya-caritamrta.* I'd started painting Advaita Acharya praying for the appearance of Lord Chaitanya, and I went to Srila Prabhupada's quarters with my sketch of Advaita Acharya performing *arati* while he prayed to a Deity of Krishna. Prabhupada said, "No, this is wrong. Advaita Acharya was praying to his *shalagram shila.*" And with a pen and paper he started doing the drawing for me. He first drew a little *asana* and then he drew the *shalagram shila.* As he drew, he described everything. And at one point I said, "That's the umbrella?" And he said, "No, the canopy." I felt wonderful that he was personally instructing me, and I took it as a great gift. Immediately I took Prabhupada's sketch, went to work on my drawing, and then put that into the final painting. It was a wonderful experience.

Nanda Kishor: Prabhupada was on a morning walk through Central Park when he went past a sculpture of the head and chest of a man and underneath the sculpture it said, "Webster." Prabhupada said, "Oh, the dictionary man?" And a devotee said, "No, Prabhupada, Daniel Webster." Prabhupada said, "Ah, Daniel has come." Now, "Daniel has come," is a line from a play, 'The Merchant of Venice,' by Shakespeare and Prabhupada, who had studied that play in college, began to tell the story—how the merchant wanted the pound of flesh and he couldn't get it and was frustrated. Then Prabhupada said, "And the purport of this story is that in this material world you can never get what you want." No materialist person can ever get what he wants in this material world. Why? Because only in spiritual life can you get what you want.

Madhavananda: From the very beginning, I always loved *kirtan* and once in Calcutta after I had lead a *kirtan* in front of the Deities, Prabhupada's servant came and said, "Prabhupada wants to see you." I went and Srila Prabhupada said, "That was a very nice *kirtan*." I said, "Oh, thank you." And he said, "But it is not GA-dad-hara, it is Ga-DAD-hara." So sometimes even today I cringe when I hear devotees saying GA-dad-hara, *sri-krsna-caitanya prabhu nitya-nanda, sri-advaita gadadhara srivasadi-gaura-bhakta-vrnda*, and I remember Prabhupada saying that to me. But I was moved by Srila Prabhupada's generous compliment.

Nanda Kishor: Another time at an airport Prabhupada was sitting waiting to take a plane somewhere when he said, "The scientists are very proud." When Prabhupada said that, he made a fist and drew his arm across his chest. We laughed to see this. We were immediately entertained by it. Then Prabhupada withdrew his senses like the tortoise pulls his legs within his shell. It was as if Prabhupada said to us, "I am your spiritual master, I am not here to entertain you." Subtly, almost unconsciously, we had taken what he said and did it the wrong way. It's an amazing thing.

Vaikunthanatha: In the Radha-Damodara Temple in Vrindavan I once had the fortune to go into in Prabhupada's rooms. Srutakirti, Prabhupada's servant, was kind to the smaller devotees, and allowed us to visit Prabhupada. I'm eternally grateful to Srutakirti for that.

Nara-Narayan had told me that the moon was self-illuminated and I went before Prabhupada and said, "Some devotee had told me that the moon is self-illuminated." Prabhupada pinched the bridge of his nose and closed his eyes for about two minutes. Then he opened his eyes and said, "I don't find that."

Guru Kripa: In Vishakhapatnam, Srila Prabhupada stayed for seven days at the Krishna Chaitanya Mission, which was the temple of Bhaktivaibhava Puri Maharaj. Anand prabhu, a *brahmachari* disciple of Srila Bhaktisiddhanta, was working in that mission. He could do the work of ten men. He would cook ten preps for 200 people with one or two assistants. Later he came to Vrindavan—all the devotees from Vrindavan know him—and worked there when the Krishna-Balaram temple was being built. So, in Vishakhapatnam he cooked two feasts a day. And as we were eating, Srila Prabhupada used to walk up and down and say, "Eat more, eat more," and he would be so satisfied to see us taking this *prasadam*. *Catur-vidha-sri-bhagavat-prasada-svadv-anna-trptan*. And as neophyte as I was, I was overeating. I would eat breakfast, and come lunchtime I had zero hunger, but I would eat again. And at nighttime, no hunger, *prasadam* was still in my stomach, but I would eat again because it was so good. After the third day, I finally threw up everything and in the afternoon went to sleep for about eight hours.

Once, Prabhupada went to Govardhan Hill on *parikram*, and we brought a big basket of *puris* and *subji* for lunch. We were sitting on the veranda eating when many dogs came around and some devotee threw a rock at the dogs. Srila Prabhupada said, "No, this is Govardhan, everyone eats." Srila Prabhupada took the puris from his plate, threw them to the dogs and said, "Feed the dogs now. All the dogs must eat, then they will be satisfied." Everyone got *prasadam*. No one went away without some *prasadam*. Anybody who visited also, Prabhupada would say, "Give him some *prasadam*."

When I had been out serving and I came back to Vrindavan, I'd come into Prabhupada's room, and sometimes he would give me *prasadam* with his own hand. He would say, "Take this *rasagulla* and take this." A few times we would eat together. He would share his meals with me and he would ask me, "How is everything?"

How can one leave the guru? I don't know. *Trnad api sunicena*. Humility will bring you the mercy of the Lord. Otherwise, you have not yet come to the position to understand. When, by humility, you come to the point of understanding, then you will be worthy of getting some mercy.

Pariksit: When Prabhupada came to the Art Department, one of the paintings I had in progress for the *Caitanya-caritamrta* was of Krishna carrying Nanda Maharaja's shoes on His head. I had put a little thread around Krishna's waist. Prabhupada said, "What is that thread?" I said, "That's something that Yasodamayi put around Krishna's waist to protect Him." Prabhupada said, "Where did you read that?" I said, "I think it's in *Nectar of Devotion*, Prabhupada." He said, "No." Then I remembered that Rukmini, Baradraj's wife, had told me that parents in India put that little string around their children's waist to protect them. Prabhupada said, "You must be very sure that everything you put in your paintings are taken from my books. Don't put anything in that is not described there." So I learned a lesson.

Nanda Kishor: At the International Students' Association on the Harvard campus in May '69, an Indian man said, "In the *Bhagavad-gita,* Krishna says that 'all paths lead to Me,' so, no matter what we do, won't we naturally come to Krishna?" Prabhupada quoted the Sanskrit and said, "All paths lead to Me, that is very good. But if we will naturally go to Krishna, why does Krishna instruct Arjuna? It is not that we will necessarily come to Krishna naturally. Therefore, Krishna instructs us in the quickest way to come to Him."

That was the first wave of the answer. The second wave was, "If we acted naturally, we will come to Krishna. But when we come to this human form of life, we do so many unnatural things. In the human form of life, with human intelligence, we begin to act unnaturally." Many people there could relate to what Prabhupada was saying, as it was the era of LSD and many other drugs. There were so many ways to fall into lower species of life.

Guru Kripa: I would write Srila Prabhupada sometimes and complain, "These Japanese are not taking to Krishna consciousness. It is very difficult here." It was a great austerity, no Sunday Feast. Everybody was out on the road. We used to chant in the street four hours a day, two in the morning and two in the afternoon, and the only people who would ever question us was a tourist looking for directions or some half-cracked Japanese trying to practice his English. Nobody came with any question. So Srila Prabhupada informed us that we should continue because there was such benefit. By giving some money, the Japanese people were doing some service.

There was a similar situation in Hong Kong. I closed the Hong Kong center because no one was coming. Then later, Srila Prabhupada asked me what happened and I told him. He said, "Now you go back, open one office, and sit and chant on your beads sometimes." So what do we know of the effect of the holy name, the pure name? Chernobyl leaked a gross substance—toxic fumes that spread all over Europe. But the holy name is the most divine, subtle substance. It will go everywhere and a very far distance, and the effect will be there on the consciousness. So this is why we have to hear correctly from Srila Prabhupada and accept that. He can understand the potency of the name. We have slightly experienced that, but not in full.

Nanda Kishor: In the summer of '68 in Montreal, Prabhupada was lecturing in a big, eight-lane bowling alley. He was speaking calmly for about twenty minutes or a half an hour. At the time, there were a lot of new yogis giving different teachings in America and there was one who taught that by meditating for six months you would become God. When Prabhupada spoke about this yogi, he started roaring. I was looking around thinking, "Who's he yelling at?" He's the spiritual master of the universe, and he was roaring at the universe. Anyway, at a certain point he said, "What is this nonsense that you can meditate and become God? God is God! He is God when He is sitting in the lap of His mother, He is God when He is speaking on the Battlefield of Kurukshetra, He is God when He is playing with the cowherd boys in Vrindavan. He is substantially God!" Prabhupada made his point most absolutely. He absolutely made every point.

Pavamana: We traveled from Bombay to Ahmedabad where we had another huge *pandal* program. The size of the *pandal* tent was as big as a city block and it would fill up every night with 15,000 people. When Srila Prabhupada sat on the *vyasasana* and preached he was fire and brimstone. That was wonderful.

The Indian people are very intelligent and many of them are very well versed in the *sastras*. So, when Prabhupada preached, he would say things that they could understand was correct, even though he was chastising them. Many times Prabhupada would speak in the local language, Hindi or Bengali, and because of the verses that he cited, we knew that he was extremely stern. But, when we went to a Life Member's house, he was the most wonderful guest. He would make small talk and he was concerned about every single person.

Srila Prabhupada was like an amazing jewel that had many different facets. For us to try to describe him is like a blind man describing an elephant. When the blind man touches the elephant here, it seems like it's big and round. When he touches it there, it's small and round. It's got so many different aspects.

Srila Prabhupada was an absolutely perfect judge of time and circumstance. He always had exactly the right thing to say at the right time for the right person. And sometimes, if we read the letter books and other anecdotes about Srila Prabhupada, perhaps he's saying to one person, "Yes, very good idea, you should get married." Then in another situation he writes, "No, it's better not to get married." Srila Prabhupada knew how to engage each person and make that person enlivened in Krishna consciousness. On one hand, he had disciple scholars like Pradyumna. On the other hand, he had disciple ex-bikers. And he had everything in between. He could engage all these different people and make them work together. The fact is that all of Prabhupada's senses were in complete control. He was never out of control.

Nanda Kishor: During the summer of '68, the temple needed some money, so I worked at the McGill Library and helped support the temple. Once, when I was coming back from work, some devotees had just arrived who I didn't know. I had no idea what was going on at the temple. Of course, a lot of people were coming, so it was no surprise. There were two or three initiation ceremonies during the week, as well as Monday, Wednesday and Friday classes by Prabhupada. Prabhupada was there for all these functions as well as the Sunday program. Practically, he was in the temple seven days a week.

I remember walking up the stairs to the Montreal temple, which was on the third floor, and hearing a woman's voice, "All glories to Swamiji." I thought, "Boy, Jadurani has gotten a stronger voice." But it wasn't Jadurani. It was Janaki. When I walked in, I saw seven new devotees who looked halfway between hippies and devotees. In their own way, they were far out. Shyamasundar, Malati, Mukunda, Janaki, Gurudas and Yamuna, and Saradiya. Saradiya didn't go on to England with the others, but she came to Montreal with them. So I came into an ecstatic *kirtan* with Prabhupada and all the devotees who had just arrived. Nobody had told me that they were coming or who they were or what they were going to do. When the kirtan ended, all the devotees were sitting in a circle and Prabhupada was sitting on the floor, in the place where he performed sacrifices. Prabhupada said, "This is all by the grace of my beloved spiritual master," and a big tear came out of his eye and the whole room became absolutely caught up in his mood. He said, "In 1959, when I was a householder, my spiritual master came to me in a dream and he said, 'Take *sannyasa* and go and preach.' But I was thinking, 'I am a householder, how can I give up my family?'" And then Prabhupada said, "So, this was *maya*." He was criticizing himself. We said, "Oh, no, Prabhupada."

Then he got specific. He said, "So I am very pleased to see these devotees who have come here from San Francisco. They are going to open a center in London." It was as if he knew what was going to happen, as if he was already celebrating what they were going to do.

We had no idea they were going to meet the Beatles, that they would preach in different ways. But Prabhupada saw it all. He said, "I am very pleased. My Guru Maharaj sent so many *sannyasis* to London, but they could not do anything. Now I am sending these householders," and it was almost as if he was saying, "and they are going to be a great success." Of course we accepted, and that's exactly what happened—it was a great success.

Guru Kripa: Srila Prabhupada was your friend. The guru is friendly with us and he is also our friend, but we are not equals. That will never be. But he is our best friend because he is our well-wisher. At times he is friendly with us, and at other times he is stern with us.

What impressed me from the beginning was the way he took time to make you satisfied, the way he would go out of his way. I would ask him to chant some mantra on the tape, and he would do it.

When George Harrison came to see him in Vrindavan, Srila Prabhupada did not flatter him. Srila Prabhupada was not enamored. He told him, "Yes, you are very famous, but what is your guarantee for the next life? You must accept a spiritual master and learn the spiritual science." Afterwards I said, "Srila Prabhupada, I have increased my faith so much today by seeing the way you dealt with this person." We grew up admiring the Beatles, but Srila Prabhupada did not cater to this world-famous person or try to get something from him.

And, Srila Prabhupada never backstabbed people. Once he was speaking about the way a certain devotee managed the temple, and that devotee was informed by one of the persons in the room. Srila Prabhupada became disturbed. He said, "What I said was for your ears, not for his ears." He had spoken about it for our understanding. But if something happened, he immediately would protect you, and especially me. Everybody was criticizing me, people would write letters to him criticizing the way I did something, but he defended me. "The udder of the cow is giving good milk, so you have to take the kicks." That is a friend. And as I go through life, I find it very difficult to find another person who will stick with you like that.

Nanda Kishor: A newcomer sitting up front said to Prabhupada, "I can't understand why all these young people are bowing down to you." Prabhupada said, "Just as you are thinking they shouldn't bow down, they are thinking that you should bow down. This is a democracy, is it not? And the majority is bowing down." Prabhupada was always perfect like that.

Guru Kripa: When Srila Prabhupada woke up from his afternoon nap, he would drink juice from a fresh coconut or have some fresh fruit juice and I used to take the drink to him. He would ring the bell, we would bring the drink, and he would take it.

Resting was *samadhi* for Srila Prabhupada, and he would be intoxicated from the *samadhi* he had been in. Every single time I came in, Prabhupada would speak about the conditioned souls and quote Prahlada Maharaj or something. One day he asked me, "So who is coming this afternoon?" I said, "One man was supposed to come at 4:00, but it's quarter after four." "Ah, who will come?" he said. His mind was constantly absorbed, "How I will help these conditioned souls?" That was his compassion. He felt great stress at seeing the conditioned souls in stress. Since that was his mood, that is why he is, 'His Divine Grace.' He had no other motive than to help people. He never tried to take personal service or credit.

Nanda Kishor: Shivananda brought an Indian Christian from the West Indies to see Srila Prabhupada. Prabhupada was a perfect gentleman with him. When the man said, "I am a Christian," I expected Prabhupada to say, "You're born in India, the land of religion, and you're following meat-eaters?" and so on. But no, Prabhupada said, "That is all right, we don't say you change your religion. We say that whatever religion helps to awaken your dormant love of God, that is perfect." Prabhupada was a perfect judge of place, circumstance and time—*desa-patra-kala*—and he was always a perfect gentleman. Of course, sometimes he did rip the ether with his lion-like voice. He was sometimes as ferocious as a lion and sometimes as soft as a rose. He had everything. I've thought this: that Srila Prabhupada is the greatest person who has ever set foot on the incontinent continents of North and South America. The greatest person ever to set foot here. That's something to contemplate.

TAPE 32

Aniruddha das
Jagadatri dasi
Karandhar das
Vidya dasi
Jayadvaita Swami
Stoka Krishna das
Giriraj Swami
Makanlal das

Aniruddha: There were a lot of prospective initiates waiting, so Mukunda and Gurudas arranged for me to stay with Prabhupada in his house for a day or two. That was a wonderful experience because my initiation was a one-on-one in Prabhupada's house. When it was my time to get initiated, I was told to bring some *dakshin*—a gift. I brought Prabhupada some sandalwood oil, some cloth and some incense. I was very timid and shy in those days. And I was anxious and nervous as well.

I went to Prabhupada's room with these things and knocked on the door. Kirtanananda and Hayagriva were with Prabhupada and I was so nervous that they had to calm me down. They said, "Just a minute, the Swami will see you in a little while." I sat there and after a while Swamiji, as we called him, called me in. I didn't know how to act, what to do, how long to stay, nothing. I offered him my respects and the first thing he said was, "Oh, so you want to be initiated?" Due to arrogance and false pride I took offense at that. I felt condescending, as if to say, "Well, of course I do. Why else am I here?"

But that feeling easily dissipated and I said, "Yes." Then Swamiji asked me if I knew what the requirements were, and I told him the rules and regulations. I noticed there was something very special about Prabhupada's eyes and I was very attracted to them. They were glowing. There was also something about Prabhupada that was different, that soothed me. Prabhupada said, "All right, you can go now and we'll call you back in a little while." I offered my obeisances, and since I didn't know how long to stay down, I just stayed there until Prabhupada said, "All right, you can get up now." Then I got up, went out and sat outside for a while. Later, Kirtanananda nudged me and said, "Come in, the Swami wants to see you."

Prabhupada was sitting on his bed and I sat on the floor. His room was narrow, maybe four or five feet wide and eight or nine feet long. On one side of the bed there was a picture of Jagannatha Puri and on the other side, a picture of his Gurudeva, Srila Bhaktisiddhanta Sarasvati Thakur. Prabhupada checked with me again to see if I knew the four rules and regulations. I told him, and then he chanted on my beads. There was no fire sacrifice for my first initiation. And then he said, "Your name is Anirud*dha,*" with emphasis on that "dha." I said, "What does it mean?" He said, "It's the grandson of Krishna."

I couldn't think of anything else to say. I was fidgety. Then Prabhupada said, "Do you have any questions?" I was so foolish that I couldn't think of anything intelligent to ask, but I remembered reading that one of the qualities of a devotee is that he is grave. So I said, "What does grave mean?" It was a silly question. Prabhupada looked at me, smiled and told me what it meant. Then I again offered my obeisances and went out.

Jagadatri: The implication of what I was doing began to dawn on me, and I blurted out, "Srila Prabhupada, how am I going to remember you and surrender to you for the rest of my life?"

Prabhupada was quiet for a second, but he liked

that question. He chuckled and said, "If you chant sixteen rounds a day and follow the four principles, you'll remember me and you'll surrender to me." Then he paused a moment, laughed again and said, "And don't forget to feed me."

In later years, I thought how kind Prabhupada was because he knew I'm a simpleton. I'm so simple that this is all I have to do and I'll go back home to Godhead. If you remember Prabhupada and surrender to him, you'll go wherever he goes, and he's definitely in the spiritual world. So my task is to remember him and surrender to him properly. I've been told also that "don't forget to feed me," means to distribute his books, to preach. But I think he meant that I shouldn't forget to offer him food, so I don't take anything that isn't *prasadam*.

Karandhar: I developed personal contact with Prabhupada when the temple moved from La Cienega, which was rented, to the place we purchased on Watseka Avenue. Gargamuni and Dayananda were working closely with Prabhupada in the negotiations with the Methodist church group and I was going on *sankirtan*. Then Gargamuni said, "We need somebody to build the altar." And somehow I got volunteered, although I didn't have a background in construction. Gargamuni said, "Okay, you're the person, and Prabhupada has a plan." So, I went to Prabhupada's room, he made a little diagram of how he wanted the three doors (this was when the temple was in the hall in the back), and then that construction became my full-time job. Everybody else went on *sankirtan* and I was only involved in making the altars. Prabhupada would frequently take a look and say, "Oh, yes," and "let's do this and let's do that." And I would be called to his room to give a progress report or to hear his comments. In that way I spent a lot of time with Prabhupada, always on practical matters. "Should this be tile? What color should this be?" and so on.

I didn't know what was going on in the politics of the devotee leadership, but all of a sudden it was announced that Gargamuni and Brahmananda and Vishnujana were going to take *sannyasa,* travel and preach. By default, the presidency of the Los Angeles temple fell on me. I was prominent in the sense that I'd done a lot of practical work, but I hadn't shown any distinction doctrinally or philosophically. In fact, I'd spent the previous several months just working in the temple alone. But somehow or other the presidency fell on me. And shortly thereafter, Prabhupada decided to organize the GBC and the BBT. And because I was the president of the L.A. temple, which was one of the bigger temples and was where Prabhupada spent a lot of time because it was conducive to his writing, I got drafted into those positions also. It all came about quickly, and it was dramatic for me. I didn't know exactly what was going on or if I was qualified or could handle it, but that's how it developed.

Aniruddha: A little while later, Prabhupada called, "Aniruddha," but I had already forgotten my name, and so I just sat there. Kirtanananda nudged me, "The Swami is calling you." Then I went in Prabhupada's room, but I was so nervous and uncertain that I don't remember what happened. However, my overall impression was overwhelming. Although I was bewildered initially, a short time later the impression had a great effect upon me. I spent one night and two days with Srila Prabhupada and I remember that his life was so perfectly organized that everything was at a certain time. He had a time for waking up, for *japa*, for bath, for massage, for the mail, to take *prasadam*, to take a walk. My life had been so disorganized for so many years that I was attracted to and impressed by his organized way of doing things.

Vidya: In his last days, when he was sick, the devotees would take Prabhupada in front of Gaura-Nitai and then Krishna-Balaram and then Radha-Shyamasundar and then bring his rocking chair in front of the *tamal* tree. There, under the *tamal* tree in the courtyard of the Krishna-Balaram Temple in Vrindavan, Prabhupada would give silent *darshans*. During that time, I felt he was training us to communicate with him after he left the planet. A *gurukula* boy would play *kartals,* two or three boys would dance, and one boy would sing for Prabhupada. Prabhupada would at most nod his head. All of us vied to sit in front of him.

Usually I was in the back because I was one of the newest devotees and I felt I didn't have a right to push forward. But one day, everybody was pushing and shoving and I was about to get a seat in front of Srila Prabhupada. I couldn't believe how lucky I was. When I sat down, there was a retarded girl, who was a daughter of one of the devotees, who was about to sit down where I was sitting. The devotee next to me pushed that little girl out of the way. I thought, "She shouldn't have pushed that child." Then I saw that Prabhupada was looking at us. I thought, "Prabhupada, I didn't do it! I didn't push the child! She did it!" But Prabhupada was looking as intently at me as he was at the woman who had pushed the child. I realized that I was just as responsible as she was because I hadn't done anything. I hadn't placated the child or found her a seat. My heart had not shown the compassion that it should have. So ever since, I've been trying to develop that quality. My lesson was that simultaneously we have to be humble and we also have to be compassionate toward everyone.

Aniruddha: In the morning, I walked with Srila Prabhupada on the beach and later we had a *kirtan* that was a little fast. Prabhupada said, "A little slower, a little slower." Afterwards, when I was going back to the temple on the bus, I thought, "I expected to feel something different but I don't." I thought that the spiritual master was magical and gave some charge. I didn't feel a charge, but I did feel a surge of enthusiasm to be serious and strict with myself. I wanted to remain celibate, a *brahmachari,* and do the things Prabhupada had talked about.

I went to the temple with this mood of enthusiasm and the

devotees told me, "You'll get over it." In those days, the San Francisco temple was very loose compared to New York, which was very strict. In San Francisco we were all wearing flowery clothes, and after some of the *kirtans*, devotees would go to the local coffee shop and have donuts and so forth. But, I was attracted to what Prabhupada said. I wanted to be serious.

Karandhar: From the very first time that Prabhupada gave me that little drawing of how he envisioned the front part of the temple room in Los Angeles, ninety-five percent of my contact and association with Prabhupada had to do with specific practical matters—like dealing with the printer Dai Nippon, managing Book Trust funds, the Mayapur-Vrindavan Trust funds. If there was a dilemma about a philosophical point, sometimes I asked questions, but mainly our contact had to do with practical management affairs. Only on the morning walks on Venice Beach in L.A. was there an occasion for philosophical debates, and somehow I was the protagonist for impersonalists and scientists. I would qualify my arguments with, "This philosopher said this, or this person said that," but I was also expounding my own ideas and doubts. Prabhupada perceived that. It wasn't just an exercise in academic objectivity.

Aniruddha: I mentioned to the producer of the TV show that we had an album called *Happening* and I gave him a prospectus. The first thing the interviewer said to Srila Prabhupada was, "Oh, Swami, I understand you have a record album. You must make a lot of money." Prabhupada smiled at him and said, "Yes, a thousand dollars a week." The interviewer was immediately defeated. The interview went along like that, and afterwards the producer couldn't look us in the face because he saw that Srila Prabhupada was genuine. Prabhupada was not, as he had thought, some strange cult figure that he could cut apart

On the other hand, The Les Crane Show was wonderful. Prabhupada chanted the *Vandeham* prayers at the beginning of the show. They allowed the singing to go on for a longer period than they had planned, and then Prabhupada chanted Hare Krishna while they had beautiful visuals of him and the devotees. Then they interviewed him, asking him general questions about *sadhana*. Prabhupada made the audience friendly right away. He was a perfect *Vaishnava* gentleman. He spoke kindly, smiled and said, "And I am such-and-such of age, and I even have my original teeth." Prabhupada let Mukunda do a lot of the talking because Mukunda was calm and cool-headed and made a good impression. Mukunda spoke on basic things like *tilak* and so on.

In the latter part of the show, a dogmatic Youth for Christ group was on—"Christ is the only way." The audience didn't like them much. In the parking lot after the show, people came over to Prabhupada and could see how genuine he was. Prabhupada had that quality. He was not like any bogus guru. Prabhupada said, "Before I came to the West, other yogis came here and only speculated on the mental platform."

Jagadatri: One morning in Mayapur, I was helping Daivishakti cut fruit for Srila Prabhupada when Prabhupada's servant, Srutakirti, told us, "Srila Prabhupada said that before you put the watermelon on the plate, you should taste it to make sure it's okay." I thought, "I can't taste the watermelon before I put it on Srila Prabhupada's plate. I just can't. I'll put the best watermelon on his plate." Of course, that watermelon wasn't good. The next day I heard, "You didn't taste the watermelon and it was no good. Srila Prabhupada was displeased." So, Prabhupada reciprocates. The way he's done it for me is to reciprocate through others. I haven't had the association that other devotees have had, but somehow or another his mercy is always there.

Aniruddha: The UCLA college engagement I had arranged was a fiasco. We didn't have much *laxmi* to advertise and due to my inexperience, I didn't organize it properly. When Prabhupada came, nobody was there. Prabhupada looked at me and said, "So, Aniruddha?" I was shy, I felt tiny, and I wanted to hide somewhere. Prabhupada said, "That is all right, let us have *kirtan*." So we had *kirtan*, and some Indian student saw Srila Prabhupada and came in to speak with him in Bengali. This student was intelligently challenging and arguing, like an impersonalist *brahmana*. Then in English, Srila Prabhupada said, "Tell me, young man, where are your Indian countrymen?" The young man was quite flustered. He didn't have an answer. Prabhupada said very gravely, "I will tell you, they are lost. Hare Krishna."

Jayadvaita Swami: I didn't go on many morning walks with Srila Prabhupada because I was a rank-and-filer. Mostly I used to watch the *sannyasis* and GBC men pile into the cars to go off for the walk, but sometimes I went. Once, as Srila Prabhupada was walking on Venice Beach, I said, "Srila Prabhupada, everyone says that since you've come the Deities look even more beautiful." Prabhupada said, "That is my anxiety." I didn't know how to process that. I stayed silent. Then Prabhupada said, "That is my anxiety, that after I leave you will neglect the Deity worship and everything will be spoiled."

Aniruddha: We bought our incense at the Vedanta Society, a nice private *ashram* at the bottom of the hills on Vine Street in Los Angeles. At that time, they had the best incense. When I mentioned that to Prabhupada, he said, "I want to see that place." I took him there and he walked around the property. He was aloof from the whole thing. Prabhupada said, "I would like to have an appointment with the *swami* in charge here." His name was Swami Pravhavananda. He and a co-author had written the Penguin edition of the *Bhagavad-gita*—the verses with some interpretation—that many of us had read. Swami Pravhavananda was the head of this chapter of the Vedanta Society of the Ramakrishna Mission founded by Vivekananda in 1918.

So, I made the arrangements and Prabhupada, some other devotees and I went to Swami Pravhavananda's office. This swami wore a Nehru jacket and looked like a businessman. He conversed with Prabhupada and right away there was a strong challenging mood. We didn't understand what was going on, but it wasn't enlivening. Prabhupada was aglow, saying, "Oh, Chaitanya," and this man was saying, "No, no, Swami, Chaitanya, no, no, no, no, no." Due to my immaturity, I thought that they were arguing about placing our books in their stores. But later I understood that they were all impersonalists, that they would never put our books there.

In the car on the way back, we were quiet. There wasn't much enthusiasm. We were chanting and then Prabhupada said, "This Vedanta Society was introduced in America by Swami Vivekananda, who preached about Ramakrishna. Ramakrishna was not very popular in India. But Swami Vivekananda was an intellectual type and he told everybody how great Ramakrishna was. He attracted a lot of elderly people, got money, and became famous. Then he went back to India. Since the Indian people follow anything that's famous in America, Vivekananda became famous that way." But before he went to America, Prabhupada said, he wasn't much of anything. Then Prabhupada said, "You know, Swami Vivekananda came here fifty years ago and now they have seven centers." Then he smiled and said, "And we too have seven centers." Everybody said, "*Jaya*!"

Prabhupada always lifted us up and made us understand how much power this movement has and how it is growing. I just read a letter from Prabhupada to Janardan in Montreal where he wrote, "The other day I met Swami Pravhavananda, and I talked with him. To speak plainly how I found him—a great rascal . . . Pravhavananda said that in Ramakrishna's previous life he was Lord Chaitanya. Similarly it is said that he was formerly Rama and Krishna. If actually he was Rama and Krishna and Lord Chaitanya, why there are so many contradictions between Rama, Krishna and Lord Chaitanya's teachings on one side, and the Ramakrishna Paramahamsa's teachings on the other side? Do you think that Ramakrishna was Lord Chaitanya and after 400 years he changed the whole philosophy? Lord Chaitanya propagated worship of Krishna; Krishna propagated that one should worship Him, Krishna; how is it that this Ramakrishna worships the material goddess Kali? Ask this question. So, such rascaldom is going on all over the world. We have to be very careful in understanding Krishna Consciousness." Because Prabhupada was saying these things to the so-called swami, the swami was getting upset. But at the time, I had no idea what was going on.

Jagadatri: Prabhupada was visiting the Dallas *gurukula* when we had one of the most ecstatic *kirtans* I've ever experienced. Vishnujana Swami was there, along with many others. Everyone was five feet off the ground. Jayatirtha was flying in the air and twirling on the way down, while waves of devotees were running back and forth. There was a great feeling permeating the entire room. Then I thought in a demoniac way, "Everybody loves Prabhupada, everybody's worshiping Prabhupada. I want to see if he's really transcendental." The affection, love and honor that everybody was giving to Srila Prabhupada was palpable. I thought, "I want to see what he does." So, after the *kirtan* was over and everybody was paying obeisances, I sat up and looked at him. I wanted to see his expression—if he was gloating from the worship. He glanced to the other side of the room, then he glanced at me, and in a fraction of a second I was shocked that I could be so gross and fallen. I immediately knew that he was totally transcendental and not bothered by worship. And I could see that he was embarrassed for me. It was a great lesson for my stone-like heart to see that all the time he was a humble servant of Krishna.

Jayadvaita Swami: On one occasion in New Dwaraka, Prabhupada said, "This balcony system is very nice. And if possible, there should also be separate entrances for the men and the ladies."

Karandhar: Prabhupada quoted a lot of Bengali proverbs, practical things like "If you can make twelve dollars running around, you can make thirteen dollars sitting down." Once, when I was the treasurer for the BBT and the Mayapur-Vrindavan Trust, he told me, "The treasurer never reveals to the devotees in general how much is in the treasury room, because as soon as you reveal how much is there, then everybody will want to plunder it." So I was always tight-lipped.

Once I told Prabhupada, "I'm always exhorting the devotees to pay their bills because it's an emergency—the BBT has to pay its bill." And sometimes that was the case, but a lot of times there was money in the account and I was trying to keep money coming in. Prabhupada said, "Yes, this is correct." He wasn't authorizing me to be overtly deceptive or dishonest, but to be practical, not to get carried away by ideological absolutes of honesty. Everything in the world has to be done with an eye to the time and the place.

In that way, I got a lot of what Allen Ginsberg, in his review of that first Macmillan *Gita,* called, "Prabhupada's practical Hindu granny-wisdom." Most of us came out of the hippie milieu and had a lack of down-to-earth sense about how to do anything in an organized or systematic way. We were still detoxing from the drugs and hallucinogens we had been taking. Although we were idealistic and had presumptions of being philosophically sophisticated, which we weren't at all, we were spaced out and more or less incompetent when it came to practical matters. Most of Prabhupada's input to me was about that.

Aniruddha: As the sun came up, we were walking with Srila Prabhupada on the pier at Venice Beach. There was a lone woman fishing at the end of the pier, and as we came closer, she got up, clasped her hands and said, "Oh, Swami, I saw you the other night on the Les Crane Show. It's so nice to meet you." That's all she said. Afterwards Prabhupada said, "Just by the fact that she gave respect to a saintly person, she will advance so much."

Once we were riding on the freeway in Los Angeles when we saw a sign that said 'Santa Cruz such-and-such number of miles ahead.' Prabhupada said, "What is this Santa Cruz?" I told him that in Spanish it's a name for Lord Jesus that literally means 'Saint of the Cross.' He said, "Ah, yes, in India also there is a place called 'Santa Cruz' that was founded by some missionaries. 'Santa' comes from the word '*shanta*,' which means 'saintly.' You can call me Shanta Bhaktivedanta."

His words seem simple, but it's ecstatic to realize how Prabhupada implanted knowledge in us and cultivated the devotional love that we gradually felt for him and which completely changed our lives. We're so grateful.

Vidya: The other quality I admired in Prabhupada was how he comprehended the person he was speaking to. He spoke to that person exactly where that person's philosophical understanding and self-realization was. It was as if Prabhupada came directly inside the other person and then convinced him step-by-step that Krishna is real. Prabhupada did that in my life and I think he did that with everyone. He had that ability.

I pray for even a small part of that ability. I pray not be at all threatened by the other person and to somehow open their heart a little bit to be able to see Krishna and accept Krishna consciousness the way Prabhupada did and is still doing so expertly.

Aniruddha: When Prabhupada was trying to acquire a permanent visa, he had to see a doctor to get a health statement. A friend of mine recommended a doctor in La Crescenta, and Subal drove Prabhupada to see that doctor in an old Volkswagen that some favorable hippie had donated. This car had huge colorful daisies painted on it, so you could see it a mile away. Naturally, some policemen stopped us because he knew something had to be wrong just by the way the car looked. Subal had an outstanding number of traffic violations, and the policeman immediately took him away. Prabhupada was there in the middle of the freeway. But Gaurasundar was also there so he continued driving. Prabhupada said, "Krishna is telling us that we need a better car."

Jagadatri: Once in Detroit, when Madhavananda was the temple president there, I went on a morning walk with Prabhupada. Prabhupada wanted Govardhan to be president there again. Then, when Prabhupada went to New York, I joined him there and went on another morning walk. We women weren't able to walk close to Prabhupada, but that morning Prabhupada stopped walking, everybody else stopped also, and we all looked down at the crack on the pavement. Prabhupada said, "Look at this plant. The living entity is so powerful that it's pushing through the cement." He pointed out how the *atma* is so strong that it can crack cement. It was wonderful.

Karandhar: The devotees couldn't get Nair, the owner of the Juhu property, to give them the title to the land even after they had met all the requirements. So, Prabhupada asked me to help. I'm a babe in the woods in India. The levels of sophisticated manipulation and deception there are light years ahead of what exists in the West. So, I couldn't help. I was puffed up. I thought, "The American management know-how is going to set everything straight," although I didn't have any idea what I was going to find in India. After two weeks I realized it was a morass that I didn't have the slightest notion of how to deal with. I was completely naive. When I tried to make a phone call from the little Juhu office to downtown Bombay, it took me three or four hours. Finally I said, "My God, I just want to get out of here. This is a nightmare."

In fact, I copped out. Although Prabhupada wanted me to stay longer, I was in India only for a couple weeks. I told Prabhupada, "I've got to get back, I've got these problems with Dai Nippon and I've got to do this and do that so please let me go." Prabhupada said, "Okay, go ahead." I went back to escape the difficult problems there. By that time, I had become accustomed to being the wonder boy of business among the devotees. In several letters, Prabhupada had praised me, saying that I was a good manager and so on, and I'd started to believe it. Juhu was a good lesson. Prabhupada was like a father figure, encouraging immature children just to keep them motivated.

Aniruddha: When Prabhupada first arrived, I got a call from a freelance photographer working with *Life* magazine in New York City. Since public interest in swamis was growing, *Life* was doing an article on the 'swami circuit,' as they called it. The reporter and photographer had gone to our 26 Second Avenue temple, but Prabhupada was in L.A., so they came to L.A. and a woman reporter interviewed Srila Prabhupada. I sat in on it. Prabhupada first described the mission he was on, but she didn't write any of those things down, which was very typical of reporters in those days. Whenever Prabhupada spoke philosophy, they would gloss over it. They wanted to know why we wore *tilak* and what was the bead bag and so on.

At the time, I was a little confused because I didn't know that reporters were like that. I was anxious to see the article. Not a word of what Prabhupada said was in the article. But they did say that of all the groups that they contacted, the song that we sing, the Hare Krishna mantra, stayed in your head. And they did mention something that Prabhupada said, "The Swami said Lord Krishna descended at such-and-such a time to this planet." The fact that they mentioned Lord Krishna, Prabhupada said, was wonderful. And he said that any sincere person who saw the pictures in the magazine would benefit. There was a wonderful picture of Prabhupada, done with filters to make it more attractive. That was very nice.

Vidya: In the very old days, *grihastha* couples, like Govinda dasi and Gaurasundar, were allowed to be Prabhupada's personal servants. My husband and I both desired to do that too. Perhaps that's why I was given *tulasi* service—I couldn't serve Prabhupada, but I could serve her. That personal service helped me a lot.

When Prabhupada was in L.A., I was always in the back. The managers had promised that whoever worked thirteen hours (I did service thirteen hours a day) could take Prabhupada's personal *darshan* or at least go on a morning walk. But I didn't belong to any particular club or department, so I didn't get to do that.

Then, one day we were standing outside the door, waiting for Prabhupada to leave for his morning walk. We were in the back because we were unimportant new devotees. We were scuffling around feeling sorry that we'd come to the movement so late and could not be with Prabhupada much. Prabhupada got in his car, and started to drive off. And somehow as the car came forward we ended up being at the edge of the driveway and Srila Prabhupada was looking right at us. All I could see were these red orbs like suns piercing through me. And in my heart and also in my husband's heart we felt as if Prabhupada said, "So, what do you want to say? What do you want?" Instantly we both reeled back from that sidewalk. Obviously we weren't ready for his association. His eyes were like suns that pierced into our hearts and cleansed our minds and us as well.

Karandhar: In Los Angeles I asked Prabhupada about the devotees' diet. He mentioned that devotees should eat simply. He also told me that mung *dahl* should always have a little bit of ghee in it otherwise it creates problems with the eyes. And he mentioned that ghee should be made from unsalted butter. But, when we had a chance of getting surplus salted butter from the government, Prabhupada said, "Oh, okay. Get it and make it into ghee. It can be used but it's not ideal."

Aniruddha: We went on many walks with Srila Prabhupada in San Francisco. One of his favorite places was Stowe Lake, a beautiful lake in the middle of Golden Gate Park. Prabhupada called it a garden because it's architecturally landscaped—it isn't natural like Griffith

Park in Los Angeles. Every morning, the same woman would come with her dog, and Prabhupada would always say, “Hello, good morning, how are you?” And she’d smile. Prabhupada never said, “Hare Krishna.” One morning one of our god-brothers said, “Swamiji, why don’t you say ‘Hare Krishna’ to her?” Prabhupada said, “She would not say ‘Hare Krishna’ back, but this way she gets the benefit of giving respect to a saintly person.”

Jagadatri: Once, all the devotees went from the Hyderabad farm to Hyderabad while Palika, Kaushalya and I were swimming. We were left behind. Prabhupada was at the farm then, feeling relaxed and happy. He asked us if we had enough *prasadam*, if we had enough saris, if we were comfortable, if everything was okay, and why were we there. We had to say that we got left behind, and Prabhupada arranged for a lorry truck to bring us to Hyderabad. He was very caring and loving.

Once, after *sankirtan* had been introduced, I wrote to Prabhupada from Dallas on behalf of our *sankirtan* party—ten other women and me. This was before *sankirtan* was in full bloom. We were bothered by the heavy pressure for women to be chaste, humble, shy and submissive and at the same time, at nine o’clock every morning we went out the door in pants to stand on an island in the middle of a highway. I wrote, “I want to be chaste, shy and submissive, but this is what we’re doing during the day. Do you know this?”

Prabhupada wrote back a wonderful letter. The gist of it was that aggression for the cause of Lord Chaitanya Mahaprabhu would purify you of all your desires for sense gratification. I didn’t think I was asking about my desire for sense gratification, but obviously he was telling us to go on being aggressive. Aggression for the cause of Lord Chaitanya Mahaprabhu’s preaching is purifying. And we were all trying to get purified. We were thinking we were victims, but actually we were in the process of purification.

Aniruddha: Govinda dasi told me that, “Swamiji prefers to be called

Srila Prabhupada." This was a little disturbing to me because I was attached to the name 'Swamiji.' So, on a morning walk with Srila Prabhupada, I said, "Swamiji, I understand that you prefer to be called Prabhupada," and he said, "Where did you hear this? Who told you this?" Then his mood changed and he said, "Actually I do not prefer, but it is better."

Stoka Krishna: When I was head of the *gurukula* in Dallas, one afternoon it turned dark as night, and the wind started howling and blowing hard. For fifteen minutes there was an incredible storm, and afterwards we went into the courtyard of the school to find that a huge tree was leaning on the wall against one of the buildings. Although I was young, I had fairly large responsibilities, and I felt myself capable of making a decision. I brought a professional to check the tree and he told me that the roots were not in good shape and the tree needed to be cut down. So, I immediately contracted to have the tree cut down. Several weeks later Srila Prabhupada arrived, the story was related to him, and he wanted to know which fool had made this decision. I immediately came forward and took my instructions. What I later learned was that Prabhupada was the consummate businessperson, and that I should have gotten two or three different quotes and found the truth rather than proceed as I did.

Giriraj Swami: Srila Prabhupada had to struggle very hard to build the Juhu temple. The first struggle was to get the land, the next struggle was to get permission to build the temple, and the last struggle was to actually build the temple and install the Deities. We had worked hard to get permission to build, which, in India, has many conditions. They give you permission, but you must fulfill certain conditions. One of the conditions was that we had to have an access road of a certain width, and it happened that there were some palm trees where the access road was to go. Once, when Srila Prabhupada came to Juhu after being away for some time, he noticed that one or two of the palm trees had been cut down and he was upset. He asked, "Why did you cut down the trees?" We thought we had the best answer—we had to get permission to build the temple. But Srila Prabhupada said, "No. You go to the municipality and tell them it is against our religion to cut down trees." We had no choice. We did it and, of course, they argued. It struck me how concerned Srila Prabhupada was for the trees. The next time Prabhupada went on a world tour, he stopped in Tehran just before he returned to Juhu, and one of the first things he said was, "I was in Tehran and I have seen they have trees in the middle of the streets there. So we can also have trees in the middle of our street, it's not so strange." In the end, on Srila Prabhupada's order, we held our ground and they gave us permission. The tree that Srila Prabhupada protected is still standing there with asphalt all around it. Srila Prabhupada has so much care, concern, and even love for a tree, then what to speak of us. It's just because of Srila Prabhupada's care, mercy and protection that we are able to stand in Krishna consciousness no matter what else is around us.

Aniruddha: Srila Prabhupada used eucalyptus twigs to clean his teeth. They had to be a little longer than the length of a finger, and not too green. We would cut them, and he would soak them in water overnight, then bite the tips between his teeth and use the bristles as a toothbrush. We took turns getting these for Prabhupada. Here in Los Angeles there were a lot of eucalyptus trees. About sunrise one morning, I went to MacArthur Park on Wilshire Boulevard wearing my hat, my bead bag and carrying a huge knife. It was quiet—nobody was there. I parked my car and then cut down a large eucalyptus branch with a lot of tributaries so I could pick the right size. I was sitting on a bench with a knife cutting up this branch, when a patrol car pulled up. The police check through the park at certain hours. A policeman arrogantly strutted up to me and said,

"Well, what do you have there, young man?" I said, "I'm cutting these for my spiritual master. He uses them as a toothbrush." He said, "Have you been in a mental institution?" and then he said, "What do you have in that bag there?" and I explained my japa beads to him. He said, "I can arrest you for carrying that weapon." He was using his power but he saw that I was okay. I told this story to Srila Prabhupada and he said, "Well, did you ask him if he was crazy?" Prabhupada was teaching me to be bold.

Jayadvaita Swami: Another time on a morning walk Prabhupada said, "These days I am not eating. But I am working. So you are saving money."

Aniruddha: In the early days, we had easy access to Srila Prabhupada. I was twenty-seven and a little older than most of the devotees, and I'd get in anxiety that the others would take my things, so I'd go to see Srila Prabhupada. Many of my god-brothers also experienced this—that we'd be in such anxiety but as soon as we came into Prabhupada's presence we understood right away that we should chant Hare Krishna and our problems would disappear. We couldn't even approach Prabhupada with our questions. Prabhupada said, "I created your good fortune," which is the truth.

Once, I went into Prabhupada's room—it was a large room—and I sat down on the floor and chanted. I was alone with Prabhupada and he said to me, "Sit on a pillow because sitting on the floor creates hemorrhoids." He was so practical. Then I closed my eyes and became engrossed in my chanting and all of a sudden it dawned on me that I was taking up too much of Srila Prabhupada's time. I opened up my eyes and said, "I should go, Srila Prabhupada," and he said, "No, no, that is all right, you can stay." So I asked him, "Is it really true, Srila Prabhupada, that we can talk to Krishna just like I'm talking to you?" He looked at me and said, "Yes." That was all I needed to know. It was very clear and matter-of-fact. That was a wonderful experience. We all had our doubts. We were practicing but we weren't fully knowledgeable, even to this day. So Prabhupada's words were very reassuring.

Karandhar: Devotees had a tendency to be a little more rigid, inflexible, and doctrinaire about diet and about how many hours to sleep and the like. If somebody was sick on an extended basis, couldn't come to mangal arati, and had to have special food, it upset things and would create dilemmas in the group dynamics. I was probably a big part of maintaining the military rigidity, to "follow the program or go somewhere else. Everybody else has to eat this, and everybody else has to get up." But Prabhupada was always a little more flexible. "Okay, if they can't eat this, give them that." Prabhupada said, "If a person's really hungry, he can eat anything," but that a diet of rice, *dahl*, *chapattis*, and *subji* was the best overall. But if somebody needed steamed vegetables, okay, arrange for it somehow. Once Prabhupada said, "A young child cannot eat too much and an older man cannot eat too little."

As far as medicine, we were trying to follow the Eastern tradition, although in the West there wasn't much known about Ayurveda until some devotees went to India and discovered the herbal formulas. But there was the old macrobiotic thing, "Should we eat brown rice, macrobiotic rice? Should we eat raw sugar?" Prabhupada said, "No, not generally, because we should eat what Krishna wants. We should eat what we offer to Krishna."

Jayadvaita Swami: Srila Prabhupada said, "Suppose a man is walking down the street and he sees a stick. Is it worth anything?"

"No, Prabhupada, it's not worth anything."

"And that man walks on and he sees some wire. Is it a very valuable thing?"

"No, Prabhupada."

"And he goes on and he sees some gourd. Is it a very valuable thing?"

"No, Prabhupada."

Then Prabhupada said, "Yes, but an intelligent man, he fixes the stick on the gourd, attaches the wire and makes a musical instrument. Similarly, I have picked up all you American and European boys and girls."

Aniruddha: I had an ecstatic experience at the wonderful San Francisco Ratha-yatra, and I wrote Prabhupada a letter about what I felt. He answered, "The Car Festival was very simple. After all, it is a car with four wheels, but it attracted the people so enthusiastically because there was His Lordship, Jagannatha. Atheistic people may say that Jagannatha was made of wood, and the car was also made of wood, but spiritual bliss can be exacted from anything, simply in Krishna Consciousness. Even accepting the whole affair as wooden, a Krishna conscious person can understand that wood is nothing but a display of Krishna's energy. So it is the Krishna conscious energy that gives us transcendental bliss, just like it is the electric energy passing through a copper cable that gives us electric light and heat. Simply the Krishna conscious electric energy can immediately be attractive by developing our sense of Krishna consciousness, which I am sure you are experiencing gradually how easily it can be done . . . To implement this transcendental bliss to the people of your country there is immense work to be done ahead and this Ratha-yatra festival is only a sample. If we get the opportunity we shall be able to over flood your country with waves of transcendental bliss, by the grace of Krishna. We can introduce various other ceremonies in connection with Krishna and His different expansions or incarnations in such a nice way that people are sure to be attracted by such a thing and become immersed in Krishna consciousness . . . There is not one incident like Ratha-yatra, but there are many hundreds of thousands of incidents in different appearances of the incarnations of Lord Krishna. In different cities and different centers we can introduce such multi-pastimes ceremonies of Lord Krishna. And certainly people will be engladdened to observe such transcendental and happy ceremonies." That was a very enlivening letter.

Makanlal: In 1969, the temple was located on La Cienega Boulevard and Tamal Krishna Maharaj wanted a *vyasasana* for that temple like the one Nara-Narayan had built in San Francisco. So, for the Los Angeles temple, Nara-Narayan built another *vyasasana* for Srila Prabhupada. When Srila Prabhupada accepted that *vyasasana*, with tears in his eyes he declared before all the devotees, "I am not fit. But on behalf of my Guru Maharaj, I must accept."

We could understand that a *mahabhagavata* pure devotee is always fit to receive that level of honor. But Prabhupada was humble. Not artificially, but from his heart he humbly felt, "This should be offered to my Guru Maharaj, to Bhaktisiddhanta Sarasvati Thakur. I will not take it for myself. As his representative I will accept it. Only on those terms."

Nara-Narayan had designed the *vyasasana,* which had a wooden gold-leafed railing around it, after an old black-and-white photograph of the throne of the King of Jaipur. Srila Prabhupada, being well educated, must have known exactly where the design came from because he said, "This is meant for kings." And he accepted it with great humility. Then, on the Appearance Day of Srila Bhaktisiddhanta Sarasvati Thakur, Prabhupada would not sit on the *vyasasana.* To honor his Guru Maharaj, Prabhupada sat on a cushion on the floor, and he put a photograph of Srila Bhaktisiddhanta Sarasvati Thakur on the *vyasasana.* That is the proper etiquette.

Aniruddha: Makanlal, Nara-Narayan's brother, was in San Francisco when I was there. He and his brother joined in San Francisco in the early days and were sincere devotees. Prabhupada said that they were very nice but a little eccentric (Makanlal said it was all right for me to say this). Makanlal and Nara-Narayan were long-haired hippies who wore typical clothes of those days and were a bit

Shakespearean when they spoke. With a sonorous voice, Makanlal would chant, "Hare Krishna Hare Krishna, Krishna Krishna Hare Hare," and it used to irritate me terribly. I would get disturbed during the *kirtans*. Then once, Makanlal had a preaching engagement at the YWCA in Berkeley, and I drove Srila Prabhupada there and back. The engagement was very nice, but all of a sudden who was leading the *kirtan* but Makanlal and I showed my distaste—I left the room. I was not very tolerant and didn't have the right understanding. So, when I was driving Prabhupada home, he looked at me and said, "Aniruddha, this Makanlal sings very nicely, don't you think?" I had to say, "*Jaya*, Prabhupada."

Gradually I understood, *trnad api sunicena taror api sahisnuna, amanina manadena kirtaniyah sada harih*. In a humble mode you can preach and chant incessantly, and that was Prabhupada's mode. He knew exactly how to utilize everybody's service. Even though there were some qualities that were not very nice, he never found fault. He found only the good. He used to say, "It's very easy to be critical, but to find the good is rare." I didn't have the ability to see only the good, but I'm beginning to understand how magnificently Prabhupada had it. To see the good in others is the way to preach, the way to not disturb anybody. Prabhupada was a perfect *Vaishnava*. One of the qualities of a pure *Vaishnava* is that he's a perfect gentleman. He doesn't disturb anybody's mind. He's able to see the good in others and evoke it. That's why we all wanted to serve Prabhupada, and that's why we have difficulty with people who don't evoke the good in us. It's very rare to achieve that ability in fullness. But we can achieve it if we follow Prabhupada's example.

Jayadvaita Swami: Since 1968 I had a question that I'd been thinking about in different ways. Finally I was on a walk with big men, *sannyasis* and GBC, when I screwed up my courage and asked Srila Prabhupada my question. Here, from the recording, is the way it went:

I said, "The spiritual masters know everything and they're

perfect in everything. But sometimes, from our material viewpoint, we see some discrepancies." Prabhupada said, "Because material viewpoint, the viewpoint is wrong. Therefore, you find discrepancies." I said, "So we should think that we have the defect." Prabhupada said, "Yes. *Acharya* is explained: 'One who's preaching the cult of devotional service, he's *acharya.*' Then why should you find any discrepancy?" I replied, "Because for instance, sometimes the *acharya* may seem to forget something, or not to know something. So from our point of view, if someone has forgotten, that is an imperfection." Prabhupada retorted, "No, no, no. Then you do not understand. *Acharya* is not God, omniscient. He is servant of God. His business is to preach *bhakti* cult. That is *acharya.* Perfection is how he is preaching *bhakti* cult. That's all . . ." I then stated, "Krishna says in *Bhagavad-gita* that one who knows Him knows everything." Prabhupada said, "Yes. Because if he knows that Krishna is the Supreme Personality of Godhead, then he knows everything. That's all. Not that he should know as Krishna. If he accepts Krishna, the Supreme Personality of Godhead, the Absolute Truth, then he knows everything."

Then I gave the example of Gaura-kishora, who could not write, although he knew Krishna. Prabhupada said, "Yes. He knows everything. Otherwise how Bhaktisiddhanta accepted him as guru? He knows Krishna. That's all."

After the walk, several GBC men and *sannyasis* jumped on me: "You have a lot of nerve." "How could you ask Srila Prabhupada that kind of question?" "Who do you think you are?" "That was offensive."

I was a little concerned, so after the class I went to Srila Prabhupada's room in the Lotus building in Mayapur. Srila Prabhupada was finishing his breakfast when I came in and offered obeisances. I said, "Srila Prabhupada? That question that I asked this morning . . ." He said, "What is that?" I recapped the question. I said, "Srila Prabhupada, was that question offensive?" Prabhupada said, "Not offensive, just ignorant."

Aniruddha: Vishnujana Swami was a wonderful devotee who sang beautifully. Prabhupada said, "By his singing alone, he can go back to the spiritual world." And Vishnujana Swami was expert in playing the tamboura, the mridanga, the harmonium, and in making up his own melodies. He was a little embarrassed to play his own melodies for Prabhupada, but he wanted to be recognized. Once, in the La Cienega temple, where Prabhupada had a small private room adjoining the main temple room, Vishnujana was elaborately playing his melodies on the harmonium in the temple room when Prabhupada came out of his room and said, "What is wrong with the melodies I have given you?" Today the movement has grown and we have many different melodies, but I'm fond of Prabhupada's original ones.

Prabhupada knew that we were attracting all varieties of people and he was broad-minded. When Vishnujana Maharaj started the road shows using guitars and a lot of music, Prabhupada said, "This is very good to attract people, but the devotees shouldn't get attached to it." Today, however, in some places it's common for devotees to play all these songs. Whatever brings a person to Krishna consciousness is all right—Prabhupada taught us to be broad-minded—but we have to be careful not to compromise.

Karandhar: One day a devotee in Prabhupada's room was upset that the breakfast oatmeal was too sweet. We all had sweet tooths but this devotee said, "Prabhupada, we eat too much sugar." Prabhupada looked at him and said, "Why do you eat so much sugar?" Prabhupada was saying that we had to work on our compulsions ourselves, although institutionally it was true. Devotees living in the temple had to eat what was served in the temple, and a lot of the time the food was probably not the healthiest or the best prepared.

Aniruddha: I came to Hawaii in 1973, when Sudama Maharaj was in charge and when Ambarish prabhu had bought a beautiful home where Srila Prabhupada could translate without being disturbed.

One day when we were chanting *sri-guru-carana-padma* during *gurupuja*, Prabhupada said, "We should enter into the meaning of this." I didn't grasp what he meant, but his statement stayed with me all these years. The *gurupuja* song has a very deep meaning and from that song I'm beginning to get a little flash of the importance of seriously following Srila Prabhupada. For the first time I'm beginning to attain a serious attitude. "Entering into the meaning," means to understand what Prabhupada is doing. The spiritual master's lotus feet are the only way to achieve pure devotional service, and to achieve that goal—pure devotional service—we have to be burning with the desire for it.

In his lectures, Prabhupada would say, "You have to be very anxious for this and develop this." We heard his words but we could not understand what he meant. It is not easy, but when you change your heart and become serious, then you can enter into the meaning of these things and feel them with great emotion. Then you can feel reciprocation with Srila Prabhupada. It comes from meaning it when you say, "I'm going to follow strictly." Sometimes we say, "I'll try" because we're not always ready to be strict, we have a lot of distractions. It takes a while. Everybody goes at a different pace. But sooner or later, that's the goal. So, if you can achieve that, it's very nice and very important. Prabhupada would like that.

Karandhar: Siddhasvarupa came to L.A. He split up his group and sent some to San Francisco, some to L.A., and some to New York. He himself came to L.A. and right away we butted heads because I was critical. I thought his group was dilettante. His people were nice, charming and sincere, but I thought, "This is the real movement and you guys are interlopers. Now you've come to us and you have to follow our program." A couple of his close associates wanted to put him in a special position, and I was against that. I said, "No, you're going to have to follow the program like everybody else." There were a couple of spats. Siddhasvarupa went to Prabhupada and complained about me and Prabhupada called me and said, "Be a little patient and tolerant. Let's try and work this thing out. He's a sincere boy. He's come with his people and we have to try to make them comfortable" and so forth. But my ego was too big. Siddhasvarupa left after a short time. I don't know where he went, but he had to go someplace where he could find his own space and be his own GBC, which was no different than a lot of other devotees. I was like that more than anybody else. As long as I was in L.A. in my own domain, I was comfortable. As soon as I went somewhere else where I didn't have so much control over my environment and my schedule, I didn't like it and I wanted to get back to L.A.

Aniruddha: One morning I was sitting on the steps that led to Prabhupada's apartment, telling a devotee some stories about Prabhupada, and when I turned around, Prabhupada was coming up the stairs. I offered my respects, and he said, "Oh, Aniruddha, how are you?"

I had to be honest. I couldn't say, "I'm fine." I said, "How can I be, Prabhupada? I'm not living in the temple." Prabhupada got very grave and said, "So?" That's all he needed to say. I understood that he meant, "You're speaking like that, but why aren't you acting in that way?" Then he said, "Hare Krishna!" and went upstairs.

When Prabhupada was leaving Hawaii, we all went to the airport to see him off. In the airport at that time, the gate was separated from the main thoroughfare of the terminal with a glass partition. Everybody went inside the gate and was sitting around Prabhupada, but I was on the other side of this partition. I was staying away. I wanted to join everyone, but I was listening to my mind. Bhumna came to the glass and said to me, "Prabhupada wants to see you." My heart started to pound – boom, boom, boom, boom, boom. I went inside very shyly. Sudama got up and I sat next to Prabhupada. I later on learned that Satsvarupa Maharaj Goswami, who was traveling with Prabhupada, had seen me and said to Prabhupada, "Oh, there's Aniruddha, Prabhupada, you remember him." Prabhupada had said, "Yes, tell him to come in."

So, I sat next to Prabhupada, he looked at me and said, "Oh, how have you been? You've been with your father?" Immediately my mind thought, "Why is he asking that?" But now I understand that Prabhupada knew that many of my problems were due to my bad relationship with my father. That's one reason why I couldn't relate to others and why I was so shy. What I wanted to say was, "No, Prabhupada, you are my father." But I couldn't say that so I said, "No, Srila Prabhupada. Ever since I have had anything to do with Krishna consciousness, my parents don't want to have anything to do with me." And we both smiled. Prabhupada's face lit up. Before that moment I was morose, but after that moment my whole spiritual life came back to me again. I felt so enlivened. It was wonderful.

During this exchange, I was just focusing on Srila Prabhupada, as if he and I we were the only ones there. I was oblivious to all the devotees until Prabhupada turned to speak to them. They were in awe, seeing me have this communication with Prabhupada. They were transcendentally envious, which is beautiful. Prabhupada said to them, "Aniruddha was with us in the beginning in L.A." I felt ashamed of myself. I knew that Prabhupada was leading up to giving me some instruction. Prabhupada knew my heart and he knew how to bring me out of illusion. I wasn't envious of Prabhupada, I was covered over by gross bodily identification. But that cleared fairly easily.

At the time the Hawaii temple was having difficulty and because of Prabhupada's words to me, I felt responsible to help. I had a lot of experience from L.A. Then it was announced that it was time for Prabhupada's plane to leave, so Prabhupada walked to the gate. As he walked he turned around and looked at me from the corner of his eye. He said, "Aniruddha, you take charge of *sankirtan*." That was the instruction I feared. I said, "Take charge, Prabhupada?" I wasn't even chanting my rounds. He said, "Yes. Hare Krishna," and he went on the plane.

What can you do? I'm sure Prabhupada knew that I wouldn't

do it right away but that eventually I'd be ready. His words have never left me. They have been repeated in my mind for years but I haven't acted on them. Now I feel determined to do the things that Prabhupada said. In one letter he wrote to me, "You can do tremendous service for Krishna." But when I read that at the time, I thought that Prabhupada was flattering me like my father did, just to get me to do something.

Prabhupada knows our potential. If we follow everything he says, if we chant and try to hear, then automatically we'll become detached, we'll get rid of this ego that's holding us back, the false idea that "I'm the doer." If we follow Prabhupada's teachings, then Krishna does everything and Krishna consciousness becomes ecstatic—very enlivening—because we don't have to worry about the results. We don't have to think, "Oh, I cannot do this." If we're doing something for recognition, for position, for any ulterior motive, we're not free. Prabhupada gave us real freedom but we couldn't really grasp it. We were attracted to Prabhupada's energy, to his love. For some of us the philosophy was difficult.

Karandhar: I wasn't a special soul. I was a spoiled, self-centered, immature brat. And I had low self-esteem. But Prabhupada nurtured me psychologically. In that sense, we had a profound and deep relationship that did a lot to rehabilitate my damaged and dysfunctional personality. But then my faults swung to the other side. I became egotistical and puffed up and began to think I knew more and I knew better.

My remembering Srila Prabhupada's qualities is like a child remembering the qualities of a parent. I'm not a great judge of character or saints. I don't know who Prabhupada is or who he was. He was kind and nurturing, and that's what attracted me to him. For most of the devotees—Tamal Krishna, Gargamuni, Silavati—that I was involved with in those early days, my formative years, their relationship with Prabhupada was like mine. In most ways we were childish, and Prabhupada gave us the attention and patience that our parents were unable to give. The time, the history, the circumstances and the culture all contributed to our neediness. Prabhupada was a father figure and we were children who needed tolerance. He was practical and sensible and he was definitely dedicated to his mission. Prabhupada was really alone. Although he told us how much we helped him, we were at least as much trouble and gave him as many headaches as we did any service. But he was centered. He carried on with his mission despite all of the hassles and the turmoil that we provoked and generated.

Aniruddha: Upendra was a wonderful devotee—warm, kind, and affectionate, and one of the god-brothers from the early days. He was a young man and Prabhupada took him under his wing. From Hawaii, Upendra went with Prabhupada to L.A. before Prabhupada sent him to Fiji to open up a temple. So, Upendra said he was sitting in Prabhupada's room when Prabhupada looked at him and said, "You know, Upendra, those were the good old days. They will not be like that anymore." I certainly would not exchange my experience of those early times. Everything has its purpose.

TAPE 33

Indradyumna Swami

Indradyumna Swami: I first saw Srila Prabhupada when he arrived in the Detroit airport on July 16, 1971. Devotees had come from everywhere—Chicago, New York, St. Louis, even the West Coast—to receive Srila Prabhupada. Prabhupada had been away for some time, and many of us had never seen him, so there was a tumultuous *kirtan*. I was looking through my camera lens when Prabhupada turned the corner in the airport. In those days, a photograph of Srila Prabhupada was something rare and special and if a devotee had one, he would treasure it. The few photos I'd seen were black-and-white and often during our *japa* sessions, we'd sit around one of them and chant. I was eager to get my own photo of Prabhupada, and when I saw Prabhupada through my lens I thought, "Prabhupada looks just like he does in the photographs." Meanwhile, all around me there was a huge *kirtan* and devotees, especially devotees who had had Srila Prabhupada's association before, began to cry and to offer their obeisances. My god-brother Bahulasva prabhu was next to me—he was a hero for me because he was a good preacher, a leader and a tough devotee—but he was on the ground crying, "Prabhupada! Prabhupada!" I thought, "Why am I not crying? I must have so many material desires in my heart that I can't cry when I see my spiritual master." So I put my camera in my bag and fell to the ground saying, "*nama om visnu-padaya . . .*" Then Prabhupada embraced Kirtanananda Maharaj and patted Bhagavan das on the head. It was very sweet. And he sat on a chair we'd set up for him and lectured. I'd been meditating on him for a few months and I was so mesmerized by seeing him in front of me that I couldn't hear what he was saying. But there is one sentence that other devotees who were there (like Bhakta-bringha Govinda Maharaj and Praghosa prabhu) and I remember from this lecture. Prabhupada said, "Our first proposition is that, 'You are not this body; you are spirit soul. Some way or other, you are in contact with this material world, and you have got this material body, and under illusion, you are accepting something which you are not.'" That entered into my heart and convinced me, "Oh, I'm not the body, I'm a spirit soul." I'd read it often in Prabhupada's books and heard it in lectures, but when Prabhupada leaned over a little and said those words, it was powerful to hear it from his lips.

The first morning in the Detroit temple, Prabhupada came down the stairs to give class. Bhagavan's wife, Krishna-bhamini, along with her first child, one-year-old Vaishnava das, were standing near Prabhupada's *vyasasana* and I was standing near Krishna-bhamini. When Prabhupada walked in, *kirtan* was going on and Vaishnava was expertly playing the *kartals*—sweetly and in time. Prabhupada saw this and said, "Oh, this is very nice." Then he sat down on the *vyasasana* and instead of picking up his *kartals* and chanting *jaya radha-madhava,* he said, "So these children who are born in our Krishna consciousness Society, they could not finish Krishna consciousness in their last life. They have been given the chance to take birth in the family of a devotee husband and wife; therefore this child is playing the *kartals*. Otherwise it is not possible. He had practice in his last life; therefore again he's remembering and playing. This is the fact." Krishna-bhamini was so happy to hear that. Prabhupada also quoted the *Bhagavad-gita* on how the unsuccessful yogi takes birth again either on a higher planet or in a family of wealthy merchants or, Prabhupada said, "In a nice devotee or *brahmana's* house." He said, "These children are special. You must take very good care of them." That impression remained with me.

Another time, at the chateau in New Mayapur when I was a *grihastha,* one afternoon I was taking my one-year old son on my shoulders while I chanted my *japa* around the castle. Prabhupada came to look out the window from his quarters upstairs and my son, Gaura-shakti, saw Prabhupada and said, "Prabhupada! Prabhupada! Prabhupada!" He was so excited that I thought he was going to fall off my shoulders. I said, "Okay, hold on! Hold on!" Prabhupada waved to him and that night in his *darshan,* Prabhupada brought up this incident. He said, "There was one young boy going around the castle with his father and when he saw me, he started chanting 'Prabhupada! Prabhupada!'" Prabhupada said, "We don't know who these children are. They're so enthusiastic when they see me, maybe there is some relationship from a previous birth." I said, "Ah, my son."

I'd been a devotee about eight months and I really wanted to be initiated but Bhagavan said that none of the devotees he'd recommended for initiation had left and he was very strict about devotees waiting one year before they were initiated. This was unusual because in those days devotees were getting initiated after six months, four months or even one month. But since Bhagavan didn't authorize me to be initiated I thought, "I want Prabhupada to know that I'm aspiring to be initiated by him." So, when Prabhupada was going to the car to leave the Detroit temple, I thought, "I'll give Prabhupada a donation," and I ran upstairs. I'd heard something about the BBT, the Bhaktivedanta Book Trust. When I'd joined the temple, I'd given all my money—two or three thousand dollars—to the temple, and the temple president had allowed me to keep ten dollars. I was saving that ten dollars for an emergency—it was some kind of security—and for me it was a lot. I put it in an envelope and I wrote a short letter: "Dear Srila Prabhupada, please accept my humble obeisances. All glories to you. Thank you for coming to Detroit. It was a short stay, but I learned so much during your visit and I became attached to you. I'm sorry to see you go and I'm going to feel your separation."

I put it in the envelope with the money, sealed it, and ran downstairs. Prabhupada was outside, just getting into his car and I was at the door thirty or forty feet away. I yelled, "Srila Prabhupada!" All the devotees stopped and looked around. Prabhupada said, "Oh?" I said, "I have a letter for you." I ran up to him, paid my obeisances, and gave him my envelope. Prabhupada folded his hands and said, "Hare Krishna." Those short encounters with Srila Prabhupada made such an impression in our hearts. *Lava-matra sadhu-sange sarva-siddhi haya*. By even a moment's association with a pure devotee, one can attain all success.

Prabhupada put my letter in his *kurta* pocket but it was sticking out. I thought, "Is he going to lose it? Will he read it?" Then he drove off. I thought, "Prabhupada's so busy, he probably won't reply." Two weeks later a letter from Srila Prabhupada came in the mail. In those days, whenever a letter would come it was a special event. The temple president would get the letter, and he wouldn't say to whom it was addressed. We'd assemble in the temple reception room, someone would blow a conch, "*Woooooooo!* A letter has come from Srila Prabhupada!" and whatever we were doing—working in the kitchen, cleaning the temple room, preparing the books for *sankirtan* —everyone would drop it and run to hear a few drops of nectar from Srila Prabhupada. We didn't think, "Oh, this letter is for this particular prabhu." We'd thought that whatever Srila Prabhupada said was for the benefit of all of us, so every devotee would hang on every word in the letter. So, Bhagavan said, "Today we've received a letter from Srila Prabhupada addressed to Bhakta Brian." I said, "That's me! Prabhupada wrote a reply to my letter!" Bhagavan said, "Bhakta Brian, you can come forward and read the letter." So I came forward, my hands shaking, and I read, "My dear Bhakta Brian, please accept my blessings. I want to thank you very much for your donation of ten dollars towards my book fund. I have information from the authorities in your temple that you are doing very nicely in Krishna consciousness. So my request to you is that you always follow in the footsteps of advanced devotees and in due course of time I will be very happy to accept you as my duly initiated disciple." I was elated that Prabhupada had agreed to initiate me in due course of time. That gave me a lot of spiritual strength.

Some months later, Srila Prabhupada wrote to Bhagavan das that he wanted Bhagavan to go to Europe to help with the new temple in Paris. A few devotees were there—Hari-vilasa, Locanananda, Umapati prabhu (who is now Umapati Swami)—but Prabhupada wanted a GBC man there to organize the preaching and get things going. So one day Bhagavan mentioned that he was going to France and he wanted an assistant. I raised my hand and said, "I traveled around Europe once." He said, "Do you know how to travel?" I said, "Of course. I've been to France, Germany and Spain. Take me and I'll organize the traveling."

Bhagavan and I were already quite close. He said, "All right, you can come but on one condition—that you get us on the same flight as Srila Prabhupada." Prabhupada was scheduled to fly to London in about a week. So Bhagavan said, "If we're going to go, we'll try to go on the same flight. I said, "Okay." I got on the telephone to New York and found out from the devotees what flight Srila Prabhupada was on. Then I called the airline ticket agent and said, "Do you have an A.C. Bhaktivedanta Swami, a Mr. Swami on this flight?" The ticket agent replied, "Yes, we do." I said, "I'd like to reserve two seats on that flight." She said, "I'm sorry, the flight's completely booked." My heart dropped. I said, "Isn't there anything you can do? This is my spiritual master." She said, "Your what?" I said, "He's my spiritual master." She said, "What's a spiritual master?" I said, "He's my guru, my spiritual teacher. In Christianity you have Jesus Christ who's your life and soul and also your teacher." She said, "Ohhhh. Okay, just one minute. I'll go talk to my supervisor." Two minutes later she came back and said, "Sir, we've made an arrangement so you can be with your guru on the flight. We've got two seats for you." I gave her Bhagavan's name and my name, and some days later we drove to New York City.

At that time the temple was on Henry Street in Brooklyn. Prabhupada was lecturing and initiating and devotees I'd heard about and wanted to meet, like Baradraj and Vishnujana Maharaj, were leading *kirtans* and having *harinam* on the streets every day. Bhavananda had made a pop art *vyasasana* for Srila Prabhupada with different colors and patterns. I was impressed, "This is an amazing *vyasasana*." But Prabhupada would struggle not to slip when he sat on it, and I always wanted to hold the cushion for him.

When it was time to go to the airport for our flight, Bhagavan and I left a little early. In those days everyone in the temple would go to the airport to see Prabhupada off, but this time most of the other devotees got stuck in traffic. Somehow we avoided the jam and got to the airport first. Srila Prabhupada and Pradyumna arrived just behind us. We checked in our bags and went to the passport control, and by that time hundreds and hundreds of devotees had arrived. It was chaotic. Everybody wanted to see Prabhupada, offer their obeisances, and maybe ask a few questions. After the passport check, an officer checked our hand luggage. I was next to Prabhupada when that officer said, "I want to see inside your white bag." Prabhupada kept all his important papers, his glasses, his *kartals*, certain documents, and medicine in a white bag he carried whenever he traveled. I was curious to see inside that white bag, but when the officer asked him, Prabhupada had trouble with the locks. The bag was old and it was made in India. The officer became rough, "Open that bag, I said!"

I leaned over the counter right into his face and said, "If you speak to my spiritual master like that again, I'm going to break your face." The officer stood back and said, "I thought you people were nonviolent." I said, "You're speaking to a pure devotee. You should know the proper etiquette." He said, "Okay young man. You open the bag." I said, "Okay." I turned the bag around and it opened, just like that. I became mesmerized—looking into the bag was a confidential insight into Prabhupada's possessions. The officer said, "Excuse me, I want to see in the bag." I turned the bag around, the officer looked in it and said, "Okay, thank you."

While Pradyumna and Bhagavan went through the same check-in formalities, Prabhupada and I walked to the plane. Just the two of us were in the hallway. It was the first time I'd been alone with Prabhupada. Prabhupada turned to me and said, "Because people in this material world associate with the modes of nature, they have no good qualities. Do you understand, Indradyumna?" Prabhupada was speaking to me! I didn't really understand but I said, "Yes." We walked a little further, then stopped, and he said, "They are hovering on the mental platform without Krishna consciousness, but with all bad qualities. Do you understand, Indradyumna?" "Yes." Just before we got on the plane, Prabhupada stopped again and said, "Because people associate with the modes of nature, they're going down. But if we can revive their Krishna consciousness, they will develop all good qualities. Do you understand?" I said, "Yes, now I understand." Hearing the same knowledge three times had a special potency—it entered my heart. I said, "Yes, I understand that they have bad qualities because they're associating with material nature. But if we revive their Krishna consciousness, then all their good qualities will come out." I felt, "Wow, okay, now I understand!" It was a mystical experience.

We went on the plane, Srila Prabhupada sat down and I nervously sat down next to him, not knowing what to do. There were no other passengers. I chanted, "Hare Krishna Hare Krishna, Krishna Krishna Hare Hare, Hare Rama . . ." and thought, "Prabhupada will see I'm chanting good rounds." Prabhupada looked out the window. A few other passengers came on and Prabhupada said, "So, *prasada*?" I thought, "What *prasada*?" At the time, Pradyumna was Prabhupada's secretary and servant and had Prabhupada's *prasada* for the trip, but as we were going through the crowd of devotees at the airport, somebody had handed me a bag and said, "Here's some oranges for Prabhupada. Tell him it's from such-and-such." So I had that bag. It had a little plastic knife, some paper plates and three oranges. I pulled down the tray table, took out the knife, cut the oranges, and gave them to Srila Prabhupada. Prabhupada sucked the juice out of the slices, his jaw making a noise, and ate them all. He put the last one down and said, "Hare Krishna. So, Indradyumna, you'll take *prasada*?" Neophyte devotee that I am, I said, "Srila Prabhupada, there's no more *prasada*." Prabhupada said, "There's *maha maha prasada*." I said, "Ohh . . ." and I took the plate feeling happy that my spiritual master had ordered me to take his remnants. I was in bliss. I put the peels in my mouth and started chewing. Orange peels are sour and my lips and mouth burned, but I thought, "This is *maha*!" I took two, three peels, and tears came to my eyes, "*Maha prasada*!" Prabhupada looked at me with an expression of amazed approval. I sucked the rest of them.

Then the plane took off, some time passed, and we were asked to close the window blinds because a movie was starting. I thought, "A movie is *maya*. I'm going to show Prabhupada that I'm not going to watch this movie." It was dark, the movie started and I picked up my *Bhagavad-gita* and read different verses, ". . . *dehino 'smin yatha dehe . . . dhiras tatra na muhyati . . . sarva-dharman parityajya* . . . I'm not watching this movie." I heard Prabhupada chuckle. And then he started to laugh. I looked over and Prabhupada was watching the movie! I put the book down, looked up, and saw it was one of Charlie Chaplin's humorous movies. Prabhupada liked the movie. He was laughing, Pradyumna was laughing, and I was also laughing. When the movie ended and the lights came on, I thought, "We aren't supposed to watch movies. What's going on here? Prabhupada must have some explanation." I leaned over to Pradyumna who was on the other side of Prabhupada, and said, "Pradyumna, can I speak to you?" He said, "I'm busy now." I said, "I need to speak to you, I have an important question. I'll meet you by the bathroom." I got up and went toward the bathroom. Pradyumna got up, went past Prabhupada and joined me in the aisle.

I said, "Pradyumna, we're not supposed to watch movies, so what am I supposed to think?" He said, "I don't know." I said, "Maybe we should ask Srila Prabhupada." He said, "Okay. Go ask Srila

Prabhupada." I said, "No, you ask Srila Prabhupada." He said, "No, you ask Srila Prabhupada." We went back and forth like this and finally he agreed to ask Srila Prabhupada. He sat down next to Prabhupada, they spoke and eventually a big smile came on Pradyumna's face. I was in the aisle waiting. Pradyumna walked over, still smiling. I said, "What did Srila Prabhupada say?" Pradyumna said, "Prabhupada said, 'we don't generally watch movies, but Charlie Chaplin's humor is very original and Krishna is the origin of all original things.'" Even as a young boy, Prabhupada liked the innocent humor of Charlie Chaplin.

I was excited as we landed in London because I had heard how Malati, Shyamasundar, Mukunda, Janaki, Gurudas, Yamuna and all the other devotees there had done a lot of service and built a new center and I'd heard how the Beatles had taken an interest in Krishna consciousness. Srila Prabhupada's receptions were always special, but I was expecting that this would be an extra special, big reception.

After we landed, Prabhupada chanted his japa while we collected the luggage, but an important bag, the bag with commentaries by the *acharyas* that Prabhupada used for his writing, didn't arrive. We waited and waited. We could hear a big *kirtan* in the reception hall, but there was no bag. Shyamasundar was upset. He said, "Someone has to wait here for the bag." I tried to hide behind a pillar. Shyamasundar said, "Prabhupada, Indradyumna can stay and bring the bag to the temple." Prabhupada said, "Yes, it is very important." Oh no, I'm going to miss the reception! Prabhupada walked out the door, the other devotees left with him, and I could see the *kirtan*, Hare Krishna, Hare Krishna. I had to wait for this bag! Why did they lose the bag? I waited by the ticket counter for about an hour-and-a-half, and finally they found the bag and brought it to me. It was a huge heavy suitcase packed full of books. I could hardly lift it. I put it on a trolley and went outside. It was raining and cold. There were no devotees around and I was miserable that I had missed the reception. I hailed a taxi, put the bag in and got in. The taxi driver said,

"Where do you want to go?" I said, "7 Bury Place." He looked back and said, "Are you all right, son?" I said, "No." He said, "Anything I can do to help you?" I replied, "No, I missed the reception of my spiritual master." He said, "Your what?" I said, "I have a spiritual master. I'm a devotee in the Hare Krishna movement." "Oh," he said, "the people who sing on Oxford Street. Well, sorry about that. Anyway, there's always a better day."

It was even raining harder when we got to the temple. I paid the driver, walked up the stairs with that big bag, knocked on the door, and some devotee with a blissful face answered, "Oh, Hare Krishna! Who are you?" I replied, "I'm Indradyumna das. I came on the flight with Srila Prabhupada and I had to wait behind for his bag." The devotee said, "Ah, come in."

I came in, put the bag down and thought, "Well, God, at least I'll get some of the *prasadam* feast." The devotees were sitting around with paper plates that were empty except for yellow turmeric stains and a few finger marks in the *ghee*. I said, "Prabhus, is there any *prasadam*?" One devotee said, "Oh, prabhu, you missed the *prasadam*. You should have come a couple hours earlier. And you missed the reception! The reception for Prabhupada was so ecstatic! Prabhupada spoke so nicely and we had a big *kirtan*!" I said, "Oh, please. There's no *prasadam*, not even a *pakora*?"

"Nope."

"Okay, well, Prabhupada's upstairs?"

"Yeah, he has a room upstairs."

"Can you help me carry this bag upstairs?"

"I'm so full. I can't help."

So I did it myself.

I was starting to get angry at that bag. Later I understood that bag was the source of all good fortune for me. The steps were very steep in Bury Place Temple. I took that bag up—boom, boom, boom, boom. Prabhupada's room was on the second floor and I was hungry, exhausted, and hadn't showered. I saw a door with a sign, 'His Divine Grace A. C. Bhaktivedanta Swami,' and I thought, "Prabhupada's there." I didn't knock. I didn't think of etiquette. I was excited to see Prabhupada again and I was a little confused. I opened the door, turned around and started dragging Prabhupada's suitcase in backwards when all of a sudden Nanda Kumar, Srila Prabhupada's servant in London, said, "Hey, watch out! You're going to bump into Srila Prabhupada!" I dropped the bag, turned around, and Prabhupada was standing close to me. He said, "Hare Krishna." I said, "Oh, Srila Prabhupada," and I fell down to offer my obeisances, *"Namah om visnu-padaya krsna-presthaya bhutale, srimate bhaktivedanta . . ."* All of a sudden there was a slap on my back. I thought, "Prabhupada slapped me on the back," but I couldn't figure out if it was out of love or anger. Of course, either would be a blessing. I can still feel Prabhupada's blessing right there on my back. I continued, *"Namaste sarasvate . . ."* and Prabhupada said something softly. I couldn't hear him. I was near Prabhupada's feet, and after a few moments his feet walked to another room. I got up and Prabhupada wasn't there. Nanda Kumar's mouth was open. I said, "Prabhu, what happened?" He said, "Prabhupada slapped you on the back." I said, "Yeah, I know. Really hard. And what did he say?" Nanda Kumar smiled and said, "Oh, it was so nice. Prabhupada said, 'So much endeavor in this material world. But when I take you back home, back to Godhead, everything will be easy and sublime.'"

We receive so many instructions from Srila Prabhupada's books, but if a disciple gets a personal blessing from the spiritual master, he treasures that and keeps it in his heart forever. Over the years, when there was opposition as the Krishna conscious movement spread and when there were daily difficulties in going out on *sankirtan*—too cold, too hot, too tired—then I remember Prabhupada's words. "So much endeavor in this material world. But when I take you back home, back to Godhead, everything will be easy and sublime." When difficult days come, those words also come to me. Let us struggle to serve Srila Prabhupada, to push on the *sankirtan* movement in this world, because in the end Prabhupada's going to take us all back home, back to Godhead. And when we go back to the spiritual world, everything's going to be easy and sublime.

We spent a couple of days in London and once someone said to Bhagavan and me, "Prabhupada wants to see you." We knocked on the door, Nanda Kumar answered and invited us in. Prabhupada was sitting behind a low desk. We paid our obeisances, and Prabhupada preached about the importance of the *sankirtan* movement. He appreciated that we were going to help the *sankirtan* movement in Paris. He looked at me and said, "My instruction to you is to preach boldly and have faith in the holy names. Krishna will give you all facility." Again his instruction went into my heart and I meditate on it constantly. "Preach boldly and have faith in the holy names."

Then Prabhupada said, "I'll give you something to encourage you," and he pulled out some of his clothes from a drawer. He handed something to Bhagavan das and he handed me one of his *dhotis*. I took that *dhoti* to my heart and I said, "Wow, now I have something that I can treasure. I have the instructions from Srila Prabhupada to preach boldly and have faith in the holy names and I have his own *dhoti*." Although I was a *grihastha*, I used to wear that *dhoti* like a *chaddar*. Once a *sannyasi* came to Europe and said to me, "You're a householder, you can't wear saffron." I said, "Maharaj, yes I can. This is Prabhupada's *dhoti* and no one's going to make me take this *dhoti* off." He said, "Oh, it's Prabhupada's *dhoti*, eh?" I said, "Yes." And I wore that *dhoti* until it wore out.

So with Prabhupada's blessings, we went to Paris. In America things were building up, we had big temples, Deities and organization. But as we walked in the Paris temple, a little house on the Fontanay-aux-Roses outside of Paris, the devotees were having a big *kirtan* and the altar—cardboard boxes with a couple of sticks to hold a picture of the Panca-tattva—collapsed. We thought, "Oh, my gosh, where did Prabhupada send us? Look at this place!" The temple was an old, cold building with no heat. But Locanananda was leading an ecstatic *kirtan*. A couple of weeks later Prabhupada came to Paris and we received him in that little temple. We had a program downtown in the American Center that Hansadutta and all the devotees from Germany came to attend. At that program, some ruffians tried to make problems outside but we didn't want to tell Prabhupada.

On a morning walk with Srila Prabhupada, I was impressed by the nice little French gardens and houses, but Prabhupada wasn't impressed. He looked at me and said, "These French, they are so expert at sense gratification."

Prabhupada visited France several times. On August 10, 1973, he installed Radha-Parisisvara in a simple ceremony. I was standing next to the *vyasasana*. As the devotees bathed Srimati Radharani, Prabhupada thought that the marble on Her cheek had become discolored from the *abhishek*. Prabhupada got off his *vyasasana* and with so much concern and care and love, he walked towards the Deity of Radharani. He got up close to Her, folded his hands and then carefully rubbed Her face. Prabhupada thought what was on Her face could be removed, but it was in the marble. I thought, "Prabhupada doesn't see the Deity as marble. He's actually seeing that Radharani is there and he's treating Her with so much love and devotion." That one incident convinced me about Deity worship.

Before they do *puja*, devotees pray, "My dear Lord, You are not a statue. You are directly the son of Maharaj Nanda." Although I didn't know that quote then, Prabhupada's intimate dealings with the Deity convinced me the Deity is not stone, but is actually Krishna, actually Radha. When Prabhupada installed the small Radha and Krishna in Los Angeles, he said, "So we have to keep ourselves always in the fire of Krishna consciousness; then everything is all right. Otherwise, it will become dull and it will be simply idol worship. That's all. That is the difference between idol worship and Deity worship. If there is no life, then it is idol worship, hedonism. And when there is life, feeling, 'Where is Krishna? Here is Krishna. Oh, I have to serve Krishna, I have to dress Him, I have to serve Radharani. She is here. Oh, I must do it very nicely. And as far as possible decorate Her to the best capacity.' In this way, if you always feel Krishna conscious, then you are fire. And if you think it is a brass-made idol, then it will remain a brass-made idol to you forever. But if you elevate yourself to the higher platform of Krishna consciousness, then Krishna, this Krishna, will talk with you. This Krishna will talk with you."

Prabhupada made monumental achievements around the world but because he was a pure devotee, the little things he did were also wonderful. Just as Krishna is greater than the greatest and smaller than the smallest, so by the Lord's grace, His pure devotee is able to do huge things. But because even the small things he does are imbued with pure devotion for the Lord, they are also significant and endearing. The way Prabhupada played *kartals*, the way he moved his fingers and chanted, captivated me. He was doing it in pure devotion for Radha and Krishna.

The next year Prabhupada was scheduled to come to Paris again, and to collect funds to renovate the temple for his arrival, we started a marathon. We went to the Metro (the underground subway) to distribute small books and pamphlets on chanting Hare Krishna. We were competing—the first two persons who won the marathon would bathe Prabhupada's feet. Every morning, the other devotees and I got up, chanted our rounds, went into the Metro before sunrise and left at eleven o'clock at night. For one month I didn't see the light of the sun. If we got tired, we slept in the Metro chairs. We ate down there too—we just kept going. I slept three or four hours a night that month. I'd heard that the dust of the lotus feet of the pure devotee, the water that washes those feet, and the remnants of his *prasadam* are very conducive for advancing in Krishna consciousness and I was determined—beg, borrow or steal—to get that mercy. My god-brother, Bhugarbha, and I were a team. We went out a few extra days, distributed many small books and pamphlets, and won that marathon. Then we made a plan—and we got an extra-big silver pitcher and bowl for washing Prabhupada's feet.

So, when Prabhupada arrived he had a big reception at the airport and then he came to the temple. Bhugarbha and I had our big silver bowl and pitcher filled with warm water, rosewater and petals. Prabhupada offered his obeisances to the Deities and sat down to receive *gurupuja*. I put the bowl under his feet and Bhugarbha started pouring the water. I thought, "Wow! This is the perfection of my life! Touching the feet of a pure devotee." The *kirtan* was raging as Bhugarbha and I gathered the many liters of water, *charanamrita*. I had the key to the president's office in my pocket and I said, "Okay, one, two, three, let's go!" We took that bowl, ran upstairs into the office, slammed and locked the door just in time to keep out the *brahmacharis* who were following us. Usually you throw *charanamrita* on everybody's head but we wanted every drop of it. Boom, boom, boom, boom, boom, the *brahmacharis* were banging, "We want the nectar! We want the nectar!" Bhugarbha and I sat down and took new cups out of our pockets. Behind us the *brahmacharis* were hitting the door. I said to Bhugarbha, "Do you hear something?" He said, "No, no, nothing to worry about." I said, "Let me do the honors," and I put *charanamrita* in a cup and gave it to Bhugarbha. Then I dipped my cup in it and—cheers! We began drinking slowly, savoring every drop. I was remembering that the water that washes the lotus feet of the pure devotee has so much mercy. The *kirtan* was going downstairs, and we were drinking and drinking. I don't know how two young men could drink that much *charanamrita*. At the end there was a couple of drops left, so we divided it, he took one and I took one. Then we sat back, "*Ahhhh*." I think that mercy is probably the reason that I'm still in the International Society for Krishna Consciousness.

After that I opened the door. Twenty *brahmacharis* tumbled in because they didn't expect the door to open. They all got up. One asked, "Where's the *charanamrita*?" I said to Bhugarbha, "The mercy?" He said, "What are they talking about?" I said, "I don't know." We still had our cups in our hands. The boys said, "You took all the *charanamrita*!" I said, "Oh, *charanamrita*! Sorry, boys. Hare

Krishna. Beg, borrow or steal, you've got to get the mercy." Then Bhagavan came and said, "What are you all doing up here?" I said, "Nothing, nothing, I'll be down in a minute, I have to use the toilet."

We came down when Prabhupada was playing his *kartals* and chanting, "*jaya radha-madhava kunja-bihari, gopi-jana-vallabha giri-vara-dhari.*" Hearing Prabhupada sing about the spiritual world, Radha and Krishna, Giri Govardhana, Yamuna, everything around us stopped. We were mesmerized. We entered the spiritual world through Prabhupada's transcendental sound vibration. Prabhupada was looking at Radha-Parisisvara and suddenly he started shaking. I thought, "Oh, no, Prabhupada's sick, something's happening." "*Kunja-behar . . .* ," and Prabhupada stopped singing. I was sitting in front of Prabhupada's *vyasasana*, and I noticed that Prabhupada's eyes welled up and then overflowed with tears. We hear Lord Chaitanya's prayer, "O Govinda! Feeling Your separation, I am considering a moment to be like twelve years or more. Tears are flowing from my eyes like torrents of rain." In the same way, Prabhupada's tears were flowing. I thought, "Here I am in the material world and Prabhupada's in the spiritual world, in Vrindavan, and by his causeless mercy I'm getting a glimpse of what it's like to be in Vrindavan, to have love for Radha and Krishna."

That was another impression that is forever etched in my heart, like lines etched in stone. If there's anything that convinced me about Krishna consciousness, it was that one incident of Prabhupada shedding tears of love. I couldn't understand it and it's still far beyond me, but it convinced me. Then Prabhupada opened his eyes and said, "Chant Hare Krishna." We started chanting and after that Prabhupada gave a short lecture and went upstairs.

In Geneva, Guru Gauranga had given me two bars of Swiss chocolate, a light and a dark, and he had told me, "Ask Srila Prabhupada if he'd like some chocolate because Swiss chocolate is the best." I said, "Okay." So, after his reception, when Prabhupada had gone upstairs to his room, we paid our obeisances and I said, "Srila Prabhupada, we have some chocolate for you." He said, "Oh?" I said, "Guru Gauranga says that Swiss chocolate is the best chocolate." He said, "Oh, so I will try some." I opened up the light one, broke a little piece and gave it to him. Prabhupada tasted it and said, "Ah, very good." He pointed to the other one and said, "And that?" I said, "This is dark chocolate, it may be a little bitter." He said, "No, no, we'll try." I took a little and gave it to Prabhupada. He said, "Hare Krishna."

When my traveling *sankirtan* party was distributing books in the French island of Corsica in the Mediterranean, Prabhupada came to Paris again, this time unexpectedly. Prabhupada was ill in England, and Bhagavan had begged Prabhupada to come to France. Bhagavan spoke about the activities that were going on in France, how many books had been published and were being distributed and the wonderful Deity worship. Bhagavan didn't want to pressure Prabhupada, but he wanted Prabhupada to know how intensely the devotees were serving and how much they loved him. When Bhagavan walked out of the room Prabhupada turned to one of his secretaries and said, "All right, we will go. Bhagavan is the Supreme Controller." So, in Corsica we received a phone call that Srila Prabhupada had arrived in Paris and we were to go there immediately.

I was giving a lecture in a yoga club when someone said, "Prabhupada's just arrived in Paris and you're supposed to go right now." I said, "I'll finish my lecture." "No," he said, "we want to go right now. We don't want to miss it." I said, "We'll finish the lecture. Prabhupada would want us to finish the lecture. This is our duty." So I finished the lecture in 10 or 15 minutes and I said to the audience, "My spiritual master, a pure devotee of the Lord, has just arrived in Paris. If any of you want to, you can come with us and meet him. Can any of you come?"

At the back a man in uniform raised his hand. He said, "Yes, my family and I will come. This is the first time we've been to a yoga center, but what you've said is interesting and I'd like to meet the person who explained this to you—your *guru*." I said, "Sir, who are you?" He said, "I'm an admiral in the French Navy." I said, "You're an admiral in the French Navy? All right." He said, "Don't worry, I'll get off duty." I said, "Well, we'll leave in about a half an hour." He said, "No problem," and made a few phone calls. He got off work, his wife packed a few belongings and got their two kids, and within a short time they were back. We jumped in our *sankirtan* van and went off for the 13-hour drive to Paris with the French admiral in tow behind us.

When we got there Prabhupada was about to have *darshan*. After driving all night we were unshaved and unshowered, but we weren't going to miss one moment of Prabhupada's association. We came in the temple and I told the devotees, "An admiral came with us who would like to meet Srila Prabhupada." They said, "All right, come on up."

Prabhupada had just started speaking when we walked in. I was so happy I could bring this person to my spiritual master. The etiquette is you bring your *guru* some *dakshin*, some flowers or fruits, and here we were bringing an admiral in the French Navy. I was bursting with pride to be the disciple of my *guru* and, "this is my alms, I've brought this person for you to preach to."

Prabhupada saw the admiral, and "Ohhh," he beamed. I asked the admiral and his wife, "You sit down here in front of Srila Prabhupada." They were respectful. They sat down and I sat next to them and told Prabhupada, "Srila Prabhupada, we were doing a program in Corsica, and when we heard of your arrival, I asked if anyone wanted to come and this admiral…"

Prabhupada said, "Oh, very nice," and began explaining how the *Bhagavad-gita* was spoken to Arjuna, who was a warrior. He described what *brahmanas, kshatriyas, vaishyas,* and *sudras* do and how everyone's focused on offering their service to Krishna. Prabhupada said, "Even though you are a warrior, you can also be a devotee of God. You can use your work to serve God." The admiral was drinking in every word of it, "Oh, yes." Then Prabhupada started speaking of reincarnation and *karma*, which was new to the admiral, but he listened carefully. Prabhupada preached to him for forty-five minutes and in the end the admiral said, "What do I call you?" I said, "Call him Srila Prabhupada." He said, "Srila Prabhupada, this is very interesting for me. I don't know what's happened. My wife wanted to go to a yoga club and now I'm sitting here in front of you, a very special person. If I want to understand this philosophy, what should I read?" Prabhupada said, "*Bhagavad-gita.*" One of the servants got a French *Bhagavad-gita*. Prabhupada said, "This is our French *Gita*. Read this." The admiral looked at it—it was a big book. He said, "I may not have time to read the whole book—of all the chapters, which one should I concentrate on?" Prabhupada said, "Read the Ninth Chapter and then you'll understand everything about Krishna." The man took the *Bhagavad-gita* that he received from Prabhupada and left. We were so young in those days, I didn't get his address or telephone number and he was gone. I thought, "Boy, I wish I had gotten his contact information."

Years later I was distributing books near the mayor's office in Paris when there was a big function. The police cordoned off the area, police cars and lights were going, and I thought, "Wow, this is great—a big event with a lot of important people. I'll get in somehow and distribute books—maybe I'll get a book to the mayor." I got in and the police threw me out, "Get out of here." Then I saw a group of Navy personnel who were part of the function and who saw how I'd been roughly thrown out. And who did I see? The admiral in his uniform. He went to the police and said, "Let this boy come." I thought, "Oh, this is a good opportunity." I said, "Admiral, it's good to see you again," and I gave a few books to the people around there. I actually didn't sell any books. The admiral said, "Yeah. Not a day goes by I don't remember your spiritual teacher. Not a week goes by I don't read the Ninth Chapter of *Bhagavad-gita.*" I said, "Thank you very much," and we shook hands. Then the police said, "All right, that's enough! You have to go." I went out of the ropes and I thought, "Oh, my God, again I didn't get his name and address." But I thought it was Krishna's mercy that this man met a pure devotee and that he would have the opportunity to meet Prabhupada again.

Another time we were getting ready for Prabhupada's arrival in Paris when there was a knock on the temple door. We opened it and there was a 19 year-old disheveled bum who hadn't bathed in weeks and had intoxicated eyes and hair matted with dirt. "Food," he grunted. "All right," I said, "I'll give you *prasadam*." He said, "I will come in." "No," I said, "first bathe, you're too dirty." We gave him *prasadam* and he went away.

Later in the afternoon I was on a *japa* walk on a prestigious Paris boulevard near the Arc de Triomphe when I heard a noise in the bushes. I looked and saw that this boy had made a little place for himself there with some newspapers. He'd been there a few days. The next day I came by and he popped out of the bushes, "Food!" I said, "Come to the temple, we'll give you some *prasadam*."

Other devotees heard about him. We nicknamed him Pig Pen, and after that I forgot about him. Then, after Prabhupada arrived, one morning all the devotees except the *pujaris* (who were on the altar dressing the Deities) went for a walk in that same area. Suddenly this boy lunged out of the bushes and tried to grab Prabhupada's feet. Someone said, "Get that boy!" and the devotees threw him back in the bushes. Oh, my God, Pig Pen almost touched Prabhupada's feet!

We all walked around a lake, then went back to the temple, and I noticed that the temple door, which we had left closed, was wide open. Somebody had come in while we were away. I was next to Prabhupada when we went into the temple room, and there was Pig Pen. He lunged and grabbed Prabhupada's feet. Somebody said, "Get that . . ." But Prabhupada said, "No." Prabhupada let Pig Pen hold his feet. Prabhupada massaged Pig Pen's head saying, "That's all right, my boy, that's all right. Hare Krishna, Hare Krishna. It's all right, it's all right." It was completely silent. Nobody moved. We were watching, stunned. "It's all right, my boy."

Then Prabhupada said, "All right, Hare Krishna." Pig Pen fell back and we greeted the Deities, "*Govindam adi-purusam tam aham* . . ." The temple was crowded and Pig Pen was sitting in the middle of the floor but nobody dared move Pig Pen out of the temple room because we'd seen how affectionate Prabhupada was towards him. Prabhupada gave class and afterward somebody said, "Pig Pen should leave." But someone else said, "No, Prabhupada gave him some mercy. Let's see. So Pig Pen, do you want to stay?" Pig Pen grunted. He had been taking drugs. I said, "Take him upstairs and clean him up." He went upstairs, had a shower and someone helped him put on a *dhoti* and *kurta*. I didn't recognize him when he came downstairs, but he still couldn't speak well. He stayed around that day and then he spent the night. Some devotees thought, "We can't have him around, he can't do anything." But Pig Pen started cleaning things. He endeared himself to the devotees by cleaning. Sometimes we'd say, "Pig Pen, how are you doing?" He'd reply, "Prabhupada saved me, Prabhupada saved me." We'd say, "Okay, Prabhupada saved you." Then he'd start chanting.

A couple of weeks later it was time for me to go on traveling *sankirtan* in my van. We packed the van, went inside to get some more books, came out, and Pig Pen was sitting in the front passenger's seat. I said, "Pig Pen, what are you doing here?" He said, "Go on *sankirtan*." I said, "Pig Pen, you're doing a good job cleaning the temple." "Go on *sankirtan*," he said. I said, "Pig Pen, why?" He said, "Prabhupada saved me." I said, "Oh, Pig Pen. All right. We'll give you a chance. You can clean the van." He said, "All right."

We got his few things together, put them in the van, and we left with Pig Pen in the front seat. I was driving, looking over and thinking, "Oh, God, look at this guy." Somehow he had a book bag and he put some books in it. In those days we distributed books in parking lots. We got to the parking lot and the first one out of the van was Pig Pen in his *dhoti*. I thought, "Oh, my God, what's this guy doing? He's going to get us arrested." I said, "Somebody go get him!" Someone said, "How should we get him?" I said, "Never mind, he'll get scared and be back in a minute."

We had a big breakfast and were packing our bags and talking, and then, "It looks like Pig Pen's doing a book at the entrance to the shopping market. Hey, Pig Pen!" An hour later, as we were getting ready to leave, Pig Pen came back with no books in his bag. I said, "What happened?" Someone replied, "He probably dumped them." Another said, "No, no, we saw him distributing the books." I said, "Pig Pen, how'd you do that? What did you tell the people?" He said, "I told people that Prabhupada saved me."

That was his *mantra*. Prabhupada had transformed him. In one verse, Sanatan Goswami says that just like bell metal can be changed into gold by a chemical process, so someone who has training and *diksha* from the pure Vaishnava devotee of the Lord can become more than *brahmana*—he can be Vaishnava. That transformation was quick in Pig Pen's heart. His transformation renewed our faith in the process of Krishna consciousness and in Prabhupada's mercy. Prabhupada transformed that boy by rubbing his head, "It's all right, it's all right, my boy. Hare Krishna, it's all right." Who can understand what Prabhupada gave during those twenty seconds that the boy was holding onto Prabhupada's feet in the temple room?

Pig Pen's speech cleared up, he started talking nicely, and he became a big book distributor and started giving classes. Eventually he was initiated as Rasada das and for many years served in France. Years later I heard that he was still distributing books in New York. All glories to Srila Prabhupada's mercy that transforms the Jagais and Madhais of the modern era!

One time Prabhupada arrived in New Mayapur when we were on traveling *sankirtan,* and later, when we arrived in New Mayapur, Prabhupada was giving *darshan* on the lawn. At the end of the *darshan*, Prabhupada asked for questions and I thought, "If I ask a question, my spiritual master will see me. He'll know that I'm his disciple, that I'm here." There were so many devotees that we didn't get much intimate association. I raised my hand and said, "In your lecture, you said that because of his love, the pure devotee of Krishna sees

Krishna everywhere. But in the Siksastaskam prayers, Lord Chaitanya's feeling separation from Krishna and thus He's feeling a moment to be like twelve years or more. So how do we understand that on one hand the devotee is seeing the Lord everywhere but on the other he is also feeling separation?"

I was sitting close to Prabhupada, and he closed his eyes. It's a deep subject, *vipralambha-bhava*, feeling loving sentiments for the Lord in separation from Him. Prabhupada opened his eyes, leaned forward and only said, "This is a difficult question. Someday when you're advanced, you will understand the answer to this question."

In the *Caitanya-caritamrta* there's a story of Sri Mukunda. Srila Prabhupada writes that, "Sri Mukunda, a great friend and associate of Lord Chaitanya Mahaprabhu, used to visit many places where people were against the Vaishnava cult. When Lord Chaitanya Mahaprabhu came to know of this, He punished Mukunda, forbidding him to see Him again. Although Chaitanya Mahaprabhu was soft like a flower, He was also strict like a thunderbolt, and everyone was afraid to allow Mukunda to come again into the presence of Sri Chaitanya Mahaprabhu. Mukunda, therefore, being very sorry, asked his friends whether he would one day be allowed to see Lord Chaitanya Mahaprabhu. When the devotees brought this inquiry to Lord Chaitanya, the Lord replied, 'Mukunda will get permission to see Me after many millions of years.' When they gave this information to Mukunda, he danced with jubilation, and when Lord Chaitanya Mahaprabhu heard that Mukunda was so patiently waiting to meet Him after millions of years, He immediately asked him to return." So, when Prabhupada said, "One day when you are advanced, you will understand," I thought, "Okay, by Prabhupada's mercy, one day I'll achieve some level of Krishna consciousness where I'll get the answer to that question."

A devotee is a perfect gentleman, and I saw that Prabhupada was willing to preach to anyone and everyone. He always had time for anyone who came. He was the perfect listener, and he was always able to give expert advice. He was so expert that he could touch even an antagonistic person's heart. In one *darshan* in Paris Prabhupada said, "Are there any questions?" A lady raised her hand and said, "Swamiji, what was I in my last life?" Prabhupada ignored that question and took another question. The lady stood up, "Swamiji, I want you to answer my question. What was I in my last life?" Prabhupada ignored her again. The third time she asked, Prabhupada said, "This is not a relevant question. *Pariprasnena sevaya.* Questions to the spiritual master should be relevant, how to advance in Krishna consciousness, how to render service to Krishna. It's not so important what you were in your last life but what you'll be in your next life." That got her. She said, "Ohhhh. So what I can be in my next life?" Prabhupada said, "You can be a devotee of Krishna if you chant Hare Krishna Hare Krishna, Krishna Krishna Hare Hare, Hare Rama Hare Rama, Rama Rama Hare Hare."

In Prabhupada's association, I saw that whether an admiral, or a hippie boy, a scholar or a devotee's mother, Prabhupada somehow expertly interested each person in Krishna consciousness. Each person went away with a favorable impression of Krishna consciousness. That's a perfect gentleman.

But Prabhupada could also become angry defending his beloved Krishna. I heard that at a big *pandal* program in Bombay, Prabhupada became angry when one boy said, "Krishna is not God. I am God." In front of 30,000 people Prabhupada exploded, "You are not God, you are dog!" Many people walked out of that *pandal* program thinking, "What kind of *sadhu* is this? A *sadhu* should not get angry." But this **is** *sadhu*. If Krishna is blasphemed and if one really loves Krishna, then that person will stand up to defend his beloved. In every situation Prabhupada reacted to give Krishna conscious instruction to each individual.

TAPE 34

Radhanatha Swami
Vaishesika das
Jagat Shaksu das
Shanka das
Rasa Lila dasi
Bhakti Vikas Swami
Brahmananda das
Vishnu Gada das
Rajendranandana das
Prasanta dasi

Radhanatha Swami: When Prabhupada left India to travel to America, only five people saw him off—a Mr. Bhagavati, a Mr. Sen Gupta of the Scindia Steamship Lines, Mr. Ali, and Srila Prabhupada's smallest son, Vrindavan Chandra De. That was his send-off.

I asked his son, Vrindavan, "What were you thinking when your father, just going on 70 years old, was walking alone up the steps to the Jaladuta, carrying only forty rupees and not knowing anyone in America to help him?" With tears in his eyes, his son told me, "I was proud of my father."

Vaishesika: I first met Srila Prabhupada in San Francisco in 1974. When I joined in 1973, I washed pots for a while and then became part of the San Francisco book distribution team. In 1973 Prabhupada started emphasizing how everyone should distribute books.

In lectures in Los Angeles, Srila Prabhupada said, "*tad-vag-visargo janatagha-viplavo, yasmin prati-slokam abaddhavaty api, namany anantasya yaso 'nkitani yat, srnvanti gayanti grnanti sadhavah.*" For someone to come in touch with the *Bhagavata* is not an ordinary thing. The *Bhagavata* is so powerful that if they read one word, or one line or even if they touch the book, their life will change. By seeing Srila Prabhupada's demeanor, by hearing the sweetness of his voice, by being taken up in his energy, he instilled in young people—some who were just walking in the door—faith in his books. Armies of devotees were distributing books.

When Srila Prabhupada was in his room in San Francisco, our temple president, Bhaktadas, introduced some of us to Srila Prabhupada. Bhaktadas said, "These are the book distributors. They are sacrificing so much to go out and sell your books every day, and they're selling so many books." We were listening, thinking, "Oh, this is nice." Srila Prabhupada said, "You must also read the books," and he preached for twenty minutes about how he wanted every one of his disciples to take full advantage of the *Srimad Bhagavatam.* "Every word," he said, "I've translated from Sanskrit into English. I've painstakingly translated these books for your benefit because I want you all to become pure devotees."

At that time I could see that Srila Prabhupada's real interest was for us to be completely serious about Krishna consciousness and to take full advantage of the process of Krishna consciousness. I've always been inspired that, although Prabhupada is pushing book distribution and it is very pleasing to him, he wants us to take advantage of everything he's given us. Srila Prabhupada wants us to take the process seriously and come to the highest platform of Krishna consciousness.

At the opening of the Krishna-Balaram Mandir in 1975, a group of us—Tripurari Maharaj, Sura das, some others and me—were working for the BBT party. After Prabhupada did the first *arati* for Krishna-Balaram, his disciples were given the opportunity to do the next *arati*. Tripurari Maharaj grabbed Sura das and me and pushed his way into the *pujari* room and said, "We're doing it!" Bhagavan came in, pushed Tripurari away and said, "No, we were here first." Gurudas came in and said, "No, we were here first." We said to Tripurari, "Maharaj, just let them do it," because we weren't fully trained in *pujari* work. But we were allowed to perform the *arati*. We were instructed to wait until Srila Prabhupada came in, then to open the Deity doors and offer the *arati*. Before we went into the Deity room, the *pujari*, who had been up for three days said, "You had better do the offerings properly because Srila Prabhupada will be watching along with all the biggest *pandits* from all over Vrindavan, and we want to make a good impression." We were very nervous. We waited and waited, and finally Srila Prabhupada came for *darshan*. We opened the doors, and we walked to the front where all the *arati* paraphernalia was. I froze. I'd never seen such *arati* paraphernalia before—long ghee wicks and so forth—and I had never done a simultaneous *arati* before. That's very difficult in and of itself.

I was at Radha-Shyamasundar's altar, Tripurari Maharaj was at Krishna-Balaram's altar, and Sura das was at Gaura-Nitai's altar. There was a fan going full speed over Gaura-Nitai's altar and no one knew where the switch for it was (the temple had just opened and everything was new to everyone). Sura das could barely light the ghee wicks or offer the *chamara* properly. Srila Prabhupada offered his obeisances to Gaura-Nitai and Krishna-Balaram. Then he came to Radha-Shyamasundar's altar and stood there. All the GBC men and the *sannyasis* stood behind Srila Prabhupada, and when I turned around to offer the incense to the devotees, I practically fainted because Prabhupada was standing there. I continued to fumble through the process and it went from bad to worse. The whole time I was thinking that Srila Prabhupada might ask me to burn my *brahmana's* thread afterwards. When I threw the offered water to the assembled devotees, it hit Tamal Krishna Maharaj squarely in his glasses and I could see he was furious.

After the *arati*, we came into the *pujari* room and Tripurari

Maharaj said, "Now is the time to pray for forgiveness." I went to the dark recesses of my room and thought that I would stay there for a long time and pray for forgiveness. Meanwhile, after the *arati,* Prabhupada went back to his room, and, according to Ramesvara, Srila Prabhupada said, "Who was doing *arati*?" Someone said, "Prabhupada, it was Tripurari Maharaj and his men. They don't know much about *puja*, but they distribute your books." Prabhupada said, "Oh, that is all right." After that I felt even more gratitude for Srila Prabhupada's mercy, and I also took it upon myself to learn how to do *puja*.

Jagat Shaksu: When *kirtan* was over, Prabhupada said the *prema-dhvani* prayers, and then he told us, "It is very nice that tonight we have with us these two Prabhus," indicating the Gaura-Nitai Deities. "There is a very nice song. Can you please follow me?" and Prabhupada started to sing Locana dasa Thakura's very beautiful song, *parama koruna, pahu dui jana nitai gauracandra, saba avatara-sara siromani, kevala ananda-kanda.* But when Prabhupada said the first two words, *parama koruna*, his voice choked and he couldn't sing anymore. He closed his eyes and put his head back on the *vyasasana*, and we saw tears gliding down his lotus face. The room was completely silent. I don't know how long that lasted, but it was like an eternal moment entered the temple room. Everything was still in ecstasy, watching the pure devotee have such a wonderful experience of his love for Gaura-Nitai! .

Then gradually Prabhupada came back to external consciousness, although he was still affected by spiritual emotions, and he said, "*Parama koruna*, so merciful. In this dark age of Kali-yuga, if Krishna incarnated to kill the demons, practically nobody would be left. In Kali-yuga, the demonic spirit and the devotee spirit is in the same body. So Lord Chaitanya didn't kill demons, He killed the demonic spirit by the *sankirtan* movement and by the association of devotees." At the end he said, "You are very fortunate. Now you must make others fortunate too. If you chant 16 rounds, follow the four regulative principles and preach, I assure you in this same lifetime you will see Krishna face to face."

Some people may say, "Well, generally it takes more than one lifetime to see Krishna face to face." But because Prabhupada made that promise, Krishna will surely have to make Prabhupada's words true.

Shanka: In a room conversation in 1976, I asked, "Srila Prabhupada, when you offer flowers to Krishna or to your spiritual master, what benefit do the flowers get?" Srila Prabhupada replied, "The plant the flower came from becomes a human being in its next life." So, my *sankirtan* began.

Rasa Lila: My initiation was a wonderful moment. It was one of those moments that Srutakirti describes—when you're so bewildered you can't remember even your own name. To be in front of Srila Prabhupada for the first time was that kind of a feeling.

The devotees in New Vrindavan had put Prabhupada's *vyasasana* on a landing about halfway up the stairs leading to Kirtanananda's cabin. To get your beads from Prabhupada, you had to climb up those stairs. It was very dramatic. The moment was so awesome you felt like you were climbing Mount Sumeru.

The night before, my husband, Narada Muni prabhu, had jokingly said, "And you better get a nice name from Srila Prabhupada." I said, "Well, yeah, I hope so. I'll try, what can I say?" So, when I went to get my beads, the sound system was reverberating and I could barely hear His Divine Grace's words. Besides that, I was practically stunned anyway. I thought I heard him say that my name was Rasa Lila but I wasn't sure. I heard all the devotees gasping and cheering. In those days we were studying Krishna Book intensely and we had contests and quizzes about it. When Prabhupada spoke my name, I experienced what he describes about the gopis during the *rasa-lila*—that as they sang and danced, their movements, their smiling, their clothes, their earrings, and their hair with flowers combined together to appear like clouds, snow, thunder and lightning. That passage flashed through my mind. When he said my name it was an experiential moment. Even though I wasn't positive what he had said, that was what I experienced. I walked down the stairs stunned and asked someone, "What did Prabhupada say my name is?" It was incredible. In one moment Prabhupada can reveal the spiritual world to you. That's his potency.

Bhakti Vikas Swami: When I received my brahminical initiation from Prabhupada in Vrindavan in 1976, I had my only one-on-one exchange with him. I'd been waiting all morning for a few mornings, and just before it was my turn to go into Prabhupada's room, Pusta Krishna, Prabhupada's secretary, wanted to stop the initiations until the next day since there were so many initiates at that time. Then he saw that I looked disappointed so he said, "Okay, go in." Now, my god-brother and close friend, Satyavak prabhu, a devotee from Britain who left his body about two years ago, had heard from the *Hari-bhakti-vilasa* that when you say *gayatri* you should face in a certain direction in the morning, another direction in the evening, and another direction at night. And he heard that you should say *gayatri* so many minutes before sunrise and so many minutes after sunset. There were many detailed rules about *gayatri*. I thought that if I got a chance, I'd like to ask Prabhupada about those rules.

I went in and Prabhupada had me pronounce the words. I thought I knew how to pronounce Sanskrit quite nicely. I read the first mantra, said every word wrong and Prabhupada corrected me. Then Prabhupada gave up trying to correct me. After I had said all the mantras, he said, "Chant this morning, noon and evening. Do you have any questions?"

I wanted to confirm the things I'd heard, so I said, "Prabhupada, is there any particular time for chanting *gayatri*?" Prabhupada had just told me "Chant morning, noon and evening," and again he said, "Yes, chant morning, noon and evening." Again I asked, "But Prabhupada, is there an exact time?" Prabhupada looked at me and said, "Morning, noon and evening." After that, I didn't think of asking the other questions. I said, "Yes, Prabhupada," offered my obeisances and left.

Brahmananda: In Montreal, there was a devotee, Dayal Nitai, who was a yogi and was also into health. He strongly criticized our diet—white rice, white sugar, butter—and said that we should eat brown rice, natural sugar, and no butter. At that time, Prabhupada was in Montreal and his apartment was a few blocks from the temple. Since the devotees didn't have a car, Prabhupada had to walk from his apartment to the temple. So, one day after class, I was walking next to Prabhupada back to his apartment while Dayal Nitai was complaining to Prabhupada about how our food was not healthy and how we were all going to get sick. Prabhupada stopped walking and said, "You see Brahmananda here? He's been eating this food for so long. Does he look sick?" But Dayal Nitai didn't get the message. Again he went on about the health thing and the way foods are processed and how we should change our diet. We walked some more and Prabhupada finally stopped and said, "You know, our Brahmananda here is so healthy that he can kill you. If I just say, he can kill you." I was shocked. What's Prabhupada doing? But I got ready. Then Dayal Nitai understood that *prasadam* was okay.

Vishnu Gada: When Bhavananda was president of the New York temple, he initiated an all-night *harinam sankirtan* party on Broadway. After being out all night, the devotees came back, attended *mangal arati* and then rested. To facilitate their schedule, *mangal arati*

was offered at 3:45 a.m. instead of the usual 4:30 a.m., and we had to wake up the Deities earlier also.

Then when Prabhupada came, he greeted the Deities, looked at Them for some time, and then spoke with Bhavananda. We were wondering, "What's Prabhupada saying?" Later we found out that Prabhupada said, "Krishna looks tired. All day He plays with the cowherd boys, He needs proper rest." Prabhupada had just arrived and I don't think anybody had told him about the all-night *harinam sankirtan* party, which was a little questionable anyway. After that, we moved *mangal arati* back to 4:30.

Rajendranandana: The pure devotee is not under the influence of the modes of material nature. When he sleeps, the pure devotee is not in ignorance but is engaged in Krishna's service. One morning when Srila Prabhupada woke up, Tamal Krishna Maharaj helped him rise and Prabhupada immediately began preaching enthusiastically. With a loud voice he said, "I want you to go to the West and preach. Ask people, 'Do you want to grow old?' No. You are forced to grow old. Do you think I want to get old? Nobody wants to grow old, but this is the law of nature. You are forced. You must surrender to Krishna if you want to become free of birth, death, disease and old age."

For Srila Prabhupada to wake up and in one moment preach on the transcendental platform, it would seem that during his sleep he was meditating on how he wanted his disciples to carry on.

Jagat Shaksu: Prabhupada called me. I went to him and paid my obeisances. He gave me my *japa mala* and said, "Your name is Jagat Shaksu das," and he explained that my name meant that we should feel the eye of the Lord watching us. Then he looked straight in my eyes and, pointing his finger, he said, "You cannot hide from the eyes of God." I thought, "Oh, my God." I wanted the earth to open up and swallow me because everybody was watching and thinking, "Maybe he did something wrong."

Actually, before I was initiated, I used to steal *maha* sweets from the kitchen, hide and eat them. When Prabhupada told me what my name meant, I immediately felt caught. I felt that Prabhupada read my mind and knew everything about me.

The next day I came back from *sankirtan* a little early and, forgetting that I was not supposed to pass through Prabhupada's garden, I passed through it. Prabhupada was sitting on his rocking chair chanting *japa*. I paid my obeisances, and was going to go back, when Prabhupada waved me over and asked, "Where have you been?" I said, "Prabhupada, I was distributing your books." We were very enthusiastic to distribute his books because we knew that Prabhupada was blessing all the people of Venezuela through his books. Prabhupada said, "How do the people in Venezuela like my books?" I said, "Prabhupada, the people here are simple but pious. As soon as they read these books, they like them and they want to buy more." Prabhupada moved his head indicating that he was satisfied and said, "Come, I have to give you something."

I followed him to his room, and on his table was a tray full of sweets. He gave me one and said, "Thank you very much for helping me." I was so moved that I was crying. I was a new devotee, yet Prabhupada gave me so much mercy. Then I thought, "He is telling me that I don't have to steal sweets, that he will give them to me." Srila Prabhupada *ki jaya!*

Shanka: When I went to Juhu in '73, the devotees there were living very austerely and worshiping the Deities, Sri Sri Radha-Rasabehari, in a small temple. In front of the temple was a fenced-in area where 14 or 15 *tulasi-devis* were growing. One day on a morning walk Srila Prabhupada asked me, "Why are the *tulasis* dying?" I said I didn't know and that I would do some research. That day I dug around the *tulasis* and found that termites and ants were eating their roots. The next morning on the walk I told Srila Prabhupada what I had found and Srila Prabhupada said, "Take one part lime and one part sulfur, mix it with ten parts of water and sprinkle it all around *tulasi-devi*. Then the ants will go away." I did that, and then Prabhupada went on his world tour. While he was gone, all the *tulasis* died. I made some nice beads for myself, took the fence down, and there was only dirt where the *tulasis* had been.

When Prabhupada had come back from his world tour, I was offering him flowers during *gurupuja* when he said, "Where are the *tulasis*?" I said, "Srila Prabhupada, I tried to save them but they all left the planet," and then I offered my obeisances and slithered out of the temple to avoid getting chastised. On the next morning walk, Srila Prabhupada stopped everybody in front of the big garden that I had made, where 54 *tulasi-devis* were growing. Srila Prabhupada asked me, "How are these *tulasis* doing?" I said, "Oh, Srila Prabhupada, they are doing very well except there are spider mites, aphids and other bugs crawling all over them." He said, "Leave the insects alone. Let them eat as much as they want. Who are you to kill them?"

Radhanatha Swami: Every year, 20,000 people who are remnants of the hippie generation, go into a deep forest and have what they call a Rainbow Gathering. We went to one of these gatherings and every night we cooked *prasad* for about three or four thousand of these people and had dramas, *kirtans* and lectures. One day I was serving *halava prasad* when a 65 year-old man with long, gray, matted hair and a long gray beard and no clothes said, "Are you a disciple of Swamiji?" I was wondering if this person was some *sadhu* from the Himalayas. I said, "Prabhupada?" He said, "Yes, I know Swamiji. He is my friend." I said, "How do you know him?" He said, "In 1965 I was going to Dr. Misra's yoga classes. Dr. Misra would not allow Swamiji to speak. Swamiji would sit in the back and pray on his beads. I would go to meet him and he would say to me, 'Whatever Dr. Misra is saying is all nonsense.' I invited Swamiji to my house, and sometimes he invited me to the tiny flat where he stayed. He cooked for me, served me, and taught me about Krishna. He was the kindest, most gentle, most loving man I have ever met in my life."

This was how Prabhupada lived. Although Dr. Misra and Srila Prabhupada had very strong philosophical debates, when Dr. Misra was sick—actually dying—Prabhupada, in Dr. Misra's own words, said, "He fed me and brought me back to health. By his love and kindness Swamiji saved my life." Although philosophically Srila Prabhupada was adamantly opposed to Dr. Misra's beliefs, Prabhupada still saw within Dr. Misra's heart a pure spirit soul, a part of Krishna, and he still showed him love and compassion.

Rajendranandana: In his final days, when Srila Prabhupada was lying on his bed and had not eaten for a long time, he said, "Now I am finished with eating. I have conquered sleeping. There is no question of sex life, and now all material activities are finished." And he asked the devotees, "Why do you pray for me to stay? This bag of bones is useless." Devotees don't like to see the film of his last days. They don't like to see pictures of Srila Prabhupada in the *antya-lila*. But, the *goswami* that our spiritual master was, he stayed with us so we would develop more and more attachment to him. At the time, he said as much to Bhavananda Maharaj that, "It is my duty to draw from you this attachment to me."

At this time, some of Srila Prabhupada's god-brothers and Gaudiya Math *sannyasis* came to visit him in his room. Srila Prabhupada asked to be propped up on some pillows and he said to them, "Please excuse me for not being able to receive you properly." And he said, "Please forgive me for all my offenses. Sometimes strong words are spoken in preaching, and I would like to ask your forgiveness for those words." Prabhupada was so humble. And his god-brothers and the Gaudiya Math *sannyasis* appropriately responded, "No, no, there has been no offense. The offense is ours. Please forgive us." And then they began talking in Bengali. Later I asked a Bengali-speaking devotee what they had said. This devotee told me that Prabhupada said, "Also please forgive my disciples. Sometime they think that only they are devotees. I've had time to teach them *prachar* but not *achar*," meaning he taught us preaching, the essence, but not proper behavior. What else could he do in the short time that he had with us? He had to send us out—an army of monkeys—to spread the glories of Lord Chaitanya via book distribution, *harinam* and all the other wonderful activities of ISKCON. Prabhupada said, "I didn't have time to teach them etiquette, so sometimes they fall short in that regard."

Prabhupada's every move, every thought and every word was dictated by the Supreme Lord, and only out of compassion for us did he remain with us in those last months. The Christians glorify Jesus Christ by saying, "He died for our sins," and for myself, my love for Srila Prabhupada was secured during his last months. It is his glory that he chose to stay with us longer than it was convenient for him. Prabhupada's doctor said that when Srila Prabhupada was lying on the bed with no body fat left due to fasting, it was like he was on fire—his skin and nerves rubbed against his bones. But did Srila Prabhupada complain even once? No. Did he ask for morphine for the pain? No. He simply wanted to be with his disciples and for his disciples to chant Hare Krishna. Out of love, he instructed all of his disciples to come and be with him for his passing. He loved us so much. He didn't forget any single service. We've heard devotees share insignificant things that they've done for Prabhupada and how he responded with, "Jaya!" That is Srila Prabhupada. How can we give up his service? How can we turn away from him or forget him? We owe him everything.

Shanka: On Bhaktisiddhanta's Disappearance Day in 1975, I was in charge of the Bombay temple kitchen and I made 98 of the 108 preparations we offered at the ceremony. When all these preparations were taken to Srila Prabhupada, Gopal Krishna, who was a young *grhastha* at the time, said, "Shanka das come and tell Srila Prabhupada what you made." So Gopal Krishna and I went to Prabhupada's room where he was sitting at a table with these 108 preparations. Prabhupada asked, "What is this preparation?" and I told him what it was and he tasted it. He asked, "What is this preparation?" and I told him what it was and he tasted it. He asked, "What is this preparation?" and I told him what it was and he tasted it. He asked, "What is this preparation?" and I told him what it was and he tasted it. Then the fifth time he asked, "What is this preparation?" and I told him what it was and he tasted it. Then he said, "Radharani has prepared this feast, you can go."

I'll also tell of a few significant chastisements that I got. One day Mother Palika asked me to go to the market to buy fruit for Srila Prabhupada. I was buying fruits when I saw a big pile of oranges. I said, "Wow, beautiful oranges." I had one cut open, it tasted great, and I bought a big bag of oranges for Srila Prabhupada. About three days later, towards the end of a morning walk, Srila Prabhupada started talking about how the material world is a perverted reflection of the spiritual world. Then he said, "Who has bought me those oranges?" I was puffed up thinking, "I'm going to be glorified." I said, "Srila Prabhupada, I bought the oranges." Srila Prabhupada said, "Those oranges are tenth class just like you." He said the oranges had been picked during the ripe season, refrigerated, and then sold for a high price during the off-season.

Another time I used a Gujarati recipe to make five-vegetable *samosas* for Srila Prabhupada. It took me a long time to grate the vegetables for the beautiful filling. Then I rolled out *puris* and flipped them in half over a little of the filling to make 35 six-inch, half-moon *samosas* that I sent to Srila Prabhupada. A couple of days went by and when I saw Brahmananda Swami, Prabhupada's secretary, I said, "How did Srila Prabhupada like the *samosas*?" Brahmananda Swami said, "He didn't touch them." Later, my good friend Harikesa, who was a *brahmachari* at the time, said, "Why don't you cook lunch for Srila Prabhupada with me?" Srila Prabhupada had invited many guests for lunch and before Harikesa and I started cooking, an Indian gentleman had made a big feast for all the guests, including a pile of little diamond *samosas*. When Harikesa and I were cooking Prabhupada's lunch, Srila Prabhupada came in. We offered our obeisances. Srila Prabhupada looked at me and said, "Did you make these *samosas*?" I said, "Oh, no, Srila Prabhupada, the other cook made them." Prabhupada said, "You don't know how to make *samosas*. You only know how to make footballs!" Srila Prabhupada looked at Harikesa, he looked at me and he said, "You two are expert in messing everything up," and he walked out smiling. After that I served him lunch for two days in a row.

Rajendranandana: In the garden we were reading the Sanskrit, the word-for-word translations, the verse and the purport from the First Canto of *Srimad-Bhagavatam*. When we read the word-for-word translation of the word *muni*, it wasn't a noun—*muni* means a thoughtful person—but it was a verb. Srila Prabhupada said, "Read that again?" The devotee read it again and Srila Prabhupada said, "Who has done this? Who has changed this? Who is that rascal?" Some prabhu's name was mentioned and Prabhuapada, said, "If you change one word of my books it can ruin our movement." He was emphatic and heavy about this point.

Not to be misuderstood, let me explain that I offer all respects to the devotees who Srila Prabhupada assigned as editors, like Dravida prabhu, but my understanding is that we can't change the message of the spiritual master. There's a great danger in that and I personally saw how Srila Prabhupada was fiery in making that point.

Shanka: Once Tamal Krishna Goswami said, "Shanka das, you're a gardener. You should offer Prabhupada a flower every day." After that I became Prabhupada's flower boy. Every time I'd see Srila Prabhupada I'd give him a flower. Sometimes he would touch my hand taking the flower. Sometimes he would grab the flower and start chastising me. Sometimes he would grab it and glorify the flower and me. Prabhupada said, "Mogra is the king of flowers."

Later on I traveled from Bombay to Calcutta on the slowest, cheapest third class train—we had very little money for anything. By the time I got to the Calcutta temple, my suitcase and shoes had been stolen and all I had was the *dhoti* and *kurta* I was wearing. And I was completely full of dirt from three days on the train. Finally, I got to Mayapur when Srila Prabhupada and the devotees were going for a morning walk, and Bhavananda Swami told Prabhupada, "Oh, Prabhupada, your gardener from Bombay is here." Prabhupada didn't say anything. We walked to Srila Bhaktisiddhanta's temple and when we returned to our property, we walked under our archway and on the left-hand side there were some cows. I didn't know anything about cows but I started fooling around with them while everyone else continued towards the temple. Then about 500 yards before they got to the temple Prabhupada stopped, turned around and said, "Shanka, come here!" I went running to him and said, "Srila Prabhupada, what would you like?" He said, "I want you to plant trees on both sides of the road here." So Jayapataka Maharaj, two Bengali boys and I planted coconut trees along that pathway. Today those trees are producing coconuts—they have survived floods and other disasters and are still going strong.

Prasanta: My favorite day of the year is Srila Prabhupada's Disappearance Day because on that day Prabhupada is fully present through remembrances of him and through the presence of his disciples. Every year I'm thankful for the opportunity to hear Srila Prabhupada's disciples speak wonderful stories about him.

When I saw the banner here, 25 YEARS OF SERVICE IN SEPARATION, it occurred to me that mine is a lifetime of service in separation because I am Srila Prabhupada's grand disciple. When I joined in '84, Prabhupada had already left. I never saw Srila Prabhupada.

In honor of Srila Prabhupada's Centennial in 1996, devotees in England produced two CDs called *A Garland of Songs*. On one CD, Jayadeva das sings a heartrending song, "I Never Knew You." I cried. I was part of the team that helped celebrate Srila Prabhupada's

Centennial and for me this recording of glorifications of Srila Prabhupada was our reward. In this song, "I Never Knew You," one line is, "Where was I when you were on the planet?" I meditated a lot on that.

Sometimes I think that one day during *mangal arati* there will be a horrible announcement that the last Prabhupada disciple has left the planet. I already apprehend the day when there will be no more Prabhupada disciples. When Prabhupada was on the planet, devotees would tell stories about him—what he was doing and saying—and the news would travel. For us grand disciples it's like that. When there is a Prabhupada disciple, we get the stories. We get to hear about the flower boy or the bathroom scrubbing, and all these little things that we don't find in Srila Prabhupada's books or on his tape recordings. And we get to love Srila Prabhupada.

As Krishna gave us *Srimad-Bhagavatam,* which has all kinds of stories about Him so that we can develop not just knowledge of Him and His teachings, but also an attraction for His personality, similarly, by hearing these beautiful stories about Srila Prabhupada, we can love Srila Prabhupada. Prabhupada explains that unless there is love, we cannot fix the mind. We cannot fix the mind on something we don't love. So we must love Srila Prabhupada. And one of the ways to love him is to hear about him. The stories we hear are significant because they teach us the heart of the pure devotee and the concerns of the pure devotee. And they can melt our reluctance to surrender.

TAPE 35

Hansadutta das

Hansadutta: One day Kirtanananda said, "We're going to meet the Swami and be initiated." At that time Sivananda—Sam Greer—had joined, and we imposed on him to lend us his green Volkswagen bus. He was attached to his bus and said, "Please, you've got to bring it back." We said, "Yeah, don't worry." So, Kirtanananda, Pradyumna, Himavati and I drove to New York in this bus but it blew up on the way back. Anyway, on the way down we stopped at my mother's place near Brewster, about an hour north of New York City. We were shaved up, wearing *dhotis* and *tilak* marks. I wouldn't sit in a chair, I had to sit on the floor, and I had to cook. But my mother was quite happy because she was spiritually inclined. Then we went to 26 Second Avenue and Kirtanananda took us upstairs to Prabhupada's little apartment.

As soon as Prabhupada saw me he said, "Oh, you have come," as if we'd already known each other. Immediately my entire muscular system felt as if it had melted away and I sank down to the ground. I bowed down, just as Kirtanananda had taught us to do. The muscles in my face and in my arms began to twitch. Finally I seated myself against the wall and looked at Prabhupada, who was shining, and I thought, "It's because I'm nervous that I'm staring," and I started to blink. But it wasn't my eyes. Prabhupada's complexion was golden, and he had effulgence streaming from him. He began to speak about how *karmis* like bitter things and the devotees like sweet things. That was my first encounter with Srila Prabhupada.

We knew that when you get initiated you get another name. My name had been Hans Jurgen Kary. Since my childhood I never liked my name because it revealed me as an immigrant and separated me from my peers. I was anticipating getting an exotic name like Hanuman or Hari das, but when I bowed down to receive my beads, Prabhupada said, "Your name is Hansadutta." I didn't quite hear him and I said, "What was that?" Prabhupada said, "Simply add *dutta*."

I was disappointed. I thought, "Oh." Not only was my name still the same, it just had the suffix '*dutta*,' but my last name also remained the same because it got the prefix, '*adhi*.' I was Hansadutta das Adhikari, and I was disappointed. After the initiation I thought, "I should find out what my name means." I went to Prabhupada and asked, "Swamiji, what does my name mean?" Prabhupada said, "I don't know."

I was bewildered. I really wanted to know what my name meant. I said, "Swamiji, is there some place where I can find the meaning of this name?" He said, "Yes." That's all he said. I wandered away but I was determined, so a third time I approached Prabhupada. I said, "In which book can I find the meaning of this name?" He said, "In *Srimad-Bhagavatam*." In those days *Srimad-Bhagavatam* was a big book even though it was only three volumes as compared to the many we have today. So I let it go. But years later in Montreal, Prabhupada was musing over different devotees' names. He casually said, "Oh, Sivananda means such-and-such, Krishna das means such-and such…" and he was going on like that. I thought, "Here is my opportunity." I said, "Prabhupada, who is Hansadutta?" He said, "You are." For some reason, Prabhupada simply wasn't going to tell me what my name meant. That was a curious incident.

When we were at 26 Second Avenue, some hippies donated an old green school bus. I thought, "This is great." I was enthusiastic. I asked Prabhupada, "Why don't we test it out by making a trip to Boston?" He agreed and in the front of the bus, next to the driver, the devotees rigged up a chair for Prabhupada. When we got going, the bus was lurching, the transmission wasn't quite in order, and the dash started to smoke. Prabhupada said, "It is like an Indian bus." I thought, "This is a great compliment." We thought anything Indian must be good because Prabhupada was from India and Krishna appeared there. Then after some minutes Prabhupada said, "Maybe it would be better to sell this bus and get some money." I wondered, "Why would he want to sell the bus?" Anyway, we made it to Boston in the bus and later I understood what Prabhupada was talking about.

In 1970, I was among the first American disciples Prabhupada took to India. Prabhupada's coming to India was a sensation something like the Beatles coming to America. It was absolutely phenomenal and the Indians were completely captured to see so many white people shaved up, singing and dancing and talking about Krishna consciousness, eating *prasadam,* sitting on the floor. In one place we went, a very important city named Surat in Gujarat, every business in the town shut down, and everybody in town—including the mayor—came to the train station to greet Prabhupada. The mayor said that even if Indira Gandhi came, she would not get that kind of reception.

In Surat we stayed at the house of Bhagubhai Jariwala. (Jariwalas are people who make gold threads). Early every morning Prabhupada would have a program, which generally only devotees attended, but in the evening local people came for *darshan.* At one evening *darshan* a man said, "Ramakrishna says that he was Krishna and Rama. What do you think of that?" From Prabhupada's previous vociferous reactions toward this kind of question, I thought, "Prabhupada is going to lay into this guy." But he didn't. Prabhupada said, "I don't know, maybe he was." Then he held up the *Bhagavad-gita* and said, "but I know for sure this is Krishna, so why should I take a chance?"

The same question could be asked of Prabhupada ten times, and each time he'd answer it in a different way. Once I heard a reporter ask him, "Are you a pure devotee of Krishna?" Prabhupada said, "Yes." "So that means you see Krishna?" "Yes." "So that means you can show me Krishna?" "Yes." The reporter said, "So show me." Prabhupada said, "Yes." The reporter said, "Well?" Prabhupada said, "First you become like them," and pointed to his disciples with their shaved heads. The reporter said, "Oh."

But at other times, to answer the same question Prabhupada would say, "No, I'm not a pure devotee." *Panditah sama darsinah.* He would say, "I'm ordinary, just like you. All I know is what I heard from my *guru*, and I'm explaining that to you." Then they would say, "Then why are we listening to you?" Prabhupada would say, "You don't have to listen. All I can tell you is what I heard from my spiritual master. Otherwise, I'm ordinary just like you."

Prabhupada's answers were always complete, irrefutable, and self-evident, but how he answered a question depended on who he was talking to. Sometimes his answers were amusing and sometimes they were so profound that they made your head spin.

Once, when Prabhupada was lecturing to a room full of hippies at 26 Second Avenue, a girl near him kept raising her hand and Prabhupada deliberately ignored her. He knew that she was going to say something foolish. But she persisted and finally Prabhupada said, "Yes?" "Swamiji, aren't there many ways to God?" Prabhupada said, "No. There is only one way. Just like food. You can't put it in your ear or in your rectum, it must go in your mouth." Everyone burst into laughter.

I was Prabhupada's secretary, which meant that when someone wanted to invite Prabhupada to a program, Prabhupada would send the person to me saying, "My secretary will take the information." Within a day or two, Prabhupada's schedule would be fully booked. Then when another person invited Prabhupada, I would say, "I'm sorry, but it's not possible because we already have a program at that time," and that person would complain to Prabhupada, "Your secretary said, 'No.'" Prabhupada would say, "Yes, I will come. Just make the arrangement." This would go on for days, as the Indian people would persist—"Prabhupada said he would come." I would say, "But it's impossible. We are already scheduled and then they'd go back to Prabhupada.

After some time I went to Prabhupada and said, "Prabhupada, you say 'Yes' to every invitation and I am supposed to make the arrangements. But when I say, 'I'm sorry but we are already booked up,' they go back to you, you say 'Yes' again, and I don't know what to do. We can't accommodate everyone." Prabhupada said, "It's my business to say 'Yes,' and it's your business to say 'No.'" I finally settled the problem by saying, "Yes," and taking all the information. Then when it was time to go, we would evaluate all the options, choose the one that had the most potential and inform everyone else that unfortunately we couldn't make it.

In Indore, another city in Gujarat where everyone tended to be devotees of Krishna, there was such a great response to Prabhupada's presence that we would be up around the clock. We would have programs all day and at eleven o'clock I'd lie down. At one o'clock someone would tell me, "Prabhupada wants to see you." For a couple of weeks I hadn't been reading and I hadn't chanted a single round. Before this I had been very faithfully completing my sixteen rounds—to miss my rounds was a mortal sin. I told Prabhupada, "I haven't chanted any rounds, and I haven't read any books . . ." He said, "Never mind, this is an emergency. You just do what I tell you."

In Indore we stayed at an *ashram* called Gita Bhavan and one day Prabhupada suggested, "Why don't you go and make some Life Members?" I said, "What's a Life Member?" He said, "Go to some merchant or businessman, show him our *Krishna* Books, tell him what we are doing and ask him to become a member by giving 1,111 rupees. Then he will receive subsequent publications and support our movement." I thought, "These people don't speak English.

What is the use of approaching them? Why would they want our books? They can't read them," and I neglected to make the effort. The next day Prabhupada again said, "Why don't you go to the market and try to make some members?" I said, "Yes," but the same thoughts were running through my mind and I didn't go. The next day Prabhupada said the same thing. I said, "These people don't speak the language." He said, "You can take an interpreter."

By this time I understood Prabhupada really wanted me to do this and I thought I should at least go through the motions, which I did. I went to a cloth merchant with the interpreter that Prabhupada had suggested. I told the interpreter what to say, and before he finished speaking, the merchant whipped out his checkbook and wrote a check. I thought, 'Well, okay.' We went to the next merchant and the same thing happened. We went to a third merchant and the same thing happened again. In a short time we had made three members. I came back and gave the checks to Prabhupada. He said, "Now do you understand?" That was my initiation into making Life Members.

Once Prabhupada and a few of us had an engagement with the king and queen of Indore. Before we left for this engagement Prabhupada told me, "Try to make the king a Life Member." I said, "Okay." So when Prabhupada finished speaking, I gave a pitch to convince the king to become a Life Member. But I failed. When we were in the car on our way back, I said, "Prabhupada, I wasn't able to convince him to be a member. Did I say the right thing about your books?" He said, "My books are like gold. One who knows the value will buy them."

In Vrindavan some years later, there was a problem with a proliferation of ladies coming to the guesthouse. Almost daily Prabhupada discussed what to do with these ladies, especially those with children but no husband. Sometimes we considered sending them to Mayapur, sometimes sending them back to America. Sometimes we thought, 'Let them stay.' It was an ongoing quandary. In the course of one of these discussions Prabhupada said, "On the one hand, we tell all our boys 'don't marry, remain *brahmachari.*' On the other hand, we tell the ladies, 'You should marry. Every woman must have a husband.' This is a contradiction in our philosophy," and he began to laugh. He said, "It's an insoluble problem."

The organizers at the Gita Bhavan realized that Prabhupada was a great draw, like a famous celebrity, so at their programs they kept the crowd from leaving by saving Prabhupada for last and they'd introduce bogus *sadhus* first. This went on every day for a number of days, and Prabhupada got aggravated that they were using him. Finally Prabhupada said, "We're going," and in the middle of the program we all got up and walked off the stage.

On another occasion in Indore, the *kirtan* was going on and we were standing up and dancing when a man kept trying to touch Yamuna, Kaushalya and Himavati's feet. These nice looking Western ladies were a sensational sight for these people. The ladies kept receding but this man was obnoxious and persistent. Prabhupada was so angry with this man that he ran towards him and tried to hit him with his *kartals*. Prabhupada was beyond all stereotyped and caricatured images of a *sadhu*.

In Surat, Prabhupada chanted his rounds in the morning while briskly walking back and forth in the sun on a concrete path outside our bungalows. One morning he stopped walking, pointed at the sun and said, "The *yogis* travel on sunbeams. I know because I have experimented in Hamburg." That's all he said.

Himavati was a very good cook and once, when Prabhupada came to London with Srutakirti, Srutakirti told her, "Don't cook very much because Prabhupada's not feeling well and hasn't been eating much." She said, "Okay," but cooked an entire feast and brought it to Prabhupada. When she returned she saw that he'd eaten practically everything. She said, "Prabhupada, the devotees said you're not feeling well and you're not eating." He said, "No, they just don't know how to cook."

On a morning walk in Mayapur, Prabhupada talked about the coming war and I asked, "Prabhupada, is there something we should do to prepare ourselves for this coming war?"

He said, "You should simply prepare for chanting Hare Krishna." I said, "That's all?" He said, "That's all."

When Prabhupada came to Montreal, where Kirtanananda had trained me, we had placed small Jagannatha Deities next to his seat. Himavati, who was a talented seamstress, had made an outfit for Them. At one point, Prabhupada reached over, picked up one Deity and deliberately examined the sewing work on the dresses and the turbans. Then he asked, "Who did this?" Someone said, "Himavati." Prabhupada said to her, "You can become self-realized just by sewing." She replied, "Yes, Prabhupada, but I want a sewing machine and Hansadutta won't buy me one." The one she wanted, the best one, cost $300 and that was a lot of money. Prabhupada said, "Oh? No, you must have a sewing machine. You must have the best." Himavati, of course, was grinning from ear to ear. I said, "Yes, Prabhupada."

I was trained as a cook in the Navy. My father was a chef and the rest of my family were hotel-restaurant people. I liked to cook. When Himavati and I joined the Krishna consciousness movement, Kirtanananda was going to teach Himavati to cook and I said, "You have to teach me to cook also. If you don't teach me, I'm leaving." Of course, I wouldn't have left, but I was excited to learn the different techniques, spicing and preparations.

On one occasion in Montreal, we had a big feast and afterwards I was walking with Prabhupada from his *vyasasana* to the door, which was quite a distance because the temple was a converted bowling alley. Prabhupada suddenly stopped, turned to me and said, "Your sweetballs were very good." I got heady. Then he said, "But mine were better."

When we were in Bombay on our first trip to India, we were crammed into the apartment-cum-temple in the Akash Ganga Building. The devotees were sick, the toilets didn't work, the water didn't run, and it was uncomfortably hot. Every now and then Himavati needed something but she and I had no money. I didn't know what to do so one day I decided to ask Prabhupada. I said, "Prabhupada, I'm a householder traveling with you and preaching, but when Himavati needs something I don't have any money to get it for her. It's very embarrassing." Prabhupada said, "Yes, householder life is embarrassing." I said, "What should I do?" He said, "What can be done? By hook or crook get money." Prabhupada didn't say, "Well, here's twenty dollars." He said, "Yes, it is embarrassing, that's what it is."

Once three or four other devotees and I were taking a train with Prabhupada and just before we departed, Prabhupada opened a pot of sweetballs someone had given him and began distributing them. One devotee said, "Prabhupada, are those offered?" Prabhupada said, "Oh, you don't have to have any."

In the early days at 26 Second Avenue, Kirtanananda tried to impose austerities on everyone. Every Sunday there'd be a lot of sweetballs left over from the feast and for Monday's breakfast we'd drop those sweetballs in our hot farina cereal. It was a delightful breakfast. But Kirtanananda insisted that we couldn't have more than two sweetballs each and that became an issue we haggled over at istagosthi. We couldn't resolve it, so it came to Prabhupada's attention. Everybody assembled. The problem was laid out before Prabhupada and Prabhupada said, "So everyone can have as many sweetballs as they like. But Kirtanananda can only have two." That was Prabhupada's sense of humor.

Once I asked Prabhupada, "Is it possible that a devotee's relationship with Krishna is preaching and that devotee remains in this world to preach—he doesn't go back to Godhead?" Before I could finish, Prabhupada said, "Yes. The *acharyas* never go back to Godhead. They remain in the material world, traveling from one planet to another, preaching Krishna consciousness." I said, "Since the *acharya* is a pure devotee, then isn't he simultaneously in the spiritual world even while he is preaching in the material world—so it doesn't make any difference that apparently he's in the material world?" Prabhupada said, "Yes, something like that."

Once Prabhupada said that Hitler was a *saktyavesa-avatara*. I said, "A *saktyavesa-avatara*?" "Yes," he said, "A *saktyavesa-avatara* means one who descends empowered to do something. It doesn't always mean he does good—he may be destructive."

These types of topics may have been triggered because I was German. Prabhupada told me that Germans were fond of Vedic culture, were the greatest Sanskrit scholars in the world—even greater than the Indians—and that the Germans had come to India, stolen technical Vedic manuscripts on how to make rockets, and from those had developed the U2 rocket.

In the early days, when Prabhupada wanted to impress his audience with the importance of *Bhagavad-gita*, he would mention that Emerson and Thoreau read *Bhagavad-gita*. And sometimes he'd mention that Hitler read *Bhagavad-gita*. Then someone told him, "But Prabhupada, Hitler's not popular in this country." Prabhupada said, "But in India he's popular because he was the enemy of the British, and the enemy of my enemy is my friend."

In 1976 I brought a large party of devotees from Germany overland to India in big Mercedes touring buses. In India these buses became a problem because every foreign vehicle required the equivalent of a visa. I was shuffling these vehicles around to keep them in the country and in the course of doing this I lost touch with Prabhupada. I was supposed to report to him at least once a month, and in India it was even more important because India was so difficult. After I had been out of touch for two months I saw Prabhupada in Bombay. While I offered my obeisances, Prabhupada said, "A rolling stone gathers no moss," which I thought was a compliment. Then he said, "Better sit down and gather some moss." Then I realized it wasn't a compliment. He said, "Where have you been?" I explained what I'd been doing. He said, "Why not go to Sri Lanka and preach?" I said, "Prabhupada, it's a small place. I could go there for a week or two but that's all." He said, "Everyone there is Krishna conscious?" I said, "No." He said, "You can go to Pakistan or you can go to Sri Lanka." I said, "I'll go to Sri Lanka."

When we were traveling in India in 1970–71, oftentimes we would parade through remote towns doing *harinam*. In one place we were pulled in a camel cart. Now, a camel is quite tall and this cart was quite low and it was hooked up close to the camel, so just imagine what that was like. Some of these places were dusty hamlets in the middle of nowhere, but no matter where it was, Prabhupada would inevitably say, "Yes, this is a very nice place," and he would find some qualification that made it a good place—it was centrally located, or the people were enthusiastic, or the food was nice. Then he would say to me, "Are you prepared to stay here and open a center?" I would think, "No!" and I'd say, "Yes, Prabhupada," terrified that he'd leave me there to open a center. That never happened to me, but it did happen to some others.

In those days Stockholm, Sweden was my zone and when Prabhupada came he lectured at Upsala University. After the lecture, a student raised his hand and said, "In his book *Siddhartha,* Hermann Hesse says . . ." and he went on talking for some time. Prabhupada let him speak and when he was finished, Prabhupada said, “Who is Hermann Hesse?” At that time Hermann Hesse was popular. If you didn’t know who Hermann Hesse was, you were nobody. The student replied, “You don’t know who Hermann Hesse is? He’s the author of this and that.” Prabhupada said, “Hermann Hesse is not one of the *acharyas*. Therefore, he has no importance,” and that was the end of it. Prabhupada swept the issue away.

In London, Prabhupada told us that astrologers are after money and women, and that astrology is a lost art. He said his Guru Maharaj, Srila Bhaktisiddhanta Prabhupada, was a great astrologer and he gave it up. Prabhupada said, “Don’t bother with astrology. Just depend on Krishna.” But one day Pradyumna, who was Prabhupada’s Sanskrit secretary and was fond of astrology, said, “I’m going to go see the astrologer B. K. Gandhi. Do you want to come?” I said, “Okay,” although I knew Prabhupada wouldn’t want me to go. When we got back, Prabhupada said, “Where have you been?” I couldn’t lie. I said, “I was with Pradyumna.” “Pradyumna? Doing what?” I said, “He took me to an astrologer.” “Astrology? Why?” “Well, Pradyumna . . .” He said, “Astrologers are nonsense. Why did you go? I have instructed you not to go.” I said, “Pradyumna asked me to go.” He said, “If Pradyumna asks you to jump off a bridge, will you jump?” “No, Prabhupada.” Whenever we did something that wasn’t sanctioned, it invariably came to light.

Prabhupada taught us not to lick the glue on an envelope to seal it but to use a little water on the finger—that was *suchi* and the other was *muchi*. Once, when we were in Chandigargh, I had finished all the correspondence, sealed the envelopes, and put everything away when I discovered one letter remained unsealed. I thought, “Prabhupada doesn’t want us to lick the envelope, but it’s too troublesome to get the water again.” And just as I licked that last envelope, Prabhupada opened the door, walked in and pointed his finger. That was Prabhupada.

Prabhupada came to Germany in 1974 when we had a castle called Schloss Rettershof. Schloss means castle and Retter refers to the knights who went to war in the 10th century. The castle was a nice brownstone building on an old, beautifully landscaped hilltop estate overlooking fields that rolled into the distance. It was picture perfect. Prabhupada liked it very much and every day he would walk through those beautiful fields.

Once, during a morning walk there with the German devotees, who had only seen him that one time in their lives, Prabhupada heard a helicopter go overhead. Prabhupada looked up at the helicopter and a devotee commented, "That's a helicopter." Prabhupada said, "Yes, I know. Once Shyamasundar took me by helicopter from Heathrow Airport," and he laughed. He said, "That was Shyamasundar's service but I had to pay." Shyamasundar had made this sensational helicopter arrangement to bypass the London traffic, but in the end Prabhupada paid for it and it was quite expensive. Then Prabhupada told a story about a *guru* who had entrusted all his money with an expert disciple who made first class programs and arrangements for the *guru*. Each place they went everything was wonderful and each time the *guru* said, "I'm very pleased with you. You have done an excellent job." The disciple said, "It's all your mercy." When they finally completed their tour, the *guru* wanted to access the money that he had entrusted with his disciple, but the disciple said, "I used your money to arrange all those programs. I told you it was all your mercy." Then Prabhupada burst into an enormous, delightful belly laugh.

The first time Prabhupada came to Montreal, I accompanied him from the airport to the temple. This was my first time in close association with Prabhupada and I thought, "I'm going to hear some profound philosophical statements." As we were driving in Janardan's beat up jalopy, Prabhupada asked what kind of car it was. Then he told a story about a man who could tell the make of any car just by hearing its sound, and one day his friends decided to test him. They blindfolded him and as one car after another went by, he'd say, "That's a Buick, that's a Chevy." Then his friends tied tin cans and scraps to the tail of a donkey and made it run by the man. The man said, "That's a Ford," and Prabhupada burst into laughter. I was trying to figure out how this was spiritually profound. I was so prejudiced towards hearing something of a philosophical nature that I was completely bewildered, "What does this have to do with Krishna consciousness?"

In our Montreal bowling alley-cum-temple, Prabhupada was sitting on the *vyasasana* after his lecture when someone raised his hand and said, "Prabhupada, would you sign this book, your *Srimad Bhagavatam,* for me?" Prabhupada said, "Yes," and he signed it. Then another person raised his hand, "Prabhupada, would you sign mine too?" "Alright." A third person asked for the same thing. Then, when a fourth person asked for his signature, Prabhupada said, "Now I will have to charge."

When the astronauts went to the moon, Prabhupada watched it live on television. At that time I'd come to L.A., and one day Prabhupada asked me to write a letter to the editor of the New York Times about the moon landing. Prabhupada said, "These are the points the editor should answer," and he listed many points. I don't remember them all, but one was: why didn't scientists internationally recognize the moon landing? Generally scientists are in a higher echelon, above national boundaries, and would applaud the scientific accomplishment of a successful moon landing. Another point was that the moon is 200 degrees below zero, so how could anything manmade function there? A third one was that the moon is made of a shiny substance, possibly ice, and therefore how could there be shadows on the surface of the moon? In this way, Prabhupada gave a number of points. The letter was never published and there was no reply to it, but Prabhupada was tuned in to the fallacies of the moon landing propaganda.

One morning in Paris, Bhagavan and Shyamasundar weren't present for *mangal arati*. Sometime later, when they finally appeared during a *darshan*, Prabhupada said, "Where have you been?" They explained, "We were with some influential people arranging preaching programs for you." Prabhupada said, "Oh? Who are those influential people?" and Bhagavan told him about a woman who owned a nightclub. Prabhupada said, "What did she say?" "Oh, she recommended another person." "Oh, so the big person recommended another person," and Prabhupada told a story about the lion and the crane. He said a lion got a bone stuck in his throat and approached a crane saying, "Please remove the bone from my throat by picking it out with your beak." The crane said, "No. If I put my head in your mouth, you will eat me." The lion said, "No, I promise I will not eat you. If you do it, I will give you a benediction." So the crane reluctantly stuck his head in the lion's mouth and removed the bone. Then the crane stood in front of the lion expectantly. The lion said, "Why are you standing there? What do you want?" The crane said, "You said that if I removed the bone you would give me a benediction." The lion said, "What? I allowed you to stick your head in my mouth and now you want a benediction!" Prabhupada's point was that big people think that they have done you a great favor by allowing you to see them. The moral is, he said, "Do your own work—don't depend on others."

One day Prabhupada asked me, "Why did I write all these books?" I said, "So that we can learn the philosophy." He said, "No. These books are there to convince you to chant Hare Krishna. If you are convinced, there is no need to read these books."

In the early seventies there were three BBT Trustees—Prabhupada, Bali Mardan and Karandhar. Not long after Karandhar left, we were in London one morning when Prabhupada unexpectedly called me into his room. He was sitting on his bed and he said, "I want to appoint you as a BBT Trustee." I understood that this was a highly confidential service because it had to do with the publication and distribution of Prabhupada's books. I was astonished that Prabhupada asked me. I said, "But Prabhupada, you have so many educated disciples with an M.A., B.A. or Ph.D. I didn't finish high school." In fact, when I had brought Prabhupada his letters a few days earlier he had said, "Why does every letter you write have two or three spelling mistakes?" I said, "Well, Prabhupada, I didn't finish school..." He saw I was embarrassed so he said, "Oh, yes. You see?" and he picked up a dictionary. He said, "I always carry a little Oxford dictionary, and so should you. When there's a word you don't know, look it up. That's how I learned English." To this day I bring an Oxford dictionary everywhere I go and whenever I see one, I immediately think of Prabhupada. That was the effect Prabhupada had on us—that everything that he referred to in the course of his preaching, either formally or casually, became a springboard for Krishna consciousness. Once he pointed out dog stool and said, "Highly infectious. This is your civilization," and now every time I see dog stool, I think of Prabhupada. Prabhupada engaged stool to inspire us to be Krishna conscious. Once he passed a man doing jumping jacks in the park. Prabhupada stopped, looked at him and said, "This exercise is for the body." Then he lifted his hand inside his bead bag and said, "This exercise is for the soul." Now when I see a man doing jumping jacks, I think of Prabhupada. This is the effect he had on me, and I imagine he affected others the same way. Anything that Prabhupada referred to became permanently impressed on our hearts just as whatever is taking place in front of the video lens is impressed on the video tape.

Anyway, when I said, "But Prabhupada, you have so many educated disciples and I can't even spell properly," he stopped me. He said, "I am asking you because without being asked you have published and distributed my books. You have understood the importance of my books. The devotees may fail, the temples might fail, but my books will live forever."

We couldn't imagine how the devotees or the temples might

fail. How could they fail? At that time there was a colossal, dynamic, energetic environment. People were coming, money was flowing, and books were being printed and distributed. Failure was unimaginable. But Prabhupada's glimpse of that made his books so important.

The copyright for the original *Bhagavad-gita* was given to Macmillan and Macmillan printed it, but the book didn't sell well. However, the contract had a clause stating that if Macmillan failed to keep the book in print, the rights would revert back to the BBT. At that time in Germany, we were translating *Bhagavad-gita* into German. I knew that we couldn't print it legally, but I was convinced that Macmillan would not reprint it, so we sent the German edition, with a few minor changes—it was smaller and had Bible paper—for printing. When Prabhupada saw the first copies he said, "It's better than the American edition."

The beauty of being Prabhupada's disciple was that he allowed us to innovate. He had confidence in us and gave us room to do things without consulting him like a schoolboy consulting his father. If we did something that was inspired by Krishna, Prabhupada recognized that, enlivened us, and caused us to expand more. An important part of relating to Prabhupada was the freedom that he gave his disciples to run with the ball. Of course, sometimes we fell on our face and lost the ball. But Prabhupada would not make an ongoing case of it and badger us every time he saw us. He dealt with it and that was it, and we continued.

Once Prabhupada asked, "Why do Christians always show Jesus on the cross?" Somebody explained why, but the explanation was insufficient. Prabhupada said, "If you love Jesus, why do you show him in this most humiliating and gruesome circumstance? If you love someone, would you put his picture on your mantel in his most embarrassing and gruesome situation?" When he said that, a world suddenly opened. It was something obvious, bizarre and perverse, but we hadn't seen it until we heard Prabhupada's comment. In many ways Prabhupada changed our perspective again and again and again.

As the years rolled on, the habit at the GBC meetings was to become more and more absorbed in secondary and managerial issues. For days the GBC members would have discussions and write resolutions and afterward those resolutions were given to Prabhupada for his approval. One year Prabhupada casually flipped through the resolutions and said, "Have you discussed how to improve the quality of chanting Hare Krishna?" We were thinking, "That's not important." At that same time Prabhupada said that the GBC meeting should not take days but three or four hours. Prabhupada was concerned with the quality of our spiritual life, especially the quality of our chanting.

Once Prabhupada told me that if a person does not chant Hare Krishna, then his devotional service becomes *karma*. In other words, his activities become *karmic*. After all, what's the difference between what devotees and non-devotees do? The difference is that the holy sound vibration, which keeps us in touch with the Supreme Lord, purifies our activities.

In India, when we were in a taxi or a car and it stopped somewhere, especially in places like Calcutta, beggars would come to the door. If Prabhupada didn't have any money, he sometimes told us, "You give them something." Also in India, well-off families all have servants and after we'd been hosted by a family and were ready to go, Prabhupada would ask the proprietor to bring all the servants, and then in order of seniority he would give them all some *rupees*. Those who were more senior got more and those that were less senior got less. Prabhupada was very concerned with everyone. He wasn't just on a high platform where he couldn't relate or interact with all others.

Once when I was in Germany I got a phone call, "Prabhupada wants you to come to Zurich." I said, "Why? What's going on?" "We don't know. He just wants you and Bhagavan to come." "All right," so we went. Even when we arrived in the middle of the night, still no one told us why we were there. Someone said, "Prabhupada wants to see everyone." We went into Prabhupada's room and in an angry mood he was talking to Shyamasundar and Bali Mardan. What happened was that some devotees had taken BBT money and other money and had bought gold. Nixon had just taken the US dollar off the gold standard and Shyamasundar, wizard that he was, knew that the value of gold was going to skyrocket, which it did. But Prabhupada was angrily saying, "How could you do that? You are gambling." Shyamasundar said, "Prabhupada, we made money—the price of gold went up." Prabhupada said, "It's against our principle, it's gambling. You cannot break our principle." Shyamasundar kept repeating, "We made money."

Prabhupada said, "No, we cannot break our principle. Our principle is no gambling, and investing money in gold is gambling." So the next day, Prabhupada and Shyamasundar marched into the bank and converted all that gold back into dollars. Prabhupada wouldn't budge from that principle.

In the car on the way to the bank, Shyamasundar knew the route and was pointing out different things. Prabhupada remarked, "Oh, you know your way around." Shyamasundar said, "Yes, when I was young I left home and traveled all over the world," and he gave a little resume of his adventures. When he finished speaking there was silence. Then Prabhupada said, "I left home when I was 50," and the way he said it put everything back into perspective.

In the same vein, Prabhupada was walking on Oxford Street when he stopped and said, "Krishna fulfills all desires. When I was a little boy I always wanted to come to London, and now I'm in London. So Krishna fulfills all desires. It just may take a little time."

Sudama was in charge in Hawaii and when someone donated a restaurant there, somehow or other Sudama claimed the restaurant as his. In a meeting about that incident, Prabhupada said to Sudama, "You are my disciple." Sudama said, "Yes." "So whatever is given to you is meant for me." Sudama said, "Yes." "So to whom does the restaurant belong? Does it belong to you or does it belong to me?" Sudama said, "It belongs to me." Prabhupada said, "Okay. Take it and be happy," and Sudama left the room. Then Prabhupada asked the rest of us, "What should we do? Should we prosecute?" Guru Kripa said, "Yeah!" Prabhupada pondered and said, "No. Then we'll become like ordinary *karmis*. Our life is based on love and trust. If we don't live that way, we won't have a spiritual life." And he let it go.

Prabhupada would not conspire or allow himself to be drawn into a conspiracy. When someone complained, he'd call the person who was being complained about and say to the complainer, "Now what did you say?" He used to say, "No *pssh pssh pssh.*" He called conspiracy, "*pssh pssh.*" He said people may speak their mind in a meeting and fight like cats and dogs but at the end, each one has to carry out whatever was agreed to.

Normally prominent people, whether politicians, entertainers, or any other celebrity, have two lives—one that they show to the public and another that is completely contrary. Prabhupada wasn't like that. He had only one life. Every time I met him, what impressed me again and again was that Prabhupada was exactly like his books. When you read his book and when you had an exchange with Prabhupada, it was the same. There was no difference. With any other person there was always another side. In this way Prabhupada was disarming. All the problems that filled your head evaporated as soon as you came into Prabhupada's presence. He would say, "So everything is all right?" "Yes, Prabhupada, yes," and as soon as you walked out the door, you were puzzled again.

Prabhupada had a big room at Bhaktivedanta Manor in Letchmore Heath. Once, near the leaded windows at the end of his room, he was sitting on a cushion behind a low table. I came in and saw Himavati sitting on the other side of the table with Prabhupada's hand in her hand. She was reading Prabhupada's palm. Prabhupada said, "What about this line? What does this mean?" "Prabhupada, that's your head line. You have a very good head line." They were casually going on like that as if they were thick and thin friends. Himavati's relationship with Prabhupada was completely different from mine. Prabhupada was very affectionate and friendly with her and she was naturally at home with him. It wasn't artificial on either side. On the other hand, my relationship with Prabhupada was in awe and reverence.

Prabhupada always related to every person individually. When Shyamasundar brought a host of celebrities, Prabhupada greeted each person differently. With Lord Brockway, a government official and a respectable gentleman, Prabhupada personally opened the door for him, walked in with him and arranged a proper seat for him. But he didn't do that with everyone. He related appropriately with everyone. Prabhupada could also be cutting. It isn't that he was gentle, smiling, soft and patronizing. While he was giving *darshan* someone might say, "What about Jesus or Buddha?" Prabhupada would say, "Do you follow Jesus? Do you follow Buddha? Or do you just talk. Oh, you just talk. Don't talk."

Some years ago I met a man in Palo Alto who had an art gallery. He said to me, "You're a follower of Swami Prabhupada?" I said, "Yes, how do you know?" He said, "I see your beads. I met Swami Prabhupada at Palo Alto University in 1967." I said, "Really? Tell me about it." He said, "He was the most unforgettable man I ever met." I said, "How is that? Did you discuss something with him?" He said, "Yes, he and I had a discussion after his lecture. I complained about the government, and Prabhupada said, 'No, you cannot complain, you elected the government officials. Since you elected them, you cannot complain.'" The man said, "I kept saying, 'but I didn't elect them.'" And Prabhupada said, "No, you elected them, that is your system. You cannot complain." This man said, "Prabhupada simply wouldn't allow me to get off this point. 'You elected. Therefore, you are responsible.'"

Prabhupada responded to enthusiasm. He did not respond to material qualifications like scholarship or even expertise in a particular field. Enthusiasm was the one factor that eclipsed everything else. If one's enthusiasm was alive and genuine, then there was no limit to the opportunities Prabhupada offered. And that's what made it possible for me to associate with Prabhupada and to serve him as I did. I was not educated or professionally experienced in any way. I wasn't an American. I was born in Germany. And I was also married. But Prabhupada gave me many opportunities and responsibilities that, under material circumstances, would have gone to other persons. This was true not only in my case, but also in the case of Guru Kripa, Madhudvisa, and many others. Prabhupada looked to anyone who had enthusiasm and determination. And Prabhupada trained, focused, and purified that raw enthusiasm. What we did for Prabhupada we did under his guidance.

In one letter to me Prabhupada wrote, "Why are my books not being printed in Germany?" I thought, "I can hardly speak German. I can't translate them." Then I understood, "Prabhupada wants his books translated into German," and I had to figure out how to do that. I wrote him, "What do I do?" He said, "Chant Hare Krishna and Krishna will give you intelligence." That was almost always the answer I got. Prabhupada wasn't the type of manager or leader who would give details. He inspired you to use your creative intelligence. In fact, Prabhupada said there's a kind of individual genius in every living entity. When I looked up the word 'genius' in the dictionary, the definition was, "in-dwelling deity." Genius is not something you or I or anyone possesses. Genius means Krishna. So if, by the inspiration of the spiritual master, we make ourselves receptive to the inflow of Krishna, then Krishna—genius—reveals how something should be done.

Brahmananda said that when Prabhupada asked him to go to Macmillan to give them the *Bhagavad-gita* manuscript, he was hesitant. Brahmananda thought, "Macmillan's a big company, how will they be interested in this?" But when Brahmananda—or any of us—submitted to Prabhupada's direction, combined with the chanting and the philosophy and the entire process or the treatment, as Prabhupada sometimes called it, then awesome things happened. As Prabhupada said, "The pure devotee doesn't do anything extraordinary, but extraordinary things take place all around him." Another example is how Shyamasundar connected with George Harrison. That was an extraordinary thing. The whole world was waiting at George's door, but by the genius, inspiration, and enthusiasm of Shyamasundar, Krishna opened George's door for Shyamasundar.

Prabhupada taught us that there is no harm in trying. In Montreal, when we had no money and could hardly pay the rent, Prabhupada saw a big government building that was for sale across from McGill University and he told Janardan, "Ask how much they want for this building." Janardan said, "It's got to be more than a million dollars." Prabhupada said, "Just inquire. Tell them we have ten thousand dollars and we'll pay them a thousand dollars a month."

From a business point of view that was an absurd proposal, but Prabhupada had noticed that this building had facility for a shop or restaurant and he asked me if I could generate a thousand dollars a month profit from running a restaurant there. I said, "I guess I could," so Prabhupada urged Janardan to make this offer. Janardan was reluctant because it didn't seem realistic. We didn't get the building, but we learned about Prabhupada's vision. Prabhupada saw that Krishna could do anything.

Because I often used to be worried about money, Prabhupada told me, "Don't worry about money. Try to do something wonderful for Krishna and money will come." That was his policy, his theme, and the basis of his operation. After all, Prabhupada came to America with practically no money but with the idea of preaching to intelligent people. By default he wound up on the Bowery with the most degraded class of people—who are the ones who heard and carried his message.

Now I hear many of Prabhupada's disciples say, "I didn't get a chance to associate with Prabhupada." But these disciples were not kept away from him. Prabhupada was accessible to everyone, but that access was conditional—you had to be prepared to accept any direction anytime, anywhere, without reservation. If that wasn't there, you couldn't come too close to Prabhupada. You had to keep a distance. At least that was my experience.

After one Sunday feast in Montreal, I made a collection and I thought, "Now I have something to write Prabhupada about." I wrote and I received a letter in response. From that time on I thought, "I must always do something that warrants reporting so that I will get a response." I needed that.

In Germany things were bleak. I'm born in Germany, but it's an awful environment and the German people are extremely unfortunate and hard-hearted. What kept me going there was that every two weeks I received a letter from Prabhupada. My letter to Prabhupada would take one week to reach him, and his response would take one week to reach me. By the time one week went by, my battery was going down. By day eleven and twelve I would walk a few blocks to meet the mailman to see if his letter had come. If it hadn't, I went back and went to sleep. I couldn't function. When Prabhupada's letter came, I was enlivened again.

To be connected to Prabhupada, to receive his sanction, that was the whole thing. Material qualifications had nothing to do with it. When I gave a lecture to the faculty at Harvard University I thought, "This is Krishna consciousness. Here I am giving a lecture to the faculty of Harvard University and they have no idea that I'm a high school dropout." After I finished the lecture I said, "This is the power of the pure devotee. By his mercy, a person who has no qualification can be in an orbit that would not be normally possible." The material world was over. I was in complete ecstasy. My hairs were standing on end and I was crying like anything. I can't even remember if I paid my obeisances. I was so stunned and bowled over by a great feeling of relief. All I had to do was follow Srila Prabhupada and everything would be taken care of.

TAPE 36

Bhutatma das
Tosan Krishna das
Atma Tattva das
Chitralekha dasi
Kuladri das
Rangavati dasi

Bhutatma: Prabhupada wanted everyone—his disciples as well as people in general—to become happy. That was clear to me when I received my first letter from Prabhupada. I had written to him expressing my commitment to Krishna consciousness, how I was becoming happy following this process, and requesting initiation from him. In Prabhupada's reply he wrote that he'd accept me as a disciple and he wrote, "I'm so glad that you're becoming happy."

From his enlightened perspective, Prabhupada saw that the only way to become happy was by realizing our constitutional position, and as we started to experience that even in a limited way, he encouraged us. The first time he communicated with me Prabhupada made that point.

Tosan Krishna: When Prabhupada rang the bell, I rushed in and said, "Yes, Srila Prabhupada?" In '68 "Prabhupada" was a new term—only months before we had addressed him as "Swamiji."

Prabhupada said, "First of all, you have forgotten to pay your obeisances." I had rushed in out of my sleeping bag and when he said that I hit the floor. Then I heard Srila Prabhupada's low chuckle. He said, "That's all right. It's all just for practice," and he called me closer and said, "Come sit down. Why did you call me to Santa Fe and then tell me to go to Los Angeles?"

I had nothing to do with Prabhupada's travel arrangements—I was barely 18 and had been in the movement for just two months. Later, it occurred to me that Prabhupada was talking to me to help me relax, but at the time I was startled. I said, "Well, Srila Prabhupada, Govinda dasi . . ." and that's as far as I got. I was a *brahmachari*, and Prabhupada was about to train me.

"Govinda dasi! Never listen to a woman." Now, Prabhupada loved Govinda dasi. Govinda dasi would go wherever Prabhupada went, or Prabhupada would send her in advance to check things out. He trusted her very much. She and her husband did illustrations for books and so forth. But in a teasing way he said, "Never listen to a woman." Then he leaned back, looked at me again and said, "So what did she say?" I said, "Srila Prabhupada, she said that Santa Fe, New Mexico, is on the continental divide and is at a high elevation." I don't know why but maybe because I mentioned the continental divide, he said, "You're an intelligent boy." I went on, "We're in the upper atmosphere here, the air is thin, you're a heart patient and . . ." "Ohhh, so you think I will come here and die?" and he opened his eyes wide. I didn't know what to say. He said, "So many people live here. I cannot come?"

Then, with just me there and without *kartals* or *mridanga*, he recited the Samsara prayers, "*samsara-davanala-lidha-loka*," and after that we chanted *japa*.

Atma Tattva: In 1977, Ravi das and I were in Kanpur distributing Back to Godhead magazines when we came to a little building with a Bengali signboard saying the marriage registration officer, Mr. Chatterjee, worked there. I told Ravi, "There's a Bengali here so let's try to give him a magazine."

We went up the narrow staircase to the third floor, and inside a first-class Bengali-looking apartment, with old paintings, a big bookshelf and an easy chair, there was Mr. Chatterjee. We greeted him and I gave him a *Back to Godhead* magazine. He said, "Do you know that when Prabhupada was distributing his *Back to Godhead* magazines, he stayed in this place?"

Mr. Chatterjee showed us around the house, "This is where Prabhupada used to sit, this is where he used to cook." There was a separate clothesline on the roof, and he said, "We never used this clothesline. Only Prabhupada's clothes dried there."

Then we sat in Mr. Chatterjee's study and he brought me a brick-red edition of the *Bhagavatam,* signed by Prabhupada, which had some translations underlined about the Lord's personal form. Mr. Chatterjee said that as a follower of the Arya-samaj he observed *yajna* performances and chanted *Rig Veda* verses but did not observe Deity worship.

Prabhupada used to joke, "I know what you Arya-samajis do. When you see a Vishnu temple, you make sure no one is looking at you, then you offer your obeisances and say to the Lord, 'I am sorry for offending You.'" Mr. Chatterjee said that he told Prabhupada, "In public I have been following Arya-samaj and in private I have been worshiping the five *murtis*—Vishnu, Siva, Durga, Ganesh, and Surya. But I don't get satisfaction from either of these processes."

For over an hour that day Prabhupada spoke to him about the personal and impersonal features of the Lord. Then later, after printing the *Bhagavatam,* Prabhupada came, underlined a certain translation, and gave the book to Mr. Chatterjee. Prabhupada said, "You are not experiencing satisfaction because you think the Lord is impersonal." Mr. Chatterjee was moved and said, "Swami Maharaj didn't return to Kanpur. But I became a personalist," and he showed us the Radha-Krishna Deities in his study. He said, "After talking with Prabhupada I came back to our grandfather's line. Now I am worshiping Radha and Krishna." He said, "Prabhupada used to take my daughter on his lap and feed her the tomato rice he had cooked. She is here now with her children for the holidays." He called his daughter, and she said, "Prabhupada told me, 'You should just take *prasad*. Don't worry about anything that your father says.'" Her father, Mr. Chatterjee, used to preach to her that God has no form and that she was not to worship the Deity. She told us, "I was a personalist all the time."

Chitralekha: Just after we arrived in Vrindavan, two-dozen devotees, including my one year-old daughter and I, went into Prabhupada's room for *darshan*. My daughter and I were quietly sitting in the back when my daughter got up and started walking to Prabhupada. The *brahmachari* at the door motioned to me to get her. He whispered, "Get her! Bring her back!" Although I saw the *brahmacari* out of the corner of my eye, I conveniently ignored him and instead made a motion to Prabhupada asking, "Should I get her?" Prabhupada saw the *brahmachari* flipping out at the door, put his hand up and told me, "Just sit down." I had no idea what my daughter, Chintaya, was going to do. She walked to Prabhupada's desk, looked around, looked at Prabhupada, walked over to him, crawled across him and sat down on his lap. All other conversation stopped as she played with his garland and then crawled off his lap. He gave her a flower to take with her and then he nodded to me to come and take her. I picked her up and took her back to sit down.

No matter who or what age the person was, Prabhupada built sweet relationships with everyone—even with the youngest children—through his sweet exchanges.

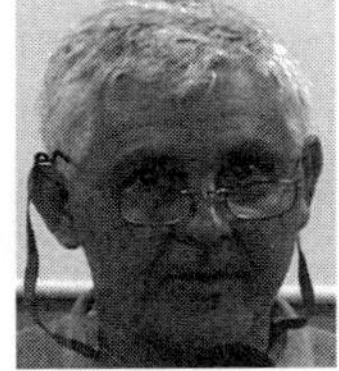

Kuladri: After evening *darshan* in Vrindavan, Srila Prabhupada would nod to me. As his servant, I would get the jar of sweetball *prasadam* on his desk and distribute them. So one evening, after he had spoken with many Brijbasis, he nodded to me. I opened the jar, and saw ants all over the sweetballs. I said, "Srila Prabhupada, ants are eating the sweetballs," thinking I couldn't distribute them. Srila

Prabhupada looked at me and said, "It is okay, they do not eat very much."

Rangavati: We were making puppet dolls in Detroit and I carried one with me when I went to have *darshan* with Srila Prabhupada. Prabhupada asked me, "What is that you have?" I said, "It's a puppet, Srila Prabhupada." He said, "You must not do this because people will think we are worshiping dolls."

My parents were also at that *darshan* and later, when Prabhupada asked for questions, my father said, "You mentioned that Christians say to God, 'Give us our daily bread,' and you mentioned that the animals are eating without such a prayer, but we Christians do not just ask for bread, we also ask for cake—we ask for everything." Prabhupada instantly cut him off saying, "What do you know?" and he dismissed my father's point. In different ways, both my father and I were dismissed at that *darshan*. My father was a bit stunned, but he didn't have a comeback and luckily he didn't argue. My father was upset that both his children—his two daughters—had joined, but when we were all squished in the room taking *darshan* with Prabhupada as the obvious authoritative figure, my father wasn't about to start a huge fight.

Bhutatma: I grew up near the beach and like a lot of other people, I always enjoyed the pleasing sound of the waves as they break and then ebb. Once we were walking on the beach when Prabhupada stopped to listen to those sounds for a minute. Then he said, "This sound of the waves retreating is the sound of the *gopis* sighing for Krishna." I thought, "No wonder it's so pleasing." Ever since then when I hear those mournful and bittersweet sounds, I think of Prabhupada's words.

Tosan Krishna: We couldn't afford to have flowers in the temple back then and we used a pay phone because the temple didn't have a phone. One day I found a beautiful piece of luxurious velvet with some trim on it in an abandoned, rustic, Catholic Church, and I brought it for Prabhupada. Govinda dasi saw it and she said to Prabhupada, "Tosan Krishna wants to know if you want this." At the time Prabhupada was directing devotees to help him pack, saying, "Put this thing away, put this here, now roll this, put this there." Prabhupada was being very exacting. When Govinda dasi asked him that question, Srila Prabhupada, who had been so sweet, suddenly said, "I want nothing!" and the room shook as if Lord Nrisimhadeva had entered.

After that I didn't know what was going to happen to that piece of cloth but two months later I visited Srila Prabhupada in Los Angeles and Srila Prabhupada was using it as a backdrop for his Deities. I thought, "He wants nothing, but he'll engage things for his Deities."

Atma Tattva: In the early '80s in Bangalore, I was required to make at least two Life Members a month. I was a bad Life Membership maker and one month I had only ten days left. I was looking in the telephone directory for Bengali names and I found a 'Ganguly.' I called and said, "I'm speaking from the International Society for Krishna Consciousness. I want to come and see you today." Mr. Ganguly sounded positive. He said, "Oh, you are from the Hare Krishna Movement? Please see me at eleven o'clock."

I took the membership form, a small set of books, a poster and so on, and I went to see him. To my surprise, I found that his was a huge place, almost equal to the aeronautical engineering place in Bangalore. I lost hope—there was no way this man was going to become a member. I went to one secretary, then another, then another, and when my appointment time came I was still with secretaries. Ganguly was the top man. I thought, "Since I came all this way, I should see him." Finally they brought me into a big air-conditioned cabin where a meeting was going on. Ganguly told everybody, "I have to talk to the Hare Krishna now, so you all go," and he closed the meeting.

I came in, spread the books on his table and put the poster up. I knew that I wouldn't have much time with him, so I was brief. I said, "I'm sure you know about this movement. We have a branch here and we have applied for land. You are a Bengali, you should be proud of this because our Guru Maharaj is also a Bengali and he has spread the Hare Krishna movement all around the world. I'm sure you appreciate this service, so would you become a Life Member?" and then I was silent. He got his checkbook and said, "What is the amount?" I said, "Two thousand two hundred and twenty-two." He said, "I'll give you a donation, and you can also make me a Life Member." He wrote a check for ten thousand and gave it to me.

I was moved. I said, "Thank you very much. This is a nice gesture." He said, "I wasn't convinced by your preaching." I said, "I didn't think I convinced you either." He said, "I want to tell you something. My father grew up in Calcutta and was a classmate of your Founder Acharya. Every day Abhay came to our house on his bike, carrying his little lunch tiffin, and he and my father played chess. The stake for the chess game was lunch —whoever lost the game had to feed the other. Almost every day Abhay won.

Later this man's father received a Ph.D. in Sanskrit and became a professor in the local university. He would tell people, "The *maharaj* who founded the Hare Krishna movement was my classmate and he came to my house every day when we were growing up." He said that Abhay told him, "You should help me later on when I do something." He would ask, "What is that something?" but Abhay did not explain what he meant.

Years later this senior Ganguly learned that the same Abhay became Bhaktivedanta Swami, went to New York and so forth, that there was a local Calcutta center on Albert Road and that Prabhupada was coming to visit. By this time, the junior Ganguly, who I was speaking with, was in high school and for three days he came to see Prabhupada in the Calcutta ISKCON temple. Since he looked like his father, Prabhupada recognized him. The junior Ganguly said, "I am the son of such and such." Prabhupada said, "Where is he? He didn't come? Tell him I want to see him."

Later, the son told the father, "Maharaj wants to see you." His father said, "How can I go and see him? He is the *guru* of the world and I am a *grihamedhi.*" His son said, "But he wants to see you and tomorrow he is going to ask me, 'Why didn't you bring your father?'" Feeling shy and small the father said, "Tell him that I am sick."

The next day Prabhupada asked the junior Ganguly, "Your father didn't come?" "He is feeling sick." "Oh, he's sick. Okay, I will come and see him." When the junior told his father that Prabhupada would come, his father said, "How will he come to our house?"

The next morning instead of his usual route, Prabhupada, followed by some disciples, walked down one alley after another, arrived at the Ganguly house and rang the bell. The son came to the door and saw Prabhupada, his disciples and a huge crowd of onlookers in front of his house. Prabhupada and a couple of devotees went in and Prabhupada went straight to the bedroom where the senior Ganguly was laying down, not sick, but tired and broken. Prabhupada sat next to him, poked him like a friend does, and said, "Hey, you didn't come to see me," in Bengali.

The senior Ganguly was shocked to see the Hare Krishna devotees in his house. He asked his wife, "Please bring something for them." Prabhupada said, "My disciples need to learn Sanskrit. I told you, you should help me. Come and teach them Sanskrit. You can travel around the world with me and teach them. Why don't you do that? You come, I will take you". Ganguly said, "Oh, Swamiji, I am very old and I don't have any spiritual energy." "No, you have the spark. The same quality that's in me is also in you. You should join this movement. It is very important. *Bharata-bhumite manusya janma haila yara.* You should perfect your life. Better late than never."

Prabhupada took a *rasagulla* and drank water. He told his disciples, "I used to come in the morning and from here we took that road to go to school. He was a very intelligent student. He used to score higher than me."

Around three o'clock that afternoon, when junior Ganguly came back from school, his father asked for some water. Then the senior Ganguly leaned back and said, "Bhaktivedanta Swami will take me," closed his eyes and passed away.

Junior Ganguly said, "In the morning, when Prabhupada said to my father, "You come, I will take you," I thought Prabhupada was saying, 'You come to ISKCON and I will take you to America or something. We understood what Prabhupada actually meant after my father passed on." Junior Ganguly said to me, "When you called I asked you to come because I wanted to share this with you. In fact, we are already Life Members." After that, even though he was a busy man, he would regularly come to our Sunday programs.

Chitralekha: Prabhupada made comments about my son, Saumya because he had poor eyesight and started wearing glasses at age two. Prabhupada would say, "His glasses are bigger than his head." If Prabhupada inquired about Saumya, Upendra would say, "He's well, Prabhupada. But sometimes he's naughty." Prabhupada would say, "Naughty means intelligent." And Prabhupada said, "Saumya should learn Sanskrit from Pradyumna."

Kuladri: I was serving Srila Prabhupada in Vrindavan when he was ill. One evening I was sitting on Srila Prabhupada's bed inside his mosquito net and massaging him with Vicks Vapo Rub, which Prabhupada liked, when somehow or other a mosquito got inside the net. Now, since the living entities in Vrindavan are not ordinary, we have to be very careful—we're not even supposed to step on an ant. I grabbed for the mosquito, but Prabhupada said, "No." I went back to massaging and when the mosquito landed on Srila Prabhupada, I flicked it away. Then Srila Prabhupada said, "Now catch it—it is attacking."

Rangavati: Manisha was a very sick 13 year-old. Her mother, Antajana, asked Srila Prabhupada, "What's the best thing to do for her?" Prabhupada said, "Simply keep her comfortable." That was a loose direction because 'comfortable' could mean medication or physical facilities or so many other things. When Manisha was near death, Antajana was distraught and one evening before *arati,* Manisha, Antajana and I met with Prabhupada in his *darshan* room. Antajana said, "Prabhupada, I don't know what to do. She's dying." Prabhupada's eyes got huge and he said, "We are all dying. You may die tomorrow, I may die next week, but we are all dying." He said those words as if to say, "Where have you been? What have I been preaching? It's just a matter of time before death comes. Chant Hare Krishna."

Prabhupada was almost outraged that dying was a surprise for us. We expected some sympathy from him like, "Oh, I'm so sorry," but there was none of that. Without soft-pedaling, Prabhupada went to the core of the matter. It threw us all back.

Manisha was a bag of bones and she was having a hard time chanting sixteen rounds every day. She asked Srila Prabhupada, "What should I do? What will happen to me if I don't chant sixteen rounds?" Prabhupada said, "You will be born in an aristocratic family or an educated or wealthy family." And he said, "Chant Hare Krishna. Simply chant Hare Krishna."

Bhutatma: About six of us were walking in Cheviot Hills around the time that Bali Mardan was involved with a Japanese woman who we thought was the heir to the Toyota fortune. Toward the end of the walk, Karandhar, Bali Mardan and I lagged behind because I was asking Bali Mardan if he could loan money to the San Francisco temple to buy property where householders could live. While we were having this private discussion, Prabhupada was walking ahead, and the three of us were still talking when Prabhupada and the other devotees were almost to the car. Then Prabhupada stopped, turned around and looked at us with a displeased expression.

Prabhupada's expressions could be very complex, but I felt that he was saying, "There you are playing with broken glass. You think that you're making some plan to expand the movement, and here is Krishna's pure devotee and you've separated yourself and are in a mental state."

When it turned out that there wasn't any money, it exacerbated the foolishness of our conversation. I clearly remember Prabhupada's look and how I thought, "Jiminy Christmas, what am I thinking? We could talk about this any time. I'm back here, missing precious moments with Prabhupada because I'm letting my little sense of self-importance run away from me."

Tosan Krishna: In 1971, I was living in Washington, D.C., the nation's capital, and I got a draft notice. I wrote Srila Prabhupada and asked, "What should I do?" He wrote back, "I'll write you a letter to present to the draft board," and the key line in his letter was, "My disciples do not have time to squander in these activities." Luckily my draft board was San Francisco, and when I presented Prabhupada's letter, it worked. Srila Prabhupada's letter worked.

Atma Tattva: I had a *Krishna Book* and on the back cover was a picture of Prabhupada looking at a *champak* flower he was holding. I showed the man this picture and said, "This is our Guru Maharaj, he has translated these books." The man looked at that picture and then brought some thread and things from a little box and for ten or fifteen minutes measured Prabhupada's forehead, ears and so on. Then he said, "This person's features show me that all the four Vaishnava *acharyas* are present in him. I wish you had a picture of his full form." So I showed him a photograph of Prabhupada's full form and he did another study, this time with a lens. Then he said, "I was not wrong. They are all working through this person. You are very fortunate to be with him. I would like to be part of a movement like that in my next life." I said, "But I thought your ultimate goal is to go to Kailash," because he was a Shaivite. He said, "Yes, if I go there I can tell Lord Shiva that I want to join some movement like this and

I want to spread *dharma* everywhere." He was happy and said, "Please give this book to me. It has given me the highest experience of studying a person's features. I want to keep this book." So I gave him a complimentary copy.

Bhutatma: Sometimes Prabhupada would speak on the way people are in the world and the way the world works from a Krishna conscious perspective. Once when he was doing that I was somehow giving good responses to his comments. He would say something, I would make an observation that he apparently liked, and he would smile. For example, he had little tissues to clean his eyeglasses. He pulled one out and said, "These cost almost nothing to manufacture yet they sell for three *rupees*." I said, "Yes, Prabhupada, that's the profit motive of the *karmis*." Prabhupada said, "Yes." It went on a few times like that and inside me my ego was swelling up. I was right there with Prabhupada having these exchanges. Then I asked Prabhupada something about Iran, because there was some question about Atreya Rishi going there. Prabhupada looked at me and then he looked away as if he'd had enough. To this day, I don't know what he was thinking, but to me it felt like he was saying, "Okay, we're going to squeeze you down to size."

In Mayapur everything is amplified. Even on into the night I felt bad about how my ego inflated. I thought, "I'm so conditioned I got full of myself." Then, as he did every morning, the next morning Prabhupada circumambulated the temple room, stopping at certain spots to ring the bell in time with the *kirtan*. When he rang that bell, the devotees chanting all around him became ecstatic. When Prabhupada made the first stop I was chanting blissfully, but my heart was still pinched by my being such a klutz. Just as I was thinking that and feeling the dichotomy between the bliss of the *kirtan* and that little pebble in my heart, Prabhupada turned and looked at me for a long time as he rang the bell. He was smiling and radiating bliss. It washed over me as if he was saying, "Don't take it too seriously, I was just cuffing you a little bit."

Tosan Krishna: One night at the lecture someone came dressed, as people did in the hippie era, in a long robe with moons and stars and with their long hair carefully arranged. This person sat erect during the entire lecture and then, almost glaring at Srila Prabhupada, said, "What about Buddha?" Srila Prabhupada said, "What about Buddha?" and stared right back at him. This person said, "Can you see God?" Srila Prabhupada said, "No, you are in the way." The funny thing was that that person was not the least bit annoyed by what Prabhupada said, but smiled and stayed around afterwards.

Chitralekha: One day in Los Angeles, Upendra, who was my husband and Prabhupada's servant, was in Prabhupada's room when Prabhupada handed him a twenty-dollar bill and said, "This is for your children." Immediately Upendra said, "Prabhupada, we can't take this from you. You're our spiritual master, we should be giving to you." Prabhupada said, "No, this is for your children. I'm not their spiritual master, they will have to take their own."

Upendra brought the twenty-dollar bill home and we knew that Prabhupada was telling us he wasn't going to be on the planet to initiate our children—they were going to have to seek out their own spiritual master. It wasn't an automatic given that all of our children would be Prabhupada's disciples.

Kuladri: I talked about how light and gentle Srila Prabhupada's body was, but once I was massaging Srila Prabhupada when his body seemed heavier than the heaviest. Prabhupada said, "Harder," and I started massaging harder. Prabhupada said, "Harder." I massaged harder. Prabhupada turned around, looked at me, and said, "Do you know what 'hard' means?"

Tosan Krishna: In '72 I was marketing the famous Radha Damodar Road Show. At the time we thought we were on thin ice with the music but when Srila Prabhupada heard the music, he liked it. Later he went to a big performance in Pittsburgh and lectured. But before that I was asked to show Srila Prabhupada our advertising. I had seen the *Srimad-Bhagavatam* cover painted by Murlidhara, which was a remake of Srila Prabhupada's original cover from India, and our poster largely utilized that art. I said, "Srila Prabhupada, this was actually your idea," because Srila Prabhupada had designed the cover of the *Srimad-Bhagavatam*. He looked at me as if to say, "Nice try." Then he said, "What is my idea? It is all in the *sastra*." Srila Prabhupada would never go for flattery.

Bhutatma: I was in Prabhupada's room with another *brahmachari* when Krishna das, who had been in Sweden trying to open a temple, came in with his wife and small son and began making excuses to Prabhupada about why he hadn't been able to stay in Sweden. The other *brahmachari* and I looked at each other because his wife wasn't wearing a *sari* or even dressed modestly. It seemed inappropriate. Prabhupada listened to Krishna das and I didn't know how he would respond. When Krishna das was done Prabhupada looked at him thoughtfully and said, "You are not Krishna das, you are Maya das!" It was heavy, but it fit. Prabhupada said, "When I came to your country, there was no question of a peaceful retreat. It was victory or death!"

Krishna das was getting smaller. "Honey I've shrunk the kids." Then Prabhupada lightened up and at the end Krishna das said, "Can my son touch your feet?" Prabhupada said, "Yes," so the boy did that and the three of them left the room.

It was a lesson for us that Prabhupada was not pleased when we rationalized things. It would have been better to say honestly, "I really couldn't cut it."

Chitralekha: Once Upendra was talking with other devotees while he waited outside Prabhupada's door. Prabhupada rang his bell to call Upendra and then asked him, "Who are you talking to?" Upendra said, "I'm talking to the devotees, Prabhupada." Prabhupada said, "What are you talking about?" Upendra said, "Just about things and other devotees." Prabhupada said, "That is gossip. Gossip will destroy this movement."

Atma Tattva: Once I showed a movie of Prabhupada lecturing to Dhananjaya and his wife, who were dance experts in Madras. Dhananjaya looked at that footage three times and then, in terms of *Bharat-natyam,* he explained Prabhupada's movements to his students. In his lecture, Prabhupada spoke intensely about the power of devotion and how, if somebody is chanting the holy name, it means that in his previous lives he has performed all sacrifices and austerities. While he spoke, Prabhupada's moods changed every two minutes. He was sometimes jubilant and sometimes frustrated that people were not taking to Krishna consciousness. It was like a dance except that Prabhupada was making *mudras* instead of moving his limbs. Dhananjaya pointed out these *mudras* to his students and quoted from the *Niti-sastra* of Bharat, "These are the different ecstasies that we learn in theory. In 28 minutes, this gentleman went through all that."

Later, in the *Nectar of Devotion*, I found three or four subheadings describing ecstatic symptoms that Prabhupada manifested while he explained the philosophy of chanting the holy name. He was not talking about *rasa lila* or any intimate pastimes, but simply about how one should chant the holy name and what happens when one does. It appeared like preliminary teachings, but Prabhupada manifested ecstasy while he explained it.

When Dhananjaya finished his explanation, I said, "There is a famous verse in the *Brahma-samhita* stating that in the spiritual world every word is a song and every movement is a dance." Dhananjaya took this so seriously that he began having that *Brahma-samhita* verse sung before his performances. This is how people were inspired, from an Arya-samaji to a business magnate to a dancer. We know Prabhupada inspired the devotees in our movement but this is how he has inspired others as well.

Tosan Krishna: The first Rathayatra in New York City was in '76. In New York it's difficult to get a permit and in 1962 the mayor had made an edict that no new parades could be held on Fifth Avenue. Yet somehow or other, with the advent of our new 55th Street temple, with Radha-Govinda moving into Manhattan, which is what Srila Prabhupada wanted, and with ISKCON celebrating it's tenth birthday, there would be a Fifth Avenue Rathayatra.

When he was in India, Srila Prabhupada telephoned us—which was very rare in those days because to even get a phone call from India was difficult—to find out if we had gotten the permit. I was in charge of getting this permit and the Police Department had initially said 'yes,' but then they said 'no.' At the very end I had a so-called last piece of paper that the Chief of Police himself, at Police Plaza One on the south tip of Manhattan, had to sign. The secretaries said, "We'll run it down, he'll sign it and it'll be over." I said, "No, I'm going to run it down." They said, "All right, if you want, you can go." I said, "I will, thank you," because Srila Prabhupada had called on the phone. I took the subway to that building, went through heavy security, went to the right floor and found the Police Chief's secretary. She looked at the paper and said, "He's never going to sign this. There's a mayor's edict—no new parades on Fifth Avenue."

I ignored her. I hopped over the turnstile, which was a minimal barricade, and went into the Chief's office. He was like a character out of a movie—a big fat guy who'd been in the force for a million years. I put the permit on his desk and said, "You are to sign this, if you will." He looked at it, started chuckling and then said seriously, "I don't know why I'm doing this." By then, I knew. Srila Prabhupada wanted it and Krishna was in this Chief's heart. He signed it.

After that, Prabhupada, the leader of the International Society for Krishna Consciousness, surrounded by disciples praising him, turned to Tamal Krishna Maharaj, who was then GBC of the New York temple, and said, "Who did it?" Prabhupada didn't say, "I did it," even though ISKCON was operating off of his energy and it was all his glory. He knew that things happen due to people, and his was a personal movement. Tamal Krishna Maharaj said, "Jayananda built the carts and Tosan Krishna got all the permits." And right then and there Srila Prabhupada wrote me a thank you letter.

Bhutatma: Once, when we had just started selling big books, Buddhimanta, Yogeschandra, Keshava and I were on a traveling *sankirtan* party and we were getting criticized because we weren't at the temple eating temple *prasadam* and so forth. We were on the front lines, and we would offer and eat sour cream and dates, that kind of food. So we went to Prabhupada in his room in L.A. and said, "We think we're doing the right thing but some people say no, we need to be eating temple *prasadam*, otherwise it's not good for our spiritual life." Prabhupada looked at us, leaned forward and forcefully said, "Just go out and sell my books! You can eat anything!"

We were totally vindicated, "We do understand what he wants. He wants us out there selling his books." Prabhupada's words smashed the critics once and for all.

Chitralekha: Prabhupada was always instructing Upendra in a gentle, loving, fatherly way and Upendra was always ready to serve Prabhupada and travel with him. But by that time I had children and Prabhupada would occasionally question Upendra, "What about your wife and children? Who will take care of them?" Upendra would try to explain to Prabhupada how we were on welfare, and Prabhupada would say, "You are foolish. You must take care of your wife and children." In some way Prabhupada always humbled Upendra.

Atma Tattva: One Ekadasi during the Kumbha-mela in Allahabad, Prabhupada was sitting back with his eyes closed, his legs stretched under his desk, talking about Ekadasi. Prabhupada said, "Lotus pods fried in ghee are very good on Ekadasi." Somebody immediately ran to the market to arrange for lotus pods, but just two minutes later a Ramanandi *brahmana* and his 9 year-old son arrived, both of them wearing Ramanandi *tilak*. They paid their obeisances, and the father put a cloth bag from his shoulder on Prabhupada's desk. Prabhupada put his hand in it and said, "Just see, it has come." It was lotus pods fried in *ghee*. He looked at the Ramanandi and said, "How are you?"

This man happened to be the priest of a Bengali family in Firozabad, U.P., where Prabhupada used to stay. Even though this person was a Ramanandi, he did the Gaura-Nitai Deity worship for this family. Prabhupada ate some of the pods, distributed the rest and said to the Ramanandi, "You haven't taken bath in the confluence, the *sangam*?" The Ramanandi said, "Swamiji, I have come to take bath in the *sangam*," and he put a plate under Prabhupada's feet. Prabhupada adjusted his feet on the plate and this man bathed Prabhupada's feet in *sangam* water from his pot while he chanted *mantras*. Prabhupada looked at him, smiling. During that time, December '76, it was rare to get Prabhupada's *charanamrita* and all of us desired it. This Ramanandi sprinkled that water on his head, drank some, and then sprinkled some on all of us.

He said to Prabhupada, "Your feet are the actual *sangam*. What will we get in bathing that *sangam*? Your feet will purify the Ganges and since you are not going to the Ganges, I brought the Ganga here. I will mix some of this *charanamrita* in the Ganga." Prabhupada smiled and said, "Give me your son. I will make him an *acharya*." The man said, "He is yours, Swamiji, you can take him any time." Prabhupada said, "No, no, any time means no time. You give him to me now. I will make him an *acharya*." The Ramanandi said, "Swamiji, now he is learning Sanskrit grammar. To study the *bhasyas*, the commentaries, he must know some grammar. Once his *vyakarana* is over, then I will hand him over to you. He is yours." Prabhupada insisted for the fourth time, "No, no, what grammar? We don't need grammar. Give him to me. I will make him an *acharya*." This man said, "Swamiji, I am not saying no. Everything mine is yours. But he is too small. He will only be trouble for you.

In a few years I will hand him over to you." Prabhupada said, "Okay, *tike, tike*," and he rubbed the boy's head. After that there were other visitors to see Prabhupada, and this man and his son left.

Years passed and the Ramananda *sampradaya* broke into many inimical sects. Then one year I was taking ten *gurukula* boys to the Allahabad Kumbha-mela and I was surprised to learn that the Ramanandas had elected one young *sannyasi* to lead their whole *sampradaya* and that they had a huge Ramananda stall at the festival. I told the *gurukula* boys, "We will have this leader's *darshan*. That one *sadhu* united a whole *sampradaya* is unheard of and you boys should meet the person who has this potency. God knows, tomorrow you may become a *guru*."

So we went to see him. We were given priority because some of the boys were from South America, Australia, and so on. There were about a hundred people with this young *sannyasi*, men with long beards and matted locks of hair, all three times older than him and leaders in their own right. This young *sannyasi* was sitting on a big seat and people were fanning him with a *chamara*. We paid obeisances and a *gurukula* boy from South America loudly chanted the *sannyasa-sukta*, which is a traditional way to greet a *sannyasi*. As he started chanting, everyone became silent and after he had finished, this young *maharaj* composed a Sanskrit poem about Prabhupada. He recited, "If I say that neither in the past nor in the future will there be an *acharya* equal to the *acharya* of the Hare Krishna movement, I won't be committing an offense to the founder of my line, Ramananda, because in his commentary Ramananda himself predicted that Vishnu worship would spread around the world and that the whole world would take to it."

As he was talking, I realized that this was the same person who, as a small boy, had his head rubbed by Srila Prabhupada. He finished four *slokas* glorifying Prabhupada and ended with the glorification of Lord Jagannatha. Then he honored each boy separately and when I went up to him he said, "Atma Tattva prabhu, do you remember me? You used to carry me on your back." When I traveled on *padayatra* we had stayed at his father's house. At that time I was a *brahmachari* and I used to carry this boy on my back. He used to call Lokanath Maharaj an "old man" because he had white hair.

He said, "Prabhupada spoke about me becoming an *acharya*. My father never brought me to the Hare Krishna movement, but before he passed away he told me that I had to study the *Sankara-bhasya* so that I could defeat it. That was his last wish. So for four years I stayed with the *mayavadis* in Benares and studied the commentary of Sankara. It was painful. Our whole *sampradaya* had split up over misunderstandings and I thought that since I had Prabhupada's blessings, maybe I could unite us. I tried for nine years and this year it has happened. By the blessings of your Guru Maharaj we are united. Ramananda said that as long as we were broken, we would never be able to fulfill his prediction. But Ramananda also said, 'we don't have to fulfill that prediction because it has already been fulfilled by these people.' We simply have to join and preach with them. Their movement is spreading around the world". Using us as a catalyst, this young *sannyasi* preached to everyone assembled there in that way. It was great to hear from him.

Bhutatma: I had made friends with a noted religious scholar, Mark Juergensmeyer, one of the professors in the Religious Studies Department at Berkeley University. I asked him, "What do you think about having a program with Srila Prabhupada and some of the faculty?" Juergensmeyer was enthusiastic and one of the people he invited was Dr. Staal, who had already had scholarly exchanges with Prabhupada about chanting the mahamantra. That exchange was printed as a brochure that we distributed to validate the scholarly nature of our movement. Dr. Staal was already well known to devotees. Twenty or twenty-five faculty members plus their wives attended, quite a big turnout for that kind of group. They were interested to meet Prabhupada because of the history behind our movement. We set up a room and put a *vyasasana* on top of a table, which I think seemed a little pretentious to them—a colorful, big chair with peacocks on it so high up that the base of it was head height for them. Some of them seemed to question the appropriateness of this arrangement.

When Prabhupada arrived, I accompanied him to the building saying, "Prabhupada, it's an old building, but . . ." He said, "We don't care, old or new, the building doesn't matter,"

The entrance to the room was from the back—the people were facing the other way. I held the door and Prabhupada walked in, and as everyone turned around I saw their expression. The moment they saw him, such a transcendent figure dressed in saffron, that little subtle edge melted away. Their sense of someone pretentious or pompous was eliminated and they sensed, "Here is a real saint."

Prabhupada was pleased by the turnout and he smiled and got on the *vyasasana* very naturally—"Yes, I do belong here, I'm representing Vyasa." He spoke not about Radha Krishna but about Vedic and *brahminical* culture. Pradyumna, Svarupa Damodar and I sat on the side. After the talk one of the professors asked, "You are interested in making people *brahmanas* and bringing the *brahminical* culture to the West. What about your followers here, are they *brahmanas*?" I wondered what Prabhupada would say because we were not really *brahmanas*. But Prabhupada handled it adeptly. He said, "They are trying to become *brahmanas*," with a tone that said we weren't struggling vainly but we were going to be successful, we were on the path. It disarmed the challenge and gave us the appropriate status, that we were sincere and we were following the correct process, even though we may still be conditioned by the modes of passion and ignorance.

Prabhupada also had a little exchange with Dr. Staal. He said, "I see the illustrious Dr. Staal is here." Of course that flattery made Dr. Staal happy. Every time I saw Prabhupada interact with anyone, the common theme was that Prabhupada was completely in command, not by dint of assertiveness, but because on some level everyone knew he was a bona fide representative of God. Prabhupada never had a trace of lack of confidence. Neither did he have any hubris or pride. He had that overwhelming sense of self-confidence that comes when one's self-realized. Everyone at this scholarly gathering sensed that.

After we left the meeting Prabhupada said to me, "This was an important meeting," because he had met scholars and had established the credibility of our movement. And later one of the scholars told me, "I was a little skeptical in the beginning. I thought, 'maybe this will be some kind of elderly Bengali *brahmana* who is caste conscious,' but after I heard him speak I understood that this person was someone very special." That comment confirmed what I had perceived that evening.

Tosan Krishna: What I remember most about Srila Prabhupada was that he was always youthful. When he walked it was hard to keep up with him. In Los Angeles, when we delivered tapes of the Road Show to Srila Prabhupada to receive his comments on the music, there were five or six of us on a walk one morning, and we were puffing and couldn't keep up with Srila Prabhupada.

Amidst his concerns for his worldwide mission, his age and all his responsibilities, he remained a Vaikuntha man. He was always above it. In one sense he seemed to be right with us dealing with all the details, but it was quite apparent that he was with Krishna. He was a transcendental man, a Vaikuntha man, as he described his own Guru Maharaj.

Chitralekha: Sometimes when a devotee fell away or had an illicit relationship, other devotees advised that person not to come to the temple or they shunned and humiliated that person so much that he or she wouldn't come to the temple. That disturbed Prabhupada. He would write, "Now you have driven him away. You have humiliated him so much that he won't be able to continue his service." In that way Prabhupada would chastise us.

Prabhupada was accepting of anything that anyone could offer on any level. No one would have become a devotee had Prabhupada been very strict. He was strict with himself but accommodating with anyone who was inclined to offer any loving service to him or to Krishna. In my eyes that is Prabhupada's most magnanimous quality. That's the mood with which he began this movement and, if we can imbibe that quality of Prabhupada's and carry on with loving compassion for one another, that's how this movement's going to continue. Be strict with ourselves, yes, but have loving compassion for one another. To go back to Godhead we need each other's support.

TAPE 37

Umapati Swami
Sacinandana Swami
Narada Muni das
Dinadayadri dasi
Bhakti Caru Swami
Vaiyasaki das

Umapati Swami: I'd been reading Buddhist books that said, "You cannot say it is, you cannot say it is not, you cannot say it both is and is not, you cannot say it neither is nor is not." So, when Srila Prabhupada said, "The Supreme Absolute Truth is a person," I thought that was the most intelligent thing I'd heard in my whole life. It made so much sense that I knew that I had found the person I was looking for.

But before I joined I still had a doubt. I thought, "I can see the Swami is honest, he's not looking for money, but how do I know he has real knowledge? He could be misled." I didn't say anything to Prabhupada, but in his next lecture he said, "I teach only what is in scripture." Then I thought, "If he teaches only what is in scripture, there's no danger," and I started going regularly to the temple.

Sacinandana Swami: Srila Prabhupada received the rose each one of us offered him. He gave another rose back to us, and he lectured. While he lectured, like so many of my god-brothers, I felt that Srila Prabhupada was speaking just for me and was looking at me. I felt personally addressed by Srila Prabhupada. It reminded me of how, when Krishna ate lunch surrounded by His cowherd boyfriends, He communicated to each one of the thousands of them. Prabhupada's eyes were wandering over his audience, and sometimes he closed his eyes in deep concentration, but somehow he connected to every one of us.

Then, because I felt so personally addressed by Srila Prabhupada, I put a challenging question to him. Foolish as I was, I wanted to test Prabhupada to see if he was really the perfect spiritual master I could surrender to for my whole life. Such surrender would have serious consequences as far as money and my position in life were concerned.

Since my mind was not spiritually developed, to see how Prabhupada would react I asked a question which I felt he could not answer. I said, "If God is all good, why did He create this *maya* which inflicts suffering upon the living entities?" Prabhupada looked at me and requested Shyamasundar to repeat the question. Shyamasundar had not heard my question, maybe due to my accent, and I repeated it. Prabhupada again asked for the question to be repeated. I became insecure but I again asked, "You say God is all good. It can't be because He has created *maya*, which is certainly not all good. So either He is not all good, or *maya* is no longer under His control and makes us suffer against the good intentions of God."

Prabhupada looked at me intently and then said, "Krishna has not created *maya*, you have created *maya*." I was startled. Philosophically I couldn't understand what he was saying—I created the whole material world? I could not even create a house because at that moment I was insolvent. Later I understood his explanation, but at the time all I understood was that Krishna was not at fault for my situation. I was at fault. I thought, "What a brilliant answer. I have understood the point. I better surrender to Krishna and Srila Prabhupada," who seemed to be very close with the Lord. It was my first memorable encounter with Srila Prabhupada and he had demolished, like a *sadhu* always does, my concept that I could challenge him. And besides answering my foolish question, he effected a transformation in my heart.

Umapati Swami: Prabhupada talked so much about impersonalists and Buddhists that Hayagriva and I began to think, "The Swami is not liberal enough," and for a short time we stopped attending his lectures. We were sitting around Mott Street talking about this when Kirtanananda came in and said, "I've decided to leave the Swami. I don't like what's going on."

I said, "We've been talking about that too." Kirtanananda said, "You fools! Do you think I could leave the Swami?" He had tricked us and he insisted that we talk with Prabhupada. When we saw him, Prabhupada said, "If you have some doubts we can discuss them." I said, "We don't like what you're saying about the Buddhists and Sri Ramakrishna."

Prabhupada said, "Okay, I will explain. I have never criticized Lord Buddha. In fact, I have always called him 'Lord Buddha'. But his followers eat meat, they don't believe in God and they don't believe in the soul. They are atheists. The Buddhist scriptures do not talk about God or the soul. As for Ramakrishna, I have always said and I will always say that he was nothing but a crazy priest. Ramakrishna said that you could worship Kali or worship Krishna and it's the same, but Krishna says, 'If you worship the demigods you go to the demigods, and if you worship Me you come to Me.' Ramakrishna has contradicted Krishna. It's as if he's saying that by buying a plane ticket to Chicago you will get to Los Angeles." I said, "What about all the wonderful things in his books?" Prabhupada said, "His disciples took them from the Vedas, put them in his books and said that he said them. Besides that, Ramakrishna's followers eat meat. They go to the doctor and get a letter saying they'll die if they don't eat meat. All the *sadhus* in India know this." Prabhupada told me about a gathering of holy people in India where some *sadhus* saw a dead fish floating on the water. They laughed and said, 'Quick, call the Ramakrishna Mission!'"

Prabhupada also said that when Vivekananda, Ramakrishna's principle disciple, met Ramakrishna, Ramakrishna touched him on the forehead and Vivekananda felt electric shocks. Prabhupada laughed and said, "You have read about the Universal Form, where does it say anything about electric shocks?" After that Vivekananda fainted and when he woke up, Ramakrishna was crying. Vivekananda said, "Why are you crying?" Ramakrishna said, "I have given you all my power, I have none left." Prabhupada said, "Is spiritual knowledge like money, that if I give it to you I have none left?"

That was the clincher.

Narada Muni: The first time I saw Srila Prabhupada was in Los Angeles in 1969. I was picking lemons to get money to go to a Zen Buddhist monastery when I saw a poster from the Santa Barbara ISKCON temple about meeting a real spiritual master. It was a small temple by the ocean and even though there was no one in the temple when I entered, by Srila Prabhupada's mercy I immediately knew that I had found what I had long been searching and praying for.

On Sunday I got a ride to the Los Angeles temple where Srila Prabhupada was performing an initiation ceremony. Prabhupada was somber and grave, yet I could also see love and compassion emanating from him when he initiated the devotees and I saw a spiritual bond forming between him and them. I immediately thought, "I want this."

Before one particular devotee received his beads, Srila Prabhupada, as always, asked him to recite the four regulative principles. When he said, "No intoxication," Srila Prabhupada laughed and said, "And this means no more LSD?" Though I'd given up drugs by then, I could relate to that.

Sitting on the *vyasasana,* Srila Prabhupada was like a universal father reciprocating an intimate mood of spiritual love with his disciples.

Umapati: One night a guest asked Prabhupada, "What about LSD? It gives you spiritual visions." That guest was trying to trap Prabhupada because if Prabhupada said, "I never took it," the guest could say, "How do you know then?" And if Prabhupada said, "I tried it and it doesn't work," he could say, "You say no intoxication but you took an intoxicant." How would Srila Prabhupada answer? Prabhupada said, "I have never taken these things, but all my disciples have given them up." That took care of that.

Dinadayadri: During an ecstatic *kirtan* in the Los Angeles temple Srila Prabhupada was laughing. Afterwards a devotee asked why he had been laughing and Prabhupada said, "I was laughing to see Narada Muni." The devotee said, "Narada Muni?" "Yes, Narada Muni was there." "What was Narada Muni doing?" Prabhupada said, "He was laughing." The devotee said, "Why was he laughing?" "He was laughing when he saw the *mlecchas* and *chandalas* dancing and chanting Hare Krishna."

Umapati Swami: Prabhupada's *Bhagavad-gita As It Is* hadn't been published yet, so Prabhupada read from the Bhagavad-gita by Dr. Radha-Krishnan, who was the former president of India. Prabhupada said that Dr. Radha-Krishnan was an impersonalist but we didn't know what that meant until one morning when Prabhupada said, "Today I will show you that Dr. Radha-Krishnan is an impersonalist," and he had Roy read Chapter Nine, Verse 34, "Always think of Me, become My devotee." Prabhupada said, "Now read the commentary." Roy read, "When Krishna says 'unto Me,' it is not Krishna to whom we should surrender but to the unborn eternal within Krishna." Prabhupada said, "You see, that proves that he's an impersonalist."

Nobody understood. What Dr. Radha-Krishnan had written sounded okay to everybody except Srila Prabhupada. Kirtanananda said, "Dr. Radha-Krishnan is right," and gave a long speech about the unborn eternal within Krishna. Prabhupada started to turn red while Kirtanananda talked. I thought, "For the first time I understand what it means to say somebody 'turned red.'" I had never seen anybody turn so red. As Kirtanananda spoke, Prabhupada got redder and redder. When Kirtanananda stopped, Prabhupada said, "Are you finished?" Kirtanananda said, "No," and continued speaking. When he finally stopped again, Prabhupada said, "Are you finished?" He said, "Yes."

Prabhupada stood up, slammed his hand down and said, "It's Krishna! It's Krishna! There is no difference between Krishna's mind and Krishna. Krishna is not an ordinary human being. He is Absolute Truth. His body, His mind and He Himself are one and absolute. There is no difference between Krishna Himself and His body." I had never seen anything so magnificent. Prabhupada was like a roaring lion. I could almost feel the room shake.

Then we understood impersonalism. Srila Prabhupada saved us on that day.

Narada Muni: At my initiation Srila Prabhupada explained the ten offenses. Regarding the offense of thinking that chanting Hare Krishna is like mundane religion, he said that you may get material benefit by mundane religion but Krishna consciousness is beyond all religion. Prabhupada said, "Just from this ceremony you can go back to Godhead." That's the importance of getting connected with Srila Prabhupada. Then Srila Prabhupada began to give the initiates their names and he explained their names. I was last. When it was my turn Prabhupada laughed and said, "You have such a nice spiritual name. Your name is Narada Muni." In the early days, Narada Muni was more popular than he is now because he was the transcendental spaceman and we were so spaced out that we related with Narada Muni. Everyone wondered who would get the name Narada Muni. When Srila Prabhupada said "Narada Muni," everybody oohed and aahed and laughed. And Srila Prabhupada also laughed. Then he said, "Narada Muni travels throughout space. So you should do this. And by chanting Hare Krishna and playing a *vina*, you can do it." I don't know what Srila Prabhupada meant, but he always had a transcendental vision of us and he saw something in us that we couldn't see in ourselves. Srila Prabhupada beautifully brought out the spiritual essence in all of us.

Umapati Swami: Some of the guys were already bowing down to Srila Prabhupada but I wasn't. Hayagriva said to me, "I don't like this bowing." I said, "Me neither." It was too foreign. There was also some talk about an initiation and Roy came up to me and said, "Wally, do you want to get initiated?" I said, "I don't know if I'm ready." He said, "None of us are, but we're going to do it anyway." I said, "Okay, me too." Roy put my name down on the list and we asked Prabhupada, "What is initiation?" Prabhupada said, "I'll tell you later."

After the morning class the day before the initiation Prabhupada said, "Now I will tell you what initiation means. Initiation means that the spiritual master accepts the disciple and agrees to take charge of his welfare, and the disciple accepts the spiritual master and agrees to worship him as God," and he got up and walked out of the room. We sat there looking at each other. I thought, "We wouldn't be this stunned if a hydrogen bomb had gone off in this room." To worship Prabhupada as God was inconceivable, especially after what Prabhupada had said about people who want to be God.

Prabhupada had Janaki, Mukunda's wife, string the beads because, as Prabhupada said, "Women have the patience to do this kind of work and they are good at it." After we all had our japa beads then we had our neck beads tied on. I said, "How do you get these off?" And somebody said, "You don't." Prabhupada picked up our japa beads one by one and asked, "Whose are these?" When he picked up my beads, I said, "Those are mine." Prabhupada motioned for me to come to him and bow down. I couldn't avoid it anymore so I bowed down. Then I repeated what Prabhupada said, he gave me my beads and he said my name was Umapati. I thought Umapati was a name for Vishnu meaning the husband of the Goddess of Fortune, but that's not what Prabhupada said. Umapati is actually a name for Lord Shiva.

I returned to my seat and I told Hayagriva, who was sitting next to me, "Getting your beads is great," because he hadn't gotten his yet. Prabhupada had all of us touch our beads to the feet of Lord Chaitanya on the Panca Tattva picture, and then he started the sacrificial fire. As he poured *ghee* on the fire the room filled with smoke, and smoke began to pour out the windows. I thought that any second the Fire Department would come and the firemen wouldn't believe what was going on there. Later I found out that everybody else in the room had the same thoughts. Finally we all went home and left Prabhupada to clean up. Nobody thought about cleaning up after the ceremony.

Sacinandana Swami: In London, while all the devotees were taking breakfast *prasadam* and the temple room was empty, Srila Prabhupada went to the temple alone to take *darshan* and pray to the Deities. After a long time he returned to his room.

In the morning I washed Sri Sri Radha-London-Isvara's dishes and at that time I was in turmoil. I thought, "What will be the consequences of my decision to surrender?" My fiancée had come to convince me to take up my old ways and my dying grandfather had requested me to come to his deathbed so he could ask me to give up Krishna consciousness. My family tradition was that you had to agree to the wish of a dying man, but I could not agree to give up the Lord's grace upon me. So I stayed in the temple but I did not clean the Lord's plates well.

One morning as I was washing the plates, absorbed on the mental platform, the temple president came into the kitchen. His face was red and he stammered, "During Prabhupada's *darshan* of the Deities, Krishna told Prabhupada that His plates are not nicely cleansed, that the old offering is still on the plates. Prabhupada said that whoever washes the dishes has to do a good job from now on." This woke me from my dreaming state. I had to be responsible. I had been pondering deeply important issues but I had not performed my service correctly and Krishna had complained to Srila Prabhupada. Besides Krishna, only the cook, who put the new offering on the plates, could know that the plates were dirty. But the cook was too fast—he put the new offering on hurriedly, without looking at the plates. Then the dirty plate was covered and only the person who ate the offering could know that the plate was dirty. It was that Person, Lord Krishna, who had detected this and He had told Srila Prabhupada. I was moved. And I was also happy that there was a direct connection between Srila Prabhupada and Lord Krishna. I became more inspired to surrender my life to Srila Prabhupada.

Umapati Swami: One morning Prabhupada said, "All of you should chant 64 rounds a day." We said, "What! Six-four rounds a day! No, we can't!" Prabhupada said, "All right, 32 rounds." We said, "Thirty-two rounds, no!" Prabhupada said, "All right, 16 rounds, no less." That's how we started chanting 16 rounds a day.

Another time Prabhupada smashed me. Sometimes I typed for Prabhupada and if there were some English mistakes I would correct them. I was typing a letter to someone in India that said, "Sri Sri Radha-Krishna." I'd heard of "Sri," but I'd never heard of "Sri Sri." Not only that, but one "Sri" was at the end of a line and the next "Sri" was at the beginning of the next line, which is a common typing mistake. I went into Prabhupada's room and I said, "Sri Sri?" and Prabhupada said, "Yes." I said, "I thought it was a mistake." Prabhupada said, "When I type in your language, you can correct me. But when I type in my language, you cannot correct me." Then somebody walked in and Prabhupada said, "I told him that when I type in his language he can correct me, but now he wants to correct me when I type in my language."

Bhakti Caru Swami: In spite of being the world *acharya,* Srila Prabhupada was humble. Once in Amsterdam, when Prabhupada was about to give initiation, the devotees hadn't organized things properly and were making mistakes at every step. Prabhupada was getting increasingly annoyed and when he saw that the sacrificial altar had no fruits on it, he was further disappointed. One devotee ran to the kitchen, cut some fruits and gave the fruit to Srila Prabhupada. Prabhupada got still more upset because such fruits are supposed to be uncut.

A hippie who used to come to the temple regularly was present, and he had noticed that whenever someone became upset, the devotees would tell that person, "Why don't you chant Hare Krishna?" When this hippie saw that Prabhupada was agitated, he told Prabhupada, "Why don't you chant Hare Krishna?" Prabhupada quietly took his beadbag and started to chant.

Umapati Swami: Prabhupada had a Robert's tape recorder, which at that time was the best amateur tape recorder. I wasn't so familiar with the Roberts but because I had a background in professional music recording, I had experience fixing multi-thousand dollar professional recorders. And I was a little proud because I knew some big recording stars. When Prabhupada said, "My tape recorder is broken." I said, "Maybe I can fix it." I looked at it and said, "What does this button do?" Prabhupada said, "You cannot fix it. If you have to ask me what that button does, how can you fix it?" Somebody walked in the room and Prabhupada said, "He wants to fix my tape recorder, but he has to ask me what a button does. He cannot fix it." I was burning with humiliation.

Dinadayadri: I was living in Washington, D.C. in early 1970, distributing *Back to Godhead* magazines and giving out incense on a college campus. It was around the time that National Guards had shot at students at Kent State University and there was unrest and a tense atmosphere on the campuses. Back then it was a big deal to sell a few magazines for a quarter each but I was upset because the students were so agitated that they weren't interested in the magazine.

Then a newspaper reporter from the Washington Post asked if he could interview me and I said, "Sure." He asked what I had done before I'd joined the movement and I told him how I'd lived on a hippie farm and had became discouraged with that philosophy. I said, "I was being misled by false rascals like Timothy Leary." I had studied some of Timothy Leary's books and I felt betrayed and disillusioned when I realized he was saying, "Have great sex, take LSD and see God." I wanted knowledge of the Absolute Truth and what Leary was saying was material—it had to do not with spiritual knowledge but with the physical body.

In those days, devotees were badly misquoted in newspaper articles. The reporters didn't understand what we were talking about and they'd write some nonsense about Hinduism. This Washington Post article was one of the first ones where we were accurately quoted. It was long, with good quotes from a lot of devotees and because it was accurate—my exact words were in the paper—it had some particular potency. My quote was at the beginning, on the front page of the Washington Post's Style section, along with a big photograph of my face. I'm camera-shy and not usually photogenic, but by Krishna's mercy I looked nice in the photograph, wearing a nose ring with a chain going to my ear.

When Prabhupada read my comments about Timothy Leary being a "false rascal," which was Prabhupada's terminology, he said, "George Harrison has given me nineteen thousand dollars for printing the Krishna Book, but by her statement this girl has given me nineteen thousand million dollars." I can't tell you how encouraged I was when I heard that. I was a young devotee and perhaps Prabhupada mercifully said it to encourage me. I wasn't parroting his words because I did have that realization about Leary, but it was definitely Prabhupada's inspiration that made me say it. Prabhupada would inspire us and if we surrendered to his inspiration, there would be a reciprocal exchange between him and us—the guru and the disciple—that was esoteric and inexplicable. Most of us understood that exchange from our personal experience.

Umapati Swami: After I was initiated I blooped. I was the second bloop in the movement. My distinction is that I was one of the first people to cause Prabhupada great pain and suffering. But the devotees would have to get me because Prabhupada's electronic equipment was always breaking down and I was the only one who knew how to fix it. Once when they had come for me, Kirtanananda and I were talking when Prabhupada came into the room, walked up to me and said, "Even if you don't want to be one of us, you must associate with us. You cannot get away from us." Prabhupada was always very concerned.

There was a seemingly ordinary boy, David Allen, from the Lower East Side who started coming. I didn't know him but Prabhupada and some of the boys who had been with Prabhupada longer knew him. Once I heard Prabhupada eagerly talking to someone about that boy, saying, "He's making advancement, don't you think?" Later I learned that this boy was formerly Prabhupada's roommate—the person who had gone crazy on drugs and forced Prabhupada onto the street. But Prabhupada's only thought was, "Don't you think he's making advancement?" That's all Prabhupada cared about.

Vaiyasaki: On a morning walk Prabhupada discussed the *api cet sudaracaro bhajate mam ananya-bhak* verse, that even if one falls down and commits a heinous sin, he's still considered saintly if he is rightly situated in devotional service. One devotee asked, "Srila Prabhupada, if it's an accidental falldown then Krishna considers him saintly, but if it's premeditated that's different—that's sinning in knowledge. How do we know if the falldown is accidental?" Prabhupada stopped walking and said, "If the devotee comes back it was accidental."

What I understood from this is that if someone bloops and 10, 15 or 20 years later and takes up devotional service again, then Prabhupada will consider his falldown accidental. That was Srila Prabhupada's ocean of compassion. He had so much mercy, so much compassion, that someone could fall away completely but when he came back, Prabhupada considered all those years in *maya* simply an accident. That really hit home.

Umapati Swami: At that time Timothy Leary, the big LSD king, was popular among the hippies. One day a few of us were sitting around the *prasadam* room talking when a young man came in and gave us all the latest hippie gossip. He said, "They had the wildest party in Leary's place in Millbrook, New York." Immediately I wanted to hear about this wild party. Just then Prabhupada looked through the window and said, "Umapati, you are not sitting properly," because I had my back to the altar. I had to turn around and face the altar, and I couldn't hear anything this fellow said. The whole thing was blocked.

Narada Muni: One evening I read the pastime of Pralambasura to Srila Prabhupada. Srila Prabhupada enjoyed hearing it and when we got to the part when Lord Balaram pummels Pralambasura, Srila Prabhupada laughed and boldly exclaimed, "This is God!" Then he explained how he used to enact this pastime with his sister when he was a child. He said, "I would play Balaram," and he laughed and laughed. That was very sweet.

Umapati Swami: Hayagriva and I were looking at the dust cover of the *Srimad-Bhagavatam* that Prabhupada had brought from India. It's a painting of the material and spiritual world with a big lotus and many bubbles. There was one bubble we both liked. We said, "This is nice!" "Wow! Far out!" "That's where I want to go." "That really looks great." Hayagriva was on his way to the temple and I had something else to do so I said, "Ask the Swami what that bubble is." That afternoon I said, "Did you ask the Swami what that bubble is?" Hayagriva said, "Yeah, he said it's the material world."

Sacinandana Swami: On a morning walk in Amsterdam we passed many sleeping hippies and Prabhupada commented on them. Finally we came to a tree with a nest that had a little bird that was just about to fly. The bird was a little doubtful if he should fly or not but Prabhupada encouraged him and finally the bird more or less tumbled down but with some idea of how to hold his little wings. Prabhupada turned to us and said, "How does the bird know how to fly?" "Instinct, Prabhupada," said someone who wanted to represent the modern scientists. Prabhupada immediately said, "That is just a name. The Lord as Paramatma is in the heart of the bird directing him to fly." Whatever Prabhupada saw, even a little bird making his first attempt to fly, he connected to Krishna. That was especially visible during morning walks.

Umapati Swami: One gray, cloudy day I was in Prabhupada's room typing and Prabhupada was busy doing something when suddenly the sun came out and filled the room with light. Prabhupada said, "When the spiritual sun comes out, it is like that."

Dinadayadri: Prabhupada liked to take his morning walks on the beautiful white sand of Juhu Beach and once, when we were walking there, Srila Prabhupada looked at the ocean and said, "What is that water?" Nobody said anything for a while. I thought, "It's Krishna's energy," but I was too shy to speak. Finally my husband said, "Prabhupada, it's the Arabian Sea." Lightning bolts shot out of Prabhupada's eyes, "Do you think your spiritual master is so nonsense that he doesn't know that's the Arabian Sea?" Obviously that wasn't the answer he was looking for. Then Satsvarupa said, "It's Krishna's energy." "Yes," and Prabhupada explained how, instead of inundating the land and flooding everything, the ocean waves stop at a certain point and how nature works under Krishna's laws. It was very instructive. When Srila Prabhupada chastised, you didn't feel bad about yourself, you felt cleansed. Prabhupada didn't give you low self-esteem but he gave a valuable lesson. Whether he chastised or praised, it was all growth and encouragement.

Umapati Swami: When Prabhupada yelled at you, your life air would practically leave your body. In Vrindavan in the winter of '76, I dressed the small Radha-Krishna Deities in the morning and then prepared Srila Prabhupada's *vyasasana* for *gurupuja*. Although so many devotees were there, nobody told me that I shouldn't be bare-chested. I thought that was how you were supposed to dress. One day I was about to do the *arati* when Prabhupada said to me, "You should have something around your shoulders." Somebody gave me a chadar to wear and I thought, "I'm supposed to wear something because I'm doing the *arati*." The next day I wasn't going to do the *arati*, so I didn't bother putting anything on. When Prabhupada came in he said, "I told you to always have a wrapper! You should listen and learn!" When Prabhupada said something like that, your life air would almost leave your body. It took me days to get my composure back. But still I see this as his being mild and compassionate.

Vaiyasaki: One morning in Mayapur in 1976, Prabhupada was walking around the ISKCON grounds with senior devotees—Bhavananda and Jayapataka—and as we approached the *prasadam* hall, we came to backlogged toilets that the Bengali devotees used—there was stool everywhere. When Prabhupada saw this he said, "What is this? It is filthy!" Bhavananda said, "These are not our toilets, Srila Prabhupada. The Bengalis use these toilets." Prabhupada said, "Why aren't you arranging for it to be cleaned? You are not cleaning it because it does not disturb you. If you were in the mode of goodness, you could not tolerate this and immediately you would have it cleaned. But you are in the mode of ignorance and this, which is in the mode of ignorance, harmonizes with you.

That's why you don't do anything about it." Prabhupada immediately ordered it cleaned up and he explained that, according to the quality of your own consciousness, you feel harmony with your surroundings. If you're in the mode of ignorance and you come across something in the mode of ignorance, it doesn't disturb you and you don't change it. But if you're in the mode of goodness, then the mode of ignorance disturbs you, you can't tolerate it, and you want to bring it to a higher level. He told the devotees that they were in the mode of ignorance because the stool didn't disturb them, and that's why they didn't clean it.

Umapati Swami: Today, in the entranceway to Prabhupada's quarters in Vrindavan, there's a store but that used to be a vestibule where Prabhupada's secretary, Harikesa Maharaj, would sit and type. Once I was talking to him there when Palika came. Harikesa told her, "Palika, tell me everything that's going on in Vrindavan." She told him everything that shouldn't be going on and left. Then Harikesa peeked through the door to Prabhupada's quarters and saw Prabhupada walking away. He said, "Oh, no, Prabhupada heard everything." The next day in his class Prabhupada said, "If you have illicit sex in Vrindavan, you will take birth as a Vrindavan monkey. That is Krishna's mercy because you have taken shelter of Vrindavan. But stop this monkey business."

Dinadayadri: At the entrance to the property there were huge wooden gates that were kept closed at night. But one morning around 6 am, when Srila Prabhupada came to those gates on his morning walk, they were still closed. Srila Prabhupada was livid. He said, "Why are the gates closed? Do you think *mangal arati* is just for you? No, it is for everyone. You must open these gates so the villagers can come to *mangal arati*." He was angry that we were so thoughtless and self-centered. He was always teaching us to think of others, giving Krishna consciousness to others, and that way we would save ourselves. By trying to save others, we would save ourselves. The idea of being concerned for our own advancement and to hell with everybody else wasn't Prabhupada's way.

Umapati Swami: In Vrindavan Prabhupada complained, "You are offering the Deities rotten flowers." The flowers looked okay to us but Prabhupada said, "If you offer the Deities rotten flowers, They will not say anything but your life will be spoiled." He talked about this many times. And once a devotee tried to give Prabhupada a garland that was bigger than Krishna's garland and Prabhupada made him exchange it. He said, "You cannot give me a garland that is bigger than the garland on Krishna."

Narada Muni: Gaura Hari and I cooked for the San Francisco Rathayatra, and after the parade we went to the Big Family Dog Auditorium where thousands of hippies were intensely chanting while Vishnujana Maharaj led *kirtan*, "Chant! Chant! And when you're tired, take *prasadam*! And chant more and more and more!" All the hippies were dressed in their full regalia, which made an incredible scene. Then in the middle of it all, Srila Prabhupada came walking through the crowd like a swan, untouched by the material energy. Prabhupada went up to the stage and declared, "I have come to make the hippies happies!" It was the perfect thing to say. Only Srila Prabhupada could say something so profound. That was wonderful.

Umapati Swami: I fixed Prabhupada's equipment and afterwards somebody played a Ravi Shankar record. When the music came on Prabhupada smiled. Somebody said, "Do you like this music, Swamiji?" He said, "This music is sense gratification." Hayagriva said, "That's a *raga*! They play it in temples!" Prabhupada said, "This music is sense gratification." Hayagriva said, "But it's Ravi Shankar! It's a *raga*! They play it in temples!" Prabhupada said, "No, it is sense gratification." Hayagriva kept insisting, "No, it's a *raga*." Then Prabhupada said, "Ravi Shankar is a businessman." Then somebody said, "What if he wants to be a devotee?" Prabhupada said, "Fine, let him come." Somebody else said, "But Swamiji, you were once a businessman." Prabhupada said, "Because I went naked then, I should go naked now?" Meanwhile, Hayagriva was fuming, "But it's a *raga*!" Prabhupada and I laughed at him.

Dinadayadri: I told Srila Prabhupada that I was having such a severe problem with an abusive marriage partner that I was suicidal. I didn't know what else to do so I blurted out, "Srila Prabhupada, I can't be Krishna conscious. I feel like I'm going to commit suicide." Srila Prabhupada paused and looked off thoughtfully. He was detached, not sentimental—"Oh, you poor little thing"—but he took me seriously. I didn't ask for a divorce or to marry someone else but I asked to live separately from my husband so I could be free of the stress of that situation and continue in the movement. Prabhupada's eyes opened wide, he looked me right in the eye and said, "There will not be other men?" "No, no, Srila Prabhupada." That was the last thing on my mind. I was at the stage where the thought of male-female relationships made me spit—not from spiritual realization but because on the mundane platform I was unbearably miserable. Srila Prabhupada said, "You will stay in our temple?" "Yes, Srila Prabhupada." He wasn't going to sanction a divorce and remarriage, but when I agreed to those two things he said, "All right, you may stay here and assist Palika." And that was it.

Umapati Swami: When I went with my then wife to see Prabhupada in Los Angeles, at one point my wife said, "Prabhupada, I really like to read your books." Prabhupada said, "You have a very nice wife. You should take care of her."

Narada Muni: I was selling books from a book cart at the '71 Rathayatra when I asked someone to take my place for a minute so I could run to see Srila Prabhupada on the Rathayatra cart before it left. When I saw him, I felt that Srila Prabhupada looked at me, and everybody probably felt the same thing. But I know Srila Prabhupada looked at me, acknowledged me and smiled at me, and I felt wonderful. Afterwards, I went with some others to Srila Prabhupada's apartment when he was getting a massage and we reported to Srila Prabhupada how many books we'd sold and we brought him the big bags of *laxmi* we'd collected. Srila Prabhupada said, "Very, very nice. Thank you so much." Srila Prabhupada had nothing to thank us for, we had everything to thank him for, but he thanked us. Another time he told us, "Thank you very much for your kind feelings of appreciation for my humble service unto you. You are all helping me in pushing forward this mission of Lord Chaitanya Mahaprabhu, coming down by disciplic succession to my Guru Maharaj."

Umapati Swami: Before I left with Hanuman, a Canadian devotee, to open a temple in Paris, we went on a morning walk where Prabhupada explained that love requires free will. Prabhupada said, "If you want somebody to love you, they must do it by their free will. You cannot force somebody to love you." Then he grabbed me by the shoulders, shook me and said, "You cannot say, 'You must love me! You must love me! You must love me!'" Prabhupada was very powerful.

Sacinandana Swami: My father was angry that Prabhupada had stolen his son and at a public program he confronted Srila Prabhupada. My father said, "It is not responsible to bring the Indian culture into Germany. It's as irresponsible as taking a crocodile from Egypt to the cold Rhine River. Just as the crocodile cannot survive there, so the people who are with you now will not be able to stay." Prabhupada must have understood that this man was the father of one of his disciples and he took up the challenge. He said, "You can become Krishna conscious in a suit and tie." My father thought, "This answer is too simple for my intellectual challenge." But the pure devotee's words do not necessarily act on the intellectual or mental platform that the question came from. They have a transformative *shakti* which works on a much deeper platform. From Prabhupada's answer my father understood that Krishna consciousness was more than externals. It was not a matter of Indian culture—one didn't have to dress according to the Indian culture. The Germans are used to tough discussions and in the end my father thought, "What a pleasant encounter. My son is in good hands. This spiritual leader is a sensible personality." I was very grateful to Srila Prabhupada for solving a difficult family issue.

Dinadayadri: When my parents met Srila Prabhupada, my mother took a photograph of Srila Prabhupada sitting on the floor behind his desk with my dad sitting cross-legged in front of him. They're both looking at the camera and have the same effulgent smile. I call that picture "my two fathers." It's as if my material father is reflecting the effulgent smile of my spiritual father. My parents thanked Srila Prabhupada for saving me from drugs and a degraded hippie life. Srila Prabhupada smiled and said, "Yes, many parents thank me." They also told him that they were concerned about me because it was difficult for them to communicate with me since I was in India. Srila Prabhupada said, "Yes, I am also concerned about my children." He chatted with my parents on a parental level, he gave them some *prasadam* from his plate, and he showered them with mercy. Srila Prabhupada knew how to relate with everybody.

Umapati Swami: Once I was talking with the devotees when I was blooped and somebody mentioned India. I said, "I would like to go to India." Prabhupada said, "For what, sight seeing?" I couldn't answer.

Sacinandana Swami: Our temple leader had made a big poster with Prabhupada's picture and in big letters "DER FÜHER," in small letters "of the International Society for Krishna Consciousness" and in big letters "KOMMT." Anyone would read "DER FÜRHER KOMMT," the *fuhrer* comes, reminding them of someone totally lacking divine qualities. People drew little moustaches on the posters under

Srila Prabhupada's nose. It was an example of how Prabhupada's disciples did not always serve his preaching mission well.

Srila Prabhupada had a few hostile elements in the audience, probably in part due to the unintelligent advertising. One particularly disturbed man said, "The chanting is mass self-hypnosis," maybe remembering Hitler's influential and passionate speeches. Prabhupada kindly said, "It is not self-hypnosis, it is self-purification." Prabhupada was so expert that with a few words he could alter the consciousness of those who heard him.

Umapati Swami: When I was living away from the temple as a householder in San Francisco, I learned how to program computers. Later Dayananda told me that the devotees working at Spiritual Sky, the old L.A. incense factory, wanted to know if they should buy a computer and Prabhupada said, "Yes, get a computer and Umapati can run it." I had not told Prabhupada what I was doing but when I came to Los Angeles and got back into devotional service again, I started programming the computer. One day on the morning walk on the beach Prabhupada said to me, "Can your computer tell how many grains of sand are on the beach?" I said, "No, Prabhupada, you would have to tell the computer." Swarupa Damodar said, "Does that mean there is a brain superior to the computer?" I said, "The computer is not a brain, it's just a stupid machine." Prabhupada seemed satisfied with that answer. He didn't say anything more.

Narada Muni: Once in New Vrindavan some reviews arrived from educators and scholars in different parts of the world glorifying Srila Prabhupada's books. When we were having *darshan*, Srila Prabhupada had somebody read one particular review. In it, a well-known person wrote that Srila Prabhupada was so prolific and the books he wrote were so profound that they could not be written by an ordinary soul. "It is my belief," he wrote, "that Srila Prabhupada is Vyasadeva himself." Srila Prabhupada lit up with a big smile and everyone said, "*Jaya*, Prabhupada! *Jaya*, Srila Prabhupada!"

We really don't know who Srila Prabhupada is. No one else accomplished what he accomplished and it's unlikely that anyone will for a long time. Srila Prabhupada was directly empowered and sent by Krishna and he came to the most fallen place. Prabhupada once said that Krishna asked him to come to the material world, "Will you please go and deliver them?" Srila Prabhupada didn't want to leave Vrindavan but he came out of his great compassion.

Dinadayadri: At the first Mayapur festival in 1972, when the cornerstone was laid, devotees were learning so-called Bengali-style chanting, which was quite different from the chanting Srila Prabhupada had taught us. The Bengali melodies, rather than being completely transcendental, were a form of traditional folk entertainment. When, instead of simply absorbing Srila Prabhupada's example and trying to emulate that, the devotees imbibed these Indian styles, techniques and drumbeats. Prabhupada expressed some displeasure especially in the beginning when they weren't good at it.

Achyutananda Maharaj had been in India for some time, learned these styles from some of Prabhupada's god-brothers in the Gaudiya Math and had started teaching others. Maharaj was a bit arrogant about it, "You don't know how to chant. I'll teach you how you should be chanting. In India you have to do it this way." Some devotees fell for it because the drumbeats and tunes were catchy. But the devotees weren't good at it, so the result was a cacophony of unpleasant sounds—a mess—rather than the beautiful, angelic chanting that we did under Prabhupada's tutelage. When Prabhupada heard those kirtans from his thatched hut he'd make a face and say, "It is a pinching sound," and he would close his windows to reduce the volume. When the kirtan ended he'd say, "Thank goodness it's over."

Vaiyasaki: Before going to the Mayapur festival in 1976, all the devotees first went to Calcutta. We were taking breakfast *prasadam* on the temple balcony when we noticed three musicians walking along the street. One had a harmonium strapped over his shoulder, another had a *mridanga* and the third one *kartals*, and when they saw us they started chanting Hare Krishna. Some devotees, including me, thought it was attractive but because they were singing for money, others didn't like it. Suddenly a devotee came out of Prabhupada's room, went over to these musicians and gave them a *rupee*. The musicians smiled, thanked the devotee and left. That became a controversy—why did a devotee give Krishna's money to these professional musicians? The devotee said, "Prabhupada gave me a *rupee* and told me to give it to them." "Why did he do that?" "I don't know." "Please find out." That devotee asked Srila Prabhupada, "Why did we give Krishna's money to professional musicians?" Srila Prabhupada said, "We have enjoyed their music, so we are indebted to them. We gave a *rupee* to clear the debt."

When I told this story to an Indian devotee, she said, "Yes, my mother always taught me that." And thereafter, if good singers came by when I was traveling on the trains in India, I would always pay them a *rupee* because I didn't want to be indebted to them. But if someone didn't have any talent, I wouldn't give him anything. I didn't feel indebted if I didn't enjoy it, if it was just a bother.

Umapati Swami: I saw the sun when I got to England and I saw the sun when I left a week later and in between it never stopped drizzling. When I hung my clothes up to dry they got wetter. Prabhupada said, "It says in the *Vedas* that a place where the sun does not shine is a condemned place."

Narada Muni: In his lecture Srila Prabhupada explained how nothing could shake Dhruva Maharaj's determined vow to realize God and therefore he was successful—he saw God. Prabhupada said, "Similarly, you can also see God in six months if you simply become this sincere and determined." Sincerity, Srila Prabhupada explained, is the qualification for realizing Krishna.

Umapati Swami: Srila Prabhupada would often cry when he talked about his spiritual master. Once, on Bhaktisiddhanta Sarasvati Thakur's Appearance Day, I watched Prabhupada perform *arati* and I could feel that he was really offering each item to his spiritual master. There was something about the way he stood or the way he moved his arms that showed me he meant it as an offering to his spiritual master.

Vaiyasaki: In 1976 Srila Prabhupada's god-brother Bhaktivilas Tirtha Maharaj passed away. Prabhupada was in his room in Vrindavan when he heard the news and he said, "Bhaktivilas Tirtha, now he is gone. But he went back to Godhead." Bhavananda said, "Srila Prabhupada, how is that possible? Instead of helping you, Bhaktivilas Tirtha gave you trouble. And he created a dispute that split up Bhaktisiddhanta's mission and forced the Gaudiya Math into a 40-year lawsuit. How could he have gone back to Godhead?" Prabhupada said, "He went back to Godhead because my Guru Maharaj accepted his service."

From that I understood that if a pure devotee accepts our service, then even though we may not be qualified, Krishna gives us the opportunity to go back home, back to Godhead. Although Bhaktivilas Tirtha caused a disturbance to the Gaudiya Math and didn't respond to Srila Prabhupada's requests for help, Bhaktisiddhanta accepted Bhaktivilas Tirtha's good service.

If the guru accepts our service we are safe.

Umapati Swami: I typed a list of the devotees' legal and spiritual names and since Prabhupada told me to refer to the devotees as '*prabhu,*' I typed that also. Prabhupada said, "Leave some space at the bottom of the page." When I came to the end I said to Prabhupada, "I'm finished." He said, "Did you leave some space at the bottom of the page?" I said, "Yes." Prabhupada said, "Now type this," and he dictated "*nama om visnu-padaya krsna-presthaya bhu-tale srimate bhaktivedanta-svamin iti namine,*" and the translation, "I offer my respectful obeisances unto Bhaktivedanta Swami, who is very dear to Krishna on this earth, having taken shelter at His lotus feet." I had never heard this before and I was amazed that he could dictate obeisances to himself without being embarrassed or proud. It was as if he was saying, "Get a pound of carrots and two pounds of rice."

Narada Muni: In New York a reporter asked Prabhupada, "How old were you when you realized God?" Srila Prabhupada didn't want to glorify himself but to glorify his spiritual master and Krishna. He said, "God is a person like you and me. The difference is that we are many and God is one, our leader. Now, what is the difference between the one and the many? He maintains all these many, he maintains us. But He is also a person like you and me. Do you follow?" This reporter persisted, "Yes, I appreciate your answer, but at what age did you realize the highest truth? At what physical age . . . ?" Prabhupada explained, "There is no question of age. Realization of God should be from the very beginning of life." The reporter said, "I understand that, Swamiji. My question to you was at what age did you yourself realize the highest truth?" Srila Prabhupada said, "Of course, we were born in a very nice family. Practically from the very beginning of our lives my father educated us in this way." The reporter wouldn't give up, "I understand that. I mean at what time did you have your own personal realization, Swamiji? At what age?" Prabhupada said, "From the age of four or five years."

In the *Bhagavatam* Srila Prabhupada wrote about some of his childhood pastimes and he wrote about Maharaja Pariksit and others who also had symptoms of being God conscious children. Srila Prabhupada has always been God conscious. He came into this world God conscious, he left this world God conscious, and now he's undoubtedly giving God consciousness to others on another planet. My hope is that all of us can eternally be with him and somehow serve him in his mission.

TAPE 38

Joshomatinandan das
Rukmini dasi
Tranakarta das

Joshomatinandan: Prabhupada gave a lecture in the New York temple and coincidentally he said, "*Bharata-bhumite haila manusya-janma yara, janma sarthaka kari' kara para-upakara*, that those born in India should make their lives successful by becoming Krishna conscious and by delivering others." I was in the crowd listening and I felt like he was telling me, "You're wasting your life. Become serious." The environment in the 439 Henry Street building was nice. There were 400 devotees there, and I was making rapid spiritual progress. Around 11:00 the next morning, Bhagavan prabhu took me in to Prabhupada's little room. Prabhupada was sitting alone and Bhagavan said, "Prabhupada, this boy is an engineer in Detroit. He chants Hare Krishna, he's read your books and he wanted to meet you." Prabhupada said, "Oh, yes, what is your name?" I said, "My name is Jana Yoshi." "Where are you from?" "I'm from Surat." "Surat is a very nice place. I received a good reception there. People were very pious and interested in chanting. What do you do?" "I'm an engineer." "So work as engineer and when you have sufficient money, build a temple there." This was Prabhupada's first instruction to me and it was fulfilled. Just last year we opened a beautiful Radha-Damodar temple on the bank of the River Tapi in Surat—and we also have five other temples in Gujarat.

Rukmini: I was in the San Francisco temple for a couple of weeks and then, when Malati, Shyamasundar, Yamuna, Gurudas, Janaki, Mukunda, and baby Saraswati left on Prabhupada's order to open the London temple, I went with them as far as Montreal. I was to be initiated in Montreal and then join the devotee-artists in Boston. The group bound for London also stopped in Montreal to get Srila Prabhupada's blessings for their preaching.

So, I first saw Prabhupada in a house on West Prince Arthur Street in Montreal. I went into Prabhupada's room with the devotees going to London, and my first impression was that a brilliant effulgence was coming from Prabhupada. I had read that when you see your true guru he will be effulgent, and he truly was. He was filling the room with light. Seeing him was like seeing the *brahmajyoti*.

Tranakarta: Prabhupada came to Chicago on the third of July 1974. Sri Govinda, the temple president, said to me, "Tranakarta, Srila Prabhupada is writing letters in his room. Stand outside the door and don't let anybody in. He probably won't come out, so don't worry." "Okay." Srila Prabhupada's quarters were the many different rooms of the whole *brahmachari ashram*. I stood by Prabhupada's door and a minute after Sri Govinda left, Prabhupada opened the door and walked out. I paid my obeisances and Prabhupada walked into the back bathroom. When he came back, I was still on my knees. In one swift motion, Srila Prabhupada walked past me, put his hand on my head, said "Hare Krishna," and walked into his room. When Srila Prabhupada put his hand on my head, it was like a lightning bolt had hit me. I was completely surcharged with ecstasy and I was experiencing various emotions. I wanted to start chanting and dancing. A couple of minutes later Sri Govinda came to check on me. He looked at me and said, "Tranakarta, you're glowing!" I tried to say, "Prabhupada . . ." and he said, "No, you're glowing!" I said, "Prabhupada just touched my head!" Prabhupada's touch on my head gave me unlimited mercy. It made me ecstatic.

Joshomatinandan: Kirtanananda Maharaj told Prabhupada, "Your servant has had an affair with a lady here." Prabhupada leaned back, put his hands behind his head and said, "In the old days, *kshatriyas* had more than one wife. Do whatever you want to do." Someone said, "He should not be your servant, Prabhupada." Prabhupada said, "That is all right, give me another servant." I saw Prabhupada's air of detachment and mood of tolerance. Prabhupada was thinking, "In this Age of Kali, especially in America, whatever little percentage of my teachings people accept, even 5% or 10%, I will accept. As time passes they will gradually advance."

Prabhupada never made a big thing out of a problem. In this meeting, my first with Prabhupada in New Vrindavan, I saw how nonchalant he was. He did not condone the falldown, but just to temper the devotees who were complaining he said, "In the old days, *kshatriyas* had more than one wife." But then he removed that person as his servant.

Rukmini: They presented me to Prabhupada saying, "This is Wendy, she's only 16 years old, and she wants to be your disciple." Prabhupada's compassion was so great. He said, "But where are your parents?" It's funny to think of the most compassionate Prabhupada concerned that my parents were suffering because I wasn't with them. That was very sweet.

Tranakarta: Prabhupada was walking on the beautiful college grounds of Northwestern University in Evanston, Illinois. There were about thirty of us with him, including fifteen *sannyasis*. Prabhupada walked under a beautiful tree that had little white flowers covering its hanging branches. Prabhupada stopped, looked at the flowers, picked one, put it behind his ear, and continued to walk. He took two or three steps, stopped, looked at all of us and glanced up. We blissfully picked those white flowers and put them behind our ears. It was like a picture out of the '60s. On the way back Prabhupada wanted to sit down so we made a seat for him by putting our *chadars* on the sand. Prabhupada sat and talked about how the material scientists dig up bones. Prabhupada said, "They dig up bones," and he dug in the sand with his hands. He said, "They're digging, digging, digging, just like dogs. They dig up bones and think they have conclusive evidence about how life began." He blasted the scientists. That was an ecstatic walk.

Joshomatinandan: Keshava prabhu, the president of the San Francisco temple, wanted to show Prabhupada a big bus he had bought. Prabhupada saw the bus and said, "This is very nice." Then he said, "Keshava prabhu, are you thinking of getting married?" Keshava said, "No, Prabhupada, I'm happy the way I am." Prabhupada said, "Yes, that is very nice. Marriage is a big burden. If you are walking nicely, why pick up a big stone and put it on your head? *Brahmachari* life is very nice, a simple life. Why take on a big burden?"

Rukmini: Prabhupada wanted the devotees going to London to start a trend and he told them a story about Mr. Charles Chaplin—how some naughty boys came from behind and nailed his tailcoat to the bench he was sitting on. When Chaplin stood up, his tailcoat ripped. He went into the men's room, ripped it more, came out and danced with more flourish than the other men. The other dancers thought, "This is the new trend," and they ripped their tailcoats and started dancing just like him. This was Prabhupada's instruction on how he wanted the devotees to plant the seed of Krishna consciousness in England, how he wanted them to start a trend, and they did that. They met the Beatles and started a Hare Krishna sensation in England.

Tranakarta: I was standing next to Srila Prabhupada when a man came up on his bicycle, looked at the *sannyasis* and said to Prabhupada, "How come these guys carry sticks?" Prabhupada said, "What did he say?" Tamal said, "He wants to know why we're carrying these sticks, Prabhupada." Prabhupada said, "Tell him we carry them to chase away dogs," and everybody laughed. We invited that man to the temple, but he was bewildered and I'm not sure if he came.

Joshomatinandan: Janmastami morning, when I was to be initiated, Prabhupada's servant said to me, "Jana Kumar, Prabhupada said that if you want to be initiated you have to shave your head." I thought, "What should I do?" Prabhupada was already in the temple room for the initiation. The Detroit devotees said, "Your hair will grow back. Shave up. You have a wonderful opportunity to be initiated by a pure devotee." I said, "Okay," and at the last minute Narottamananda prabhu shaved me up. After I took a shower, dressed, and went into the temple room, Prabhupada saw me, nodded his head and said, "Ummmm."

I was initiated, "Joshomatinandan das," and later I asked Prabhupada if somebody who was working outside could keep his hair. Prabhupada said, "The hair will come back, but for a Vaishnav ceremony you should shave your head." I think Krishna dictated this to Prabhupada especially for me because I was such a tough, difficult person. Since I was too embarrassed to go back to Detroit clean-shaven, I left that life and became a *brahmachari* in the Chicago *ashram*. Without that special dose of mercy and kindness of having to shave my head, I would not be what I am today. Srila Prabhupada was an expert doctor with a different medicine for every person. I can never thank him enough for the way he transformed my life.

Rukmini: Maybe because I was a young girl something about me reminded Prabhupada of Rukmini, and at my initiation Prabhupada told the story of Rukmini for the first time. Then he said to me, "Your name is Rukmini. Krishna can accept any number of beautiful girls. You are a beautiful girl, so now become beautiful within also." It was a beautiful and powerful instruction.

Joshomatinandan: I said, "Prabhupada, you say Jesus Christ is a pure devotee. But he never mentioned the name of Krishna and he never chanted Hare Krishna, so how can we say he is a pure devotee?" Prabhupada said, "Because he was free from material desires, therefore, he is a pure devotee." Ever since then I've had high regard for Jesus and I look upon him as I look upon any other *acharya*. In fact, because Jesus was a bold *acharya* and a great preacher, Prabhupada had a natural appreciation for him. No other Indian swami or yogi or teacher could have that kind of appreciation of Jesus as Prabhupada had because Prabhupada was doing the same thing that Jesus had done.

Tranakarta: On a morning walk in Chicago, an ordinary man was in awe looking at Prabhupada and he said, "What do you think about the coming of Christ?" Prabhupada said, "Your messiah has already come." We all said, "*Jaya*, Prabhupada!"

Joshomatinandan: After three or four months in L.A., I wrote to Prabhupada about getting married and Prabhupada said, "I heard that you want to get married. That is very nice. Husband and wife, double strength." Then when Prabhupada came to L.A. in December, Jayatirtha prabhu performed a fire sacrifice and Prabhupada gave my wife, who was also his disciple, a ring from his finger. And because we were going to India, he gave us a lot of blessings and encouragement. We have been married 30 years now.

Rukmini: Like a loving grandfather, Prabhupada was concerned when he saw that I was too thin. Amazingly, he said that my husband and I should live separately, so Baradraj stayed in Boston painting pictures for Prabhupada's books and I stayed in New York. Then, with the permission of the temple president, Brahmananda, I went to Los Angeles and for six months was happy to learn *pujari* work from Shilavati.

After being overseas for about a year, Prabhupada went to New York and then to Boston where he saw Baradraj and said, "Where is your wife?" Baradraj said, "You sent her away, Prabhupada. She's in Los Angeles. Should I send for her?" Prabhupada said, "Yes. Husband without the wife is only one half, wife without the husband is only one half." So I had the order to return to Boston.

Tranakarta: Prabhupada was so kind and merciful that just his glance took away my anxiety. Prabhupada first came to Chicago in '74 and then returned in '76. While he was away, I learned to play the *mridanga* from tapes. I got pretty good and when he came again I wanted to play in the *kirtan* for his pleasure. But when I grabbed my *mridanga,* the big devotees who were leading the *kirtan* said, "No, no, no, you can't play." I was hurt. I made my way back to the *vyasasana* because I was the *kshatriya* of the temple and I was supposed to be close to Prabhupada. When I got up to the *vyasasana*, Srila Prabhupada was looking at me and he gave me a big smile. He knew. He gave me his mercy and took away all my bad feelings.

Joshomatinandan: Once, when he was in his garden, Prabhupada spoke intimately about how, after Sumati Morarji had given him a berth on her steamer, the Indian government wouldn't sanction the P-forms that would allow him to come to America. He had gone from one department to another department to another department to get the P-forms, but to no avail. Prabhupada said, "I was leaving the office frustrated when a Bengali gentleman saw me and said in Bengali, "How are you? What do you want? Is there anything you have come here for, Swamiji?" Prabhupada asked him, "What is your name?" "My name is Bannerjee", and they had a conversation in Bengali. After that, that man went from one table to another and got Prabhupada's P-forms sanctioned. Prabhupada said, "That was Krishna's mercy. I tried so much and it didn't happen, but at the last minute this man helped me." Prabhupada also said, "After I arrived in America I was struggling very hard and sometimes I would go back to the pier where I had landed and ask, 'When is the next steamer going back to India?' One Indian man at the pier said, 'Swamiji, you ask many times but you are not returning to India because you have come with a mission.'" Prabhupada said, "Actually I did not want to return without some success. But I would go and ask, 'When is the next steamer going to India?'" Then, sometime later, his mission took off.

Rukmini: There was one evening where he was looking around the room and he was looking at each and every devotee and he said, "I want each and every one of you to open a temple," and he was looking into the face of each devotee. So my impetuous personality, I said, "Swamiji . . ." At that time, he was called Swamiji. I said, "Swamiji, even the girls?" He was laughing. He was always very grandfatherly. And he said, "Yes, there is no difference. When you are preaching, there is no difference." And he began to speak about Jahnava Mata, that in the absence of Lord Nityananda, she was leading the whole *sankirtan* movement. So he said, "Yes, there is no difference." It was a very nice instruction.

Tranakarta: On September 13, 1976 I arrived in India for the first time. A devotee said, "Prabhupada's in Vrindavan now." I said, "Really?" I hadn't known that. So from Delhi, where I'd arrived, I went to Vrindavan and that night I led *sandhya arati*. The next morning I was chanting *japa* after *mangal arati* when Hansadutta Maharaj said, "Tranakarta, Srila Prabhupada wants to see you in his room." I said, "You're joking, right?" He said, "No, Prabhupada wants to see you. Let's go." "Okay." I nervously went into Srila Prabhupada's room, paid my obeisances and when I was still on my knees, Prabhupada, who was standing by the door, looked at me and said, "You play the *mridanga* very nicely. Where did you learn?" I said, "From tapes, Srila Prabhupada, and from playing in *kirtans*. But it's all your mercy." He said, "*Jaya*," and then he said something that touched me. He said, "I remember you from America." I said, "*Jaya*, Prabhupada." Prabhupada said, "Can you play?" I said, "Yes, Prabhupada." Prabhupada started playing his harmonium and singing to Krishna and I played the *mridanga* for Prabhupada, or rather, the drum just played itself. Harikesh recorded some of it. To say the least it was an amazing and very transcendental atmosphere. I was awed watching Prabhupada.

Joshomatinandan: After being in India for three or four years, Giriraj was a little sick so he went to Chicago and then to Los Angeles. In Los Angeles Giriraj's parents came to meet Prabhupada. His father was a very respectable man and he said to Prabhupada, "If there is anything I can do for you I'll be happy to do it. I'll give you a huge donation or whatever, but please let my son come back to his family," because Giriraj was their only son. Prabhupada said, "Giriraj, what do you think?" Giriraj said, "No, no, Srila Prabhupada. There is no power in this world that can separate me from your lotus feet." Prabhupada smiled and told his father, "I am not keeping your son, but he stays because he likes Krishna consciousness. I do not object if he goes to you and continues this activity at home, but I cannot force him to do that. But I can assure you that he will be happy and peaceful here and he will make you a proud father." Giriraj's father was a jolly man. There were many exchanges and both his mother and his father had a positive impression of Srila Prabhupada, and were happy when they left. Prabhupada knew how to conduct himself, especially with his disciples' parents. He sympathized with them.

Tranakarta: Pundarika prabhu's father was the Managing Editor of *Playboy* magazine. His mother was a big writer and they came to see Srila Prabhupada in Chicago in '75. His mother was respectful to the devotees and wrote favorable articles but his father wasn't so convinced. When Prabhupada talked about meat-eating, the father started to debate with Prabhupada a little aggressively. Because the father was so puffed up, Prabhupada finally stopped speaking and said, "Then why don't you eat your own son?" Pundarika was sitting in the room. Whoa—there was complete silence. Prabhupada had made his point.

Joshomatinandan: When I returned to India in 1974, my parents went with me to see Prabhupada. My mother said, "He is our only son, we spent everything to send him to America, and he has now left it all and joined you." Prabhupada said, "There are so many people who go to America to make money, but your son is a very rare person. You should be proud that your son has become a devotee of the Lord and, as he has become a devotee, so can you. You can join us and I will give you a nice place to stay." Prabhupada talked with them so caringly that afterwards my mother said, "Your Guru Maharaj is a very kind-hearted person." If anybody had bitterness or resentment, it melted away when they sat in front of Prabhupada.

Rukmini: The *pujaris* in Los Angeles had a beautiful and high standard of Deity worship that didn't exist anywhere else in the society. So, after being trained in Los Angeles, when I returned to Boston, where they didn't have this nice standard, trying to introduce it was difficult. One night I had a dream that all the temple devotees were lying on the floor arguing with each other, "In New York we do it like this." "Well, in Boston we do it like this." "Well, in Montreal we do it like this." Then the curtains closed and the Deities were gone. This dream upset and traumatized me and I wrote a letter to Prabhupada lamenting about how unacceptable our Deity worship must be. I wrote, "I think we've been very negligent in our standard of Deity worship and now I had this dream that the Deities disappeared. And I know that you said that without *bhava*, Deity worship is just like idol worship." Prabhupada wrote a pragmatic letter back with a list of many items of cleanliness. He wrote, "Deity worship means to be very clean. You should try to bathe twice daily. The Deities should never be approached without having bathed first and changed to clean cloths after passing stool, etc. Keep teeth brushed after each meal, fingernails clean and trim. Be sure that your hands are clean before touching anything on the altar or the Deities. And cleanse the Deity room, altar and floor daily thoroughly. Shine the various *arati* paraphernalia after *arati*. This is described in the booklet for pujaris written by Silavati dasi. The idea is summit cleanliness—that will satisfy Krishna. Regarding your dream, it is a great blessing to you that Krishna warned you. So you should never be negligent. Always be careful, then in due course you will feel bhava." That was very nice.

Tranakarta: Once in Vrindavan we were circumambulating Krishna-Balaram with Srila Prabhupada. When we came around the side, Prabhupada stopped. His eyes got big and he looked right in my eyes and said, "Simply by circumambulating Krishna and Balaram in this way, no more traversing up and down in the material universe." Then he kept walking and chanting, "Hare Krishna, Hare Krishna..." *Jaya*, Prabhupada. Thank you, Prabhupada.

Joshomatinandan: I asked Prabhupada, "How did Lord Ramachandra disappear?" Prabhupada said, "The Vaishnavas do not discuss the disappearance pastimes of the Lord, but Lord Ramachandra entered in the Saryu River along with the whole population of Ayodhya and together they all went to Vaikuntha." Later I read that same description in the Valmiki Ramayana, but Prabhupada gave me another important principle—that the disappearance pastimes of the Lord are not discussed much by devotees.

Tranakarta: Srila Prabhupada cared about and loved the devotees. Like a concerned father, every morning he would come out of his room, come up to me and say, "How are you this morning?" and he meant it.

And there wasn't anything that got by Srila Prabhupada. One day we were chanting *japa* with Prabhupada while we circumambulated the Krishna-Balaram Temple, and when we came to the iron gate in the front, Prabhupada asked, "Why is the lock unlocked?"

From where we were, you couldn't see that the lock was unlocked and we looked at each other thinking, "You can't tell the lock's unlocked." One devotee ran over and, sure enough, it wasn't locked.

Another morning Prabhupada said, "Why didn't the *chokidar* ring the bell at two o'clock this morning?" The *chokidar* was supposed to ring the bell every hour on the hour throughout the day and night. The next day Prabhupada asked, "Why didn't the *chokidar* ring the bell at three o'clock?" Srila Prabhupada knew everything in Krishna's service, including the minute things that we were oblivious to.

Joshomatinandan: Another time I said that Rupa and Sanatana Goswamis were born in a *sarasvata-brahmana* family, an exalted *gaura sarasvata* family. They were great Sanskrit scholars and they had a powerful Vedic background. Why did they feel so low that they did not enter the temple of Jagannatha? Was it just because they associated with Muslims? Prabhupada said, "Associating with Muslim means adopting their habits, like meat-eating and so on. Maybe Rupa and Sanatana Goswamis also associated with the Muslims in that way and, due to that, they felt unqualified." Prabhupada's answer was pragmatic—he said "maybe." Then he said, "But everything they did was under the dictation of Krishna. They are eternally liberated souls, *nitya-siddha*. So it doesn't matter what they did."

Rukmini: A bearded *yogi* stayed with us in the New York temple for some time, teaching Pradyumna Sanskrit. When we went on street *harinam sankirtan*, he used to stand in the front and no one thought much about it. But in retrospect, he was posing as the *guru*. Later, when Prabhupada came, this *yogi* became highly offensive. He brought a woman with him into Prabhupada's room, and the two of them began yelling at Prabhupada. It was a terrible, embarrassing scene. Later Prabhupada spoke from the *vyasasana* about this *yogi*. With compassion and grace and an aristocratic demeanor, he looked at Pradyumna and said, "Is not a snake with a jewel on his hood even more dangerous than a snake without such a jewel?" It was amazing.

Joshomatinandan: I asked Prabhupada about a revered and famous sadhu, Dangari Maharaj, who was then the biggest *Bhagavat* reciter in India. He would shed tears when he recited the *Bhagavat*, and the people in the audience would cry too. Prabhupada said, "I don't know about him. What does he say?" I said, "He speaks about Krishna's pastimes, but he also says that you can worship whomever you believe in. You can chant *om nama shivaya* or *klim durgaya namah*. There are several *mantras* that he prescribes, even though in his own *katha* he generally chants Hare Rama Hare Rama, Rama Rama Hare Hare, Hare Krishna Hare Krishna, Krishna Krishna Hare Hare." Prabhupada said, "If he thinks that the name of Krishna and the name of the demigods are the same, then he is not Dangari, he is *dhangari*." *Dhanga* means pretension. He said, "The Vaishnav will not say that the holy name of Krishna is equivalent to anything else." Prabhupada never judged a person by his looks, his name, his title, or by the tears he shed, but he judged a person by what he said, by his philosophy and *siddhanta*.

Tranakarta: I would love to play the *mridanga* when Prabhupada sang Jaya Radha-Madhava, and since I followed him nicely, Prabhupada liked my playing. The mercy I got from him will last forever and is what keeps me going right now.

One morning I had the drum on my lap and Prabhupada was getting ready to sing when Hansadutta Maharaj said, "Let me have the drum, I want to play today." I said, "Sure Maharaj", and gave him the drum. Prabhupada chanted one line, "Jaya Radha-Madhava," and then opened his eyes and motioned twice with his finger, "Give Tranakarta the drum." I grabbed the drum. Through my whole stay in India, Prabhupada showered unlimited *mridanga* mercy on me. If we went to a village or to do a program in somebody's house, after

Prabhupada spoke he would look at me and say, "Play the *mridanga*, we will sing now."

Rukmini: In Delhi, the temple was a house in Anand Niketan, a neighborhood of embassies and diplomats, and Prabhupada's room was on the roof. One night when we came in, a *sannyasi* was playing the harmonium. Prabhupada saw Baradraj and said, "Let him play, he is better." The *sannyasi* gave up the harmonium so Baradraj could play. Prabhupada loved Baradraj's harmonium playing. After the *kirtan*, Prabhupada was quoting from the *Siksastakam* prayers. I was sitting toward the back as there were many *sannyasis* in the room as well as Pradyumna the pandit. As Prabhupada would sometimes do, he tested us by appearing to forget a verse. He said, "*Nayanam galad-a* . . . what is that? *Nayanam galad-a* . . ." There was a room full of people who were much higher in the hierarchy than I was, and none of them appeared to know the verse, so I quietly said, "*Nayanam galad-asru-dharaya.*" Prabhupada's eyes got big and he said, "Yes, what is that? What is that verse?" and I said the verse. Prabhupada teased the *sannyasis* by making sure that they noted I had spoken, and when he did that, I fell into the trap of false pride. Then Prabhupada quoted the last verse of the *Siksastaka* prayers, "*Aslisya va*...what is that verse?" I guess the *sannyasis* had memorized other verses, so I again said the verse, *aslisya va pada-ratam pinastu mam.* Prabhupada said, "Yes, what is that verse?" and made me chant the verse. Then he looked at all of them and said, "You see? This little girl knows. You don't know, she knows." He was our teasing grandfather. But then, of course, he had to take care of my false ego. Prabhupada began to talk about the *ugra-karma* civilization and about how people work long hours in hellish factories. He said, "Just like they have these...what is it called? A crucible?" I went, "Hmmm." Prabhupada looked at me and said, "Do you know what a crucible is?" I didn't but I said, "A crucible is a little room where monks meditate." Prabhupada tossed his head disgustedly. He threw my answer away and said, "Does anyone know what a crucible is?"

Brahmananda said, "Yes. A crucible is a vast form in which they melt molten steel to make beams for building skyscrapers." Prabhupada said, "Yes, that is crucible," and looked at me. I was properly chastised.

Joshomatinandan: Prabhupada's life was to give philosophical instructions about Krishna to whoever came. He used to show intelligent, prominent people Dr. Radha-Krishnan's book and say, "See what Dr. Radha-Krishnan is saying? That Kurukshetra is not a historical place, that Kurukshetra allegorically means your body, the five Pandavas means your five senses, and Kauravas means the evil desires in your mind. And Radha-Krishnan says that originally the Mahabharata was written by a poet who assumed the fictitious name Vyasa and then other people added to the Mahabharata until it became a big epic." Prabhupada blasted the Indological ideas that Radha-Krishnan had learned from Westerners and which he propounded. Prabhupada said, "Today thousands of people visit the historical place, Kurukshetra, yet Radha-Krishnan says Kurukshetra is not there. So how can anyone learn *Bhagavad-gita* or hear anything from such a person?"

One of Mahatma Gandhi's statements was, "If all the activities attributed to Krishna in *Srimad-Bhagavatam* are true, if Krishna performed these pastimes, then I refuse to accept Him as God incarnate even at the cost of being banished from Hinduism." Prabhupada was furious at this. He said that Gandhi had no understanding of Krishna, he had no understanding that Krishna's pastimes are transcendental, not material. God is the supreme and original enjoyer. We have the tendency to enjoy, and that tendency comes from Him. Our enjoying tendency is a perverted reflection of His enjoying tendency. He is the *purusha*, and every *jiva* is *prakriti*. We are all God's wives, God's *prakriti*. Therefore, your wife is His wife. God has all the rights.

In his autobiography, *Experiments with Truth*, Gandhiji said, "Since I never had a spiritual master, I never understood spiritual life and I always suffered because of a lack of spiritual instructions." He admitted it, but he still made wildly inaccurate comments and Prabhupada would explain that to visitors.

Tranakarta: Once Jagadish, a few other devotees and I were in Prabhupada's room when Prabhupada was speaking in Hindi with some big political guests. It was ecstasy seeing Prabhupada's exchanges with these people but we couldn't understand anything. When it was time for them to leave, Prabhupada graciously walked them to the door and in English one of the guests said something to Jagadish. Jagadish replied, "*Accha*," in the same way that all the devotees say, "*Accha.*" Prabhupada said, "Just see, he's speaking Hindi!" Everybody in the room busted up with laughter.

Joshomatinandan: Sometimes Prabhupada was very tolerant of his devotees. After he read some letters from New York about Bali Mardan and his wife, Prabhupada said, "The whole problem is sex life. *Yan maithunadi-grhamedhi-sukham hi tuccham. Tuccham* means insignificant. One may think that sex is the greatest platform of happiness, but actually that happiness is insignificant. In fact, sex life is a source of distress. We have so many problems because of sex life." Although the situation in the New York temple was a big problem, Prabhupada spoke in this way for five minutes and then dropped it. He reduced every problem to a philosophical understanding because he saw everything from a philosophical viewpoint.

I saw that in his every action Prabhupada never thought of himself as the doer but fully dependent on Krishna. He would pursue a certain line and leave success or failure up to Krishna.

Rukmini: The devotees wrote to Prabhupada that our new temple was like a palace and I was distraught about that because I thought, "Prabhupada will be disappointed or maybe angry when he comes. Our new temple is only slightly nicer than the first one and is simply a gala storefront." Our first temple had been right off the Bowery on

26 Second Avenue, and the second temple was a few blocks north, on the second floor at 61 Second Avenue. It had been a tuxedo shop and there were mirrors on the wall. When Prabhupada came into the new temple he sat down on his *vyasasana* and said, "I prayed to Krishna to send me one moon, but He has sent me so many moon-like boys and girls." I was amazed at his gratitude and love. I thought he would be disappointed or perhaps angry and he was grateful for even the slightest service endeavor.

Tranakarta: Prabhupada cared about and loved the devotees. It was October or November and we were sitting on the marble floor of the Krishna-Balaram *mandir*. One morning Prabhupada asked, "Are you cold?" "Yes, Prabhupada." That day Prabhupada sent another devotee and me to Agra to buy big madras carpets to cover the floor so the devotees could stay warm. Besides being the savior of the whole world, Prabhupada, like a loving father, was concerned about the health of all the devotees.

Joshomatinandan: Some devotees wanted to go from Juhu to Bombay by taxi, and being a miserly man, I agitated them by saying, "Why should you go by taxi?" I told Prabhupada, "When I tell the devotees that it's too expensive to go to Bombay by taxi, they get agitated." Prabhupada said, "Just consider that before becoming devotees they were eating flesh and blood like tigers. Now they are chanting Hare Krishna, they are dancing and they are enjoying spiritually. Haven't they accomplished something great? So if they want some extra money, give it to them. Don't worry about their faults." Then in a lecture the next day he said, "Money is very hard to earn. Money is like Krishna's blood and we should not waste it. Every *rupee* should be considered as a brick in the temple." So to me he said, "you tolerate," while to them he said "don't waste money." In other words, he helped me increase my tolerance in the service of Krishna, and he helped them increase their frugality in the service of the Lord. He approached the difficulty from different angles and instead of feeling discouraged, everyone saw a way to increase the quality of their service. This was a key principle in Prabhupada's dealings with every devotee, and that's why he was able to produce so many managers. In spite of our many mistakes, the movement grew because of Prabhupada's kind and affectionate dealings.

Tranakarta: Hari Sauri prabhu, Srila Prabhupada's servant, was kind to me and would give me little things to do for Srila Prabhupada. Once he said, "Trana, I'm going on the roof for a few minutes to hang up Prabhupada's clothes. Prabhupada is with some important guests and we just served them *prasadam*. Prabhupada probably won't ring the bell but if he does, please go in and see what he wants." "Okay." As soon as Hari Sauri left, ding, ding, ding, ding—the bell rang and I went running in. "Yes, Srila Prabhupada?" Prabhupada said, "More *puris* for the guests." "Yes, Srila Prabhupada." I ran to the kitchen, "Srila Prabhupada needs more *puris* for the guests." "Oh, we're out of flour, we can't make any more." "What? I can't go back and tell Prabhupada there's no *puris*." "Well, prabhu, we don't have any more *puris*." I'm such a fool that instead of making them myself, I went back to the room. Up to this point, Prabhupada had never chastised me but when I said, "Srila Prabhupada, there's no more *puris*," he was furious. "What do you mean there are no more *puris*? There must always be *prasadam*!" he yelled. But it was mercy. I felt bad, but it was mercy.

Joshomatinandan: The last verses of the *Nectar of Instruction* say, *vaikunthaj janito vara madhu-puri tatrapi rasotsavad*, "Greater than Vaikuntha is Mathura *mandala*, and greater than that is Vrindavan where *rasa* dance takes place. And greater than Vrindavan is Govardhan. And in Govardhan, Radha-kunda is the best place. Where is a knowledgeable person who will not serve the holy place called Radha-kunda?" When that book came out, Prabhupada's secretaries complained that devotees wanted to give up distributing books to stay in Radha-kunda. Prabhupada said, "Just see the rascals. They have not followed the first verse of *Upadesamrta* and they are jumping to the eleventh verse." The first verse is *vaco vegam manasah krodha-vegam jihva-vegam udaropastha-vegam*, "One who controls the pushes of the senses is fit to be guru and make disciples everywhere." *Sarvam apimam prthivim sa sisyat.* Prabhupada said, "Let them control their senses first, then they can think of Radha-kunda. Their mentality is called *markata-vairagya*, the renunciation of the monkeys. Monkeys also live in the forests, eating only fruits and leaves, but they are thinking, 'Where is the she-monkey?' The desire to give up one's service and go to Radha-kunda is simply monkey business."

Rukmini: Sometimes Prabhupada would give his mercy to someone who seemed undeserving, and sometimes he would not give it to someone who seemed deserving. Once an elderly, pious-looking Indian gentleman ardently said to Prabhupada, "Swamiji, give us your mercy, give us your mercy!" But Prabhupada saw his heart and off-handedly said, "I have already given everything, but you do not take it. What is the use?" I was shocked. Prabhupada said, "It's like a man who has fallen in a well but does not take the rope someone throws him." Prabhupada gave that man bittersweet compassion.

Joshomatinandan: Dr. Patel arrogantly criticized the devotees, but during morning walks on Juhu Beach he would respectfully argue with Prabhupada and Prabhupada would also respect and encourage him, although he smashed Dr. Patel's philosophy. Prabhupada was like a snake charmer. Dr. Patel proudly thought, "In a previous life I must have been Prabhupada's younger brother."

Then one day Prabhupada said that Ramakrishna Paramahamsa's philosophy—*yatha mat tatha path* (anything you do is all right) was bogus. It was atheism. And Prabhupada criticized Vivekananda's *daridra-narayana* philosophy that Narayana is not in the temple but is in *daridra*—the poor men—so serving poor men is better than going to the temple. Prabhupada said, "If Narayana is in the poor men, then why isn't He in the rich men also? And if Narayana is in a man, then He is also in a chicken. You are trying to serve the poor men and you are killing *murgi*—the chickens—to eat them. You are eating *murgi-narayana* and you are serving *daridra-narayana*, so your philosophy is contradictory." Prabhupada said, "You can be compassionate to poor men, but your service should be rendered to Narayana, to God. Narayana is never *daridra*, never poor. This kind of confusion has turned Bengalis into ruffians." So one Gujarati, Mr. Shah, became bewildered and started shouting, "You criticize everybody! You don't respect other saintly persons! You only think that you are right, that they are not good! Vivekananda was a great man!" The devotees were upset and were going to physically remove Mr. Shah but Prabhupada said, "No, no, let him speak." Prabhupada walked on calmly saying, "I am simply saying what Krishna has said. *Na mam duskrtino mudhah prapadyante naradhamah*. 'Those who are miscreants, foolish, whose knowledge is stolen away by Maya, they do not surrender to Krishna.' Krishna says they are miscreants and on behalf of Krishna, I have to say this. I have nothing against those persons, but I am trying to teach my disciples how to judge their philosophy." After that we walked back to the temple silently and attended *gurupuja*. Like the devotees, every day Mr. Shah offered flowers to Prabhupada and on that day he also put his head on Prabhupada's feet and started crying like a baby. He felt repentant. Prabhupada put his hand on Mr. Shah's head and said, "It is okay." Then Prabhupada said, "From tomorrow, we are not going to discuss. We are just going to read *Krishna* book." So starting the next morning, one of us read *Krishna* book while we walked along the beach.

Tranakarta: Prabhupada could reveal something to you that other people could not see. A few of my god-brothers and I have had that experience. Once, on a drizzly Delhi morning we walked in a park with Srila Prabhupada. Prabhupada wasn't speaking but intensely chanting, "Hare Krishna, Hare Krishna," and we chanted too. Suddenly Prabhupada walked off the path onto the wet grass, and we wondered, "Where's Prabhupada going?" He went to a little hill with a big bush tree on each side of it and another one behind it, which made a little cave. We ran ahead and laid our *chadars* on the ground. Prabhupada walked in and sat down, still chanting, "Hare Krishna, Hare Krishna." Suddenly, to my eyes, Srila Prabhupada emanated an incredible molten gold effulgence that so lit up the area that I could not make out his features. I was awestruck. Why did I see that? It was causeless mercy. Maybe I got a little glimpse of Krishna coming to sit next to Prabhupada to tell him exactly what to say. I have no idea, but it was beautiful.

Then, after a minute that seemed like forever, Prabhupada came back. He looked in the distance and saw two men walking some three hundred yards away. Prabhupada said, "I know those two men. Before I came to America I used to buy paper from them for my *Back to Godhead* magazine." "Wow, Prabhupada!" Two devotees invited those men to speak with Prabhupada and when they came they paid their obeisances and were ecstatic to see him.

Joshomatinandan: One morning as we were walking from the temple to Juhu beach, a man offered his obeisances to Prabhupada. Prabhupada said, "What do you do?" "I am a music teacher." "Oh, in that building you teach music." The music teacher was surprised, "You know this, Swamiji?" Prabhupada said, "Yes, one should be observant."

Rukmini: One night in his room in Vrindavan, Prabhupada told some stories about common sense intelligence and the ability to be observant. He said, "If a man is intelligent, when he is lying on his back he will naturally count the rafters." He said that when he was a child in Calcutta, during the rainy season a pipe dripped outside his window and he used the beat of the drips as a metronome to practice his *mridanga* beats, faster or slower according to the drips.

He also told a story about a question on a job application that read, “Have you ever ridden the Punjab Mail train, the train that brings the mail to Punjab?” One applicant answered, “Yes, many times.” And the next question was, “How many cars are there on the Punjab Mail?” The idea was that an intelligent person would notice such a thing. Prabhupada told another similar story, about a man and his assistant who were interviewing two job applicants. One of the applicants came in, sat down, had his interview, had many qualifications for the job, and left without closing the door after him. Then the other man sat down, had his interview, had none of the qualifications for the job, but closed the door properly behind him when he was dismissed. The interviewer said to his assistant, “Who do you think will get the job?” The assistant said, “Of course, the man with all the qualifications.” The interviewer said, “No, the man who has none of the qualifications will be given the job.” “Why?” “Because he closed the door behind him. So we can train him, we will be able to work with him. The other man, although he has the qualifications, he was not observant enough to close the door properly. So we won’t be able to work with him in our company.”

Tranakarta: Prabhupada loved to sit on the rooftop of the 55th Street temple in New York. Before he arrived at that temple, the devotees had cleaned the whole building and made it spotless except for one little utility storage shack on the roof. Thinking that Prabhupada would not look there, the devotees threw stuff in it and locked it. As he usually did, Prabhupada toured the whole building and eventually went to that shack on the rooftop. I can see the faces of the devotees, “No!” Prabhupada said, “What is in here?” “Oh, it’s just storage, Prabhupada.” “Open it.” I opened it and it was full of junk. Prabhupada didn’t say anything. He just made a face.” Prabhupada knew every little aspect of everything that had to do with devotional service to the Lord. He knew things that we were completely oblivious to.

Joshomatinandan: When the Vrindavan temple was going to be inaugurated, I helped with the printing of invitations and then Srila Prabhupada put me in charge of the *prasadam* kitchen, which took a lot of time—I missed most of the festivities. Prabhupada also had me invite various Vrindavan saints to the festival. I invited Karpatri Maharaj, a strict *sannyasi* who at that time was the biggest and most respected impersonalist of India and who spoke about Krishna at *Bhagavat sabdas*. When I invited him for our weeklong festival, he said, "I cannot come to your function." "Why?" "Because your guru gives *brahmana* threads to Westerners. This should not be done." I said, "Why not? If the Westerners behave like *brahmanas*, if they rise early in the morning and chant sixteen rounds of Hare Krishna every day, if they study *Bhagavatam*, *Gita*, and all the scriptures, and if they spread the message of *sanatana-dharma,* then why not give them *brahmana* initiation? Nowadays in India, *brahmanas* are bus conductors and factory workers and postmen. How can you think that those people are *brahmanas* and these people are not *brahmanas*? The four divisions are devised not by birth but according to *guna* and *karma. Catur-varnyam maya srstam guna-karma-vibhagasah.*"

Previously, in Prabhupada's presence, Vallabhacarya had had the same objection and at that time, Prabhupada said, "Open *Srimad-Bhagavatam*, Seventh Canto, chapter number eleven, last verse. In this chapter, Narada Muni instructs about the duties and roles of *varnashram* and at the end he says that, 'If one shows the symptoms of being a *brahmana, ksatriya, vaisya* or *sudra*, as described before, even if he has appeared in a different class, he should be accepted according to those symptoms of classification.' If the *brahmana* has symptom of *sudra*, he should be accepted as *sudra*. If *sudra* has symptom of *brahmana*, he should be accepted as *brahmana*. *Yasya yal laksanam proktam tasya varnabhivyanjakam, yad anyatrapi drsyeta tat tenaiva vinirdiset.*" Prabhupada made me memorize this *sloka* in 1974 and when I quoted it to Karpatri Maharaj, he opened his eyes wide in surprise and appreciation. He said, "Your guru has trained you very well. But there is the actual tiger and a tiger-like man. A man may be considered like a tiger, but he is not a tiger. Similarly, a person may be like a *brahmana* but he is not a *brahmana*." That is Mayavadi word jugglery. When I narrated this conversation to Prabhupada, Prabhupada said, "Did you tell him this verse, *yasya yal laksanam proktam*?" I said, "Yes, I said *yasya yal laksanam* and he said, 'Your Guru Maharaj has trained you very well.'" Prabhupada laughed. He said, "Yes, you are well trained, your *sloka* is accepted, but still Karpatri is so envious, so unfortunate, that he will not come to this wonderful temple opening."

Tranakarta: Pishima, Prabhupada's sister, loved Prabhupada. One day I was sitting on the large terrace outside of Prabhupada's room in Calcutta when she came with that little bottle of Ganga water that she always carried under her *sari*. She reached under her *sari*, poured some water from the bottle onto her hand and, laughing and ecstatic, threw it—poof—right in my face, saying, "Ganga jal!" That's how I remember Srila Prabhupada's sister and I enjoyed seeing her. She looked like Prabhupada. You could tell they were brother and sister, and you could tell Prabhupada really loved her, too. Once when Prabhupada was speaking with some guests, she came in the room talking in Bengali and Prabhupada said, "Old woman, sit down!" She obediently sat down and didn't say a word.

Joshomatinandan: The Governor of Uttar Pradesh, Dr. Channa Reddy, was a chief guest in the inauguration of the Krishna Balaram Temple in Vrindavan. We wanted Prabhupada to sit on the nice *vyasasana* on the inauguration day, but Prabhupada said, "No, I will not sit on the *vyasasana*. I will sit in a chair like the governor." Prabhupada knew the protocol—that no one should sit on a higher seat than a governor. Even though he is the *acharya* of the whole world, and even though it was his temple opening, he arranged to sit on a chair near the governor.

Tranakarta: We were walking in New York City's Central Park when a big, dried up, dead branch fell from a tree. Motioning with his cane, Prabhupada said, "This is our modern society, dead. Why are they dead? Because they are disconnected from Krishna." I always remember that.

Rukmini: Prabhupada's servant, Nanda Kumar, came out of Prabhupada's room one day shaking his head in bewilderment. He said to me, "Prabhupada said an amazing thing. He said that I'm too creative to be a good servant and that I should do business." At that time I thought, "What's creative about business?" I was surprised and Nanda Kumar was also surprised, but now that I'm doing business, in retrospect I can see how right Prabhupada is—business really is creative. I have often mentioned that to people.

Joshomatinandan: In 1977 another devotee and I went to Madhava Maharaj's—one of Prabhupada's god-brothers'—place. I told Madhava Maharaj, "I am a disciple of Bhaktivedanta Swami Prabhupada." Madhava Maharaj said, "That is very nice. But I am senior to Swami Maharaj. Swami Maharaj was a businessman, so he is an expert organizer. Therefore, his movement has spread everywhere very well. But that is all external. *Bhakti* is something else. *Bhakti* is the spontaneous emotion in the heart." He criticized. Then he gave me some fruit but I left it there. I said, "Preaching is the mission of Sri Chaitanya Mahaprabhu, and you consider that external? Chaitanya Mahaprabhu says whomever you meet, you talk about Krishna. And He sent Haridas Thakur and Nityananda Prabhu to preach door to door. And you say it is external?" and I walked out. I told Prabhupada about this conversation and Prabhupada was furious! For three days he blasted these misconceptions on his morning walks. He said, "Just see the envious person. He thinks that spreading the mission of Lord Chaitanya all over the world and inducing thousands of people to chant Hare Krishna is due to former business success? He thinks it is an external thing? What has he understood? He is a *sannyasi* for so many years, but what has he understood?"

Tranakarta: Once in Prabhupada's room, Sri Govinda's son Sudarshan, who was 2 or 3, touched his crayon to a picture of Srila Bhaktisiddhanta. Prabhupada said, "Don't do that to my Guru Maharaj!" Sri Govinda's wife took Sudarshan out of the room and Sri Govinda felt bad that his son had done that. Prabhupada said, "When a young child is a rascal it means he will be a great soul when he grows up." Prabhupada took away Sri Govinda's anxiety.

Joshomatinandan: Once we were sitting with B.V. Puri Maharaj, who, unlike many of Prabhupada's god-brothers, was present when Prabhupada laid the Mayapur cornerstone. In fact, Puri Maharaj invited others to come and even though many did not come, he came. Also, unlike many of Prabhupada's god-brothers, he accepted the title "Prabhupada" for Prabhupada.

Another time some big government officer from Calcutta said to Prabhupada, "Swamiji, I am following *dharma* properly. I always go to the Ramakrishna Mission." Prabhupada blasted this man. He said, "These Western disciples of mine will not go to the Ramakrishna Mission even to pass urine. You are going to the Ramakrishna Mission but what does Ramakrishna teach? Do you know what he teaches? He teaches, *yatha mat tatha path*—that whatever you do is all right, that you don't have to go to the temple and you don't have to chant. You can build your body and serve the poor. But do any of *Bhagavad-gita's* 700 verses say that? If someone does not repeat the words of Krishna, what is the use of his mission?" Sometimes Prabhupada would be bold and forceful and sometimes he would be cool.

Rukmini: Lord Krishna is described as being *bhava-grahi janardanam*, which means that He takes only the essence of a devotee's attitude. Prabhupada was also like that. He saw the essence of what was being presented. If someone approached him with arrogance, he could cut right through that. If there was a kernel of sincerity, he would take that. He saw what was hidden and what no one else could see. He was unstereotyped and transcendent. A single word can't describe him because he was also so much more. He was aristocratic yet had a child-like innocence. He was meek and humble, yet had the regal air of a king. He was beautiful, unassuming, imminently present at every moment, observant to every detail, and yet kind to everyone.

In 1968 or '69 in Boston we had a small temple with only one *brahmachari*—Devananda—and he was having some difficulties. At that time the medicine for anyone who was having trouble was to travel with Prabhupada for a while. Devananda expressed a desire to travel with Prabhupada and Prabhupada asked Satsvarupa, the temple president, if Devananda could travel with him. Satsvarupa said, "Well, Prabhupada, if you give me someone else." Prabhupada said, "Ohhh, conditional."

Joshomatinandan: In Mayapur, 1977, Prabhupada had a fever so somebody was with him constantly. I was gently massaging him about two o'clock in the morning when he woke up and said, "These rascal scientists do not accept this. Go and preach to them, tell them that you are not the body, that you are a spirit soul, and the proof is that in this life the soul is transmigrating from childhood to youth to old age." Prabhupada spoke philosophy at two thirty in the morning in the middle of a heavy fever, and after ten or fifteen minutes went back to sleep. He was dreaming about preaching and living for preaching.

Tranakarta: Prabhupada woke us up to how fragile this material world is and how we are deeply rooted in it. He wanted us to get out of here by chanting Hare Krishna. When someone asked Prabhupada, "How can we please you the most?", sometimes he would say, "Learn *Bhagavad-gita*". But most of the time he would say, "Chant Hare Krishna and be happy. Become Krishna conscious." That's what he wanted. We don't have to work like an ass to make a few bucks, Krishna will provide. We need to chant Hare Krishna, always remember Krishna, and do everything for Krishna. Krishna, Krishna,

Krishna. That was Prabhupada's mercy on us. This personality, His Divine Grace, gave us Krishna, gave us His holy names, and gave us Lord Chaitanya's movement. Wow! Jaya, Srila Prabhupada.

TAPE 39

Dhananjaya das

Dhananjaya: At 5:00 A.M. on Bhaktisiddhanta Sarasvati Thakur's Disappearance Day in December 1970, a stretch white Mercedes limousine with blacked out windows came to our temple. The chauffeur, with his cap, his dark suit and his polished black shoes, had a piece of paper with my name on it. I was called out of the temple room, I identified myself and the chauffeur said, "I've been told to take you to the fruit and vegetable market." I said, "Who told you to do this?" He said, "George Harrison is with John Lennon on a yacht on the Thames, and he remembered it was an auspicious spiritual master's day, so he gave me 100 pounds. John gave permission to use his Mercedes and I'm to take you to the fruit and vegetable market to get fruits and vegetables for a feast." While partying with his friends on a yacht, George spontaneously decided to do this.

Srila Prabhupada wrote to me, "How is the preaching in London?" That year so many boys and girls joined our temple that the *brahmachari* and *brahmacharini* rooms were overflowing. About 65 devotees were living in a property meant for 10 or 12. I reported this to Prabhupada and he wrote back, "Contact our good friend Mr. George Harrison and ask him to help us to find a bigger property." George Harrison happened to be in town at the time—that year he recorded the album later called *Living In the Material World,* which had an insert of a big color print of Krishna and Arjuna, the same picture that's on the cover of *Bhagavad-gita As It Is.* When I visited George I'd take him all his favorite types of *prasadam*, like deep-fried potatoes, cauliflower and deep-fried curd soaked in sour cream, *samosas*, cauliflower *pakoras*, different kinds of sweets like *burfi, sandesh* and Simply Wonderfuls, as well as the strawberry buttermilk nectar that we became famous for. I was seeing him once a week until he said, "If you keep bringing all this stuff you have an open invitation to come as often as you want." Then I began visiting him three or four times a week and when I felt it was the right opportunity I said, "George, now we have so many devotees in our temple that we're running out of space. Could you help us find a bigger place?" Without hesitating he said, "Sure. No problem. Visit different estate agents, see different properties and if you find something really good, call me and I'll come with you to check it out."

George was an exceptional person and he constantly thought about how to spread Krishna consciousness. For instance, although it's a single album, his album cover for Living In the Material World is double—it folds out—because George wanted to put a set of *japa* beads, a bead bag and a set of instructions how to use them into the other slipcover to be sold along with the record. And a lot of the lyrics on that album are Krishna conscious. One of the songs, called "The Lord Loves the One Who Loves the Lord," George was very clear for whom that song was meant. He said, "I wrote that for Srila Prabhupada."

George told me he got inspired when I interrupted him with my visits to his studio. Once he said, "Every time you come here I can't get any recording done. This recording studio costs 3,000 pounds a day but when you come, I don't get anything done. We sit down, eat *prasadam* and talk about Prabhupada and Krishna consciousness." He loved distributing Prabhupada's *Gita* to his friends, and we'd supply him with beads and bead bags so his friends could chant japa. He had the mood of giving to others the wonderful opportunity of

Krishna consciousness that he had received from Srila Prabhupada and the devotees. When I asked him, "Why don't you take initiation from Prabhupada?" He said, "I don't need to, I've already got a spiritual name." I said, "What do you mean you've got a spiritual name?" He said, "My name's Hari's son, son of Hari," and then he laughed—that was his Liverpudlian dry humor.

When I went with him to visit different properties, he would have one hand on the steering wheel, steering the car, and the other hand in his bead bag, chanting.

Once in 1972 an older English devotee called Bhakti Pramode, who worked as a security manager for the world-famous Midland Bank, drove Shyamasundar, Prabhupada and me in his car to see one of the properties that I'd arranged for George to see. It was called Runnymede Farm on the banks of the River Thames. Runnymede is where King John, the King of England, signed the Magna Cart in the early 13th century. The farm hadn't been used for three or four years and was overgrown. George came from Friar Park in his Porsche, walked around the property and said, "They should call this Runnydown Farm, not Runnymede Farm."

Bhakti Pramode was an intriguing person who loved to fuss around Prabhupada. He never called Prabhupada "Prabhupada," but he called Prabhupada "Your Grace." He would say, "How is Your Grace this morning? Are you feeling cold? I've got a travel blanket I'd like to tuck around your legs so you don't get cold." He also liked Scottish highland dancing. Once he and his wife, Yasodamayi, came for Prabhupada's evening *darshan* at Bury Place when Bhakti Pramode was wearing his full highland dress kit—with a tweed jacket and a kilt and the sporran and the long stockings and the sgian dubh, that little knife tucked into the top of the stockings with a kilt. He and his wife paid their obeisances and sat on the floor. Since he was elderly—in his mid to late 50s— Bhakti Pramode couldn't sit cross-legged properly. He had his knees up in the air and Prabhupada was looking straight up his kilt. Prabhupada said, "What is that you're wearing?" He said, "This is a typical Scottish dress, Your Grace, because we've just come back from some highland dancing." Prabhupada said, "You are feeling comfortable in that skirt, or would you prefer to sit on a chair?" because he was kind of exposing himself to Srila Prabhupada. Anyway, this Bhakti Pramode was Prabhupada's driver. He drove Prabhupada to Ratha-yatra or wherever Prabhupada wanted to go and sometimes he would try to get Prabhupada to go on little tours around London. He wanted to take Prabhupada to see Londinium, the first city the Romans established where there's still some Roman ramparts, and he showed Prabhupada Buckingham Palace and London Bridge. Prabhupada liked Bhakti Pramode.

Anyway, there we were in Runnymede Farm. We walked up to the main house, which wasn't a standard farmhouse but was a small stately home with impressive column pillars in the front, high vaulted ceilings and a beautiful staircase. George and the rest of us stood with Srila Prabhupada, discussing the possibility of moving onto this property. Prabhupada said, "Before we move in, we will build a bank beside this house," he pointed to Bhakti Pramode and continued, "you will be the bank manager because you have some experience in banking." Then Prabhupada pointed to George and said, "And George, you will deposit all your money in that bank and we will spend everything in Krishna's service." George, taken aback, said, "All my money will be. . . ?" We all laughed because what Prabhupada said was completely unexpected.

By the end of '72 nothing had happened. Prabhupada wrote to me, "Better to take the upper hand and begin very energetically attempting to get some place. Expending energy for Krishna, that is appreciated and not the actual result of our energy. But if there is lack of energy being devoted for some purpose, then everything will be delayed and possibly stopped. Better to seize the iron while the fire is hot, that my Guru Maharaj used to tell me." Prabhupada presumed that the iron was getting a little cold. Then in January of 1973, in a freezing cold, miserable British winter, we got information about a property called Piggot's Manor in Letchmore Heath, 17 miles from central London. This was the one and only time I didn't go as a devotee, with a shaved head, *dhoti, tilak* and *kurta*, but went disguised with trousers, coat and hat. The previous property George and I had looked at was an amazing health spa outside of the city of Oxford with an indoor heated swimming pool, a beautiful conservatory, saunas and mud baths and more than a hundred acres of land. The asking price was 330,000 pounds. After George saw that property he said, "This is a bit rich for you people, isn't it? You're supposed to be renunciates. Even I would have a hard time remaining Krishna conscious in this environment." Then we got the details on the Manor, which was being sold for 220,000 pounds—110,000 pounds cheaper than the previous property. This time George didn't come but I phoned him from a pay phone in what is now the Manor temple room and I described the details and the price. He said, "It's a lot cheaper than the previous property. What do you think?" I said, "I think it's a fabulous place." He said, "All right, I trust your judgement. I can't come to see it because we're having some meetings in Los Angeles with Allen Klein, our financial advisor, about selling the Apple Company." George gave me the names and phone numbers of legal people who could do the paper work to buy the property, and said, "Phone them up, tell them that you want to secure this property, and when the transaction is complete, I'll come and see it." The paperwork took about six months. George had set up a foundation called the Material World Charitable Foundation. He said, "The profits from the Living In the Material World LP album will go towards paying for that property, but it'll go through my foundation." And that's what happened—the Material World Charitable Foundation paid for the property and the agreement was that we would pay 10 pounds a year rent, which is called a peppercorn rent. It's the absolute minimum that you can pay for a costly property.

We acquired the Manor from a Scottish lady, Mrs. Ruffles, who was from Aberdeen, a city in northern Scotland. The story is that the Scots are quite mean, but even in Scotland, people from Aberdeen are called Aberdonians, and are considered extremely mean. Before we moved into the property, Mrs. Ruffles removed every single doorknob from every single door. She removed a pair of brass lion's head doorknockers from the front doors to the house. She removed all the pelmets and siphoned off all the diesel fuel (for the central heating) from the tanks. Mrs. Ruffles took away all the coal for the fireplaces. When Prabhupada went on an inspection, there were a couple of doors we couldn't open because there were no doorknobs or door handles or anyway to open the doors, so we had to show him those rooms later on. When we showed him his quarters upstairs, with its huge living room, a huge old-fashioned bathroom and a comfortable bedroom, he was happy. He said, "Yes, this is a nice facility for the spiritual master."

All this time the Deities that had been sent from India were in our temple sewing room. Generally when there's a new temple project, first we get the land and house and then the Deities come. But in this situation, the Deities came one year before we acquired Bhaktivedanta Manor. When Prabhupada came in the summer of '73, he asked me, "Where are the Deities that came to England in 1972?" I said, "They're stored in Bury Place." Prabhupada said, "We will install those Deities in this property." And that's what happened. On Janmastami Day of 1973, Srila Prabhupada installed the Deities and he named Them Sri Sri Radha-Gokulananda. He had intended to call the community New Gokula and the bliss of Gokula is Radha-Gokulananda.

One of the first things George did when he returned from Los Angeles was visit the Manor. We took him on a tour of all the rooms because by that time we'd gotten door handles and doorknobs and we showed him the gardens and the lake and all the other places.

George was curious about everything. He liked the Manor and thought it was a good value for the money. Then Shyamasundar brought George to the temple room and said, "Wouldn't some crystal chandeliers look great here?" George said, "Yeah, that would be really nice," and George bought a pair of beautiful chandeliers for 3,000 pounds—after he had just bought the Manor for us.

When Prabhupada first came to the Manor in 1973, it was raining and at that time he told me three things. First, he said, "This property is like gold kept in a dark place. To appreciate the value of gold requires bright light, especially sunshine, because gold naturally shines. But if you keep it in a dark place, then who can appreciate it? Similarly, this is a valuable property. But because of the weather, who can appreciate it?" The British weather is typically raining and cloudy and miserable. Occasionally, for a week or two, it would be sunny and we have beautiful photographs and films from the Manor of Prabhupada sitting on the lawn on sunny days.

Second, because he was shrewd, Prabhupada also said, "This property is like a white elephant. A white elephant is something rare and valuable, but it is expensive to maintain. Similarly, this property will be very expensive to run." That turned out to be very true.

And finally he said that he wanted the Manor to be famous for cow protection. He said that we should teach the British the importance of cow protection, *go-raksya*, and keep 150 cows there. At that time we had 17 acres of land and only 6 acres of it was an arable field suitable for cows. I said, "Prabhupada, it's not practical to keep 150 cows on 6 acres of land because each cow requires at least one acre." Prabhupada said, "So purchase 150 acres for the cows. What is the difficulty? But that's the minimum number of cows you should keep. If you need to purchase another 150 acres for those cows, then purchase it." We didn't acquire more land until 1997, when we got permission to put in a new approach road and got another 55 acres with that, so now we have about half the amount of land that Prabhupada said we should have in 1973—and now we have 25 cows. Prabhupada also wanted us to buy a double-decker red London transport bus, drive it into the center of London, fill it up with people interested in the Manor, and bring them there for some time.

Srila Prabhupada's vision was always long range and sometimes we have a hard time fulfilling it. There is no place in the UK where Krishna conscious cow protection is practiced. Prabhupada wanted us to be self-sufficient in *ghee* and milk, to sell *ghee* to the visitors, and for us to be engaged in handicrafts like spinning, weaving cloth, making brass Deities and so forth. I said, "What about the Indian community? Should we focus on the Indian community?" At that time Prabhupada said, "No, we don't need to bother with the Indian community, they are already Krishna conscious. We have to focus our attention on the British community, they know nothing about Krishna."

Once George came to see Prabhupada with Ravi Shankar. As he usually did, George offered his full *dandavats* to Prabhupada. Ravi Shankar had presumed that George was his own disciple, but George never offered his *dandavats* to Ravi. He only did that to Prabhupada, and Prabhupada immediately sensed that Ravi Shankar was a little envious. After speaking with George, Prabhupada said, "You must be hungry. Go to the kitchen and get *prasadam*," and Prabhupada asked a devotee to accompany George. When George had left, Prabhupada talked with Ravi Shankar and that placated Ravi Shankar's false ego. Their conversation centered on plane tickets, travel and the best airline to travel on because Prabhupada understood that Ravi Shankar was not interested in spiritual philosophy. So Prabhupada related to Ravi Shankar in a way that he could keep up the conversation. Prabhupada was expert at dealing with everybody. He knew George's love for *prasadam* and he knew that Ravi Shankar needed attention.

When George visited Prabhupada at the Manor in 1976 he said,

"Do you think I should move into the *ashram*, shave up, and wear *tilak* and a *dhoti*?" Prabhupada said, "No." At that meeting George came with Ravi Shankar's niece, Laksmi Shankar, and had just made the musical arrangements and written the words for a song called "Krishna, Where Are You?" that she had sung. George played that song for Prabhupada. Prabhupada listened to it and said, "Yes, this is the mood of the six Goswamis. Krishna, where are You? I have not captured You. I would love to capture You, I would love to have You in my vision eternally, but You are always disappearing from my sight. This feeling of separation, called *vipralambha,* is very pleasing. Go on writing lyrics and music like this. This is your service to Krishna. It will not be good for you to live in the *ashram*. You can do much more preaching and reach many more people if you remain outside." Prabhupada was very understanding.

By 1980 we'd been living at the Manor, worshipping Radha-Gokulananda, for seven years and many Indian businessmen wanted to get involved. There was a lot of restoration and repair work to do and we needed a car park. But these businessmen didn't want to give their money because they knew that George's foundation, not ISKCON, owned the property. They would say, "Can we trust George? One day he could decide he didn't like you Hare Krishnas anymore and say, 'Get out.' There's no binding legal document and we'd have given donations for nothing. We don't want to do that." At the time Vicitravirya was the temple president and we had had the Manor property appraised by Lloyd's Bank and Barclay's Bank and we'd also been advised by our solicitor. Vicitravirya said to me, "Ask George how he feels about us and about this property." I called George and he came over. I said to George, "We want to stay here and many people want to give sizable donations—10,000, 20,000 pounds or more—but they know that we don't own the property. So what we want is either to pay rent and get a 100-year lease from you, or to pay for the property in installments over 10 or 15 years." We walked around, and since by that time George was into gardening and identified himself as a gardener, he didn't like how we hadn't maintained the gardens. I'd seen his place, Friar Park, and over the years it was amazing what a wonderful job he'd done on his property. He'd learned the Latin names of every plant and herb. Our gardens were full of weeds because our qualified devotees were on the streets selling books, not gardening and weeding and trimming hedges and planting, and our place was a terrible mess. George said, "I'm getting a headache just walking around here. You haven't looked after this place." I was very nervous. He said, "Give me a week to think about it and I'll let you know." A week later he called and said, "I've spoken with Allen Klein, and what he's come up with is this. You put 45,000 pounds towards the cost of the property and from my side I'll put another 145, which makes a total of 190. And we'll show that we sold the property to you at a loss. I know you can't afford 190 but if you can come up with 45,000 within a week, the place is yours. Then I don't need to think about it anymore." He wanted to give the place as a donation but he couldn't legally because a charitable foundation can't donate property to another charity—there has to be some financial transaction. Since the property cost 220, through the books he was making a loss of about 30,000. But by 1980 the two banks had appraised the property at 1.5 million pounds. So we got the 45,000 pounds together, gave it to him, he signed the deeds over to ISKCON, and from that day the Manor belonged to ISKCON.

The last time George associated with a large group of devotees was when he and his wife, Olivia, visited the Manor in the summer of 1997. We had invited him to a celebratory dinner a few days after we got permission to build the new approach road. This dinner was held shortly after we had another amazing fund-raising dinner called "Prabhupada's Dream", during which guests and patron members of the Manor were invited to raise funds to buy the land for the approach road. That evening the target was to raise one million pounds. We rented a large circus tent with a stage, set many tables, and served a nice dinner. There was a positive response—within two hours we raised 800,000 pounds—but we were 200,000 short until Michael, an Irish businessman patron member who imported Indian clothing, so appreciated Prabhupada's Dream of having 150 acres of land for 150 protected cows, that he pledged 200,000 pounds. Michael had only once before been to the Manor and at that time he had taken part in *arati* and heard a lecture, but that evening was the first time he had attended a special patron's dinner and he pledged more than any other patron member. What he pledged was a substantial amount of money for anyone, especially for a person of non-Indian origin. It was an auspicious evening.

George agreed to come to our second dinner, but we didn't know if his wife would come. Both were invited but Olivia never attended our public functions. She wasn't a great fan of the Hare Krishna devotees—she followed somebody else—and she left it up to her husband to go to such things. But this time she came. A Gujarati disciple of Shivaram Swami named Sruti Dharma and I went to the car park at the Manor to welcome them. They had brought rubber Welly boots with them because they were enthusiastic to walk through the fields to see where the new approach road was going to be built, and we did that. We walked from where the main gate would be all the way to the Manor property, which is about a half a mile. We stopped to talk along the way and George observed the fields, "How far does the property extend on this side of the road? How far on the other side of the road? Are you going to have any kind of hedges or trees so that the road doesn't look ugly, so it doesn't spoil the overall beauty of the farmland?" We got into the details and when we were returning George said, "If you want to have a successful business, I suggest you start a garden center." In England, garden centers are usually incredibly successful. Families who've just moved into their home buy trees and shrubs, flowers and herbs. George said, "If you do that, I don't think you need planning permission for this." He'd put a lot of thought into this idea and as I said, he identified himself as a gardener first and a musician second.

He said, "I'll help you set it up and with whatever you need." We were happy that he was so open-minded about our project. Then we took him to the temple with Radha-Gokulananda's altar, Sita-Rama, Laksman, and Hanuman's altar and the little Gaura-Nitai Deities between Them. George offered his full *dandavats* to the Deities, Olivia offered her *pranams* and they both took *charanamrita*. Then we went into the dining room.

The history behind this dinner is that in 1982 the local District Council decided that it didn't want to have the Manor as a public place of worship because the building hadn't been planned as such. They wanted to close down the Manor. Our 15-year campaign to keep the Manor open was basically a freedom of religion case. During that time reporters were always interviewing the devotees. We were in newspapers, on television, and on the radio. At one time the Manor had been owned by Saint Bartholomew's Hospital, an old hospital in London, for a nurse's training college. Mrs. Ruffles had bought it from Saint Bart's with the idea of turning it into a nursing home, but she couldn't carry the financial burden and so she sold it. Then we moved in and suddenly festivals were going on with thousands of visitors and many cars were in the village. We didn't want the villagers to be irate with our festivals—we wanted to take the strain off the village. After a long, hard battle, in 1996 the British Government's Secretary of State for the Environment, John Gummer, announced on television that, "the government gave permission for the construction of an access driveway which by-passed the local village, plus full planning permission for the Manor to be used as a place of public worship." Before that neither the government nor the District Council had recognized us. That was a great victory for us and that's why we had this victory dinner, which was a nice feast cooked by my wife, Bala Gopala.

Everybody who had been involved in the campaign—over 200 people—were there, all VIP guests including some MP's, legal people, newspaper people and so on. Akhandadhi mentioned all the different guests that were present and praised and honored everybody. Finally he came to George and said, "We have to thank George because this would never have happened if he hadn't agreed to donate this property." George was an honored guest, but he wasn't expected to say anything. But before he spoke, Olivia stood up and said, "I am deeply touched by what I've heard and seen tonight, and I feel impelled to say that George has got true friends here, and I feel happy for him. And I feel happy that I didn't miss the opportunity to witness this amazing gathering." This was the only time that Olivia had come to the Manor. Before, when I called George and she answered the phone, she would be rude. I used to pray that she didn't answer the phone. She would try to stop me from intruding into their privacy by visiting her husband. Olivia didn't like us until that evening. After she sat down, Shyamasundar and Mukunda presented George with a little Prabhupada *murti* with a Prabhupada hat and glasses and a bead bag and a little book rest and a miniature size *Bhagavad-gita*, a little *vyasasana* and a *sannyasi danda*, and a little pair of *kartals* and a little pair of glasses. It was cute. George cradled Prabhupada and said, "I'm going to take Prabhupada home with me tonight." It really touched him. He said, "I didn't want to say anything, but I feel I've got to. First of all, I feel ashamed that I never participated in this campaign." George hadn't given any support, either verbally or in the press or in any other way. He said, "But I was following it on television or in the papers. I knew what was going on. In the back of my mind I thought if it didn't work out, if you had to close the Manor, you could move over to my place in Henley and take over Friar Park—that could be your new temple." He was so moved by what he had heard that evening that he was talking from his heart. Everybody started clapping like anything.

TAPE 40

Jayadvaita Swami

Jayadvaita Swami: When I first joined, all day I drove the devotees mad with questions, "Here it says this but there it says that, and what about this and what about that?" I was loaded with questions. When Srila Prabhupada came, some of my questions had been addressed, but I still had questions for Prabhupada. One was "How does the spiritual master know what the disciple is doing?" The intention of my question was essentially "If you do something and the spiritual master is not physically there, how does the spiritual master know what you're doing so that he'll be pleased and give you credit for it?" Srila Prabhupada answered in a different way. He said, "The face is the index of mind. So, when you are making spiritual progress, everyone can see."

Sometimes Prabhupada would say many things on his walks, but on the first walk I went on he mostly chanted *japa* on his beads. On that walk I asked him, "Since Vyasadev was present when *Bhagavad-gita* was spoken, why does Krishna say to Arjuna that over the course of time the knowledge of *Bhagavad-gita* was lost?" Srila Prabhupada answered, "That meant that the knowledge was not generally known."

When Srila Prabhupada came from Hawaii, he began his lecture by mentioning that a local paper, the *Honolulu Advertiser,* had run an article saying, "The swami is a small man, but he has got a big message." Prabhupada was quite happy with that.

On one engagement, a knowledgeable student, perhaps a grad student, asked a question in the context of *advaita* philosophy. He asked about the soul merging into the Supreme the way the drop of water merges into ocean water, and from the way he asked, it seemed that this idea seemed right to him. Prabhupada answered that the drop merges with the ocean but when the sun comes the drop evaporates and is no longer in the ocean. To merge is a temporary situation. But if you become an aquatic, then you can dive in the ocean and remain there always. Srila Prabhupada said that our philosophy is to merge deep into the ocean and at the same time maintain our individuality. Hardly anyone had come to this engagement except this one intelligent person who asked a question that Prabhupada brilliantly answered.

At an evening program in New York, Rukmini asked, "If Lord Chaitanya is Krishna, how did He show the six opulences?" Srila Prabhupada briefly answered, but the next morning he called an *istagosthi*, which meant a discussion of *Krishna-katha*. Later *istagosthi* came to mean a gripe session or a management meeting, but Prabhupada's idea of *istagosthi* was a discussion about Krishna consciousness. For Prabhupada to call an *istagosthi* was unusual. I don't recall any other time when Prabhupada had a meeting in the morning. But we all came. Prabhupada led *kirtan,* and then he said, "About Rukmini's question," and he answered it in detail. He mentioned how Lord Chaitanya was beautiful. He said, "People were attracted to fair skin, and Lord Chaitanya was very fair-skinned. He was called Gaurasundar." And "He was learned also, so He was known as Nimai Pandit." In that way Prabhupada described the Lord's different opulences. Then he said, "Lord Chaitanya's main opulence was His renunciation," and he explained how Lord Chaitanya left His wife, Vishnupriya, and His elderly mother. Prabhupada emphasized that opulence of Lord Chaitanya.

One time Srila Prabhupada asked me, "Why are you so skinny?" I said, "I don't know, Srila Prabhupada."

Satsvarupa Maharaj, the temple president, gave me some little booklets about Krishna that were published by a well-known spiritual press in India, and said, "Could you ask Srila Prabhupada whether it's all right to read these booklets?" I went into Srila Prabhupada's room with the booklets and I asked Srila Prabhupada, "Is it all right to read these?" Srila Prabhupada said, "It is not required." Prabhupada's meaning was "no," but I didn't understand that because in my experience elective subjects were optional and required subjects were obligatory. So I said to Srila Prabhupada, "All right, they're not required, but is it all right to read them?" We went back and forth that way a couple of times before I understood that "not required" means if it's not required, why do it? Forget it. The answer was no.

Prabhupada spoke in a Harvard classroom, and the professor, who was Indian, raised a question about Krishna and the *gopis*. Prabhupada became stern and strong with him, and the thrust of Prabhupada's response was "Krishna and the *gopis* are above your head. What is your qualification to understand these things? You are misunderstanding—you are taking it as mundane. Try to understand from *Bhagavad-gita*—Krishna is the Supreme Personality of Godhead." Prabhupada's eyes were flashing and he became animated. "This person is talking about Krishna and the *gopis* in some academic context. What does he know? What right does he have to talk about Krishna and the *gopis*?"

A young hairdresser named Eddie, who was a follower of some *yogi*, became attracted to Srila Prabhupada. Eddie was from New York, but he came to Boston to be with Srila Prabhupada, and he brought some friends with him. Eddie would help Prabhupada put his shoes on and off, and Prabhupada said to him, "You are nice." On one morning walk, Eddie asked Srila Prabhupada if he could be initiated. Prabhupada said, "First you should know the philosophy. If today you come on sentiment, tomorrow you will leave on sentiment," which is what happened. Eddie didn't stay.

Once, an elderly gentleman came to the temple with a letter from Srila Prabhupada that he'd received in Prabhupada's absence, and the letter said, "When I come to New York, then you can see me and we will discuss." Brahmananda had me take the gentleman over to Srila Prabhupada's apartment at 26 Second Avenue, a block or two away from the temple. The gentleman was respectful. He said to Srila Prabhupada, "Swamiji, I like your teachings, but one of your disciples said that you said such-and-such person is a rascal," and he mentioned a big spiritual person from India. The man said, "It seems to me that he's a holy person. I don't understand why you'd say he's a rascal." Prabhupada said, "Who has said this?" The man said, "You didn't say that?" Prabhupada said, "If he says that I have said that and I have not said it, then *he* is a rascal." The man became settled—he was relieved that Prabhupada hadn't said that. Then Prabhupada took a little blue hardbound volume from his shelf and opened it. He showed the book to the man and said, "Do you know this book?" The man said, "Dr. Thus-and-so. Vedanta Society! Oh, yes!" He was pleased. Prabhupada opened the book and said, "Read this verse." The verse was *man-mana bhava mad-bhakto mad-yaji mam namaskuru.* The man read, "Always think of Me, become My devotee, offer your homage to Me, worship Me." Prabhupada said, "Yes, he is a very good scholar, he has translated the verse nicely. Now what does the commentary say? Read." The man began reading, "It is not to Krishna that we have to surrender but to the all-pervading unborn within Krishna." Prabhupada said, "Just see! Therefore, I say they are all rascals." Then Prabhupada quoted, *na mam duskrtino mudhah prapadyante naradhamah, mayayapahrta-jnana asuram bhavam asritah:* "Anyone who doesn't surrender to Me is a miscreant, the lowest of men, his knowledge is stolen by illusion, he is demonic in nature." Prabhupada explained all of these words at length and said, "*I* am not saying they are rascals, Krishna is saying it. What can I do?"

After Srila Prabhupada initiated a large group of devotees at 61 Second Avenue, he walked back to his apartment gravely, with his head held characteristically high, while ecstatic barefoot devotees blissfully danced behind him. At first Srila Prabhupada didn't say anything. Then he said, "We have increased the disciplic succession from Chaitanya Mahaprabhu."

Prabhupada once quoted and explained a verse from *Caitanya Bhagavat* about *muchi* and *suchi*. He said that *muchi* is a cobbler, the lowest class of man, who skins animals and uses the skins to make shoes, and *suchi* is the most pure, the *brahmana*. But the person who is *suchi* becomes *muchi—yadi krsna tyaje*, if he gives up Krishna consciousness; and the person who is *muchi* becomes *suchi*, *yadi krsna bhaje*, if he takes up Krishna consciousness. Prabhupada liked that verse. He also said if a person claims "I am *brahmana* because I was born in a *brahmana* family," that means, "I have *brahmana* skin." Srila Prabhupada said, "He is a skin dealer, that's all. That means he is *muchi*. He is thinking, 'I am *brahmana*,' but he is a skin dealer: 'Oh, I have got *brahmana* skin.'_"

At one point a German disciple named Uttama-sloka came to 61 Second Avenue and related some of his experiences with Srila Prabhupada. He said that Srila Prabhupada had told him, "Just try to hear yourself chant sincerely."

While in New Vrindavan, Prabhupada said that Krishna is light and *maya* is darkness, and he gave an example. He said that if you hold your palm up it's in the light. And when you turn your palm down it's in darkness. It's up to us whether we turn toward Krishna or away from Krishna. Therefore, we're called marginal energy—we can turn either way.

At that time the devotees had purchased a cow, but they hadn't purchased the calf the cow had just had, and the cow was crying. In the pasture the cow ran the length of her body through the electric fence, searching, "Where is my calf?" After that, Prabhupada told them to get the calf also, but it was not possible. On some later occasions Prabhupada mentioned, "They say that the animal has no soul, but just see how the cow is crying for her calf."

When Srila Prabhupada came to Boston in December of 1969, he stayed in a little house in a suburb a long distance from the temple. The winter was not agreeing with Prabhupada. He had a serious cold, but he called the devotees who were involved with *Back to Godhead* magazine—Hayagriva and Satsvarupa Maharaj (they were co-editors), Pradyumna, Kirtanananda Maharaj, and me—to his house for a meeting. Before this meeting we just "did things," but at this time Prabhupada wanted to train us in how to have a meeting. We went through snow-covered, winding roads to Prabhupada's house, and he started the meeting by having a *kirtan,* and after that there was some discussion. Several times in different venues Prabhupada repeated that pattern, that in a meeting you first have *kirtan* and then you discuss. At this meeting Prabhupada explained the BTG editorial policy. He said that there are four levels of Krishna consciousness. The first level is how to awaken someone to Krishna consciousness. People are sleeping in illusion, in *maya*, so we have to awaken them. Then the second stage is how to train them to be Krishna conscious. Someone comes forward: "Swamiji, please accept me, please initiate me." So the second stage is training. Then the third stage is to understand Krishna's different energies, as in the Radha-Krishna *lila.* And the fourth stage, Prabhupada said, is the *paramahamsa* stage, to be always absorbed in thinking of Krishna. Prabhupada said that *Back to Godhead* should be on the first two stages—how to awaken and how to train someone. Subjects like Radha-Krishna are not meant for the general public.

Either Pradyumna or Kirtanananda Maharaj asked if we could publish *Brahma-samhita* in *Back to Godhead,* and Prabhupada was not very much in favor of this idea, because *Brahma-samhita* is very dense. Then Prabhupada said we could publish it "in small installments." He said, "It will puzzle their brains," and he said, "My spiritual master used to speak from the highest elevated platform." As Prabhupada was speaking, somehow it seemed to me that the room filled with effulgence. From the way Prabhupada spoke with such regard for his spiritual master, I pictured his spiritual master speaking from a high throne. Then Prabhupada began telling the story of how he had been dragged by his friend, Narendranath Mullik, and had met his spiritual master, how one thing led to another and Prabhupada came to the West. Prabhupada said, "Even when my spiritual master spoke in Bengali I could not understand. But I would go on hearing. That was my policy. And my spiritual master noticed that 'This boy likes to hear.' I would understand or not understand, but I would go on hearing. And because I was enthusiastic about hearing, *sravanam*, now I am enthusiastic about preaching, *kirtanam*."

When Rathayatra was coming up in 1969, Srila Prabhupada was in San Francisco, and we were at ISKCON Press in Boston, working on the Second Canto and other things. Some devotees thought that all the Press workers could pile in a van, drive across the country in two days, be with Srila Prabhupada for the Rathayatra, and then turn around, come back to Boston and keep going. Somehow this idea came to Srila Prabhupada's attention and Prabhupada said, "What do they want to come here for? They should go on with their work, their prescribed duties." From that we understood that association with the spiritual master is not just by physical proximity but also by our devotional service. We can be with the spiritual master by serving him.

It was around 1969 that it became important to identify Srila Prabhupada as the Founder-Acharya of the International Society for Krishna Consciousness. At first Srila Prabhupada was known as A.C. Bhaktivedanta Swami, then he was A.C. Bhaktivedanta Swami Prabhupada, and then A.C. Bhaktivedanta Swami Prabhupada,

Founder-Acharya of the International Society for Krishna Consciousness. The Founder-Archarya part began while we were publishing the Second Canto in chapter-by-chapter booklets. From the West Coast we heard that we were supposed to write Founder-Archarya. But the message was garbled, so we only printed "Founder of the International Society for Krishna Consciousness." Prabhupada was upset with us. Then another message came and we reprinted. We ran a black line through "Founder of the International Society for Krishna Consciousness" and put "Acharya of the International Society for Krishna Consciousness." Again it was wrong. Finally we got it right—"Founder-Acharya"—and since then that's been there. Prabhupada foresaw that his position as Founder-Acharya should be well established.

Later, when the Press was in Los Angeles, Srila Prabhupada passed by our newly occupied BBT building and saw the Bhaktivedanta Book Trust sign without "Founder-Acharya" underneath it. Even though Radha-vallabha, who was in charge, had the letters in a box, ready to go (they just hadn't been put up yet), he got blasted by Srila Prabhupada: "Why is this missing?" Prabhupada considered it crucial. In fact, at one point he issued a letter to all the centers that on all the letterhead, on all the cards, on all the publications of the Society, this line had to be there, "Founder-Acharya His Divine Grace A.C. Bhaktivedanta Swami Prabhupada." Prabhupada foresaw how significant and important it would be for us and for others to understand the Society properly with its Founder-Acharya.

ISKCON Press was in Brooklyn in 1974, and one day when Srila Prabhupada was there he called me into his quarters. His head was freshly shaved, and he was sitting on a platform looking regal and aristocratic. He asked me about the Press manager, Advaita das: "I have heard that Advaita is not attending the programs. Is that fact?" I didn't want to be a tattletale, but I admitted that it was probably so. Prabhupada said, "Go over there and tell them to close the Press. We do not need this Press. If they cannot come to the programs, better to close the Press." Up to that time, Prabhupada had been putting tremendous emphasis on the importance of our Press activities. He had given money for it, and the Press devotees were working hard. It was very important to Prabhupada that we keep up our *sadhana*, our standard devotional activities.

Another time Srila Prabhupada was having his massage in his Henry Street quarters in Brooklyn. Someone had gotten him a little vibrator, and Prabhupada's assistant was massaging Prabhupada with it. Then Baradraj Prabhu came in to ask questions about the paintings. But Prabhupada had an issue to take up with Baradraj. Prabhupada said, "What are these bust pictures?" Prabhupada was referring to paintings of the *acharyas* that portrayed only their head and shoulders. Prabhupada didn't consider those paintings appropriate, and he instructed Baradraj that their full forms should be shown. He said, "The paintings are not for decoration, they are for worship." He said, "*Vande guroh sri*" (I offer obeisances to the spiritual master), and he pointed to his foot, "...*caranaravindam*" (beginning with the lotus feet).

Sai was a young American yogi and guru who had his own Krishna consciousness movement and who, in July of 1971, surrendered to Srila Prabhupada and later became Siddhasvarupananda. Many of his followers came to New York, and Srila Prabhupada held initiations for them. They already had devotee names—the girls had poetic names like Lalita and Radharani—but Prabhupada gave them completely different names like Chaya (which means "shadow"), names of Durga, and names of Maya, the illusory energy. Prabhupada named one girl Maha-maya, and some of the devotees laughed. Prabhupada said, "Don't laugh. It is serious." Prabhupada said that several times at initiations. Devotees would say, "Ohhh!" and they'd laugh, but Prabhupada would say, "You should be grave, it is serious." To this devotee, Maha-maya, Prabhupada said, "Maha-maya is another face of Radharani."

In the summer, when Prabhupada came to New York City, devotees from many different centers also came there, and Prabhupada performed many mass initiations. Once there was a large initiation, many first initiates, many second initiates, and Srila Prabhupada asked the temple presidents and GBC men, "Have you scrutinized these lists? For first initiation we can be lenient, but for the second initiation we should be a little strict." So the presidents cut names from the second-initiation list. When one New York devotee's name was cut he became completely passionate and threw a tantrum. "What do you mean I'm not qualified to be a *brahmana*?" Prabhupada knew what he was doing.

One of the earliest devotees was named Rayarama. He joined before Satsvarupa Maharaj and many of the others, and he was impressive and dedicated to helping Srila Prabhupada. He and Hayagriva were the first editors of *Back to Godhead,* and he was the original editor for *Teachings of Lord Chaitanya.* Rayarama knew the philosophy better than anyone, at least in New York, because he was practically the only devotee who'd read all the books, and he used to be terrifyingly good in answering questions. Hippies and others would come and he would speak with them expertly. I was typing in Rayarama's office, but in 1968 or early '69, after I'd been around for a few months, Rayarama left the Society. Then in 1971, when we were at Henry Street and ISKCON Press was on Tiffany Place, he showed up at the Press. He said that he wanted to come back, and he wrote a letter to Srila Prabhupada that "I want to do some service, I want to join again." I thought Srila Prabhupada would be happy if such a long-lost devotee returned to the Society. However, from Rayarama's letter to him, Prabhupada detected that his materialistic mentality was still there. Srila Prabhupada wrote, "I welcome you for your coming back to our society and you are feeling very nicely for the association of devotees," and then Prabhupada explained, "Devotee means who are following the regulative principles. One cannot be independent and at the same time become a devotee, because all devotional activities are based on surrender. So in the association of devotees we learn this important item—how to surrender, but if we keep our independence and try to become devotees, that is not possible . . . If you want to live with us you must accept temple life, namely cleanly shaven head, observing the regulative principles, decorating the body with tilak, etc. You know all these things. As far as your editorial work is concerned, I welcome your good service but if you do not follow temple life and Deity worship, it will set a bad example." Prabhupada ended his letter with, "To associate with me you are always welcome but not with your independence. That will not help me or you."

I think Srila Prabhupada knew that his letter meant Rayarama would say, "Well, then I can't join." But Prabhupada laid it on the line, "If you want to join and surrender, then you are welcome back full-heartedly. But if you want to join but not really join, if you want to join but keep a separate mentality, to have your own agenda, then why do it? Why cheat?" Rayarama left, and we never saw him again.

We had been sending Srila Prabhupada photocopies of the layouts of the Fourth Canto of *Srimad-Bhagavatam*, the pastimes of Dhruva Maharaj, and when he was on Henry Street Srila Prabhupada called me into his office. He was looking at a photocopy and said, "Why is it 'Lord Manu?'" I said, "I don't know, Srila Prabhupada. It shouldn't be Lord Manu?" Prabhupada said, "Lord Brahma, Lord Shiva. But Lord Manu? No, it shouldn't be." Later I went back to the original tape, and the reason it was Lord Manu is that Prabhupada had said Lord Manu. So, trying to extract the purport, I took it as an instruction that Prabhupada wanted the editors to be scrutinizing. That was the word Prabhupada used most often for editors. Perhaps there was nothing wrong in those pages, but Prabhupada picked that point—"Why Lord Manu?"—to emphasize that the editors should be careful, that nothing should be passed over quickly.

When the First Canto of *Srimad-Bhagavatam* was published in 1972, Satsvarupa Maharaj and I noticed that there were things in that edition that didn't match what was in Prabhupada's original *Bhagavatams.* We mentioned this to Srila Prabhupada, and Prabhupada said, "Just print it." Prabhupada did not want the book production slowed down, especially since the books were ready to print. So we printed. Prabhupada said nothing further about it, and we said nothing further about it. But in 1975 or '76 I did a review of the First Canto of the *Bhagavatam,* and I saw that there were many places, especially in the translations to the first two chapters, where there were major discrepancies—the translations for Sanskrit words were missing or wrongly stated. Although the editor had done a wonderful service to Srila Prabhupada and to the readers, we thought the first two chapters, in particular, had been edited to less of a standard than they deserved. After all, they had been edited before Prabhupada instituted daily chanting of the Sanskrit verses and the word-for-word synonyms in *Bhagavatam* classes—that came a little later—and all of us, including the editor, were not very familiar with the books.

So, I went through the First Canto with special attention to the first two chapters, and I did a revision especially on the translations for those two chapters. I typed them up, put them in an envelope, and when Srila Prabhupada visited the 55th Street temple in New York, I went to his room to leave it for him to approve or disapprove. I had written a cover letter saying what I'd done, and I thought, "I'll just leave this here and come back or wait for a reply." But Srila Prabhupada was sitting there. I offered my obeisances, said what I was there for, and Prabhupada had me start reading the revised translations. Prabhupada listened attentively as I read the first two, three, four verses. Then he stopped me and said, "So what have you done?" I said, "Srila Prabhupada, I went through the verses and revised them, mainly to make them closer to what you originally said." Prabhupada said, "What *I* have said?" I said, "Yes, Srila Prabhupada." Prabhupada said, "Then it is all right."

Sometimes we think that everything Prabhupada said was about Krishna, but Prabhupada sometimes talked about other things. He'd talk about British history and there would be no apparent connection to Krishna consciousness. Once Prabhupada went on a walk in Central Park in New York City, and when the devotees came back I asked them, "What did Prabhupada talk about?" The first devotee I asked said, "He told the story of *The Merchant of Venice.*" I said, "What was the point?" He said, "He just told the story." I thought there must have been some point. I went to another devotee who had been on the walk: "What did Prabhupada talk about?" "He talked about *The Merchant of Venice* and told the story." "What was the point?" "He just told the story." What happened was that in Central Park Prabhupada had seen a statue of Daniel Webster, the famous American statesman, and had said, "Oh, Daniel has come," and there's a line in *The Merchant of Venice,* "A veritable Daniel," and then Prabhupada started telling the story of *The Merchant of Venice.* There was no purport, he just told the story, and that was it. Srila Prabhupada was conversant with English literature and English history, and sometimes he talked about those things. A pure devotee has the prerogative of talking about whatever he wants to talk about.

Another time I was in the car with Srila Prabhupada when we were driving back to Henry Street after a walk near the East River in Brooklyn. As we pulled up to the temple, on the corner of the street we saw a man lift a little boy so the boy could put a letter in the mailbox. The whole vignette just lasted for five or ten seconds, but Prabhupada, seeing this from the car, became absorbed in the scene. His eyes got large and brilliant, and nothing else was on his attention. I thought, "Maybe Prabhupada is remembering something from his childhood in Calcutta . . ." Then the man put his boy down, and Prabhupada said, "On his own the little boy cannot do, but when the affectionate father helps, then it is possible." So on our own, what power do we, the living entities, have? But when the

Lord or the spiritual master gives affectionate help, then it becomes possible.

When Srila Prabhupada went to San Francisco for Ratha-yatra in July of 1975, Krishna das was there. As a young man, Krishna das had gone to Germany, done a lot of nice service, and then had drifted away. Now he had come to be with Prabhupada and perhaps revive his service spirit. On a morning walk at that time, Srila Prabhupada talked about many subjects, and one of them was the feeling of separation from the spiritual master. Krishna das said, "Srila Prabhupada, you must always be feeling separation from your Guru Maharaj." His statement was a prompt—it was a way of saying, "Srila Prabhupada, could you speak about your feelings of separation from your Guru Maharaj?" Prabhupada responded, "That you do not require," which was Prabhupada's idiomatic way of saying, "None of your business," but he didn't say it in a mean or abrasive way. Then Prabhupada got in his car and left.

Sometimes I used to take a break from my stationary position as an editor to travel, especially to visit colleges with Satsvarupa Maharaj and his Library Party. In the course of this traveling, in the summer of 1976 we went to Detroit to be with Srila Prabhupada. We talked to Srila Prabhupada about what we were doing, and I said, "Srila Prabhupada, it's so difficult to convince the students to give up sense gratification." Prabhupada said, "We do not say give up—but regulate." In that way he corrected my understanding and also indicated how we should present the philosophy. Other times Prabhupada gave the example that sense gratification is like salt: too much salt and you can't eat; too little salt and you also can't eat. It has to be regulated.

The Detroit temple had been purchased with funds given by Ambarish prabhu and Lekhasravanti dasi. Since her father had been a leading labor leader in Detroit, Lekhasravanti was well connected, and once she brought a very respectful black gentleman, Jackie Vaughn, a member of Michigan's House of Representatives, to meet Srila Prabhupada. Prabhupada received him very cordially. Detroit is an opulent temple with beautiful Gaura-Nitai Deities, Jagannatha Deities, and Sri Sri Radha-Kunjabihari, tall marble Deities. Kunjabihari is black marble, and Radharani is white marble. Srila Prabhupada said to this gentleman, "Krishna is black and we worship Him. You have seen our Deity? The gentleman had been brought to the temple so he said, "Yes." Prabhupada said, "Yes. Krishna is also coming from your community.

One year in Mayapur we lived in the Lotus Building while it was still under construction—the roof was unfinished cement and rebar. That year a devotee named Gayatri dasi from Gainesville came to Mayapur with a cake she'd baked, and the *sannyasis*, as the senior guys, commandeered and consumed this cake. But Gayatri had traveled from Miami to London to Delhi to Calcutta and then she'd driven to Mayapur—so many days of traveling and so much hot sun—and this cake had become poison. The *sannyasis* were laid out on the roof of the Lotus Building writhing in pain, retching and wretched. I was glad I was just a *brahmachari*. But what should we do? These men could die. Should we take them to the hospital? Prabhupada said they should regularly take some Deity *charanamrita* and they would be all right. And they were.

Once Radha-vallabha and I were standing with Srila Prabhupada on the veranda in Mayapur. It was warm weather, and Prabhupada, standing in the sunlight, had a freshly shaved head and was wearing only an *uttariya* to cover his chest. Prabhupada rubbed his head in a characteristic way and said, "Anything good you want to do, you'll have to go through so much trouble."

On one walk we suddenly came to a kind of a *mandap,* a raised concrete platform with a tin roof over it, where music was playing.

Prabhupada got on the *mandap*, and when he saw a deity of Durga there he offered his full *dandavats* before her and then sat on his knees, looked at the deity, and quoted *srsti-sthiti-pralaya-sadhana-saktir eka, chayeva yasya bhuvanani bibharti durga*, that Durga is conducting her affairs in obedience to the order of Govinda. Prabhupada said, "We are also offering respect to Durga, but not like materialists who ask her, 'Give me this, give me this, give me this.' The *gopis* were worshiping Katyayani, which means Durga, that 'My dear goddess, you always carry out Krishna's orders. You are Krishna's devotee and are very dear to Him. Please benedict us to be engaged in Krishna's service.' In that way," Prabhupada said this feelingly; practically he had tears in his eyes, offering respect to Durga in relationship to Krishna.

Although his health was quite poor, Srila Prabhupada regularly attended *guru-puja* in Bombay. Once he said, "You should attend *guru-puja;* it's very important." He explained the song *sri-guru-carana-padma*, and at one point he came to a line and said, "What is that line? Every day you are singing these verses, but you do not know what they mean." He was cross with us. He considered *guru-puja* very significant.

The last Bombay *pandal* program that Srila Prabhupada attended was March 23 and 24 in 1977. Srila Prabhupada's health was extremely bad. He was so weak that he couldn't get onto the stage on his own strength. Bhavananda and Tamal Krishna Maharaj would carry Prabhupada onto the stage and deposit him on the *asana*. The first day Prabhupada seemed to have no energy. He had Bhavananda read from the Second Canto of *Bhagavatam*, *sva-vid-varahostra-kharaih samstutah purusah pasuh*, and then Prabhupada spoke. His opening words were "I have come to encourage you and be encouraged by you." Prabhupada didn't say much, just a little, and then he had Bhavananda read more, and Prabhupada sat, exhausted. Bhavananda read, Prabhupada said a few words, Bhavananda read, Prabhupada said a little more, Bhavananda read more, and then Prabhupada said more. Soon Prabhupada was speaking and speaking, and soon he was roaring. Prabhupada got so inspired that he began preaching with triple strength, and by the end of the lecture he was full of power and energy and strong preaching. He finished his talk—and then called for questions. One person said, "When chanting, you chant the name of Rama as well as Krishna. I see a picture of Krishna, but I do not see any picture of Rama." Prabhupada said, "The name is there." And again the man was saying, "But there's no picture." And Prabhupada said, "But the name is there!" Prabhupada just strongly preached that there's no difference between the name and the person whose name it is, and he just drove that point home.

Another time at this *pandal* program, a person with a sophisticated, intellectual demeanor said, "Sir, can you prove by logic that there is God?" Prabhupada said, "You do not know what is logic." Again the man said, "Sir, can you prove by logic that there is God?" Prabhupada said, "You do not know what is logic!" And a third time, "Sir, by logic can you prove. . . ?" "You do not know what is logic. There is a mother, material nature, and there are children, the living entities. Therefore, there must be a father. That's logic. Now take it." The crowd cheered. It was great how Prabhupada finished: "That's logic. Now take it."

Prabhupada talked about how one could become an animal in the next life, and a man stood up and said, "If I become an animal, I'll have the consciousness of an animal, and I'll be happy living as an animal—it will not be bad." Prabhupada said, "If it is not bad, then that is all right." Then he paused and said, "But we do not think that kind of life is very nice." The man sat down.

Once Prabhupada was sitting in an airport with the devotees, and someone brought *prasadam*. They offered it to Srila Prabhupada, Prabhupada took a little, and then he said, "Now distribute." Many devotees were in the airport, and many other people were there also. A devotee asked, "Should we distribute the *prasadam* to the general public?" Prabhupada said, "No, charity begins at home."

At one of Prabhupada's airport departures a devotee toddler walked a few steps away to explore the airport. Prabhupada said, "Oh, he is very brave." After a few more steps the child looked around, and when he didn't see his mother his face withered, and he began to cry. Prabhupada said, "That's like our position—we want to become independent, but when we become independent we are in so much difficulty."

Once, in ISKCON's early years, when Achyutananda Maharaj and two others were the only ISKCON devotees in India, Achyutananda Maharaj sent us an article of some discussions that he'd had with His Holiness Sridhar Maharaj. He included a cover letter to explain the article, and he said that Sridhar Maharaj was Prabhupada's *siksa guru.* Satsvarupa Maharaj wrote to Srila Prabhupada to ask if we should print these discussions with Sridhar Swami and if we should mention that "he is your *siksa guru.*" Prabhupada said that yes, the article could be printed, that the conclusions were in agreement, that it's understood that if we publish something in our magazine we endorse the conclusions. He said, "But it should be B. R. Sridhar Maharaj. Sridhar Swami was another man." (Sridhar Swami was the original commentator on *Srimad-Bhagavatam.*) And Srila Prabhupada said tersely, "There is no need of mentioning *siksa guru* in this connection."

In India, someone had improperly canvassed Achyutananda Maharaj to convince him that he needed a *siksa guru,* and Prabhupada understood that this was an attempt to alienate Achyutananda from Prabhupada and to bring him into some other society. Prabhupada had written to Achyutananda to leave that place and go to Srila Sridhar Maharaj, and he had instructed Achyutananda, "If you are actually serious to take instructions from a siksa guru, I can refer you to one who is most highly competent of all my god-brothers. This is B.R. Sridhar Maharaj, whom I consider to be even my *siksa guru*, so what to speak of the benefit that you can have from his association." So that was the basis of the statement that Achyutananda Maharaj had written to us. But when it came to publishing in *Back to Godhead* that Srila Sridhar Maharaj is Prabhupada's *siksa guru*, Prabhupada said, "There is no need of mentioning *siksa guru* in this connection."

There are various things that Prabhupada didn't do that have somehow become ISKCON convention, and we can mention some of them. One is that it has become a fashion for devotees to place their *brahmana* thread under their *dhoti* when they chant their *gayatri mantra*. It seems that someone read a statement saying that the thread should be covered with your cloth so it is not visible. But Srila Prabhupada never did that. Prabhupada sometimes chanted with his hand extended so you could see his fingers and his thread. Prabhupada didn't put his hand under his *dhoti* to hide his thread.

Sometimes devotees think that before chanting each round of *japa* one should chant the Panca Tattva *mantra—sri-krsna-caitanya prabhu nityananda sri-advaita gadadhara srivasadi-gaura-bhakta-vrnda*—on the head *japa* bead. That's another thing that Prabhupada never instructed us to do. I was at many initiations when Prabhupada said, "Start on one side of the head bead and chant Hare Krishna, Hare Krishna, Krishna Krishna, Hare Hare/ Hare Rama, Hare Rama, Rama Rama, Hare Hare on each bead until you come to the other side of the head bead. Don't cross over the head bead, but turn the beads around and come back. In this way one round, another round, another round." He didn't instruct us to chant the Panca Tattva *mantra* before each round.

In my experience, Prabhupada always did *kirtan* in the same way. In the morning he would chant *Gurvastakam,* then the Panca

Tattva *mantra (sri-krishna-caitanya prabhu nityananda sri-advaita gadadhara srivasadi-gaura-bhakta-vrnda)*, then the Hare Krishna *mantra,* and then he would stop. He would begin very, very slowly, he would gradually, gradually, gradually build up speed, reach a crescendo, and then he would stop and chant the *prema-dvani mantras.* And in the evening in the old days, when there was *kirtan* Mondays, Wednesdays and Fridays, Prabhupada would very slowly chant all of the verses of the *Mangalacarana.* Then he would chant the Panca Tattva *mantra,* then the Hare Krishna *mantra,* again gradually building up the tempo and then stopping. There was nothing else in Prabhupada's *kirtan.* There were no *nitai-gaura haribols;* there were no Deity names. Prabhupada loved the Deities more than anyone, but he didn't chant any names of particular Deities. These things were added later.

Prabhupada never referred to Subhadra-devi as "Lady Subhadra." Devotees seem to have picked that up from the British: If it's Lord Randolph, then it must be Lady Such-and-such. But for Prabhupada it was always Subhadra-devi, never "Lady Subhadra," any more than it was "Lady Radharani." It's not that because we refer to "Lord Jagannatha" it then becomes "Lady Subhadra," and "Lord Krishna and Lady Radharani," unless we're going to enter into British titles of nobility with countesses and duchesses and so on.

Someone asked Srila Prabhupada if the Universal Form was just for this universe or whether it encompassed many universes. Prabhupada said, "One universe is enough for you."

Prabhupada showed an exceedingly deep sense of duty. Many times he expressed that he was carrying out his duty to his spiritual master. I related that story of when Prabhupada conducted a big initiation and everyone was in ecstasy and Prabhupada said, "We have increased the *parampara* from Chaitanya Mahaprabhu." It was a matter of duty. Prabhupada was so balanced. He wasn't carried away by giddy enthusiasm, he wasn't depressed by setbacks, he wasn't stopped by anything. He had a duty to perform, and he carried out that duty. As a matter of duty he accepted the personal praise and gifts that were offered to him and offered them to his spiritual master and, through the *parampara,* to Krishna. The translating and publishing that he did, his priorities, the way he trained his disciples, was all in line with the duty that he'd been given by his spiritual master. And Prabhupada performed that duty with such commitment. Prabhupada was very serious about the duties that he performed, and at the same time he was joyful, he was jolly. Prabhupada said that the first symptom of a self-realized person is that he's jolly. Prabhupada could tell jokes. He could make plays on words. He could relax and have a good time with the devotees. And he could be cutting. He could be withering when he wanted to criticize. He could be sarcastic. He could be insistent. He could be many things. But it was all in line with his duty as a servant of his spiritual master and a servant of Krishna. That quality of Srila Prabhupada's stands out in my mind.

TAPE 41

Mahamaya dasi
Govinda dasi
Tulsi das
Kulashekhara das
Svavasa das
Mahavir das

Mahamaya: Prabhupada's books were so transcendental that I couldn't believe there was somebody on this planet that could write them. Although everybody in the temple knew Prabhupada, I was thinking cynically, "Does the person who wrote these books really exist?"

The night before I was initiated, we arrived in New York from Washington, D.C. We missed Prabhupada's New York airport arrival because our temple president, Damodar, felt that our business was to stay out on *sankirtan*.

Since Prabhupada was having initiations every morning for a week in New York, every night he lectured on *Bhagavad-gita*. So, the hot July night just before my initiation, I went into the temple room, which was packed with devotees, and waited for Prabhupada to come through the doors. I still doubted, "Is he really going to walk through those doors?" Kirtiraj prabhu was tapping devotees on the shoulder saying, "There's not enough room in the temple for everybody and there are people in the hallway who have never seen Prabhupada. So can you please leave?" He asked me this, but I had just arrived and, although Prabhupada had been there for a couple of days, I had never seen him. So I didn't budge. When Prabhupada walked through the doors all my doubts completely went out the window. I felt as if I was seeing an old, old friend who I hadn't seen in so long that I had forgotten about him.

Govinda: Gary and I were well situated in Texas, when we were mystically, incredibly drawn to the Haight-Ashbury area 1,500 miles away just a couple of months before Prabhupada arrived there. In San Francisco we saw some flyers that said, "The Swami is coming to town," "Chant and be high forever," this sort of thing. Gary looked at one of these flyers and said, "When this Swami comes to town, we'll go see him and we'll do whatever he says to do." We went to Frederick Street and learned about the classes and Mukunda das, who later became Mukunda Goswami, arranged for us to visit Prabhupada. In our first private meeting, Prabhupada was sitting in a lounge chair in the sunlight looking effulgent and peaceful near some bay windows in his apartment. I sat in another chair opposite him and Gary sat on the floor. Prabhupada began to ask us questions about our lives, who we were, where we had come from, what we were doing. He was personally interested in us, as he was in each of his disciples. We told him that we were artists and had studied art. He asked about our parents, our family. In the course of the conversation, I told him that I had traveled all over Europe and had studied art in various places, and he was quite surprised. He raised his eyes and said, "Oh, you have traveled so much?" I looked like I was 16, although I was actually 19 or 20. I said, "Yes, Swamiji, but none of it has made me happy." He smiled and said, "Ah, that is required, to be disgusted with material life."

Tulsi: I was initiated with Jayatirtha, Ujjvala, and some others. We sat on the floor with Prabhupada and watched him chant on our beads and do the fire sacrifice. When Prabhupada said, "Your name is Tulsi das," somehow or other I got a shocked look on my face. Prabhupada said, "Is that all right?" I said, "Oh, yes, Prabhupada!" That was my first personal interaction with Prabhupada. I was a new devotee and I hardly recognized any of the names, but because we'd done *tulasi* worship I knew the name Tulsi das.

Mahamaya: When they called me I went to the *vyasasana*. Aravinda, sitting to Prabhupada's side, said my initiated name—Mahamaya—and I was bowled over when I heard him say it. Then, when Prabhupada said my name there was shocked silence in the temple room. Prabhupada started laughing and then everyone laughed, including me. Prabhupada said, "The illusory energy is not all bad. For one who does not want to serve Krishna, the illusory energy is there." He gave the example that just as there are phases of the moon, so Mahamaya is a phase of Radharani's energy. Being in front of him I felt that he was seeing me—not the layers of false ego that I thought I was—but the soul, and it was a wonderful experience. He was definitely lifting me to his platform.

Govinda: At the time of my initiation, there were no *saris*—most of us didn't know what *saris* were. I had been an art student, and art students wore jeans. So I was initiated in paint-stained beige jeans. It didn't seem to matter to Srila Prabhupada. That was what our life was like at that time. During my initiation, I saw him put colored dyes down and build the fire, and I thought, "What is the depth of meaning to this? What is really going on?" I didn't have any background information. *Bhagavad-gita* wasn't printed yet. The only thing we had were Prabhupada's three *Srimad Bhagavatam* volumes, which we read right away. I had some misgivings during my initiation, so afterwards I went upstairs to visit Srila Prabhupada and I told him that I didn't feel liberated. I thought that when I got initiation, by golly, it was going to be immediate *nirvana*. Prabhupada was very patient with me. He said, "Just see the fan over here," as there was a fan on in the corner. "If I unplug it, it may spin a few more times. But because it has been unplugged, it will eventually stop. So it's like that. Although your material life may not cease immediately, because it has been unplugged, it will spin a few more times. But just follow the process as I have told you." He explained the concept very beautifully and gently. Then he gave us our first job—to make a four-foot-by-four-foot Radha-Krishna painting.

Kulashekhara: I had studied the pronunciation for the *Sri Isopanisad* with Pradyumna in New York, but I only knew the first six verses. Now, it's said that the *guru* knows everything about the disciple, and he's expert in engaging the disciple and using anything the disciple has to offer. So when an impersonal *mayavadi* swami came to visit Prabhupada at Bury Place, Prabhupada gave him all respects and had me put a cushion down for him. Then Prabhupada said, "Please make up a plate of fruits." I ran down, made a fruit plate, returned and offered it to Prabhupada, who said, "No, offer it to our guest." I offered it to the swami, then offered it to Prabhupada and Prabhupada said, "Sit down." I sat down. Prabhupada looked at the swami and said, "My boys all know Sanskrit." I thought, "Oh, no, what is he up to now?" Prabhupada, beaming, looked at me and said, "Chant *Sri Isopanisad.*" I started chanting, *om purnam adah purnam idam, purnat purnam udacyate, purnasya purnam adaya*...in perfect meter, as best I could. I got up to the fourth verse and thought, "Prabhupada, I only know six," but I kept going, I had faith. I got up to the fifth verse and I was sweating, but I kept going. When I started on the sixth verse, I felt like Draupadi about to come unraveled. Mentally I was saying to Prabhupada, "Prabhupada, I only know six, I only know six." On the second line in the sixth verse, Prabhupada looked at me and said, "That will be enough, you can go now." Even though I only had that little bit of knowledge, he used it perfectly and got the maximum value out of it. That was a nice experience.

Mahamaya: Every night there was a program at the *pandal*, and once, when Prabhupada had asked for questions at the end of his lecture, a challenging man came up to the microphone and said, "Can you show me a miracle?" We thought he was demanding that Prabhupada produce ashes in his hands like Sai Baba and others. Prabhupada looked at the 150 devotees sitting on the stage in front of him, swooped his hand to indicate us and said, "This is my miracle. I have changed these *mlecchas* and *yavanas* into Vaishnavas." We all cheered, "*Haribol! Jaya!*" We were so happy to be his examples of success.

Govinda: Srila Prabhupada knew that we were art students and he immediately engaged us as artists. His very first project was to have me paint a four-foot-by-four-foot painting of Radha-Krishna from the cover of his *Srimad-Bhagavatam*. Then he had me paint a four-foot-by-three-foot painting of him sitting on the *vyasasana* with a painting of Lord Chaitanya dancing in a *sankirtan* party hanging behind him, and specifically with Lord Chaitanya's foot touching his head. What I found so significant in this is that Srila Prabhupada engaged people in the work for which they had a natural propensity. Since the people already had an inclination to work in this particular way, doing that same work for Krishna gave them a taste for devotional service.

Svavasa: Throughout the morning walk all I could think about was how to maneuver myself to the front to say something because I felt I'd never get the opportunity again. On this walk, a devotee was asking Prabhupada intimate questions about Radha and Krishna's pastimes. Prabhupada briefly answered his questions and then continued chanting *japa*. This devotee would persist in asking more questions. Prabhupada didn't exhibit anger about the questions, but it wasn't an enlivening and powerful discussion. Srila Prabhupada was not absorbed in it.

That morning the walk wasn't very long. When we turned around to return I became nervous because I had little time left to say something to Srila Prabhupada and I tried to develop enough courage to do it. Finally I thought, "I've got to do this. I cannot hesitate." I zigzagged through the crowd of *sannyasis*. Doing that excited me, but I was fearful of offending Prabhupada and fearful of saying something insignificant. I yelled out, "Srila Prabhupada!" It was so startling that Prabhupada and all the devotees stopped in the middle of the street. They thought it was some crazy guy. Everyone looked at me. Out of complete anxiety I started saying, "Srila Prabhupada, we want to please you. We're distributing books at O'Hare Airport," and I told him the statistics of how many books we distributed and how we were doing it. I said everything I could say and repeatedly said, "We just want to please you, Srila Prabhupada." Srila Prabhupada looked at me throughout the whole thing, which took a matter of seconds, but it meant minutes to me—my throat became choked up and my mouth became dry. At one point all I could hear was my heart beating fast. And then I was finished. I stood there before Srila Prabhupada. Prabhupada could see I was excited and he was merciful, kind, peaceful and calming. He said, "Thank you." Then what shocked me was that Prabhupada, with his calm demeanor, wonderfully encouraged me by turning to all the devotees and saying, "Just see, this is my real devotee," referring to the book distributors. At the time I was overwhelmed with emotions, but later I thought about what happened and I felt that this was my life instruction from Srila Prabhupada. I felt that it was something that Srila Prabhupada was telling me and it meant everything. Even now, so many years later, I consider that to be the most important event in my life in Krishna consciousness.

Govinda: A significant thing that happened in Boston was that Swamiji became Srila Prabhupada. Gaurasundar was studying various forms of address in Sanskrit and he learned that "ji" is an affectionate form of address, which was news to us. I was sitting in Srila Prabhupada's room taking dictation, as I often did, and Gaurasundar, at the doorway, said, "Swamiji, is it okay if I call Govinda dasi 'Govindaji'?" Swamiji said, "No, 'ji' is a third-class form of address. You should not." I said, "Why are we calling you Swamiji if it's a third-class form of address?" He said, "It is not very important." I said, "No, it is very important. What is the best thing we can call you?" Swamiji said, "You could call me Gurudeva or Guru Maharaj or Srila Prabhupada." I said, "Which of those three is best?" and Swamiji said, "Srila Prabhupada is nice." I said, "Okay," and told all the devotees. From that day he was no longer Swamiji but Srila Prabhupada.

Mahavir: After the temple opening in Brazil, I arrived in Mayapur just before the festival. I was a young *brahmachari* and I was distracted—I wanted to become a *sannyasi.* I wanted to grow and get more prominent so Prabhupada would see me. Unfortunately in my case, beneath the surface there were other things that I wanted also.

It was the first time I'd been to India and I felt it was an incredible place, huge and beautiful and powerful. Out loud I said to myself, "I would love to manage this place." When I said that, although I wasn't aware of who he was, Jayapataka Maharaj was sitting next to me. Late that night Hari Sauri prabhu told me, "Prabhupada would like to see you." When I went in the room, there was Hridayananda Maharaj, Jayapataka Maharaj and Srila Prabhupada. Prabhupada said to me, "So you'd like to stay here?" I was overwhelmed that a question was being directed at me and I said, "Yes." They talked about it a bit. Prabhupada wanted Bhavananda to go up and down the Ganges preaching from a boat, and he wanted Jayapataka Maharaj to preach to politicians and Indians, so help was needed in Mayapur. Since I was Canadian, which helped visa-wise, and since I was a manager, I was targeted.

After I walked out of the room what I had said yes to hit me—in Brazil I was the big honcho. My doubts got so heavy that I changed my mind and asked Prabhupada if I could go back to Brazil. Prabhupada agreed, “Okay, you don’t have to stay, you can go back.” But later I was asked back into his room and Prabhupada said, “Have you made your mind up yet? Do you want to stay?” I was under the impression I was already released, but I couldn’t say no to Srila Prabhupada. I knew you’re supposed to do what he asked you to do. So I said yes, but when I walked out of the room it hit me again. I went back in and said, “Srila Prabhupada, I don’t know what the devotees in Brazil are going to do. There’s 40, 50 people there already, a BBT, temples, but I’m the only one there who has had any experience. I need to go back.” Prabhupada said, “Okay,” but sometime later he again asked me if I would stay in Mayapur and again I said yes. Afterwards I got completely overwhelmed again, went back, asked if I could leave, and again he said, “Okay.” I don’t remember how many times this went back and forth. Finally one day during his massage he turned to me and kindly said, “In the spiritual world, we all have different relationships with Krishna. So it’s okay, you can go back to Brazil.”

Govinda: After Srila Prabhupada’s stroke, he and Gaurasundar and I were living in New Jersey for three weeks in the spring of 1968, and during that time Gaurasundar was called to an Army draft appointment in New York. Gaurasundar and I were in anxiety because he didn’t want to fight a war that he didn’t believe in and that Srila Prabhupada did not support. Before Gaurasundar left to catch the train to New York, he bowed down to Swamiji, who said, “Don’t worry, Krishna will protect you. He will take care of everything.” That day Srila Prabhupada mentioned Gaurasundar several times and was thinking of him. In the evening when Gaurasundar returned, he came up the stairs with a big smile on his face. He was very happy. Immediately Swamiji called Gaurasundar into his room, “What happened?” Gaurasundar explained that he was wearing a silken cord with a three-inch high *murti* of Lord Jagannatha around his neck and he also had big red chanting beads, and the doctors, who had never seen such odd things, decided he was not psychiatrically competent for the Army. Srila Prabhupada said, "Yes, if we are sincere, Krishna will protect us. He will make all arrangements. You have chosen Krishna's service, not the Army's service, so Krishna has arranged everything perfectly."

Tulsi: When Prabhupada came to Los Angeles in 1974, I was temple president and I went on his morning walks and attended his afternoon darshans in the little garden in the back of the temple. One evening there was quite a few devotees in that garden when I came in and Jayatirtha said, "Prabhupada, I'd like to introduce you to our new temple president, Tulsi das." Prabhupada said, "Oh, I know Tulsi das." In my heart in a nanosecond I felt really good, "Prabhupada knows me! Prabhupada recognizes me!" Then Prabhupada said, "Why did you leave Bombay?" I went crashing to the bottom, my heart was beating loudly, and I started making excuses, "I was having some trouble with the management," "I was doing this or that." Finally I looked straight in Prabhupada's eyes and said, "Srila Prabhupada, I was in *maya*." Prabhupada said, "Yes!" and went on to give a lecture about the power of *maya*. That moment in the L.A. garden was a highlight for me.

Govinda: Srila Prabhupada had several disciples in Hawaii who were intelligent and charismatic and had misled some of the more simple devotees. Since I had been the first devotee in Hawaii, I felt protective of the others—they were like my children—and I was in anxiety about what was going on. I explained to Prabhupada how these people were misleading devotees, changing the philosophy and so forth. Prabhupada calmly said, "The mouse respects the cat, and the cat respects the dog. The dog respects the wolf, and the wolf respects the tiger. But we see they are all animals." In other words, from his perspective, all of the people that he had to deal with on this planet were on the level of animals. Prabhupada was coming from Krishnaloka while we were coming from low-grade backgrounds and once we realized this, there would be no chance of our getting puffed up and trying to outguess him, edit him, change his ideas or think we could do better. It's impossible, we can't. I saw many instances of this.

Unfortunately, one close-to-home instance was my own husband, Gaurasundar, who I loved very much. He was brilliant, he was educated and he was a nice devotee. He was studying Sanskrit and Bengali, and did the transliteration for the first part of *Caitanya-caritamrta*. He took Prabhupada on walks and massaged Prabhupada every day. I give him all credit for the wonderful service he did. But later on he left and although Prabhupada knew I was quite attached, he many times commented to me, "Gaurasundar is suffering from too much intelligence. He has the disease of being too intelligent. He thinks he knows more than his *guru*." This was Gaurasundar's flaw. He was brilliant in every respect. But as soon as a person thinks he knows more than his *guru*, the fall down begins.

Kulashekhara: In the early '70s, I'd been preparing to take *sannyasa* and Srila Prabhupada was giving me special attention. I went on all the morning walks—on one walk I had a beautiful vision of Prabhupada's skin changing from flesh to golden silk.

When the time had come, I got fresh cloth, shaved up, went to Shyamasundar and said, "Shyamasundar, I'd like to see Srila Prabhupada." He said, "Why do you want to see Srila Prabhupada?" I said, "I want to ask him for *sannyasa*." He said, "Kulashekhara, do you really want to take *sannyasa*?" I said, "I've been preparing for it for years and I'm ready." Shyamasundar said, "Do you ever think of sex? Do you ever think of marriage?" I said, "Sometimes the thoughts cross my mind, but I don't pay any attention to them." He said, "Kulashekhara, maybe you should get married." I said, "What?" He said, "This is a big decision. This is for the rest of your life. Go away and think about it because if you ever think of sex, you shouldn't take *sannyasa*." I didn't sleep much that night. Trying to be truthful with myself, I thought, "Sometimes I do think of sex life—it does cross my mind. Maybe I am being totally false. I should probably get married." Then I started thinking, "Who do I want to marry?" I thought about the different *brahmacharinis* and which one would be best for me to marry. I more or less went through the complete ceremony. The next morning I went back to Shyamasundar and said, "Shyamasundar, I think you're right. I should probably get married." He said, "Who do you want to marry?" I told him the name of the girl and he said, "That's a good choice. Go in and see Srila Prabhupada. Just knock on the door." I said, "Great." I knocked on the door, went in and Prabhupada was beaming at me. I paid obeisances, got up and sat there. Prabhupada said, "Yes?" I said, "Srila Prabhupada, I'd like to get married." He said, "What? What? Who has done this do you?" I was devastated. I said, "Prabhupada, I went to see Shyamasundar..." and he said, "Shyamasundar!" He said, "Pradyumna, get Shyamasundar in here immediately!" Prabhupada was furious. I sat there, looking at the floor and feeling like a dog. Shyamasundar came in and Prabhupada said, "Who are you to tell my *brahmachari* to get married?" Shyamasundar said, "Prabhupada, he said he wanted to take *sannyasa*, and I told him if he ever thinks of sex life..." Prabhupada said, "Everyone with a material body thinks of sex life." Prabhupada looked at me with compassion and said, "Look at him. He's finished." Then he said, "You have no right to tell my *brahmacharis* to get married, ever." I don't remember much after that.

Tulsi: I'd wanted to get married for some time, but Ramesvar and a couple of others were convincing me, "You should take *sannyasa*," and, although I didn't accept the idea in my heart, it seemed that Prabhupada was giving *sannyasa* to everybody as a gift of mercy. One day about 30 devotees were in a *darshan* with Prabhupada, Ramesvar was standing behind him, I was 15 feet in front and Jayatirtha was beside me. When there was a lull in the discussion Ramesvar pointed at me. I stammered, "Srila Prabhupada?" Prabhupada said, "Yes?" "I've been talking with some devotees and there's a thought that it would be good for me to take *sannyasa*." Prabhupada said, "How long have you been a *brahmachari*?" I said, "Five years." He said, "Very nice. What about the butter?" I said, "What about the butter?" Jayatirtha whispered to me, "You know, women—fire, butter." Instead of being truthful with Prabhupada and saying, "I'd really like to have some female association and all that goes with it," I said, "Prabhupada, as long as I'm traveling and preaching, everything is fine." Prabhupada said, "Okay, you can take *sannyasa*." I said, "Should we bring my name up in Mayapur and then wait a year?" He said, "No, you take this year." Oh no! What am I going to do? I'm going to take *sannyasa* in a few months time! I didn't envision myself like any of the other *sannyasis*, traveling and preaching—I was a manager.

After leaving L.A. Prabhupada went to Hawaii, and there was a boat there that the devotees wanted but nobody could skipper. I love the water, I've always lived on the water, and I thought, "This is a nice idea." I wrote a proposal for a traveling boat *sankirtan* party. I could manage the boat, sail it into towns and preach—it would be fun—and it seemed like something Prabhupada wanted. Ramesvar saw it as a way to increase book distribution. Prabhupada read my proposal and wrote back a short paragraph, "Why waste time sailing? Better to fly instead." I accepted what Prabhupada said, but I still had *sannyasa* looking at me. What am I going to do? Prabhupada was in Bombay and Ramesvar had Harikesh bring this boat idea up again. Prabhupada asked, "Why is Tulsi so anxious to do this?" Harikesh said, "Prabhupada, he's in L.A. and he's agitated by all the women there. With the boat, he'll always be out." Then Prabhupada wrote a scathing letter to Ramesvar, who wouldn't show it to me for years. In that letter Prabhupada saved me. He said I was a rascal, a fool, and a bad choice for *sannyasa*. When I heard that Prabhupada said I couldn't take *sannyasa*, in the core of my being I was thankful. I felt saved.

I had been duplicitous when I told my spiritual master that as long as I'm traveling and preaching, then I'm fine. I had been stupid. First, I had asked to take *sannyasa* and second, I was not straightforward with Prabhupada. If I'd have said, "Prabhupada, I'm not *sannyasa* material. I would like to get married and have a nice wife," he'd have probably instructed me down those lines. But I didn't give him the information he needed to give me those instructions. But by his grace he straightened it out anyway.

Mahamaya: As the others were leaving, my god-sister said, "Should we leave too, Srila Prabhupada?" Prabhupada said, "Not unless you have some questions." We said, "No, we don't have any questions," and we both offered our obeisances. But we did have questions and as we got up from paying obeisances, we started asking questions. She said, "Srila Prabhupada, in yesterday's *darshan* you said that a *sannyasi's* business is to preach, a *brahmachari's* business is to assist the *sannyasis*, and a *grihastha's* business is to do Deity worship. What about the *brahmacharinis*? Can we also do Deity worship?" At the time the *brahmacharinis* were doing most of the Deity worship for Radha-Rasabehari in the old Juhu temple. Prabhupada said, "Yes, you can also do Deity worship," and she was satisfied with that answer.

Then it was my turn. I had heard from a friend, Cintamani prabhu, that, since her husband, Sudama, had taken *sannyasa,* Prabhupada had given her personal instructions on two different occasions to make Jagannatha her husband, Subhadra her daughter, and Balaram her son. I had also heard from Nandalal prabhu that in Los Angeles Prabhupada had given her a silver Deity of Krishna right from his desk and told her to worship this Deity. These ladies were in a renounced position—one's husband was a *sannyasi* and the other was older and didn't want to get married. I was 29, and I thought I was very old. I wasn't going to get married and I wanted an instruction like them. I wanted to ask, "Can I have my own Deity?" but I couldn't do it because I didn't have a close, personal relationship with Prabhupada. Instead I said, "Srila Prabhupada, can devotees have their own Deities?" and his answer was "No. That will distract from the temple Deity." I took that instruction to mean that if you get absorbed in your own Deity worship, then you won't want to take the time to worship the temple Deity.

Govinda: In Los Angeles in September of 1968 we were going to record the Govinda record album with Prabhupada reading his spiritual master's Preface to *Brahma-samhita*, "The materialistic demeanor cannot stretch to the transcendental autocrat..." Prabhupada asked me to type this preface and then he read it to me a couple of times to see how it sounded. He would read things to me because I knew English fairly well. I listened very carefully and there was one word—"analogously"—that he pronounced "ana-*lo*-gously." I had never corrected Srila Prabhupada before. In fact, I loved it when he called watermelons "waterlemons." And when he called for some "antelope," I never told him, "That's called cantaloupe." I was fine with that. I had a very motherly relationship with Prabhupada and I thought whatever he said was wonderful. But because people who may not understand his accent would be hearing this album and because this recording was for posterity, I thought, "Oh, you want your *guru* to come with the best foot forward." I was not on an ego trip but had innocent and good intentions. I said, "Srila Prabhupada, I think that word is pronounced 'an-*al*-ogously." He looked at me and said, "You pronounce it your way, and I'll pronounce it my way."

Mahavir: Prabhupada knew I was young and passionate and when I got to Mayapur the first thing he said to me was, "Do you want to take *sannyasa* or do you want to get married?" So I knew he knew, and at that moment I had already resigned from the idea of taking *sannyasa*.

After Prabhupada had first asked me to help the Mayapur management, I set up my little office in a corner and without any instruction from anybody I immediately changed the cleanup time and generally created havoc. When Prabhupada returned from his morning walk and went into the temple room for *gurupuja*, the temple floor was wet because of my bad timing. Meanwhile I was somewhere else, changing something else. Prabhupada started going upstairs to his room while I was coming downstairs with a big smile, expecting glorification. Prabhupada pointed his cane at me and said, "Who do you think you are? You're the king?" It was just a few days before the Mayapur festival and all my older god-brothers who I looked up to were standing there looking at me. Out of embarrassment I had an out-of-body experience. I went up to a cloud and watched the conversation. I was young, had been doing something I shouldn't have been doing, got chastised, and took it hard. To make it worse, before this I'd been on the morning walks everyday, agitating people, butting in front of the *sannyasis,* and Sudama Maharaj had told me that when I stopped going Prabhupada had said, "Where's Mr. Brazil?" and had started chastising me, "Oh, he thinks he's the king." Sudama Maharaj said, "You are getting the mercy." But I thought, "Mercy? I'm just waiting for Krishna to take my life away."

Anyway, after the cleanup fiasco I went back to my room and became practically physically ill. I didn't want to go out in public. The next day I was lying in bed feeling like it was over for me. I was at rock bottom. I'd been preaching, opening centers, and I wanted my *guru* to be happy with me but instead he yelled at me worse than my dad ever had. I heard the greeting of the Deities and then Hari Sauri prabhu came in and said, "Prabhupada wants you at *gurupuja.*" I thought, "Oh, no," it just got worse. But I did what I was told. I took a quick shower, got my *dhoti* on, and went to the back of the temple room, which was full, just in time for *Gurupuja.* I hid behind Gurudas, who was a good size then, and saw Guru Kripa prabhu grab the *mridanga* to begin leading when Prabhupada stopped him. At Prabhupada's indication the devotees moved aside to make a direct channel between Srila Prabhupada and me. Prabhupada pointed at me and said to Guru Kripa, "Let him lead. He likes to chant." At that moment I melted. Prabhupada had given me the most severe chastising of my life, which till today helps me, and I had also made contact with him as my father. It was an emotional morning program for me.

It was the next day that I went to his room and asked if I could go back to Brazil, and that's when he let me go. But during these conversations he had also said to me, "You should be in India, it's good for you here."

Kulashekhara: The day after that *sannyasa* incident Srila Prabhupada let me have a private *darshan* with him to talk about the marriage system. I said, "Prabhupada, can you tell me about married life?" He said, "When the girl is 8, she is betrothed to a husband from the same social strata. The families have already worked out their astrological compatibility. Then from 8 till 12 or 14, the girl would go to her husband's house every day and his mother would train her how to take care of her son—the way he liked his food cooked and so on. Then as soon as she attained puberty, they would have sex life and she would never look at another man the rest of her life." He said, "That is marriage. Anything else, I do not know."

Govinda: At the Honolulu temple in Hawaii, one of Srila Prabhupada's disciples was a sculptor and Prabhupada spent a great deal of time giving us elaborate instructions on how to make Gaura-Nitai Deities. Afterwards the sculptor-devotee asked, "My wife would like to make silk, but in order to make silk you have to kill the silkworms. Is this okay?" After this devotee left, Srila Prabhupada expressed annoyance because he had given one instruction and instead there was talk of making silk. He said, "These Western disciples, they are so creative. Next they will be asking me if they can kill cows to make *mridangas*."

Mahavir: One morning in Vrindavan the American and European devotees complained to me that they wanted more fruit. At that time breakfast was *chapatis* and *kichari*, and lunch was *chapati, dahl*, rice and a *subji*. But I had already learned not to change anything, not to ruin a good thing. I went to Prabhupada and said, "Srila Prabhupada, the devotees want fruit in their diet." Prabhupada said, "Humans are grain eaters. If they want to eat fruit, then that's all they should eat. Don't change it." So I didn't. I was happy because the *chapatis*—fresh and hot and just a little burnt— and the *kichari* were the best. The Vrindavan *prasadam* was delicious.

Govinda: Each morning at the end of class in the Frederick Street temple, Srila Prabhupada would ask for relevant questions. One morning I wanted to hear the story of Lord Chaitanya falling in the water, but I was shy about asking since it wasn't relevant to the class. I raised my hand anyway and said, "Could you please tell the story about Lord Chaitanya falling into the water?" Prabhupada became totally quiet for about five minutes. I thought, "What have I done wrong now?" I didn't know what was going on and I was worried. Then he said, "Yes," and told the story of Lord Chaitanya falling in the water. Afterwards, the devotees said, "Didn't you see? There were tears running down his face. He was in complete ecstasy." I marveled at that. I began to see that when his Western children—we were just like children to him—asked about Lord Chaitanya it gave him great pleasure, great joy.

Tulsi: Jayatirtha was so tired that he was falling asleep and Prabhupada wouldn't let him drive from Laguna Beach to San Diego. So Jayatirtha approached me to drive Prabhupada. I felt that this was a great and rare opportunity. But in those days, we hardly slept. The only way I stayed awake in *Bhagavatam* class was to exercise my temple president privilege and stand up to fan Prabhupada for the whole class. I was just as tired as everybody else. While I was driving the hour-long drive from Laguna Beach to San Diego, I looked in the mirror and saw that Prabhupada was asleep. A bit later I looked in the mirror and Brahmananda was asleep. Then a bit later I looked over to Jayatirtha, who was riding in the shotgun seat, and he was asleep. I was the only one awake and I was dying to fall asleep. I couldn't roll down the window, I couldn't turn on the radio, I couldn't chant *japa* loud or anything. I was struggling and struggling with this—and I'd have probably fallen asleep and killed us all—but at the darkest moment when my eyes just wouldn't stay open, from the back seat of the car I heard Prabhupada softly clapping his hands to start a *kirtan*. Then everybody in the car gradually woke up and the four of us had a wonderful *kirtan* on the way to San Diego.

Kulashekhara: Once my father drove Prabhupada from the London airport to Bury Place in his white Jaguar Mark II, a car with red leather seats and an exceptionally smooth ride. Prabhupada sat in the front with my father and I sat in the back with Pradyumna and Shyamasundar. We were in the middle lane of a three-lane road by the British Museum when a red double-decker bus was in the lane to our right and another one was in the lane to our left. Then those two buses almost closed in on our car. It was very dangerous. My father spontaneously screamed, "*Haribol*," slammed down on the gas pedal, and our car took off through a small gap that opened between the buses. Prabhupada turned to my father and beamed at him. Years later my father wrote me, "Remember when I was driving Swamiji from the airport and those buses closed in on us and I screamed "*Haribol*!" and the buses parted just like the waves of the Red Sea parted for the Lord." My father equated the experience of the buses parting to the parting of the Red Sea. That was something special for me.

Govinda: We were in Boston in May of 1968 when a new *Back to Godhead* magazine was published with a black-and-white picture of Prabhupada on the back cover and the caption, "This man changed the world." It looked very slick for those days. Prabhupada called me in his room, handed it to me and said, "Look at this." I looked and thought, "What's wrong with it?" He said, "This is very serious. The spiritual master should never be referred to as a man. This consciousness, viewing the spiritual master as an ordinary man, even calling him a man, is the beginning of fall down." This seriously affected Prabhupada because one should never refer to or consider the spiritual master on the level of a man.

Mahavir: Once I was singing *Jasomatinandana* in a happy-go-lucky mood while I walked down the path on my way to the temple room. From Prabhupada's room I heard Prabhupada ask Jagadish, "Is that Mahavir? Tell him to come in." I quickly went in to Srila Prabhupada's room and Prabhupada said, "Where in the world are there rivers like the Ganges, the Krishna, the Yamuna? India has the most beautiful rivers. There's only one other place in the world that has a beautiful river, the St. Lawrence." It stunned me because I'm from Canada. I think Prabhupada spoke about the rivers in India in this way to give me the real picture—so that I wouldn't be in culture shock from India. Prabhupada talked about cleanliness and about how the *dhotis* of the local people looked dirty. He said, "Actually, none of those *dhotis* go 12 hours without being washed at least with water. Since the water has so much soil in it the clothes look gray—but they are always clean."

Govinda: Before they went to London to open a temple, Malati and her husband, Shyamasundar, Yamuna and Gurudas, and Janaki and Mukunda flew from San Francisco to Montreal to see Srila Prabhupada. Malati's new baby, Saraswati, was also with them. When Malati danced in kirtan, Saraswati was on her hip with legs and arms flopping.

When those devotees came to see Srila Prabhupada, Srila Prabhupada took little Saraswati, held her up over his head and said, "Do you remember me? I am your old friend." On many occasions Srila Prabhupada indicated that these children were special. By Srila Prabhupada's request they had been brought from higher dimensions to spread Lord Chaitanya's mission. One of the most important things we can do is to let the children know how much Srila Prabhupada counts on them, how much he cares about them, and how important they are to him. Whatever has happened is unfortunate. Srila Prabhupada loved the children and wanted to teach them everything.

Many years later I was in Dallas when Prabhupada was giving lectures about teaching the children not with a heavy hand but with love, disciplining them only with love. If you love them, they will respond, they will want to do things properly.

Kulashekhara: Since my mother and father had visited Prabhupada a few times, I spoke about my family with him when he said, "Because you are a devotee, twenty-eight generations of your family will be liberated." I said, "What do you mean by liberated, Prabhupada?" He said, "That means they will become devotees in their next life." I said, "Does that mean just my immediate family, like my mother and father and brothers and sisters, or does it mean my extended family, aunts and uncles . . .?" He said, "Extended family, everybody. Aunts, uncles, everybody, twenty-eight generations of your whole family become devotees."

Govinda: While Srila Prabhupada was in Los Angeles in 1968, we illustrated the *Bhagavad-gita* and *Teachings of Lord Chaitanya*. There were five drawings for *Teachings of Lord Chaitanya*, and they took quite a while. One was a picture of the Nawab coming to visit Rupa and Sanatana Goswamis, another was a picture of Lord Jagannatha in the Jagannatha Temple with Lord Chaitanya. At that time, I had no idea what the inside of the Jagannatha Temple looked like. Srila Prabhupada described how the interior was dark and how the *pujari* sat on the altar and handed down garlands. I did the drawings according to Srila Prabhupada's descriptions. Later when those five drawings were removed from the book, Srila Prabhupada was disgusted. He said, "Why they have removed these drawings from this book? Why they have removed them?" Srila Prabhupada had supervised every aspect of them and personally overseen them. And when he saw that the illustrations to *Krsna Book* had been removed he said, "Why they have removed these paintings? Those early paintings were full of *bhakti*." Even though the technical quality of the paintings might not have been perfect, their mood was very special.

Mahavir: Once in Prabhupada's garden my wife and I were speaking together in Portuguese while she took care of the plants and I fixed things. Through his window, Prabhupada yelled for me to come inside. I went inside the room and he said, "Are you speaking Mexican?" I said, "No, Prabhupada, Portuguese." Then he said, "You Americans ruin everything. One of you changes everything the person before you did. Then you go away and someone else comes and changes everything you did. When that person goes away another comes and changes things again. Stop changing everything. Just save it."

Since that day, that has stuck in my brain. Wherever I go, whatever I see and whatever needs to be fixed, I don't change it. I can still hear Prabhupada saying, "Don't change it." I just take what's there and improve on it—I try to make it better. Prabhupada's instruction was so overwhelmingly important that I still use it in my business and in management.

Govinda: When we were in Montreal it was Srila Prabhupada's birthday and I decided to celebrate it like Westerners do by baking a two-layer cake. I frosted it, put a bunch of candles on it, lit them all and then brought it into his room. His eyes were big with surprise to see me carrying a flaming cake and he said, "Oh?" I put it on the altar, offered it, then brought it over to him and said, "Srila Prabhupada, this is how we celebrate birthdays in America. If you blow out all the candles, you can make a wish." He blew out all the candles and then I said, "You don't have to tell anybody what you wished for." He said, "I wish only for Krishna's service." Then we enjoyed the cake, Western style.

Svavasa: I appreciate Prabhupada's strength—Prabhupada never gave up fighting for Krishna. One of my fondest thoughts is when Prabhupada was in New York at the time the anti-cult movement was prominent and giving us lots of trouble. Prabhupada said, "I want to fight for Krishna with my last breath." That statement was very significant and important to me. No matter what the circumstances Prabhupada would never give up. He was a warrior for Krishna. Whatever it took, it didn't matter. He would do anything for Krishna. He exhibited this strength on the Jaladuta before he came to America and he exhibited it in New York in the early days. Most people would have turned back, given up, but Prabhupada had a vision of so many temples, so many devotees. I personally appreciate Srila Prabhupada for his undaunting devotion and strength to the instruction of his spiritual master and, of course, to Krishna.

TAPE 42

Mulaprakriti dasi

Mulaprakriti: For two days Vishnujana Maharaj and a few other devotees preached to me so beautifully that I knew I was going to join. Then Srila Prabhupada arrived, and he was splendor on all levels. When I saw him I cried—he was the most beautiful person I had ever seen—and I knew immediately that he was my spiritual master.

Srila Prabhupada was excited that some of the book distributors had figured out how to sell books in many languages and that we were distributing books in countries where nobody else had before. When I went to train some book distributors in Hawaii, I would go to the airport wearing a *sari* and *tilak,* and one day when I returned and was walking across the temple lawn, Prabhupada saw me from his balcony. He called his servant, Upendra, and said, "She is coming from preaching?" Upendra said, "Yes, Prabhupada." Prabhupada said, "I would like to speak with her. Would she like to come up?" Upendra, who was my friend, ran down the stairs and said, "Mula! Prabhupada asked if you'd like to talk to him in his room right now!"

I had had a long day at the airport, my hair was standing in all directions, and I was nervous. I went up the stairs, not knowing what to expect. Prabhupada was sitting alone in his room at the desk that's still there now. I paid my obeisances and sat near the back. Prabhupada motioned for me to come closer. I came closer and he motioned for me to come closer still. Finally I scooted up next to his desk and he said, "Tell me about *sankirtan*. How is it going?" I was choking from nervousness and said, "Srila Prabhupada, people are taking your books. They like your books." He said, "Yes? They are liking?" I said, "Yes, Srila Prabhupada. And not only people in America, but people from all over the world." He said, "What kind of people did you distribute to today?" I strained my brain to remember and said, "Teachers and students and lawyers and mothers and old people—every kind of person." He said, "More? More types of people?" I was trying to think of more people and he leaned over, excited to hear, and said, "What are they saying?" I said, "They say that they're interested in this kind of knowledge." He said, "What do you say?" I said, "I say that it's transcendental knowledge you can't find in any other book. It will make you happy. It's about God and about love of God." He said, "Yes, this is very nice. I know what I want you to say." He asked Upendra to bring *Bhatavatam* Canto One, Part One, and he opened it right to the verse that says, "This Bhagavata Purana is as brilliant as the sun, and it has arisen just after the departure of Lord Krishna to His own abode, accompanied by religion, knowledge, etc. Persons who have lost their vision due to the dense darkness of ignorance in the age of Kali shall get light from this Purana." Prabhupada said, "See how beautifully *Srimad-Bhagavatam* sells itself. Anyone who heard this from *Srimad-Bhagavatam* would think, 'I must read that book, I must.' That's what you need to tell people. Tell them straight from *Srimad-Bhagavatam.* I am excited when I read *Srimad-Bhagavatam*, so certainly they will be as well."

Then he said, "You distribute books to people from which countries?" I started listing people from all the countries I could think of that we had ever distributed a book to, and he said, "More, more, more." He said, "I am sitting in my room absorbed in writing these literatures, and all the time I think about how these books are being received by the public. Book distribution is also popularization of this transcendental knowledge. I want this knowledge to be distributed in a way that people will appreciate it and I want it to be popularized everywhere."

It was a beautiful sunny day and Srila Prabhupada was beautiful, sitting sweetly and ecstatically with no shirt on, just his *sannyasa* cloth, and when he leaned forward to ask questions his eyes would get really big. I was young and enthusiastic and part of my book distribution technique was to sometimes interrupt people. So, at one point Srila Prabhupada started to ask me a question and when he hesitated, when he leaned back, I interrupted him to finish his question for him. At that moment, Prabhupada's *sannyasi* secretary happened to walk by, heard me interrupt Prabhupada, and loudly cleared his throat. I thought, "Oh, no!" I was so embarrassed. I closed my mouth and looked at Prabhupada. But Prabhupada finished the sentence and clarified it. We talked back and forth more and he told me beautiful sweet stories about salesmanship and about women and about preaching, and a few things about his own preaching. Then he started to make a very deep comment and again he hesitated for a second and again I interrupted, but this time I said something that wasn't what he was going to say. His *sannyasi* secretary, who was in the room, cleared his throat loudly for the second time and was furious with me.

I didn't know what to do. I was so fallen. I felt mortified and I thought my spiritual life was finished. I put my head down to make an obeisance and thought of getting out of the room backwards, but it was a long way to the door. I was down on the ground and it was very quiet. I peeked up with one eye and saw Srila Prabhupada bent way over his desk on his elbows, leaning forward right next to me, smiling beautifully and looking at me with great love. I didn't say anything but Prabhupada said to the secretary, who was standing there, "Just see, she is so enthusiastic." That was an enormous delivery of mercy that I shall never, ever forget.

As we were talking, Srila Prabhupada looked like a young boy. He was brilliant and was enjoying himself tremendously. I was also enjoying myself and giggling, although I don't remember what was so funny, but the mood was joyful. Then we heard a couple of bangs on the door and in came some temple managers, GBCs and other people. It was heavy-duty. One of them said, "Prabhupada, we have some issues we need to discuss with you," and immediately Prabhupada's face fell. He straightened up in his seat, looked at me and shrugged sadly that our conversation was over. At one point while he was talking to these managers he asked one of them, "How is your college preaching going?" That devotee said, "Prabhupada we very much like the preaching." Prabhupada said, "I hear many good things about the preaching," and pointed to me. Then he said, "Tell me," and the devotee started to describe his preaching. Prabhupada said, "And how are the books going?" The devotee said, "Prabhupada, we're not distributing your books at the colleges because we're not allowed to take any money. We give lectures and then we give out cookbooks." Prabhupada said, "I have not written any cookbook, have I? Have I written any cookbook?" The devotee said, "It's been compiled, and it has some philosophy in it." Prabhupada said, "Why do you think I am writing and writing day and night? Because I want these books to go out. You may give one lecture, but the chances are that it will go in one ear and go out the other. But if you give them just one of my books, it will stick." Then he said, "Okay, everyone out. I'm tired. We can discuss these things later." As I paid my obeisances and left, Prabhupada turned to me and said, "Thank you very much."

Every morning in Vrindavan Srila Prabhupada went on a short walk while a crew of us cleaned his rooms. It was my first time in Vrindavan and didn't know much about cleaning his rooms. However, the devotee in charge of cleaning, Daivishakti, was fastidious. She knew every tiny thing to do. She told me, "Clean Prabhupada's little desk upstairs because that's the tiniest area. Just clean it perfectly and remember to put everything back exactly the way it was." I was so nervous that I'd pick up something from that desk but couldn't remember where it was supposed to be put back down. And there were a lot of things on that desk. I started to sweat from nervousness but I dusted and did my best. Then Daivishakti said, "Prabhupada's coming! Prabhupada's coming!" I had a terrible feeling that I hadn't finished, I felt incomplete, but I had no choice. I ran downstairs and stood aside as Prabhupada went into his room. Then, with a terrible sense of shock, I noticed that Prabhupada went straight upstairs. I looked up, saw him sit down at his desk, and within a minute there was a loud, "*Haribol*! Who has cleaned this room?" Daivishakti ran up, came back down and said, "Mula, you messed up." I said, "I know. What did I do?" She said, "Prabhupada immediately noticed that his glass of water wasn't in place and the tiny silver lid for the glass wasn't dusted." I was amazed that Srila Prabhupada immediately saw that, and I've always remembered his standard of cleanliness. When I'm cleaning for Srila Prabhupada or for the Deities, I know that he's looking and can see every little thing that I might have missed.

Once we distributed a record number of books and, as a reward, got invited into Srila Prabhupada's garden for an afternoon *darshan*. It was a beautiful afternoon and just a few devotees were with Prabhupada, who was sitting regally on his dais, when a tall Indian gentleman wearing an orange *dhoti* and an Ivy League shirt and jacket, walked in. This man had been in the West for a while and was trying to integrate whatever little Krishna consciousness he had brought from India into his now westernized life. Srila Prabhupada was affectionate to him and the man was respectful to Srila Prabhupada. Prabhupada had this man sit by his side and in a masterful way Prabhupada discussed light and sweet things with him, like the weather and the garden. The man was excited and spoke affectionately to Srila Prabhupada. Then at one point the man said something impersonal and when Srila Prabhupada confronted him on it, the man balked. Prabhupada got a little heavier, saying, "You don't know that Krishna is a person, the Supreme Personality? This is all Krishna's. None of it is yours." The man looked to us for some moral support but we kept looking at Prabhupada and Prabhupada decided to give him a huge dose of mercy by getting heavier and heavier with him, "You are thinking that you are some professor, some *sannyasi*, but you are a fool. You are nonsense—you don't know anything. How can you masquerade as a teacher? You don't even know the basic teachings of *Bhagavad-gita*." The man said, "Ah, I have read *Bhagavad-gita*," and Prabhupada said, "No, you haven't because you don't know the simplest things. You are a fool, and you are a rascal." The man was extremely shocked and kept looking over at me, maybe because I was a girl, but I kept looking at Prabhupada, so the man looked back at Prabhupada—he had nowhere to go. Prabhupada leaned over and said, "You are a nonsense, a super fool and a demon! You are a demon!" At that point the man broke and said, "Yes, I am a nonsense, I am a rascal, I am demon," Prabhupada looked at him happily and nodded his head. The man paid obeisances in the dirt at Prabhupada's feet and started to cry and roll around a little. Then Prabhupada, like the most magnificent king, gently pulled his feet away, stood up and regally walked out with his head held high. A few of the *sannyasis* left with him, so just a couple of us were left in the garden, stunned and watching this man, who didn't realize that Prabhupada was gone. His eyes were closed and he said, "I am demon. I am such a demon!" After a little while he realized where he was, shook the dirt off himself, sat up, and looked at each of us with an innocent, blissful, beautiful smile. He said, "*Jaya! Jaya!* Hare Krishna!" and walked out the other door. That was the end of that.

During the later years in Los Angeles I had the privilege of cleaning Srila Prabhupada's bathroom. I used to get the nectar of the eucalyptus twigs he had used as toothbrushes and I used to collect the bathtub ring of mustard seed oil, a delicacy which I'd greedily take and distribute, along with any other little things left around in the bathroom. One day it started to rain, and Srila Prabhupada came back early from his morning walk. I was blissfully cleaning and singing, absorbed in my service. Everybody else had gone downstairs but I was still finishing the floor of his bathroom when I realized that Prabhupada was vigorously walking up the stairs, so I squeezed myself into a corner and put my head down. Prabhupada was with an Indian gentleman who said something about the sunrise being beautiful and Prabhupada said, "Yes, it is somewhat beautiful, but it is Krishna's sunrise and Krishna is so beautiful. Krishna is so beautiful!" Then Prabhupada stopped walking and said, "Even one tiny ray emanating from the tips of Krishna's toenails is a million times more effulgent and beautiful than anything in this world." Prabhupada was full of that intense vision. He said to the man, "You don't know?" The man didn't say anything. Prabhupada turned to me—he had seen me all along—and said, "Can you see?" I said, "No, Srila Prabhupada, I can't see." Then Prabhupada looked at me in a beautiful, deep way and said, "I want you to see." That was very special for me.

One day in Mayapur an old Gaudiya Vaishnav came to the *pujari* room looking for someone to talk to. He was holding a *Back to Godhead* magazine and he said, "Is anyone here a disciple of Bhaktivedanta Swami Maharaj?" A few of us said, "We are." He said, "I have to tell you something really special." He was very excited. He said, "For many years at Advaita Acharya's house in Shantipur, I humbly served as the *pujari,* doing the *aratis* and taking care of guests. Many years ago, when I was young, I noticed a *grihastha* gentleman who, in a sober and quiet way, sometimes sat at the back of the hall, chanting *japa* and weeping. I never disturbed him. I never asked who he was, but whenever he came my heart would fill with joy and I would give him some *maha prasadam*. He moved with great determination—he came in in a very determined way and he left in a very determined way. Sometimes he would chant all afternoon. After some time he didn't come anymore and one day a few years later I was doing my *seva* when I saw someone in saffron robes sitting and chanting in the back exactly as he had. I looked closely and recognized that it was my old friend, but now chanting even more deeply and weeping bitterly. He wept so much that I also wept. I got some *maha prasadam* and when that *sannyasi* was ready to leave I gave it to him and said, 'I've seen you for many years but this time I didn't recognize you at first. I'm so glad to see you. What is your name? Who are you?'

"He said, 'my name is Abhaya Charanaravinda Bhaktivedanta Swami Maharaj, and I am a humble and fallen disciple of my most glorious Gurudeva, Srila Bhaktisiddhanta Saraswati Thakur Prabhupada. I've been coming here for many years because this is the place where Chaitanya Mahaprabhu and Nityananda Prabhu and Advaita Prabhu used to gather to plan the whole worldwide *sankirtan* movement. This is such a holy place. I have been praying in the dust of this place, the dust of Their feet, for Their mercy. Many years ago my Gurudeva gave me an impossible mission. He ordered me to go across the ocean and plant Krishna consciousness on foreign soil. I do not know how to do this and I come here to pray for Their guidance and inspiration. I am feeling Their great mercy. Tomorrow I am leaving Bharatavarsa on a ship. I have no place to turn. I don't know what will happen. I only know that my Gurudeva has given me this order, and the personalities of this place have given me Their mercy. Would you also bestow your mercy upon me?'"

That devotee said, "Of course, you have any mercy that I have to give. I pray that you will be successful." Prabhupada said, "May we meet again," and Prabhupada took his little bag and walked away. So, the day before Prabhupada left India on the ship he made a visit to Mayapur—and he also went to Shantipur.

That old Vaishnav said, "I often remembered him and wondered how had he done, what had happened to him. Then I noticed a strange occurrence—white Vaishnavas started coming to our little temple. I was shy of them and didn't speak to them—I didn't speak English. I didn't know where they were from or how they had become devotees. But one day one of them gave me a *Back to Godhead* magazine with an article about Prabhupada's life and a picture of Srila Prabhupada as a *grihastha* in Calcutta. And I saw that that was my old friend, and now I am looking here and I see that the *Acharya* is also him. Bhaktivedanta Swami Maharaj has actually done it. I am so happy. I want everyone to know about your Gurudeva and his glories."

TAPE 43

Rupa-Vilasa das
Caru das
Tejiyas das

Rupa-Vilasa: Everyone was having *kirtan* when Prabhupada's limousine arrived at the temple. I'd been chanting sixteen rounds for about a week, didn't know what to expect, and had a reaction that I'd never had before. When Prabhupada got out of the car it appeared that he was being projected from some other world. When something is projected on the screen in a movie theater, you know the motion you see is coming from somewhere else. Similarly, Prabhupada's presence was unearthly and in my heart I immediately understood that this was an absolutely pure person, the person I'd been looking for, my spiritual master. I fell on the ground to offer obeisances, although I'd never offered obeisances to anyone before.

When he came into the temple he paid his obeisances to the Deities and then walked to the *vyasasana* at the far end, smiling and glancing lovingly at everyone. As everyone says, when Prabhupada looked at you, you felt that he understood everything about you and you felt completely exposed and foolish. Almost universally devotees say that in front of Prabhupada they had no secrets, that Prabhupada could understand everything essential about them.

Caru: In a letter to all temple presidents Karandhar wrote, "The etiquette is to invite the guru to your temple. It's not likely that he'll come, but invite him." As I was president in Sydney, I duly wrote a letter saying, "Please come and visit Australia," and I was shocked when Prabhupada responded, "I'm coming, send two tickets." We had no money whatsoever. We sold *Back to Godheads* and made fifty dollars on a big day. Paying the rent was a major achievement. Our temple was a storefront with a big window at a bus stop in Paddington, which was a trendy area. We held evening *arati* at six o'clock where 30 or 40 commuters, who were waiting to go home, could see it. The temple was wonderful, but it wasn't clean. We hadn't changed the carpet from when it had been a store and we didn't even know that carpets were dirty. We really didn't know anything about devotional service.

The first two devotees in Australia were Bali Mardan and Upendra. Then Upananda joined and shortly thereafter Vaibhavi and I joined, and two weeks later the others left. Upendra went to Fiji and Bali Mardan went to Hong Kong. While I was driving them to the airport I said, "Who's going to be in charge?" They said, "You are." And a few months later Prabhupada came. At this time there were virtually no books. There was just that old blue *Bhagavad-gita As It Is* and, to be honest, I couldn't understand it. Later, by listening to cassettes and taking notes, I understood the philosophy, but reading *Bhagavad-gita* was over my head.

When Prabhupada agreed to come, we let it be known that we needed three thousand dollars for two tickets, and a Baha'i guest, who later was initiated as Raghunath, donated the money. So, after the big Cross Maidan *pandal* in Bombay, Prabhupada arrived in Sydney with the Deities of Radha-Gopinatha. Prabhupada was understandably appalled at our lack of knowledge but he said, "They are sincere boys and girls," and he held an initiation ceremony. I have always been good with the media and at my invitation three or four television stations crowded into our small storefront with their big cameras and lights, and a hundred people were in a room that could comfortably only fit forty or fifty. Prabhupada installed the Deities and we got our *brahmana* initiation. We didn't know what a *brahmana* thread was. Prabhupada said, "Where are the *brahmana* threads?" and we said, "What are *brahmana* threads?" So Vaibhavi went downstairs and got a ball of string, tied the threads together, brought them up, and we had our *brahmana* initiation. Prabhupada later said that he left the Deities in *mleccha-desh*.

Tejiyas: People from all over America had come to see Prabhupada and Prabhupada started describing the Life Membership program. He said, "We have introduced this Life Membership program in India and America. In India it costs 1,111 *rupees*, and when they become a member we give them an entire set of books. This is a very good business," and Prabhupada laughed. A lot of the devotees were young and not all of them understood Prabhupada's humor. Prabhupada said, "We give them 500 *rupees* of books and we take 1,000 *rupees*. Very good business," and he exploded in laughter. He continued, "Then they invite us to their homes and give us a feast. In this way, we are eating our way back to Godhead. Very good business." Prabhupada laughed again and then everyone laughed. That was my first meeting with Srila Prabhupada—I saw his precise intelligence, his wit, his enormous humor, how he would teach with his humor, and how he was a highly developed manager and organizer.

Rupa-Vilasa: Prabhupada came to Dallas three or four times and he used to take walks on White Rock Lake, the richer section, where a famous oil tycoon, H. L. Hunt, had a home. The devotees told Prabhupada, "We tried to see H. L. Hunt but he wouldn't see us." Prabhupada said, "Oh? He would not see you? But when death comes, will he also say, 'I cannot see you'? Anyway, he may say, but death will come and do his business." Then Prabhupada said, "What would you have said if you were able to see him?" Somebody said, "We would show him your books." Prabhupada said, "No." "We'd tell him about the school." Prabhupada said, "No." He didn't like those answers. Finally Prabhupada said, "You should tell him he has become a wealthy man by stealing from the earth and at death he will be severely punished for this crime." A devotee said, "Prabhupada, if we speak to him like this, he'll become angry." Prabhupada said, "Angry? If I shake my stick at a dog, he will also become angry. You have to learn how to talk to this class of men."

Caru: During Srila Prabhupada's visit in 1971, I booked him on a number of national television shows but we'd have to travel quite a distance to get to the studios and then they'd ask superficial questions for five or ten minutes. After one interview Prabhupada looked at me, shook his head and said, "They do not know how to question." Another time Prabhupada and I were sitting in the waiting room to go onto a national TV show, and on a little TV we saw a graphic scene of a woman being violated in the woods. Prabhupada was astounded—incredulous—that these kinds of things were displayed on a public medium. He looked at the whole thing and then turned to me and said, "The world is going to hell," and shook his head.

Once, Prabhupada was on the Mike Willesee Show. Mike Willesee was a famous, cynical, acerbic, interviewer who would always damage his guests. Almost no one went away from the Mike Willesee Show without bleeding from several wounds. Prabhupada sat between Mike Willesee and a picture of Krishna. Mike Willesee said, "This is your Hindu God?" Prabhupada said, "No, this is God. Tell me whatever you'd like to about God as He's described in your scriptures—His name, fame, qualities, and pastimes. If you're saying that this is a Hindu God, then tell me about your Christian God, as much information as you'd like to share with me and the audience." Willesee said, "There isn't much." Prabhupada said, "We have all the information in our scriptures and if you're interested, we'll show you that Krishna is not a Hindu God, He's God, He fits all the qualifications, and you have to accept Him. You failed to present me with a superior description of God. I have His picture right here. You have not even a word to say. So you please accept Him as God right now." Mike Willesee was devastated. No one had turned him upside down like that before.

Sometime later, Prabhupada asked me not to book him more television engagements. Even though he was reaching a million people, the questions weren't deep and the time was too short. I canceled a couple of national shows because Prabhupada wanted to give Krishna consciousness in depth, even if to a smaller audience.

Tejiyas: Srila Prabhupada told a story about people in Spain who said it was an accident that Columbus discovered America—since he never intended to do it he shouldn't be glorified for it. In every way they discredited Columbus. When this was brought before the Queen, Columbus said, "It wasn't an accident." So the Queen posed a challenge: "Whoever can answer this challenge should get the credit. Without any extraneous devices, make an egg stand on its end." Everyone thought of different ways to get an egg to stand on end. When the others had finished, Columbus boiled the egg, tapped its end, and stood it up. Everyone protested but the Queen understood that Columbus was intelligent and he got the credit. Prabhupada told this story in relation to his god-brothers being envious of him and not wanting him to have credit for spreading Krishna consciousness.

Even now people say, "It was really Lord Chaitanya who spread Krishna consciousness throughout the world." It's audacious and impersonal to say this, although in his humility and meekness, Prabhupada also said the same thing. He would say, "Everything that has happened is the mercy of Lord Chaitanya. It is all the kindness of my spiritual master. My spiritual master has sent me all of you to help me." When Prabhupada said that, you knew he had no false ego. But at the same time, amazingly, Prabhupada knew who he was. It's almost impossible to understand this—except from the position of pure devotional service.

Rupa-Vilasa: On another morning walk at White Rock Lake, Prabhupada observed different things. Somebody pointed out a horse running in a field on an estate, and Prabhupada said, "A horse is the most beautiful of animals." Satsvarupa Maharaj, playing a straight man, said, "Prabhupada, I thought a cow was the most beautiful." Prabhupada thought that was funny. He said, "A cow? A cow is not beautiful." Then Prabhupada said that amongst women, Jewish women are the most beautiful, which amazed everybody. Satsvarupa said, "But Prabhupada, the black people say that they're the most beautiful," and Prabhupada said, "Everyone will say like that." It was light and fun.

Caru: I booked Srila Prabhupada two speaking engagements in one day. The first was at nine o'clock in the morning at the very exclusive North Sydney Boys School. Two or three hundred third and fourth graders in uniforms sat in the auditorium along with their teachers to hear from Prabhupada. We always carried Prabhupada's *vyasasana* with us, we always had a *kirtan*, and there was a lot of brouhaha. Prabhupada began by asking the boys to chant the maha-mantra responsively, word-by-word, and Prabhupada chided them in a friendly way when they weren't enthusiastic enough. Then Prabhupada asked, "Do you know what is God? Can any one of you stand up and tell me what is God?" One boy raised his hand and said, "God is self-realization, and God is found in the unconscious mind." Prabhupada asked that boy to come forward. Prabhupada was kind and gentle with him and steered him in the right direction, until the boy got the idea that consciousness is the spark of sensation within the body. From there Prabhupada discussed the supreme consciousness as it's described in the Thirteenth Chapter of *Bhagavad Gita: ksetra-jnam capi mam viddhi sarva-ksetresu bharata* . . . about the field of activities, the individual soul, and the supreme soul. It was a technical lecture, but Prabhupada unfolded it in a way that was perfectly palatable for these young boys. They were satisfied and I felt that they had ingested most of what Prabhupada had said.

In the evening we went to the Wayside Chapel, which was a gathering place for radicals, fanatics, homosexuals, and Nazis. The moderator was Reverend Ted Noffs, who delighted in increasing attendance through sensationalism and controversy. His constituency was eloquent but morally bankrupt and politically extreme. Prabhupada gave a brief and simple lecture. He sensed that this was not a good forum. Those persons were used to haranguing and weren't interested in surrendering. Prabhupada calculated, "Let's make this as brief and painless as possible." Compared to what he'd talked about in the morning with the boys, he spoke more simply, as if they were less intellectual than the boys, which, in spiritual terms, they were. Spiritually they were totally unqualified. Then Prabhupada asked for questions, and the questions were challenging. In a very elongated way one person said, "What's the practical good of it?" Prabhupada answered with a tone that said, "You wouldn't understand, but this is what it does," and he said, "The practical result of chanting Hare Krishna is that it saves you from death." After the program Reverend Noffs escorted Prabhupada to the car, and Prabhupada asked him, "What do you do here?" Reverend Noffs said, "One of the things we do is help kids with drugs." Prabhupada got in the car and asked Ugrasrava, "So they give young people drugs?"

Rupa-Vilasa: To help us organize the *gurukula,* Prabhupada met with all the teachers and at that time he discussed other things as well. Once he said the big *mayavadis*, Ramakrishna, Vivekananda, also study *Vedanta,* "But," he said, "They could not understand." He asked us, "Why they cannot understand?" He liked to put us on the spot to see what we could come up with. One of the devotees cited a verse, *naham prakasah sarvasya yoga-maya-samavrtah*, that because of *yoga-maya*, the illusory potency, they're bewildered. But Prabhupada wasn't satisfied with that answer or other answers that were offered. Finally Dayananda sat bolt upright and said, "Because they haven't got *Bhakti*vedanta!" Prabhupada said, "Here is the answer!" The rest of us felt envious that Dayananda had given the answer that pleased Prabhupada.

Tejiyas: Srila Prabhupada was asked, "Have you ever seen Krishna?" He said, "I always see Krishna in front of me." Once, in a public *pandal,* a boy challenged, "Do you see God?" Prabhupada hesitated a second and then said, "Yes." Prabhupada understood his position. It's hard for us to estimate Prabhupada's vision, how, although he's the master of teaching Krishna consciousness, he sees that everything is not done because of him. Prabhupada knows precisely what he's doing. But he's very humble because he knows that somehow or other he has the mercy of his spiritual master. Prabhupada's acknowledgement of his powers was in his statement, "My spiritual master liked me. I listened to his words very carefully." Prabhupada took those words very seriously and that's his acknowledgement of how somehow or other—miraculously—he is given this credit.

Caru: Two young interviewers asked Prabhupada, "Have you seen God?" Prabhupada said, "What do you think? Before you buy gold, you should first educate yourself so you can recognize gold. So to know whether my answer is right or wrong, you need to know who God is and the qualifications for seeing Him. Do you know who God is and who is qualified to see Him?" They said no. "Since you don't know, for better or worse you have to accept whatever I say. Will you do that?" "Yes." "Then I have seen God." That was powerful.

Rupa-Vilasa: We had a guest who had been visiting the temple regularly and had won a Teacher of the Year award and I wanted him to meet Srila Prabhupada. But when he came, that man was in distress from a great misfortune. On Valentine's Day he had been driving a school bus and when the children got off at a certain stop, one of them crawled under the bus to get a card that had blown there. This man didn't see the child and had run over and killed him. The man was thinking, "How can I meet Prabhupada in this state?" I said, "Just tell Prabhupada what happened." I wasn't sure that was the right thing to do but when we got into the room I told Prabhupada the situation. I was amazed by Prabhupada's compassion. Prabhupada questioned the man at length to get the whole story, "Did you look both ways?" and so on. Prabhupada got a sense of exactly what happened, how the parents reacted, and how the school staff reacted. Then Prabhupada said, "It's not your fault. You didn't do anything wrong and you will not be blamed for this." This man was pacified and he began to ask Prabhupada different questions.

In his answers, Prabhupada brought up a rocket scientist, Werner Von Braun, who, at a large scientific conference, had declared that the real purpose of science was to establish the existence of God. This caused consternation for some people, but when Prabhupada read about it he deputed some of his disciples to speak to Von Braun and give him books. I got excited and said, "Prabhupada, this is wonderful. He's a famous person. If he becomes interested in Krishna consciousness, it will be a great boon for the movement." Prabhupada said, "I am not interested in speaking to him because he's a famous man. I am interested in speaking to him because he has come to the right point." Throughout Prabhupada's preaching, whether people were low or high, little or big, he would spend sometimes hours with them answering their questions and being merciful to them because of their sincere interest.

Caru: Srila Prabhupada gave many speaking programs in Sydney —in Paddington Town Hall, in Ormond Hall, in Sydney Town Hall, and, since we advertised them, they were all well attended. But the people who came weren't completely happy because Prabhupada didn't fit their preconceptions. At a public speaking engagement in a big hall in South Melbourne, someone asked a long question about what Prabhupada thought of Guru Maharaji, who was very popular at the time. Although Prabhupada knew him, in public he would never criticize anyone by name. Prabhupada asked, "What is his philosophy?" "God is the light between your eyes." Prabhupada looked at that person and said, "Thank you very much." Someone else asked about Lobsang Rampa and someone asked about Meher Baba and Prabhupada said, "What is their philosophy?" and didn't give any of them any credence. People complained, "How come he's like that?" We said, "That's our *guru*; Unalloyed devotional service, nothing less."

Rupa-Vilasa: Srila Prabhupada visited us one very hot summer. There was no garden or a nice spot for him to sit outside so Prabhupada, wearing his dhoti and his *sannyasa* top, sat in a chair on the lawn next to Graham Street, which is a busy road. We sat around him while cars zipped by and someone fanned him with a peacock fan. Then a man walking on the sidewalk did a double take—it was more than he could handle. In a demanding voice he said to Prabhupada, "Why is that man fanning you?" Prabhupada, relaxing in the chair said, "It is hot." This man didn't know what to say. He turned on his heels and walked off. Prabhupada demolished his whole irritation with three words, "It is hot." That was humorous.

Caru: I arranged a program at St. Pascal's Franciscan Seminary and Prabhupada gave a wonderful lecture about the universality of God consciousness—how God consciousness is for everyone. He said that a religious person is not necessarily Christian, Hindu, Muslim or Jew or one who pays lip service to this or that denomination but one who follows the laws of God. *Dharmam tu saksad bhagavat-pranitam*. At the end one of the seminarians asked, "What do you think of St. Francis?" Prabhupada said, "What is his philosophy?" The seminarian said, "He talked about brother tree, sister bird." Prabhupada said, "That is real God consciousness. One who is pandita, learned, his vision is equal. So if St. Francis was thinking like that, that is the highest standard of spiritual understanding." Prabhupada's appreciation was greater than the seminarians, and they were followers of St. Francis. Prabhupada had never heard of St. Francis and yet based on a two- or three-sentence description of how St. Francis saw the world, Prabhupada immediately recognized that he was a kindred spirit, another *guru*, another spiritual master, and Prabhupada said, "That is real God consciousness!" His statement profoundly affected the seminarians.

After the question period Prabhupada said, "God's name is Christ or Kristo or Krishna. So let's join in glorifying God. You say Kristo and we'll say Krishna." And the frocked and collared seminarians stood up and started chanting, "Kristo, Kristo, Kristo, Kristo, Krishna, Krishna, Krishna." They were young men, some of them bearded, a little older than us. We were in our early 20's and they were mostly in their mid or late 20's or early 30's and older mentors were there also. The place was rocking. Many of the seminarians had tears rolling down their faces. It was a moving, nondenominational glorification of God's names.

Tejiyas: Prabhupada was speaking to Giriraj and me about the different *kendras* and *kalamandirs*—the many big cultural halls in Delhi. As he talked, we walked past these halls, one after another because we were in the center of Delhi where they all are. Prabhupada said we should organize programs in them, and Giriraj asked Prabhupada a question about how to progressively spread this movement. At that time Prabhupada gave a *sutra*: "Simply it takes intelligent organization."

We can take this as a clue from Srila Prabhupada—that if in our hearts we seriously want to facilitate Lord Chaitanya's mission and see it fully manifest as soon as possible, then we should intelligently organize.

Rupa-Vilasa: In 1976, when we only had four or five kids in the *gurukula*, once Harikesa—Prabhupada's secretary—pulled me to the side and said, "You're not running this *gurukula* properly. You should be like a *guru* figure to these children. You should not have such friendly, familiar relations with them." I have never been submissive so I said, "Maybe that's your opinion but Prabhupada never instructed us that way." I went to my room and a few minutes later somebody came knocking at the door, "Prabhupada wants to see you right away!" I had never been summoned before, so I was shocked. I checked to make sure I had *tilak* on, then went into Prabhupada's rooms and offered my *dandavats*. Prabhupada was sitting behind his desk looking grave. He said, "So? You think you are guru?" I said, "What?" He said, "You think you are guru?" I said, "Prabhupada, I never said that!" I was looking around the room desperately, saw Harikesa, and said, "He said that!" Prabhupada said, "What is this?" Harikesa attempted to explain to Prabhupada his idea but after a couple of sentences, Prabhupada waved him off, looked at me again and said, "You are not guru. I am guru." I said, "I know!" He indicated that I should be quiet and said, "You are the experienced disciple, you are teaching the inexperienced, but you are not guru! Is it clear?" I said, "Yes, Prabhupada!" "All right," he said, and then he dismissed me. I walked out of the room completely crushed and thinking, "What have I done? I never thought I was a *guru*, and now I'm being chastised for it."

Years later, after Prabhupada left and when some unqualified people thought that they were gurus, I realized that I never had any illusions about my situation and that my freedom from illusion was Prabhupada's mercy. If I had any seeds of desire to be a guru, they were crushed from that experience—it made quite an impression on me.

Caru: On a morning walk in Sydney, I asked Prabhupada about the power of the *kshatriyas*. Based on our philosophy, I thought that having many wives and being sexually active would decrease a person's spiritual and physical power. Once, Prabhupada said that Gandhi was successful in driving the British out of India because he was continent after the age of 35. So I asked Prabhupada, "How is it that the *kshatriyas* were the most physically powerful people in society and yet at the same time they were dispensing their seed profusely?" Prabhupada said, "System of eating." That's all he said.

Rupa-Vilasa: Venkata Bhatta prabhu told me that at the Kumbha-mela a devotee asked Prabhupada about bathing at auspicious moments. The devotee said, "Is this something we *Vaishnavas* should do?" Prabhupada said, "*Vaishnava*? You are *trying* to become *Vaishnava. Vaishnava* is not an ordinary thing." In other words, we are at the stage of *Vaishnava praya*, which means almost a *Vaishnava*. We're thinking we're *Vaishnavas* but we are only approaching the precincts of becoming a *Vaishnava*. Prabhupada indicated, "You're thinking this is not for you, but you need all the help you can get, so go ahead and bathe at auspicious moments."

Caru: In Paddington, a fellow asked Prabhupada for permission to interview some of the disciples to see what their backgrounds were and try to find some keys as to why certain types of people became devotees. Prabhupada said, "You don't need to do that." The man said, "Why?" Prabhupada said, "Because their backgrounds are all black. It doesn't matter if they were a Nobel Prize winner or a Ph.D. or a beggar on the street. Before they came to Krishna consciousness, it was all black. Don't pay any attention to what they were before."

There's a verse, "One who sees a *Vaishnava* as a member of a particular sect or creed, the spiritual master as an ordinary man, or the Deity as stone has *jada-matir buddhi*, he has hellish consciousness." This fellow was thinking, "This *Vaishnava* has a B.A., this *Vaishnava* took drugs, or this *Vaishnava* worked for the Defense Department," but Prabhupada was saying, "A *Vaishnava* is a *Vaishnava*. Do not distinguish higher and lower *Vaishnavas*." For example, sometimes the sky is cloudless all day long and sometimes there are clouds in the morning but they dissipate and in the evening the sky is cloudless. Under the clear evening sky, what difference does it make whether or not there had been clouds earlier in the day? Either way the sky is cloudless now. Similarly, Prabhupada said, "Just see them as *Vaishnavas*, that's all. Don't see them in terms of where they came from or make relative determinations that this one was good and this one was bad. It was all bad, it was all black and now it's all white."

Rupa-Vilasa: Sometimes Prabhupada sat under the *tamal* tree in the courtyard of the Krishna Balaram temple and we would be honored to have *kirtan* or *bhajan* for Prabhupada's pleasure. One flamboyant devotee—he wore his silk *dhoti* in an elaborate style, his *tilak* was perfect, and he considered himself to be an expert *kirtaniya*—began to chant in a showy way. Prabhupada listened for a few seconds, then waved him off and pointed to one of the *gurukula* boys. This particular boy could not sing. He had a voice like a strangled frog and he didn't know how to play the *mridanga* either. He began whaling away and his face went bright red. He was trying sincerely, but the sound was atrocious. Prabhupada sat there smiling and nodding his head and tapping his finger, obviously enjoying it, but the flamboyant devotee was so upset that he left. Prabhupada appreciated heartfelt chanting. He didn't appreciate a showbottle.

Tejiyas: Several times I heard Prabhupada talk about change. "In general," he said, "your whole disease is that you want to change everything," Devotees changed Prabhupada's instructions. For example, Prabhupada mentioned how devotees in Los Angeles had taken down the glass windows although he didn't want that. But, at the same time, there were things that Prabhupada did want changed. For instance, he asked the editors to change the incorrect wording in the *Gita*—Hayagriva had put "cattle raising" instead of "cow protection"—and because of that and other mistakes, Prabhupada had once joked, "Bhagavad-gita As It Is Not." There were many such mistakes that needed correcting and Prabhupada sometimes got angry when we were slow to change those.

So there were things we weren't supposed to change, and also, on his instructions, other things that some devotees were to change and review. But in general, unnecessary changes were the overall disease. So we shouldn't abuse those who were authorized to make changes. And those who were authorized should make only appropriate changes. But overall, better safe than sorry: don't change. Like *kirtan*. In the beginning, after Prabhupada finished chanting Hare

Krishna he would stop. Then devotees started introducing *haribol* from the Gaudiya Math. Prabhupada said, "What is this '*haribol*'? Don't simply say '*haribol*', but do it. Chant His name." Or the "*jaya jaya gurudeva*." Prabhupada said, "Which *gurudeva*?"

One of Prabhupada's pet peeves was "Prabhupada said." He said, "Who said 'Prabhupada said'? When did I say? I never said. You are always saying 'Prabhupada said.' Stop this." It became a problem.

Rupa-Vilasa: Prabhupada came into the room to show us how to teach but there was nothing for him to sit on. He stood there while somebody ran to the temple, got a large seat and put it down behind a desk. Prabhupada sat down and said, "What are your questions?" Devotees began to ask questions but some of them were sitting almost behind Prabhupada. Prabhupada said, "You come to the front, then ask." So they moved in front of him. Later on I read in the Manu Samhita that the etiquette before the spiritual master is never to sit to the side of or behind him but always to sit in front of him and to put questions humbly.

At one point Prabhupada held up two sticks and said, "This stick is for the students if they misbehave," and he tapped his own hand with the stick. Then he said, "The other stick is for the teachers if they misbehave." Unfortunately that instruction wasn't well understood.

Caru: On one morning walk Prabhupada was told that two ladies, Swati and Shasti, had observed *Ekadasi* every day for a year. Prabhupada said, "That is very good. Grains are for animals." A month later I was in Vrindavan and went on another morning walk with Prabhupada, when Prabhupada said something about grains building strength. One devotee said, "But Prabhupada, I thought you said grains were for animals." Prabhupada said, "I eat grains. Am I an animal?"

Rupa-Vilasa: Prabhupada's friend, Bhagatji, was helping with the management of the ISKCON temple in Vrindavan and he was also the patron of the *gurukula*. Prabhupada and Bhagatji had a friendly relationship and he used to see Prabhupada regularly. One day when Bhagatji was going into Prabhupada's room I thought, "I am running this fledgling *gurukula* so maybe I could go in too," and I said, "Can I come with you?" Generally, we were afraid to see Prabhupada because there was an intimidating wall of *sannyasis* and older devotees around him. Bhagatji said, "Yes, come, come."

Prabhupada was with a couple of Indian guests in the garden with the lotus fountain. Bhagatji and Prabhupada greeted each other and then Prabhupada pointed to me and said, "Go and get some *asanas*." I thought, "Oh, my gosh." I ran out, found Hari Sauri and said, "Prabhupada wants some *asanas*." Hari Sauri said, "I don't think we have any." He rummaged around in a closet and found a rumpled, terrible-looking *asana*. He said, "This is all I've got," and gave it to me. I was in a sweat. I went back with my *asana* and as soon as I walked into the garden, Prabhupada said, "Get them some *prasadam*," because the guests were leaving. "Yes Prabhupada." I ran to Hari Sauri, "Prabhupada wants *prasadam* for the guests." He said, "It's on the table." I gave it to the guests. "Whew, I did something right." I went back to the garden and stood in the back with my one crumpled *asana*. Prabhupada said, "So? I asked you to get some *asanas*. What is the difficulty?" I said, "Prabhupada, we only have this one *asana*." He shook his head and rolled his eyes. I seemed to be destined to make an idiot of myself. I said, "Prabhupada, what should I do with this *asana*?" He said, "Take your one *asana* and sit down!" And he and Bhagatji laughed uproariously. Prabhupada said, "These Westerners, what can you do?" I was the object of the laughter, but somehow I started laughing uproariously too. I had gone in there with aspirations to be recognized as one of the big devotees and Prabhupada crushed me completely. He made me realize that I'm an insignificant servant and I can hardly do anything right. He immediately reduced my false ego to its proper perspective. It was an instructive experience.

Another time, Prabhupada was circumambulating the temple with a group of us. At one point he came to the corner of the building and stopped so suddenly that devotees almost ran into him. He turned around and said in a grave voice, "You are blind, but I can see." We didn't know what to say. Nobody said anything. We went around again. When we got back to the same spot and without saying anything Prabhupada pointed to a light that was on. The sun had already come up and the light was on. In Vrindavan, Prabhupada's mood was that not a *paisa* should be wasted. Whenever water was dripping, whenever there was any neglect, whenever a merchant was trying to get the better of us in a business deal, he was on top of it. And that was his comment, "You are blind, but I can see." It worked on every level. It was true in terms of the management of that temple and it was true in terms of our spiritual condition. It was a statement in truth, and it had a practical application.

Tejiyas: Another instruction I received was in a letter Prabhupada wrote to me. He said, "Now strain your brain to think of more and more ways to introduce my books to the intelligent class of men." At that time I was alone in Delhi, really alone. No one would stay and no one even came there except to make trouble. I was enduring all that and I was always in anxiety.

Prabhupada said, "I always want to hear from you," and told me to report to him regularly, so I reported that I had made ten members of Parliament Life Members. Prabhupada wrote back "You have opened up a whole new history in Krishna consciousness." I thought, "Wow." Besides being sweet and encouraging, the way he wrote it was as if this was earth-shattering news, "Tejiyas made ten Life Members!"

It was amazing what went on by Prabhupada's mercy. The biggest members of Parliament, the hardest to crack, even *mayavadis*, were inviting Prabhupada to their homes. Kamla Patri Pati, who, after Indira Gandhi, was the most respected person in the Congress Party—he was called Panditji—invited Prabhupada and all the ministers and top members of Parliament to a program at his house. At that program Prabhupada was on fire as he spoke about Rupa and Sanatan Goswamis and how they left their prestigious government posts to take up the mission of Lord Chaitanya Mahaprabu.

Rupa-Vilasa: After a lecture, Jnanagamya, a friend of mine, stood up and asked Prabhupada, "Prabhupada, how can we ever repay our debt to you?" Prabhupada said, "You can never repay your debt. Remain always indebted."

Another time, after a *Bhagavad-gita* lecture, an Indian man in the back of the temple said, "Why was Krishna trying to tempt Arjuna to fight, to become violent? This seems to go against the principles of humility and peacefulness." Prabhupada looked irritated and got fiery. He motioned for this person to come forward and said, "Come up here!" the way a grandfather would speak to a grandson who was out of line. When the man sat in front of Prabhupada like a student, Prabhupada said, "Now repeat your question." By this time the man's challenging attitude had diminished but he stammered his question out again. Prabhupada began to roar at him saying, "Do you think that Krishna, the Supreme Being, Who is all-compassionate, would try to get Arjuna to do something that was against religious principles? Krishna is the origin of all religious principles, *dharmam tu saksad bhagavat.* Would He advise Arjuna to do something against his own self-interest?" Prabhupada hammered at this person and when he was through, waved him away. The man almost crawled back to his original seat. That's what Prabhupada thought that person needed at that instant.

Caru: At the end of a lecture, I asked, "If Christians would give up eating meat, would they be Krishna conscious?" He said, "Yes, definitely. Krishna is pure, you become pure, you will understand. Krishna will be revealed to you if you are pure."

Rupa-Vilasa: After one lecture someone asked, "What is it like to be always in touch with God, to be situated in God consciousness?" Prabhupada pondered the question for a few seconds and then said, "Without fear," and he smiled one of those gargantuan smiles. When I heard this, I started grinning like an idiot. I felt emotional and ecstatic and the hairs on my arms were standing on end. I thought, "Boy, I don't want to make an idiot of myself." But I looked around the room and everybody else was in the same state—a wave of ecstatic feeling passed through the room. For that moment, nobody had any fear and everybody had symptoms of ecstasy.

Later I read in *Caitanya Siksamrta* that by associating with someone on the *uttama-adhikari* platform, you can briefly, by their grace, experience symptoms of *bhava*.

Tejiyas: I wrote a letter to Prabhupada about my anxiety. I was disheartened because the devotees I trained would abandon me three weeks later. Even my wife would argue and run away. Prabhupada's reply was, "Actually we are not after making members, we are not after collections, we are not after selling books, we are not after any of these things. These are just different ways to engage in service to Krishna and thus to become Krishna conscious. You need not worry. Do not be in anxiety."

Two weeks later I got another letter from Srila Prabhupada increasing my responsibilities five-fold. He wrote, "Make the members of Parliament Life Members." I had so many responsibilities that I was getting more and more anxious. I hadn't made a Life Member in 45 days. I was trying to follow Prabhupada's instructions of being detached, thinking, "I'm a servant of Krishna and whatever I get is Krishna's arrangement." But I was also thinking, "Why am I in such anxiety?" The daily reality I faced was that the devotees in Vrindavan would starve if I didn't send money, and I had to take care of the devotees in Delhi also. At the same time, Prabhupada put me under stringent financial directives. I had to give 50% of the Life Membership money to the BBT and 50% to construction. So I had no money for maintenance and I was the little maintainer of the

Vrindavan and Delhi ISKCON temples. Beyond this, there were always new problems, more things to do and not enough *prasadam*. I got sick. The devotees revolted.

Every afternoon Srila Prabhupada would take a leisurely hour-long massage. He had so many things to do, but he was leisurely about everything he did. I went and sat there for a while. Then I told Srila Prabhupada, "I'm worried that I'm not progressing correctly in spiritual life. In *Bhagavad-gita* it says, *brahma-bhutah prasannatma na socati na kanksati*, that when one attains the *brahma-bhutah* platform or is Krishna conscious, anxiety and lamentation are gone. But I'm always in anxiety and I'm concerned that I'm making an error in my spiritual life. Srila Prabhupada, please correct me."

Prabhupada's reply was amazing. Prabhupada looked at me softly and kindly and said, "No. Your anxiety is all about pleasing Krishna. Mother Yasoda is always in anxiety, that this demon Trinavarta might steal Krishna or that Krishna might be hungry. So, all your anxieties are simply in relation to pleasing Krishna and are transcendental." He was so kind.

Rupa-Vilasa: The *gurukula* building in Vrindavan was under construction and Prabhupada liked to go there every couple of days to see the progress. Once, Prabhupada went in the early morning with a contingent of *sannyasis* and senior devotees and from the back windows of the building they looked at the workers. Some of the workers were bathing with water that gushed out of a pipe. Some of them were making *chapatis* over fires and some of them were brushing their teeth with *neem* twigs. A lot of these workers were *brijbasis* and were chanting songs about Krishna. Prabhupada watched this whole scene, turned around and said, "Just see. They will rise early in the morning. They will work all day long in the hot sun and for what?" Somebody said, "Three *rupees*." "For a few *rupees*," Prabhupada said, "they will take bath, they will chant some *mantra*, and they will live in this simple way." He appreciated the simplicity of their life and how sincere and innocent they were.

Hansadutta Maharaj said, "Prabhupada, we should learn to live like this." Prabhupada laughed and said, "You will never learn. You will never learn."

Caru: Prabhupada sat on the *vyasasana* and the first question the reporter asked was, "What's going to happen to the movement after you die?" Before he'd even finished the sentence Prabhupada said, "I will never die!" A long pause, "I will live forever in my books."

Going back to Australia, before Prabhupada arrived I would inform the press and make his arrival a media event. Reporters would follow him from the airport to the temple. Once, Prabhupada spent quite a bit of time with a reporter for the *Melbourne Age*, the largest daily newspaper in Melbourne. Prabhupada treated the reporters as individuals. He didn't give them a media package, a slick presentation for newspapers. Prabhupada tried to get them to be Krishna conscious, and he really gave this fellow a lot of mercy. But the article that came out the next day had a picture of Prabhupada and the heading, "Swami says he'll be an animal in his next life." We were aghast and upset at the ingratitude and dullness of this reporter. We showed Prabhupada the article, "Look what he's written..." Prabhupada smiled and said, "Caru, count the number of times that Krishna is mentioned in the article." It was eight or ten times. Prabhupada asked, "What is the circulation?" It was two or three hundred thousand. "How many people read it?" We figured and it turned out that the name of Krishna was repeated or read more than a million times as a result of that article. Prabhupada said, "How can that be bad? The name of Krishna has been intoned mentally or verbally more than a million times on this day. That cannot be bad."

Rupa-Vilasa: Another time Srila Prabhupada was circumambulating the temple when he came to a strange-looking pattern of stone in the path. Originally the *parikram* path around the Krishna-Balaram Mandir was made from red stone that was laid out in a particular pattern. But this area, where there was a curve, was different. Prabhupada pointed to it with his cane and said, "What is this? This is not a proper pattern. They have cheated you. They have given you the rejected stone and have charged you the rate for the good stone."

Harikesa would regularly either try to correct or to argue with Prabhupada, and this time he began to argue, "No, Prabhupada, actually it is a pattern," and he explained why. Prabhupada said, "It's obviously not a pattern," and they went back and forth. Finally Prabhupada yelled at him, "Yes! It is a pattern! It is a clown's pattern, and you are the fool!" Harikesa began to laugh hysterically and everybody was in awe that he had the nerve to argue with Prabhupada about this, but that was the nature of his relationship.

Caru: The whole temple room in the Lotus Building in Mayapur was packed with devotees. Prabhupada was lecturing and for a moment he looked at us—20-year-old kids—and said, "I am an old man, I may go at any time. But there are hundreds of you young men and women, and all of you have at least 50 years left." I got a sense of how exciting every day was for him, preaching Krishna consciousness, captaining a world movement, as it was exciting for all of us who participated in it. At that moment, Prabhupada was transcendentally envious of us, that he was going to have to go and we had 50 years—so he started crying out of sheer enthusiasm to preach.

Rupa-Vilasa: Prabhupada was in his room in Vrindavan discussing various preaching plans with Akshayananda Maharaj when Prabhupada said, "So, what should we do?" Akshayananda Maharaj replied, "Prabhupada, we'll just have to become Krishna conscious." Prabhupada said, "Another impractical suggestion." That was one of the most hilarious exchanges I heard.

Another story is when a devotee said, "I'm the most fallen, Prabhupada," and Prabhupada said, "You're not the most anything." This devotee was trying to show how humble he was. He wanted credit for being the most something, and Prabhupada said, "You're not the most anything." Prabhupada was so quick and so funny, so sharp and so sarcastic, but you never felt offended by him. Even if the joke was at your expense, you had to admit it was really funny, and it always had an instructive edge to it. And it was merciful because he was trying to help you. The false ego is such an obstacle, and Prabhupada was cutting through that to put us more in touch with reality.

Caru: Before Prabhupada first visited us in Australia, we had a couple of his books and we knew something of him as an author. One tends to think of the author and his works as being separate and one is curious to know what the author is like as a person. Having read his commentaries, I wondered what Prabhupada would be like in person.

I was in charge the first time Prabhupada came to Australia and I was with him more than anybody. Whether I was alone with him or whether there were 20 or 30 other people, he was the personification of the *Bhagavatam* and the *Gita*. There wasn't any difference between his work and himself. He was truly the person *Bhagavat*, and early on I realized that one need not be in the physical presence of Prabhupada because Prabhupada is perfectly and completely present in his books. Since there is no difference between Prabhupada and his books, I always had plenty of inspiration in my devotional life. When Prabhupada left the planet it was the worst day of my life, but everything was still there. The books, the senior devotees, our international society, our vision, our goal, our inspiration—and to this day I haven't faltered for any lack of inspiration.

Tejiyas: I was staying at the Hyderabad farm, which was important to Srila Prabhupada. When I heard that Srila Prabhupada was not feeling well and that there was a chance he might leave the world, I went to see him in Vrindavan—around November 8th. Prabhupada's room was packed with devotees and I tried to be as inconspicuous as possible, to not disrupt the mood. Everyone was very quiet, and I could see Prabhupada's condition. He hadn't eaten for almost six months. He was lying in bed, emaciated, weighing maybe 70 pounds if that much, drinking one spoon, two spoons of water, maybe eating a little bit. I was sitting in the back, listening. There was *kirtan*, and Kirtanananda came in and offered Srila Prabhupada strawberries from New Vrindavan. Srila Prabhupada asked, "What is the value of strawberries?" No one knew what to say. Several devotees poked me to say something, as I'm known as a walking encyclopedia. I didn't want to intrude on Prabhupada, but I said, "Srila Prabhupada, the value of strawberries is that they are very high in fructose and that provides immediate energy." Even lying on his departure bed, not eating, Prabhupada was pragmatic. The devotee next to Prabhupada said, "Tejiyas says that . . ." and he repeated what I'd said. Prabhupada said, "Oh, Tejiyas is here? How is the Hyderabad farm?" Even in his state he was so cognizant. I gave him a report that we were growing corn, rice, mung beans and so on. As soon as I said corn, Prabhupada said, "Oh, corn. You can grind the corn and then there are big pieces which you can cook with water like rice," it was called *bhata*. "And the fine powder, you make that like a *chapati* and you cook it on the cooking pan. The villagers like this very much." From a physical point of view Prabhupada was starving, but what was he thinking? How we could make corn in the most delicious way to make the villagers happy when they took *prasadam*. This is a person of unlimited compassion.

Rupa-Vilasa: During Prabhupada's last days, 24-hour *kirtan* was going on in his room and devotees would chant for him in shifts. I went with a group of *gurukula* students. Prabhupada couldn't take too much sound so we used tiny *kartals* and made as little noise as possible. Tamal Krsna Maharaj asked me to lead the chanting and I thought, "I'd really like to please Prabhupada with this chanting." I tried to remember every tune that Prabhupada had chanted the Hare Krishna *mantra* to and I chanted those. I really concentrated, then our shift ended and we left. The next day when we went to chant, Tamal Krsna Maharaj grabbed me by the arm and said, "You have to chant for Prabhupada." I said, "Sure, but why?" He said, "The other day after you left Prabhupada called me over and said, 'Who was that chanting?'" Tamal, always the guardian, said, "Was there anything wrong, Prabhupada?" Prabhupada said, "No. It was very nice."

Another time, Ayodhyapati, who is now B.V. Govinda Maharaj, and I were in Prabhupada's room and we were asked to help massage Prabhupada. Devotees were massaging his head, arms and legs, and Ayodhyapati and I each massaged one of his feet. I felt, "I've always wanted to get the dust from Prabhupada's feet but I never had the opportunity," and I turned to Ayodhyapati and said, "This is *Vaikuntha*." It was. We felt like we were in the spiritual world with Prabhupada, serving him by massaging his feet.

During the last couple of months it seemed inevitable that Srila Prabhupada would be leaving us and we couldn't stand that thought. We felt helpless and desperate. Then when we were chanting for him on the last day, at first there was a lead singer and a response as there usually is, and in the final moments everybody began chanting together. It felt like there were many more people in that room than were actually there. It felt like there was a heavenly chorus with many personalities from other places present, and there was tremendous feeling as this glorious chanting was going on. It was a spectacular ending.

With his last breath Prabhupada uttered the syllables "Hare Krishna," and we could almost sense, "He's ascending now, he's with Krishna." Some devotees were completely stricken and cried hysterically—one threw himself on the floor weeping. Others were stoic—there were so many different kinds of reactions. It was intense but there was nothing inauspicious about it, it was completely auspicious. Sometimes the scriptures describe the sentiments of the gopis as being simultaneous nectar and poison, and Prabhupada's leaving was like that. It was ecstatic because Prabhupada had perfectly executed the mission of human life and gone back to Godhead, but it was an irretrievable and irreplaceable loss for us.

TAPE 44

Gokularanajana das
Udayananda das
Arjuna das
Jnanagamya das
Bahushira das
Jayapataka Swami

Gokularanajana: We grew up in the '50's with black and white TV and when color TV came it was exciting, like eye candy. When I first saw Prabhupada, it was like the first time I saw color TV—everything else was black and white or shades of gray. Prabhupada actually knew who he was, he knew who God was, and he knew what his purpose was. He was the only person I knew who was in reality and the first time I saw him was the first time I saw reality. I had taken some theater and drama courses in college and there was always a discussion about your inner monologue that motivates you and makes you efficient with your movements. I could see that Prabhupada's every movement was saturated with devotion. If he was walking to see the Radha-Govinda Deities in New York, he was walking to see Krishna. He wasn't just walking in front of people, he was walking to see Krishna, and everything was devotional. His every movement was very efficient. There was nothing frivolous in him.

Udayananda: The day after Srila Prabhupada gave me *brahmana* initiation was the first morning that I said my *gayatri* mantra, and I thought, "I'll go down to Lake Michigan and when the sun starts rising, I'll say my *gayatri* mantra." We were in Evanston and there was a nice park along the lakefront. So I chanted *japa* there, got all set to say my *gayatri* mantra, and up drove the Ford Lincoln Continental. The door opened, and maybe thirty yards from me out steps His Loving Divine Grace Srila Prabhupada. I said, "Jaya, Srila Prabhupada!" and I offered my obeisances, but Prabhupada's back was to me. All these *sannyasis* were there, Brahmananda, Satsvarupa, and when everyone was ready, Prabhupada turned and started walking right towards me. I hadn't even memorized the *gayatri* mantra yet, and I was saying it as Prabhupada walked by. Prabhupada said, "Why is he not offering obeisances?" I had offered obeisances, but Prabhupada's back was turned. And they said, "Prabhupada, he's chanting his *gayatri* mantra." I couldn't hear Prabhupada's answer, but he said, "What is the value of such chanting when the spiritual master comes by and you do not offer obeisances?" and then he walked on.

I chanted my *gayatri* quickly and I ran to catch up with the devotees. Sudama Maharaj saw me and went to the back of the group to talk with me. I said, "Maharaj, is it all right if I come?" He said, "Why didn't you offer your obeisances?" I said, "I did." He said, "When?" I said, "When Prabhupada got out of the car, I offered my obeisances." He said, "Prabhupada didn't see it," and told me what Prabhupada had said. Immediately I couldn't breathe, I was suffocating. I felt, "Oh, God, what is my worth? Why should I live another moment?" I carried that for a long time.

Twenty-five years after that incident, I wrote a Vyasa-puja offering apologizing to Srila Prabhupada for committing that offense and thanking Srila Prabhupada for impregnating my heart with his few words. By his grace I was never familiar or took him lightly ever, ever again. Even though I didn't think I was taking him lightly then, but after that I redoubled my determination to appreciate what it means to be in the association of the *jagat guru*. His words helped me for the rest of my life. Since that time I have offered my obeisances before and after saying *gayatri* mantra. If I'm sitting in front of the Deities and the curtain opens and there's *jagat guru* sitting on the altar, I offer obeisances. Sometimes I see devotees chanting *gayatri* mantra when the Deities open and they don't stop chanting. I think, "What is the value of this chanting?"

Arjuna: In Mauritius, Sir Seewoosagur Ramgoolam, one of the Prime Minister's right-hand men, was very friendly with the devotees. In those days, although officially there was no apartheid, the apartheid mentality of South Africa had spilled over into Mauritius and the few French families employed the rest of the population. When Ramgoolam heard that white people bowed down to Prabhupada, he was impressed and wanted Prabhupada to come to Mauritius. Ramgoolam asked the devotees, "Please draft a letter to induce your spiritual master to come and I will sign it." The devotees wrote, "Will Your Holiness please come and bless our island, and please bring your Krishna Consciousness Movement," and Ramgoolam signed it.

At that time Prabhupada was a little reluctant to travel but since a head of state had invited him, he came. Mr. Tilak, Secretary of Parliament for Agriculture, escorted Prabhupada off the plane and then Prabhupada attended a very nice reception in the VIP lounge, where foreign heads of state are honored. It was the first time Prabhupada had had such a reception.

The first thing Prabhupada said was, "*yad yad acarati sresthas tad tad evetaro janah.* Whatever the leaders do, common men will follow." Throughout his visit he was meditating on this and he gave many instructions on how to set up a perfect Krishna conscious society. Mr. Tilak brought 40 members of Parliament and heads of state to meet Prabhupada, and for about 40 minutes Prabhupada gave them a blueprint of how to set up an ideal society. In January 1976, a transcript of part of that talk was printed in *Back to Godhead* magazine. Srila Prabhupada said that Vedic society is based on love and a perfect society can be set up in a small place like Mauritius—it is no longer possible to do this in a highly industrialized state. And

Prabhupada said, "We don't have to invent anything new. The Vedic histories have already given examples of perfect Vedic societies. A perfect society is based on love, not on law. If the citizens love you, then they will automatically want to follow your laws. But first there must be love. So, *Bhagavad-gita* teaches that we must put Krishna in the center. If we govern according to *Bhagavad-gita*, we will get perfect society."

Jnanagamya: I was invited by Satsvarupa to go on a morning walk in Dallas. We went into a fairly well-to-do subdivision where there was a sign, "Beware of the dog." Prabhupada commented on this "Beware of the dog," and we understood that he was talking about the man in the house, not the dog. Prabhupada had an incredible sense of humor and sometimes a great sense of sarcasm.

Bahushira: After Prabhupada's disappearance I began helping Satsvarupa with the *Lilamrta* by interviewing people in India who had known Srila Prabhupada. One of them was Acharya Prabhakara Misra, Prabhupada's first disciple. Acharya Prabhakara was clean-cut, well behaved and articulate. His demeanor impressed me. He had an M.A. and Ph.D. and was a very cultured Sanskrit scholar and teacher. In Jhansi Prabhupada had told Acharya Prabhakara, "I met you here because I saw you in a dream and I knew I was supposed to come here." Prabhupada and he would do *bhajan* together, they'd hold Rathayatra festivals, and they'd have programs in villages in the area.

Acharya Prabhakara said that on Krishna Janmastami in 1954, he had to go to Delhi. When he came back to Jhansi, he took a little rest, woke up at 1:00 a.m. and heard Prabhupada ecstatically playing *mridanga* in the temple room. Prabhupada was chanting in total bliss. Acharya Prabhakara went upstairs and saw Prabhupada bouncing around the temple room doing *kirtan*. Prabhupada was wearing a *kadamba* flower garland that went all the way down to his feet. *Kadamba* flowers are very rare in Jhansi and when they are available they are usually the size of a golf ball, but the ones on Prabhupada's garland were big—the size of tennis balls. And he said the atmosphere and aroma was *aprakrt*—nonmaterial. It was surcharged and smelled like the heavenly planets. Acharya Prabhakara wanted to ask Srila Prabhupada, "Where did this garland come from? You can't buy it in a market." But Prabhupada wouldn't answer. He just kept doing *kirtan*, bouncing around the temple room chanting. The next morning Acharya Prabhakara asked Srila Prabhupada, "Where did you get the garland, why did it smell so much, and why were you feeling so blissful?" Srila Prabhupada told him, "I was chanting to Krishna and feeling some love for Him, and He appeared and gave me this garland. I went to touch His feet, and He disappeared. Because of that, I was dancing around the temple room." Prabhupada was crying.

Acharya Prabhakara was very believable and I felt that what he said was valid. He also said that sometimes Srila Prabhupada's mood was to do *kirtan* intensely. He would chant on and on and on—for three days straight without eating and sleeping. Ordinarily we never hear about Srila Prabhupada chanting for two or three days straight. We hear that sometimes he wouldn't eat for long periods, especially near the end, but remarkably, in Jhansi, he was doing *kirtan* for a long period of time without eating and sleeping. And the result of his *bhajan* was that Krishna appeared.

Jayapataka Swami: Srila Prabhupada went to Birnagar to make a courtesy call to Lalit Prasad Thakur, the brother of his spiritual master, Om Visnupada Srila Bhaktisiddhanta Saraswati Thakur. Birnagar is Bhaktivinoda Thakur's birthplace and Bhaktivinoda Thakur spent a good part of his childhood in that beautiful place, which is about an hour drive from Mayapur.

It was impressive to see Lalit Thakur, a pure soul who was from a whole other century. At that time he was 97 or 98 years old and he would chant nonstop all day. He had been a lifelong *brahmachari* and had worked for the government until he retired in his 50's. But throughout his life he practiced *sadhana-bhakti*. It was nice to know that Bhaktivinode Thakur had more than one child who was active in Krishna consciousness.

The Deities Lalit Thakur worshiped were on the second floor and he had a library of Bhaktivinode Thakur books. He was doing *nama-hatta* preaching in Bangladesh as well as in different parts of Bengal and he had a lot of disciples. One of his more intimate disciples was an elderly lady, in her 60's or 70's, called Bhakti Ma. Another disciple, Sacinanda, was actively preaching in the villages.

Lalit Prasad Thakur used to sit on his bed in a little room and not move much. He was bathed in his bed, he went to the bathroom in his bed and his disciples bragged that even though he would go to the toilet there it smelled like roses. And I did notice that there was no bad smell in the room.

When we first went there, Lalit Prasad Thakur seemed agreeable to ISKCON having a temple to honor Bhaktivinode Thakur at his birthplace in Birnagar. Prabhupada talked about building a library, a display, an exhibition, an *ashram*, a preaching facility, and fixing up the temple at Bhaktivinode Thakur's birthplace. At that time a small, broken-down temple marked that spot and when Prabhupada saw the poor condition it was in he practically cried.

However, later some of Lalit Prasad Thakur's followers insisted, "We shouldn't give ISKCON any land," and so the second time Prabhupada went to finalize everything there was a different mood—they weren't agreeable to having an agreement with ISKCON. Neither did they themselves have the capacity or the wherewithal to develop the birthplace of Bhaktivinode Thakur. Prabhupada became impatient and upset that everything was being canceled with no reason and that Bhaktivinode Thakur, who was so great and who deserved to have a wonderful monument for his greatness, was not being properly honored.

Suddenly Prabhupada became intense. In a loud voice he said, "Isn't it sinful that you cannot develop the birthplace of Bhaktivinode Thakur and you won't let anyone else do it either?" In other words, the birthplace was their responsibility but they couldn't develop it, and although we could develop it they wouldn't let us. It was going to stay in an undeveloped state and in fact today it's in worse condition than it was then. Prabhupada loudly and intensely asked this question four or five times very loudly, almost...I wouldn't say shouting, but I would say just maybe one level below that. Nobody said anything. Then as Prabhupada walked out he turned to the few of us secretaries and assistants who were with him and said, "Because I asked a question, there was no offense."

Srila Prabhupada was talking to the brother of his spiritual master so the etiquette of seniority was there, but at the same time, from Prabhupada's point of view, Bhaktivinode Thakur was being offended. Therefore Prabhupada expressed that he had a right to question the situation and that questioning wasn't an offense. To accuse, to say, "You are nonsense, you didn't give," would have been offensive. But questioning, "Isn't it offensive? Isn't it sinful?" was not offensive. So if somebody intensively inquires, it's technically not an offense.

Gokularanajana: One morning everybody else was scrambling to get out of the cars and for a few seconds just Tripurari and I were with Prabhupada. Some ducks were quacking and Prabhupada turned to us and said, "We must save these *mudhas*," the quacking of the materialists. Tripurari said, "Srila Prabhupada, is it true that the spiritual master will come back if the disciple falls down?" Prabhupada said, "Yes, but don't take advantage."

Udayananda: I was on the Radha-Damodar party for a little over two years, and occasionally we met Prabhupada in different places—Chicago, Atlanta, Rathayatra in San Francisco—and he would speak to us. In a personal *darshan* in Atlanta, Prabhupada stressed the importance of *brahmacharya* in spiritual life. He encouraged us to remain *brahmacharis* and he said, "If you stay *brahmachari* then you have a 75 percent chance of going back to Godhead in this very life, but if you take up the *grihastha ashram*, 25 percent. Therefore, try to see all women as *mataji*, as mother, and address them as, 'my dear *mataji*.' *Mataji* is a respectful term that means you love and respect that person just as you love and respect your own mother. A *mataji* is one of the gurus—the Bhagavatam says you should not become father or mother unless you can save your dependents from repeated birth and death. So if you address all women as *matajis*, you will not look at them as objects of sense gratification."

Arjuna: When Hari Sauri prabhu was ill, a good friend of mine, Godrum das *brahmachari*, massaged Prabhupada. Godrum, one of Prabhupada's bodyguards, was strong bodied and the first time he massaged Srila Prabhupada's chest, which was soft, it made him think of a woman's breast. Immediately Prabhupada said, "The allurement of the illusory energy takes the form of breasts of a woman." Godrum was devastated that Prabhupada could read his mind. Godrum said, "God, I'm not qualified to do this service!"

Gokularanajana: With his cane Prabhupada pointed to the skyline and said, "You see this city? This city and all cities will collapse very soon. Do you know why?" Everyone hesitated, wondering, but Tamal Krsna quickly said, "Because the people here don't know how to grow food." Everybody else was searching for some esoteric reason but Tamal gave a practical reason. Prabhupada said, "Yes." Growing food is the whole purpose of our farm communities and we still are trying to grasp their importance.

Udayananda: All the devotees were in a particularly ecstatic mood and chanted and danced in ecstasy for almost an hour in a huge *gurupuja*. Prabhupada was sitting on the *vyasasana* and at the end he said the *jaya om* prayers while everyone offered their obeisances.

Then Prabhupada said, "If you go to *gurupuja* every day with your god-brothers and god-sisters, then any problems you have between each other will be resolved." Prabhupada stressed the importance of *gurupuja* and I've had experience that when we really get into *gurupuja* we really appreciate our god-brothers and god-sisters and we especially appreciate Srila Prabhupada.

Jayapataka Swami: When Srila Prabhupada was going from Calcutta to Mayapur he would leave early in the morning and stop to have a breakfast picnic at a little mango orchard that was owned by a devotee—it was his favorite picnic spot. Once, on the way to this spot, Prabhupada noticed a picture of Krishna and Balaram on the windshield of his car and he asked the devotees, "Who is more powerful, Krishna or Balaram?" Someone said, "Balaram is more powerful, He's the older brother," and someone said Krishna is more powerful. Prabhupada said, "See, Balaram has His hand on Krishna's shoulder—Krishna is holding up Balaram—so Krishna is more powerful."

At this time one of Prabhupada's god-brothers, Damodar Maharaj, was with us and when we got to the mango orchard Prabhupada had some mats set up and he took *prasadam* with Damodar Maharaj and the rest of us also took *prasadam* a short distance away. It was a little picnic in the garden. After Prabhupada and Damodar Maharaj had taken fruit, Prabhupada said, "You can serve Damodar Maharaj water." Damodar Maharaj said, "But after fruit we shouldn't drink water." Prabhupada said, "The secret is you take a sweet, then after the sweet you must take water." If you take water after fruit, the water washes out the fruit's nutrition. But if you take a sweet, that somehow caps the fruit's nutrition and you can take water after that. So when you get thirsty after taking fruit just take a nice *maha prasad sandesh* or *rasagulla*, remember Srila Prabhupada, chant Hare Krishna and then drink a little water.

Gokularanajana: Tripurari asked Prabhupada if we get *karma* by shaking the *karmis'* hands when we are distributing books. Prabhupada said, "I hope not."

Bahushira: Kailash Chandra das was a heavy controller—Mars exalted, ready to fight. When he got initiated in Chicago, Srila Prabhupada saw right through him, as he could see right through everyone. It's a sensitive moment when a controller bows down to someone because at that time that person doesn't have control. So, as Kailash Chandra bowed down, Prabhupada said, "Your name is Kailash Chandra das...das, das, a thousand times das! Not God ...das!" Kailash Chandra jerked while he was bowing down because Prabhupada was being so strong and direct. Kailash Chandra was amazed at how Prabhupada treated him. He thought, "What am I supposed to do with this?"

Udayananda: One morning Prabhupada was walking towards the Ganga with the temple presidents, GBC and *sannyasis*. Some of the leaders took the opportunity to complain to Prabhupada, "This person in my zone is doing this," or "He isn't authorized." One after another, these leading devotees were lodging complaints and backbiting. Prabhupada walked on without speaking until all of a sudden he stopped, turned around, whipped his cane around with a big sweeping motion of his arm and said, "All of you have come simply to discourage, and I have come only to encourage." And he repeated, "All of you have come simply to discourage, and I have come only to encourage." Then he turned around and continued walking. All of a sudden those devotees started saying, "Please accept my humble obeisances, prabhu," "Please accept mine," "Forgive my offenses." I took this to heart and thought, "Whatever happens in my life and whoever I associate with, I can make a better impression if I follow this instruction of Srila Prabhupada."

Gokularanajana: With Prabhupada's permission, Jayasacinandana prabhu sang a *bhajan* for Prabhupada while Prabhupada waited for his flight. He sang one of the classic ones that Prabhupada also had sung and Jayasacinandana made every intonation, every syllable just the way Prabhupada had done it. Prabhupada closed his eyes and every now and then he'd look over at Jayasacinandana. When the song was finished, Prabhupada leaned over and said, "You listen very well," which I thought was interesting. He didn't say, "You chant very well," he said, "You listen very well." Prabhupada said that the qualification his spiritual master had noted in him was that, "You actually know how to hear and listen."

Udayananda: In a class in Chicago in 1975, Prabhupada talked about how Visvamitra Muni had performed heavy *tapasya* for 60,000 years. Then he talked about *sankirtan* and book distribution and he said, "You can get the same benefit of this *tapasya* on a few days of *sankirtan*." A few days on *sankirtan* are the equivalent of 60,000 years of *tapasya* by Visvamitra Muni! Everyone said, "*Haribol*!" After that there was a big installation of four sets of Gaura-Nitai Deities, one for each of the four buses. Srila Prabhupada's mercy was to give us this great process.

Jnanagamya: I had studied film in college and I was determined and anxious to make Krishna conscious films. I wrote Srila Prabhupada some letters about that and he wrote back, "Hitler and Napoleon and many others made so much propaganda and then what happened? Nothing happened. They're over, finished." Prabhupada emphasized book distribution and was not enthusiastic about my making films. I tried to appreciate that, but I also sent Prabhupada an outline I had written for a film and when I went to Vrindavan, Hari Sauri introduced me to Prabhupada by saying, "This is the boy who has sent you the draft." Prabhupada said to me, "Who is stopping you from doing this?" I could understand that Prabhupada understood me very well, that I was holding myself back, stopping myself from doing what I said I supposedly wanted to do.

Anyway, I continued to play with the idea and Atreya Rishi,

who was a GBC, encouraged me. He said, "Why don't you come to Iran, get a job and develop some skills." I said okay. Then, on one of his last stops on his last tour of the world, Prabhupada came to Iran and again I presented the idea of filmmaking. The complete dismay on Prabhupada's face was incredibly devastating. I thought, "Oh, my gosh, what am I doing?" It was an amazing experience.

It seemed that Prabhupada always chastised me. Once I was sitting down in Vrindavan and Prabhupada gestured, "Cover your feet." So I covered my feet. And then another time before I even sat down, Prabhupada gestured again, "Cover your feet." He remembered my faux pas.

The first time I came to India, at the big Delhi *pandal* in '76, I was one of the many bodyguards assigned to keep the crowds a little distance from Prabhupada. At the end of the *pandal* Prabhupada walked back stage and, when he was about six or eight feet away from me, two girls dove at Prabhupada's feet. There were a hundred people following Prabhupada and I thought, "My gosh, these girls are going to trip Prabhupada and all the people behind him will fall on him." So when these girls were diving, I tried to restrain them but it was useless. Although I never got close to them, Prabhupada said to me, "Why are you pushing? Why are you pushing?" I thought, "My God," and everybody stopped. Prabhupada was looking at me totally upset. After that I wandered around in a semi-conscious state until Dayananda said to me, "You really got the mercy." I thought, "Is that what it was?" I was relieved but every time I pushed anybody after that, I remembered what happened—Prabhupada was warning me.

Anyway, these personal chastisements—the conversations and letters about filmmaking, the dive-bomber devotees, covering the feet—were Krishna's arrangements. I had a more intense false ego than anybody else, and Krishna arranged for my spiritual master to smash me. For some time I took it in a negative way, especially when my *sadhana* started to slide a few years ago, and I made up a lot of stories, "Prabhupada always liked the others best and he didn't like me that much." But after some soul searching the conclusion I came to was that that is my story.

Prabhupada loved every one of his disciples no matter what their faults or their problems and he wanted all of us to go back to Godhead. Otherwise, he wouldn't have bothered to come in the first place. If he showed some exasperation with us that was good for us—it was to help us get our act together. I feel very blessed to have had Prabhupada's association in that way. If he had encouraged me or flattered me I would have probably doubted his perceptions even more. Prabhupada gave me an incredible life, all the things that I've been able to do in ISKCON, places I've been able to go, and the basic service, the *sadhana*, the chanting, the association of devotees. Nobody could offer that to anyone else unless that person was a pure personality. It could not come from anyone who had any taint of greed or selfishness. Prabhupada was a wonderful beacon of light and his concern and efforts for all of us show us that Krishna wants us to reappear in the spiritual world.

Gokularanajana: When Balavanta became a GBC in 1976, I became the temple president in Atlanta. I had been used to having the guidance of an older god-brother and I felt alone. I felt that I had risen to my level of incompetence. I thought, "Why is everybody going to stay because of me?" I was meditating in that way over and over again for a couple of months, and I was getting up the nerve to tell Srila Prabhupada, "Srila Prabhupada, I'm honored by the opportunity to serve as the temple president, but you should think about someone else. I'm not competent or ready."

Before the Rathayatra in New York I went into Prabhupada's room, paid my obeisances, looked up and Srila Prabhupada was engaged in conversation. All I knew was that I wanted to tell Prabhupada how alone I felt. Prabhupada looked right at me and with such compassion said, "One thing is, even though I was in a foreign country and I didn't know anyone, I never felt alone." I thought, "How did he know?" He said, "As long as I was following my spiritual master's instructions, I knew he was in my heart." I didn't have anything to say. I was going to be temple president for a while.

Udayananda: As the 80 of us were leaving, my dear friend Praghosa prabhu stopped, went to Prabhupada and said, "Srila Prabhupada, thank you for bringing us to Sri Dham Mayapur." Prabhupada said, "Sri Dham Mayapur is your home. This is your home. The West is only for preaching and sense gratification. So, if you're not preaching you should be home in Sri Dham Mayapur."

Jayapataka Swami: After the welcome address, Prabhupada came upstairs, sat down on his seat, leaned back relaxing, took his golden goblet, held the cup high to drink a little water, and sighed a sigh of relief and satisfaction. He said, "To be in Mayapur is wonderful. If you live in Mayapur or if you die in Mayapur, it's all the same." We thought, "Living or dying is the same? How is that, Srila Prabhupada?" He said, "Mayapur is the spiritual world. So if you're living in Mayapur, you're living in the spiritual world. And if you die in Mayapur, you go back to the spiritual world. So both are the same."

Bahushira: All six vans were lined up near the Lotus Building, the original building in Mayapur. Srila Prabhupada was on his morning walk and I was feeling weak from diarrhea. I thought, "If I get some rest before Srila Prabhupada's morning class, then I won't fall asleep in it." And I thought, "If Srila Prabhupada were to look in a van, which one would he look in?" I was trying to outwit my spiritual master. I figured he'd check Gargamuni's because that was the first one and he was coming from that direction. He might also check the last one and maybe the middle one. But he wouldn't check the second one from the last. So I crawled in that one and went to sleep. The next minute the door slides open and I see Gargamuni and Prabhupada looking at me. Gargamuni had thunder burning me. I looked up, "Oh, my God!" I offered my obeisances and said, "I'm sorry, Srila Prabhupada, I'm sick." Prabhupada said, "Ohhh," and walked away. I thought that I could outsmart the pure devotee, but you can never outsmart the pure devotee. He knew to check the second van from the end. Another lesson from Srila Prabhupada was that you could never outsmart your spiritual master.

Udayananda: It was Rasa-purnima, the full moon night in the *sarat* season when Krishna performs His *rasa lila* with the *gopis*. Panca-dravida Maharaj said, "Srila Prabhupada, do you want to hear the chapters of the *rasa lila*?" Prabhupada said, "Yes, that would be nice," and Maharaj started reading. It takes about three hours to read the five chapters. At that time somehow or other I was Prabhupada's foot massager and I was massaging Prabhupada's feet. So, there I was at the lotus feet of the *jagat guru* on Rasa-purnima at Krishna-Balaram Mandir in Sri Vrindavan Dham, listening to the *rasa lila* of Krishna and the *gopis* with His Divine Grace. Panca-dravida Maharaj read and read and I thought, "I can't get any higher than this. If I had any pious credits, I could die right now. That would be perfection." But I'm so sinful, here I am 25 years later still alive. Anyway, everyone was listening and Srila Prabhupada had his eyes closed. I thought, "Maybe he dozed off." After about two hours Maharaj mispronounced a word in a Sanskrit verse, and immediately Prabhupada corrected him and then closed his eyes again. I realized that Prabhupada was in rapt attention, he was in *samadhi,* and all the hairs on my body stood on end. Prabhupada was absorbed in hearing the pastimes of Krishna from his own Krsna Book. At the end Maharaj said, "Prabhupada, maybe we can do this every night." Prabhupada said, "Yes. We are simply here to enjoy."

Arjuna: Someone had forgotten to bring Prabhupada's *prasadam tiffin* on the train and a devotee came to ask us if we had anything that Prabhupada could eat. I gave some fruit I had purchased. Then that devotee told us that when Srila Prabhupada had been informed that his *prasadam tiffin* was missing, he didn't say anything but as the train pulled out of one station, a *samosa-wala* was going by the windows calling, "*Garam samosa*! *Garam samosa*! *Garam samosa*!" Prabhupada put his hand out, stole a *samosa,* popped it in his mouth and then said, "A *sadhu* never goes hungry." One lucky *samosa-wala* was missing one *samosa* that day.

Gokularanajana: Before the fire *yajna* began at a first initiation, Prabhupada was sitting on the *vyasasana* while Kirtanananda Maharaj lectured on the ten offenses. At one point Kirtanananda said, "You can chant any name of God," Prabhupada said, "Any bona fide name of God." It was a little reminder.

Udayananda: We had *kirtan* competitions. Devotees from the Chicago temple would do their thing, the L.A. devotees would do their thing, the Radha-Damodar party would do their thing and the London devotees would do their thing, like that. Everyone was fired up about chanting. But one of our god-brothers didn't like it. He was in Prabhupada's room with the Radha-Damodar boys and he said, "Prabhupada, it's getting completely crazy out there, all the dancing like wildmen." Prabhupada stopped him and said, "Yes. When you become a lover of Krishna, you dance just like a madman." All the Radha-Damodar boys went, "Haribol!"

Gokularanajana: There was a local pop star, a drummer in a band, who had been coming to the Sunday Feast regularly. Then at one Sunday Feast he showed up wearing a turban and he was with the Yogi Bhajan group. He'd always loved the devotees but he was challenging in a playful way. He asked a question and Prabhupada said, "You are very fortunate. You have accepted a bona fide guru, Guru Nanak. Now don't be a hypocrite. Follow. Study the *Grantha,* chant Hare Rama and read Bhagavad-gita."

This is the same instruction that Prabhupada gave to Christians. In that Sunday Feast lecture, a devotee's father and his girlfriend were there, challenging. Prabhupada basically said the same thing, "We accept Lord Jesus Christ as our guru." Prabhupada also told them, "You should be following the ten commandments," They said they did. Prabhupada said, "What about thou shalt not kill?" They said, "We don't kill." "Do you eat meat?" Prabhupada handled them very well. At that time I kept thinking how Prabhupada had said, "I can speak like this because I'm an old man. But you cannot."

Jayapataka Swami: In Mayapur Prabhupada told us that the devotees in the Gaudiya Math are expert at taking care of guests, but we are not yet so expert. He said, "You should take nice care of guests, feed them nice *prasadam*, give them personal attention, ask them how they are doing and what they need." At that time a VIP came, a commissioner from the government, and Prabhupada said, "Now I will show you," and he sat there and instructed us, "Give him more water, give him more rice, give this…" The person was flattered, "The *acharya* is personally overseeing my meal." While he was eating, Prabhupada told jokes—we never saw him tell so many jokes. Prabhupada said, "During *prasad* the talk should be light, it's good for digestion. Do not preach heavily when somebody's trying to eat."

Gokularanajana: Srila Prabhupada was definitely pleased during his visit to Atlanta, and he did many things he hadn't done before, like give a drum class. Everyone could see that he was pleased. Afterwards someone asked him, "What was it about Atlanta that pleased you so much?" Prabhupada said, "I was pleased when I saw how all the devotees were cooperating together to please me." In his last days Prabhupada gave the famous instruction, "The test of your love for me will be how you cooperate together after I am gone."

During those three days Prabhupada was in Atlanta, Tamal Krsna took the *brahmacharis* to Srila Prabhupada's room and introduced each of them to Srila Prabhupada. It was very sweet. And on Sunday, during the question and answer period after the lecture, one of those *brahmacharis* asked Srila Prabhupada, "What pleases you the most?" There was a hushed pregnant pause. Everyone was in suspense. Prabhupada chuckled and said, "If you love Krishna, if you chant Hare Krishna." I still get goose bumps thinking about that.

Udayananda: Bhakti-caru Swami came in early '77 and Prabhupada immediately gave him first and second initiation and said, "He is not a new man in this movement." Then a couple weeks later, Prabhupada was walking on the roof of the Lotus Building with Bhakti-caru Swami when Prabhupada said to him, "You have had billions of births. All of us have had billions of births, and we have always given those lives simply to sense gratification. If you give one birth to Krishna you will not be the loser. Just give one to Krishna. And if you're not satisfied, you still get more births." Prabhupada spoke matter-of-factly, just like saying the sun rises every day. He was considering transmigration, "Don't worry, you can get billions of more births. But give one to Krishna and see what happens." A week later Bhakti-caru Swami took *sannyasa*, and he's maintained his *sannyasa* vows ever since. He's given this one birth to Krishna. At any point in time we can also give our life to Krishna and that's what I'm hoping to do.

Bahushira: Dadhi Bhaksha das was innocent, boyish, and small, and an albino. He became Prabhupada's disciple in an unusual way. During one *kartik* he was going around the Krishna Balaram temple on a morning walk with Srila Prabhupada. Prabhupada had said that if you circumambulate the temple it's like seeing all the holy places. Dadhi Bhaksha was in the back and many different *sannyasis*—Tamal Krsna, Adi-keshava, and others—were walking with Srila Prabhupada. Prabhupada was saying, "And so Krishna likes sweets." From way in the back Dadhi Bhaksha interjected, "Srila Prabhupada, I like sweets!" Everyone stopped, turned around and looked, and you could almost see the arrows from the eyes of the *sannyasis*, "What is this?" Prabhupada said, "So your name is Dadhi Bhaksha das ['servant of Krishna, the yogurt eater']!" He was initiated on the spot, and everybody said, "Jaya, Prabhupada!" It was completely perfect. Prabhupada was like that, soft as a rose, hard as a thunderbolt. Dadhi Bhaksha prabhu thought the thunderbolt was coming, but the rose came.

Gokularanajana: After we performed the plays Srila Prabhupada said, "You should do more plays of the same standard. That will be good for you and good for all who see them." I took that instruction to mean that we should do plays of pastimes directly from Prabhupada's books and we should rehearse them well. Prabhupada himself said that he was in a play that was rehearsed for one year. We hadn't rehearsed for a year, but we rehearsed almost every day for several weeks and we did a dress rehearsal the week before. That's what I take "of the same standard" to mean.

Udayananda: Once, not long before Prabhupada left his body, he called Bhakti-caru Swami over. Maharaj went to Prabhupada with a humble service mood and Prabhupada talked to him in Bengali. Bhakti-caru Swami smiled sweetly and laughed and Prabhupada smiled and laughed, enjoying this *rasa* with him. I was completely envious. They were sharing an intimate Bengali moment and I thought, "He's so fortunate, he can talk to Prabhupada in his native tongue. I wonder what that joke was about." Finally Prabhupada said, "Look at this body, it's completely useless. I am practically proving that life does not come from a bag of bones." We half chuckled and were half stunned in amazement. Srila Prabhupada transcended the whole situation. He defied the "logic" of science by saying, "I am practically proving that life does not come from a bag of bones."

Bahushira: In 1977 in Bombay, we were on the library program and were getting a lot of reviews of Srila Prabhupada's books. Vaiyasaki had collected a lot, as well as Maha Vishnu, Prabha Vishnu,

Birsringha, Yajna das, Nrsingha Caitanya, Abhinanda and I. We had taken these reviews to Srila Prabhupada and Prabhupada started crying when he read them. If Srila Prabhupada cries from joy at some service, that service is the utmost a disciple can do. When Gargamuni told us how Prabhupada had responded, we felt we'd done something in our life that was very pertinent. We felt successful and complete.

Udayananda: Govardhan das and I arrived in Vrindavan and checked into a room in the Krishna-Balaram guesthouse. Three minutes later Upendra knocked on the door and said, "Prabhupada wants to see you right away." Prabhupada had asked for Govardhan because in Detroit, where he was temple president, they'd just had a magnificent wedding for Lekhasravanti, Walter Reuther's daughter. Ambarish was the best man. So it was Ford and Reuther, and the ceremony was covered by Time magazine, the New York Times, the Chicago Tribune, the Detroit Free Press— there was tremendous publicity throughout the country and it was a magnificent preaching opportunity.

We were on our way to Prabhupada's room when Tamal Krsna Maharaj stopped us and said, "You've never seen Srila Prabhupada look the way he does now. He's not robust and healthy and it might be a shocking and painful sight for you. But don't cry and don't say anything negative. Just say encouraging things." Maharaj didn't want Prabhupada to be anxious. He said, "We're trying to encourage Prabhupada, to uplift his spirits, to make him enthused to go on preaching for at least another 10 years. So don't look shocked, don't be sad." We thought, "Okay, we're prepared to do this."

Prabhupada was lying in his bed and we offered our obeisances. Then we stood at Prabhupada's feet and saw him. We were shocked. Govardhan immediately lost it and quietly sobbed, covering his mouth with his *chaddar*. Prabhupada smiled and said, "Who has come?" Tamal said, "It's Govardhan and Udayananda from Detroit, Prabhupada." Prabhupada said, "Are your accommodations in the

Krishna-Balaram guesthouse okay? Did you get *prasadam*? Are you comfortable? Is everything all right?" Govardhan, who was saddened by Srila Prabhupada's condition, couldn't talk, so I said, "Yes, Srila Prabhupada, it's first class. Thank you for taking such good care of us." Prabhupada said, "Are the devotees in Detroit happy in Krishna consciousness? And how are Lekhasravanti and Ambarish? How is the temple and how is the Deity worship? Are you preaching in the neighborhood?" Prabhupada went on talking about everyone else's well-being.

The *kaviraj* who was treating Srila Prabhupada had treated thousands of people with the same condition and he had said, "This disease is so painful that others have writhed in pain—they can barely tolerate the pain—and they become incoherent, delirious." But Prabhupada's consciousness was crystal clear and he was simply concerned about the well-being of others. Never once did he say, "Look at my condition. Look at how I am suffering." I was trying to wrap my mind around how a person in such a condition could be so selfless.

Arjuna: Prabhupada had a dream about an excellent *kaviraj* from Calcutta. This *kaviraj* came to Vrindavan and was treating Prabhupada. He was *dhira*, a sober practitioner, brahminical, and very reverential to Prabhupada. He was from the Sri Sampradaya and wore big white and red *tilak*. One day he said, "At first I doubted that your Guru Maharaj was a *paramahamsa*. But I have treated thousands of dying people, and in this condition—when there's no more muscle and fat to cushion the nerves from being pressed against the bone—usually people are in such agony that I have to administer morphine. However, your Guru Maharaj never manifests the slightest expression of pain."

I also saw this in March-April in Bombay. At that time Srila Prabhupada's whole jaw was swollen. When we get a toothache, we can't tolerate it. But Prabhupada tolerated it. We never saw any difference in his mannerisms, in his way of dealing with anyone, and he never complained. In fact, when the devotees were trying to induce him to take care of his body, Prabhupada wasn't agreeable. He transcended his body. It was very evident that Srila Prabhupada was a successful *astanga-yogi*, that he had totally transcended his bodily conception and was a true living saint.

Jnanagamya: On one of his visits to Dallas I asked Prabhupada, "How can we repay you?" Prabhupada was quiet for a minute and then said, "You can't repay me but you should always feel very obligated." For me, even when I don't feel confident in or turned on about devotional service or when I allow politics to get in the way, I still feel obligated to my spiritual master. This sense of responsibility, this feeling that there is something important for us to do, that is Prabhupada's perfect gift to his followers.

As a child I remember feeling, "There's something very important I have to do in this life. I have no idea what it is, but I'm going to do something that's going to be very important." So that could translate into becoming successful in the material sphere, or it could translate into becoming a loving servant of Krishna.

Prabhupada was a simple person and his activities were simplified. He didn't complicate his life with so much stuff. Once at *gurukula*, the children gave him their drawings of Krishna and Prabhupada looked through them. I thought, "These are wonderful pictures of Krishna from little pure devotees." But Prabhupada put them down and walked away. He wasn't interested in taking anything. He accepted things and then distributed them again. While I would have taken such pictures to put on my wall and to treasure, he was going on and on and on, constantly accepting adulation from people, their worship, and then offering that to Krishna everywhere he went. He never got bogged down or overwhelmed by it. His ego was never out of joint by doing those things. The incredible impression I had of Prabhupada is that he was a perfect living being and that his desire was to make us also perfect in our relationship with Krishna.

Udayananda: My god-brother Praghosa prabhu went to Washington, D.C. to distribute books at the airport and when he came back from *sankirtan* one day, Srila Prabhupada saw him and said, "Where have you been?" Praghosa offered his obeisances and said, "I've been distributing books, Srila Prabhupada." Prabhupada said, "Come with me," and together they went into Prabhupada's room. Prabhupada said, "Where are you doing your service these days?" Praghosa said, "I'm in New York, Prabhupada, in the 55th Street temple." Prabhupada said, "Oh, you're in New York? I also started in New York" as if every single devotee in the movement did not know everything about Prabhupada, especially where he started.

In his last days, Prabhupada talked about going on parikrama around Govardhan, but he wasn't focused only on Govardhan. When news and letters arrived about the preaching and the book distribution that was going on, Prabhupada became inspired and once he said, "I should give up lying here in Vrindavan and go out and preach. You should take me to the New York temple. And if I die, put my tomb on top of the Radha-Govinda temple on 55th Street. I want to die preaching with my New York preachers." So we know how important that temple was to Prabhupada and what a catastrophe it was to have lost that temple. Prabhupada said, "Place my tomb on the top of the 55th Street temple."

Arjuna: In 1978, Yasodanandan Swami and I went with the *gurukula* boys for the Magh Mela in Allahabad, and at that time we met Devraha Baba, an 800 year-old saint who lived in a house on stilts. Usually he never came down from his house because everyone tried to touch his feet. But when we went he came down and for almost ten minutes he spoke in Sanskrit glorifying Srila Prabhupada as a *saktyavesa-avatar*. He was so old that even his eyebrows hung down in dreadlocks. He called some of his disciples, who were two, three, and four hundred years old. It was very significant how this great, highly respected saint of India wonderfully glorified Srila Prabhupada.

When Prabhupada departed, a cyclone swept through India. I was in Vrindavan and had delayed returning to Mayapur for about two weeks because we all felt that Prabhupada was close to departing. But then I thought, "No, I have to go and do my service." I got to Mayapur Sunday night, and around three in the morning my *brahmachari* roommate, Siddhartha, woke me up. He said, "Prabhupada's here!" I immediately got up and offered my obeisances. Then Siddhartha said, "Oh, it must have been a dream." We tried to take rest again but a cyclone swept through and a huge *nim* tree keeled over, wham! It woke up the whole neighborhood. Then the next morning we heard that Prabhupada had departed. We *brahmacharis* thought, "Wow, Prabhupada came and took his *nim* tree." And the newspaper reported that a weird snap storm swept throughout India. On the front page there was a photo of a tidal wave in Madras with flames on top of it. We thought, "Wow, how a pure devotee's departure creates inauspicious symptoms."

TAPE 45

Candramauli Swami
Prajapati das
Sukadev das
Pita das
Sumati dasi
Jagajivan das
Sarvabhavana das
Dhanesvara das

Candramauli Swami: Prabhupada was sitting outside surrounded by a large group of devotees and he glanced in my direction. It seemed like he was looking at me and looking through me. I'll never forget that look. I thought, "Oh, my God, he's seeing what I don't want him to see." The fact that he noticed me was a nice experience but the other half of it was, "I'm afraid of what he's seeing."

Prajapati: We'd come from Dallas to Los Angeles to get initiated and the first time we saw Prabhupada he was getting out of a car to go into his quarters. His effulgence seemed to fill the whole street. Everybody couldn't help but have tears in their eyes. Prabhupada was not only effulgent, but also his love of Krishna was contagious—we all got a glimpse of his ecstasy just by being with him.

The next morning was the day I was supposed to get initiated and after *mangal arati* I was stringing my neckbeads. In those days, we didn't have neckbeads with clasps. When you got initiated, your neckbeads were fastened together with a knot so they were tied on for life. One devotee came over to me and said, "Prabhupada wants you on the morning walk." I said, "What do I do?" He said, "Meet at the foot of Prabhupada's stairs." I went there and a devotee said, "Where's your flower?" I said, "What do you mean, flower?" He said, "If you're going to greet Prabhupada, you have to have a flower." I said, "Where do I get it?" "You have to find one." I looked but I could only find one insignificant little rosebud, so I held it in my hand and waited for Prabhupada. He came down the stairs, we offered our obeisances, and then they introduced me. I again offered my obeisances to Prabhupada, and when I got up they had all walked out to get in their little Ford compact two-door car that said "Hare Krishna" on the side. Prabhupada was sitting in front, Karandhar was driving, and there were four or five of us in the backseat—somehow I got in on the bottom and devotees piled in on top of me, all wanting to go on the walk with Prabhupada.

Just as we pulled out onto Venice Boulevard, a bearded, older drunk guy, who had been thrown out of the temple earlier, was sitting on the curb dejected. When he saw Prabhupada in the car, he looked up and said, "Hare Krishna" in a gruff voice. Prabhupada laughed in such a musical, contagious way that all of us in the car also laughed hysterically, not knowing exactly why we were laughing except that Prabhupada had laughed.

On the ride to the beach Prabhupada asked me, "What is God?" Now, Mohanananda had primed me, "This is one of the questions Prabhupada might ask you." So I'd learned, "The Supreme Person complete in six opulences, all wealth, all beauty..." I was nervous but I said, "Prabhupada, God is the person..." and I started telling him what I thought was the correct answer. He said, "That's what *we* say. What do *they* say?" Prabhupada wanted to know what I had learned as a theologian. I said, "Prabhupada, they can't make up their mind. They have no idea who God is." He said, "You must defeat them. These people don't know who God is. Therefore, by claiming they know God when they don't, they are cheating."

Sukadev: Daily I had been going on morning walks with Srila Prabhupada and once when we were driving back in the car I said, "Srila Prabhupada, you said that if a tree has fruit then it becomes beautiful, and if a woman has a child then she becomes beautiful. When does a disciple become beautiful?" I was praising myself, thinking, "This is such a nice metaphor and I asked such a nice question about it." Prabhupada immediately laced into me. He said, "Oh? You have not read our books? What is the meaning of this verse, *ar na koriho mane asa*? What is the meaning?" I said, "I don't know, Srila Prabhupada." Prabhupada looked at me and said, "Hmm, parrot-like chanting." I was driving so I could not jump out of the car, and there were heavy-duty *sannyasis* in the car—Brahmananda, Guru Kripa—who gave me the *sannyasi* sour look, "Sukadev, what are you doing asking Prabhupada this question?" I thought, "Oh, Krishna!" Then Prabhupada said, "What is the meaning of *yasya prasadad bhagavat-prasado*?" I said, "By the mercy of the spiritual master one gets the mercy of Krishna, Srila Prabhupada." Prabhupada said, "Yes. When the disciple is strictly following the order of the spiritual master, then he is beautiful. Otherwise he is ugly."

Pita: One by one each boy came in to meet Prabhupada and when we were all there Prabhupada said, "You all are gems. You are a hundred percent engaged in devotional service, you are all *brahmacharis*, and you are selling my books. Thank you very much. Just do your level-headed best." I felt great relief when I heard this because I was under a lot of pressure on that party—the devotees pushed us hard and hyped us up to sell Prabhupada's books. But Prabhupada said, "Just do your level-headed best." And the idea of level-headed sunk into me. I thought, "This is logical and spiritual, this is the truth. Prabhupada only wants our level-headed best."

One devotee asked, "Prabhupada, if we die on *sankirtan* will we go back home, back to Godhead?" Prabhupada said, "Whatever state the mind is in at the time of death, that state you will attain. If you think of Krishna and you die on *sankirtan*, you go back to Godhead. If you don't think of Him, then maybe not." Everyone in the room sighed—they hadn't gotten what they wanted. Then Prabhupada said, "But I promise you this: if you distribute my books until your dying day, Lord Chaitanya will personally come and take you back home, back to Godhead." Then the devotees were relieved, "Ahhh!"

Sumati: I received my second initiation from Srila Prabhupada so that I could care for the Deities, but I didn't know anything about *gayatri* mantra and I didn't know that there was a way that you counted the mantras on your fingers. Prabhupada showed me the finger movements for *gayatri* but I didn't know what he was doing. When he did the same movements again I thought, "Oh, maybe he wants my beads," so I took my beads out of my bead bag but he said, "No." Then he took my hand in his hand, took my thumb and put it on each of the places to show me how to chant the *gayatri* mantra. Many years later I became aware that there were times when the *guru*, knowing his disciple was not pure enough to care for the Deities, would touch that person to purify him or her enough to be with Krishna on the altar. I felt, "Oh, that makes sense. I certainly needed that purification."

Jagajivan: In Mayapur and other places I started making 16 mm films of Srila Prabhupada. Sometimes I wouldn't have film in the camera, but I would use it as a trick to go on the morning walks: "I'm filming." The devotee in charge would say, "The camera crew is okay." On one morning walk there was a pole sticking up with a bull's path around it and Prabhupada said, "That pole is a *griha*." The bull was connected to the pole and couldn't leave the area.

All our macho *grihasthas* out there are the bulls connected to the pole.

Pita: Prabhupada told us that he wanted us all to be *brahmacharis*, to never marry. He said, "If you all remain *brahmachari*, you'll have a 90% chance of going back home, back to Godhead. As soon as you marry, there's only a 50% chance. As soon as you marry, you must have an apartment and then you must put so many things inside. If you are a *brahmachari*, you can sleep under a tree."

Sarvabhavana: At first I found some of the management policies regarding the restaurant, the guesthouse and the cooking a little strange, but later on I understood. For example, in Vrindavan Prabhupada wanted three separate small kitchens, each with a little mud-caked oven that burns wood or coal. Prabhupada said, "I don't want our life members to go outside to drink tea. If they want it, let them brew their tea here. Provide this facility." So we made three small cubicles where life members could make tea for themselves. Initially, you might think that tea is an intoxicant that devotees are not supposed to take, and here Prabhupada is providing tea facilities for guests and life members. I asked, "Prabhupada, sometimes fanatic devotees say, 'How can you do that?'" He said, "When a guest comes to the house, then you try to fulfill all his wishes as long as it doesn't involve sinful activities. We may not drink tea because that is part of *sadhana* and because drinking tea is in the mode of ignorance, but it's not sinful. There is no harm if you provide facilities for guests to make their own tea."

Candramauli Swami: Before the class, Ambarish das, a New Vrindavan cowherd boy, led *gurupuja*. When he finished singing, Pusta Krishna Maharaj, Prabhupada's servant, picked up the *mridanga* and started to chant the Hare Krishna maha-mantra. We wondered why he did that because it seemed like Ambarish had already ended the *kirtan*. Later we learned that Srila Prabhupada never liked to be worshiped without Krishna also being worshiped in the same *kirtan*. In other words, even in his *gurupuja kirtans*, we had to chant Hare Krishna because Prabhupada felt that worship of the spiritual master must include worship of Krishna. This experience taught us something important.

Prajapati: Since I had a degree in theology, Prabhupada wanted me to write theology. The first morning I walked with him he said, "You must defeat the rascal theologians who mislead innocent people." Then, on a series of morning walks that started in December of '73, Prabhupada said, "Theologician, you must write on the necessity of God." I said, "Yes, Prabhupada." The next day he said, "Did you do it?" I went home, quickly wrote something and gave it to Prabhupada's servant. Then the next day Prabhupada said, "Very good. Where will you have it published?" He really pushed me in that area.

And he pushed me in the area of theater also. The temple in Juhu had a big theater and Prabhupada wanted us to perform there. One of his last requests to us was that we have a theater troupe performing Krishna *lila* six months of the year based in Juhu and six months in the West. Once we did a play for him in Los Angeles called "The Cry of the She-Jackal," from a chapter in the *Bhagavatam* called, "The Pandavas Retire Timely." Prabhupada liked it very much. He blessed us that we were all going back to Godhead and afterwards in his quarters he said, "You must perfect this play. You don't need to do a lot of plays. Just take this one and one or two others, and perform it everywhere in the world." And in a letter about the theater and dance troupe he said, "You can have a party of about 15 people that can go everywhere. Sell tickets to cover the expenses." He was enthusiastic about plays based on Chaitanya *lila* and Krishna *lila*, stories from the *Bhagavatam*, as well as contemporary plays dealing with philosophical issues, all as part of the Hare Krishna cultural expansion.

Dhanesvara: After I received my master's degree from the University of Florida I wanted to blend science and Krishna consciousness, so I asked Prabhupada by letter how I should use my scientific credentials in Krishna's service. Perhaps through experiments I could demonstrate how the light from the moon nourishes vegetables, based on Lord Krishna statement in *Bhagavad-gita,* and in that way convince scientists. In his reply, Prabhupada suggested something different than what I anticipated. He wrote, "The topmost science is this Krishna consciousness and that is a fact. The so-called modern science has become spoiled for lack of this perspective. Real science means to acquire perfect knowledge from the parampara, not by so-called academic and empirical research. Such technique is bogus and will not help us in obtaining perfect knowledge.

Yes, you should use your scientific credentials to present this Krishna conscious philosophy. Everything may be used in Krishna's service. It may not be possible to convince the rascal scientists of this Krishna consciousness philosophy because after all, Krishna gives everyone free will and if it is their determination to remain atheistic how shall it be checked? Our principle aim is to challenge their nonsense proposition so that the layman and common people may be saved from this rascaldom . . . Krishna consciousness is perfect so it can be substantiated by all means of argument and logic. The main theme is that life has come from life and not generated from matter as they foolishly claim. You just prove this point and it will be a great victory."

That letter was very instructive for me because I saw that Prabhupada had a practical way of approaching things and that he was aiming at the mass of people. Over the years I've come to see how, especially in the universities, it's practically an academic requirement to be atheistic, so it is very difficult to try to convince the professors of something otherwise.

Pita: At Ratha-yatra, Srila Prabhupada told us the story of how Krishna took the form of Jagannatha. He said, "One day Krishna was walking through the halls in His palace in Dwaraka when He heard Rohini and Rukmini talking. Rukmini said to Rohini, 'Last night when He was sleeping, I heard Krishna saying the name Radha, Radha, Radha. Who is Radha?' Rohini said, 'Radha is very special and the relationship between Radha and Krishna is very special. Let me tell you the story of Radha-Krishna's relationship.' Krishna listened while Rohini told the story and as He listened He became stunned and He took the form of Jagannatha with big eyes and a big smile." Prabhupada smiled broadly, "Later Subhadra came by, saw Krishna stunned, also listened, became stunned and took the form of Subhadra as we see in the Deities. And the same thing happened to Baladev."

Sumati: The large Jagannatha Deities in Boston were badly cracked. Satsvarupa asked me to write to Prabhupada to ask what we should do about it. I did that and Prabhupada wrote back saying they should be put in the sea and we should carve new Deities. At the time Lord Jagannatha's clothes weren't being changed at night so I also asked Prabhupada if Lord Jagannatha could wear pajamas at night. Prabhupada wrote back and said, "Yes, that would be very nice."

Sukadev: Somehow or other in 1976 I wound up as president of the Hawaii temple. When Prabhupada was there I said to him, "Prabhupada, I don't want to stay here. These devotees don't like me, I'm having trouble, and I want to get out of here." Prabhupada said, "No, you will stay." "I want to go, Prabhupada." "No, you will stay. Depend on Krishna and Krishna will save you."

At that time I had been praying to do some direct service for Srila Prabhupada and one day Hari Sauri came to my office and said, "Prabhupada wants a Coleman burner." I said, "What for?" He said, "Prabhupada's going to cook his own *prasadam*." "Why would Prabhupada cook his own *prasadam*? We have so many devotees here.

No one's sincere enough to cook for Prabhupada?" He said, "The girl who's been doing this service has been adding too much salt even after Prabhupada told her to put less." I said, "Although there's so much going on, I'll cook for Prabhupada." Of course, I had no instruction. Here I had to cook for the spiritual master of the universe and I had no instruction. Afterwards I asked Hari Sauri, who was his personal servant, how my cooking was and he said, "Prabhupada said everything was good but the *dahl*. It was untouchable." I was in shock and I asked Hari Sauri, "What has to be done?" Prabhupada wanted the *dahl* cooked thoroughly so that it was all soup. I said, "No problem." I cooked the next day and I then asked, "How was the *prasadam*?" Hari Sauri said, "Prabhupada said everything was perfect." Just by hearing those words, I felt such intense happiness that I wanted to run outside and jump up and down. I never felt so much ecstasy as when Prabhupada said that everything I had cooked was perfect.

Sarvabhavana: Regarding translating, Prabhupada gave me some wonderful instructions that I treasure and try to follow. He told me there are two ways of translating. One is literal and the other is *bhavartha*—to capture the spirit, to convey the deep spiritual and devotional mood of the acharya who wrote the original work. Prabhupada said, "I prefer *bhavartha*, to translate the spirit and mood of these writings rather than to translate literally. I want you to read the original Bengali or Sanskrit or Hindi, understand it, formulate it in your own words and write it."

Once in Vrindavan when Satsvarupa Maharaj was there, Prabhupada told him, "You should edit *Renunciation Through Wisdom*, it is a very important book." And it truly is an incredible book—it's a gradual unfolding of the philosophy and purport of *Bhagavad-gita* in which, in the original Bengali writing, Prabhupada excelled himself. In English Prabhupada wrote simply but his Bengali writing was scholarly and erudite. To translate this work was quite challenging and every single day Prabhupada asked me to read the English translation to him while he read the Bengali. He liked my work and that made me blissful.

Jagajivan: Some man said, "Buenos dias" to Prabhupada. Prabhupada asked Hridayananda Maharaj, "What is he saying?" Maharaj said, "That means 'good day' in Spanish." Prabhupada said, "Ah, buenos dias." Prabhupada began his Spanish speaking at that point. I was surprised and impressed because his pronunciation was perfect. Prabhupada was a great linguist.

Pita: One time when he was speaking from the *vyasasana* Prabhupada said, "Don't use this philosophy like a knife. This philosophy is very strong and you can use it like a knife, you can cut with it." Another time Prabhupada said, "Jumping, jumping, jumping, just like a monkey, over the head of your spiritual master. You'll all become monkeys in Vrindavan for deviating from the order of the spiritual master."

Prajapati: Prabhupada saw a *Bhagavad-gita* dance and a Pralambasura dance that we did in Los Angeles and he asked us to perform these at the opening of the Krishna-Balaram Mandir in Vrindavan. We also performed in Mayapur and the way the stage was arranged there our backs were to the Deities. Earlier we had been told that that was not acceptable, that the deity doors should be closed, and so we had some argument with the authorities that had made the arrangement in Mayapur. But since they were GBC and we were lowly dancers and actors, we did it their way. Prabhupada didn't see the performance, but in his quarters he saw photographs of it. He said, "Backs should not be to the deity." Instead of saying, "Yes, Prabhupada," we tried to explain that we were told that Krishna is all-pervasive, therefore it was okay if we had our backs to Him. Prabhupada got furious and animated. He said, "Krishna is all-pervasive? Then you should dance on the roof!"

Once in New York, we performed the Krishna-Rukmini play

and Prabhupada said some wonderful things. He said, "These plays are better than reading my books," because they were bringing the books to life. And of course, his books should be brought to life.

Candramauli Swami: On a morning walk in Central Park I was way in the back when Prabhupada was talking about how, in this materialistic civilization, everybody rushes around in different ways. He said, "The man is running on four tires and the dog is running on four legs. So what is the difference? No difference. They are both doing the same business, running. Running for what? Sense gratification."

Pita: In the middle of a class Prabhupada began a sentence and I realized that he was going to say something grammatically incorrect. I thought, "Just see, he's a perfect master yet he's going to say something grammatically incorrect." Prabhupada stopped speaking, looked right at me (even though there were 300 people in the room), looked back up, said the whole sentence perfectly, then looked at me and nodded his head. I melted into the floor and thought, "That couldn't have happened. I hope he didn't know what I was thinking." It was amazing. Then I thought, "Wow, Prabhupada is the perfect master. He really knows."

Sukadev: Prabhupada said that you have to become like the bumblebee and not like the fly and Prabhupada proved it by his own example. Once Nara-Narayan—who does not sing like a nightingale—was in the temple room singing and Prabhupada said, "Who is that singing?" Karandhar said, "It's Nara-Narayan, Srila Prabhupada." Prabhupada said, "Hmm, he keeps very good time."

Sumati: The temple in Boston used to be an old house on North Beacon Street. Between the men's and ladies restrooms there were a couple hooks on the wall and when Prabhupada was going into the men's room he noticed *japa* beads hanging from one of those hooks.

He took them and said, "These beads are crying. They should never be left here next to the stool room. They should always be around your neck or in a bead bag." When he said, "These beads are crying," it was an important lesson about how sacred the beads are.

Pita: Srila Prabhupada went through the doll studio and when he saw the changing bodies exhibit he said, "From boyhood to youth to old age the body changes but the soul remains the same. This is not a Hindu problem or a Muslim problem or a Christian problem. This is a universal problem. This Krishna consciousness movement will stop this death business. This is nonsectarian—it is not a religion. This is how to stop the birth, death, disease and old age problems."

We showed Prabhupada the *murti* of himself that Locan prabhu had made and when the head of the *murti* moved, Prabhupada liked it very much. He said, "Now that you've done this I will never leave. In this form I will sit on the *vyasasana* and I will always be with you." Prabhupada told us that his *murti* form was non-different from him and that he will always be present there.

Dhanesvara: I asked Amarendra that if Prabhupada is *jiva-tattva*, not *krishna-tattva*, how could he expand in so many pictures to receive the offerings of his disciples? The *jiva* is localized yet we offer *bhoga* and prayers to Prabhupada's picture. My question was, "How can Prabhupada be present in all these places to receive the offerings?" Amarendra said, "Why don't you write to Prabhupada and ask him?" I was pleased that he suggested that because at that time the movement was very large, with thousands of devotees, and Prabhupada couldn't possibly deal with everybody one-on-one. I didn't want to burden Prabhupada with my question. But since my temple president had ordered me to, I thought, "Great, I'll write." I asked Prabhupada that question and several others as well. The reply letter was to Bhakta Don, dated 1 December 1973, and it is in the *Siksamrta* book under "Spiritual Master," as well as in the Folio. Prabhupada said, "The spiritual master is present wherever his sincere disciple is trying to serve his instructions. This is possible by the mercy of Krishna. In your attempts to serve me and in all your sincere devotional sentiments I am with you as my guru maharaj is with me. Remember this always."

In his letters, Prabhupada sometimes gave specific instructions to individuals and sometimes he gave general instructions. I consider this a general instruction that applies to me and to all the devotees. The wonderful thing about this is that Prabhupada did not say he was with us only "in your successes and in your accomplishments." No, he said he was with us, "in all of your attempts and in all of your sincere devotional sentiments." This is wonderful and I always remember it.

Prajapati: On that first morning walk Prabhupada asked us a question. He said, "What if the mind wanted the eyes to see?" It wasn't until years later that I understood that question. We can't see without the help of the sun or some form of electricity—our eyes are completely dependent. Inwardly also the light of consciousness and the Supersoul allow our eyes to see, and in that sense we are totally dependent on Krishna. Prabhupada was pointing out that everything that we take for granted, like vision, is totally dependent on Krishna. We can't do anything independently. Our disease, *maya,* exists not in the world around us but, as Prabhupada writes in the Prayers of Lord Brahma in the *Krsna Book*, "The existence of *maya* is only within the mind. *Maya* is nothing but ignorance of Krishna's personality. When one forgets His personality then that is the conditioned state of *maya*. Therefore, one who is fixed upon Him both internally and externally is not illusioned." Our vision is incorrect. When we are Krishna conscious, we see everything as Krishna's energy.

Prabhupada was not Krishna, but he was as close to Krishna as a living entity could come. He was totally transparent to Krishna, as was Jesus Christ and Mohammed and other great religionists. On one side there's a danger to minimize Prabhupada and maximize somebody else, and on the other side there's a danger to elevate Prabhupada to be the Supreme Person. As Prabhupada himself explains in *Caitanya-caritamrta,* he is the Supreme Personality of Servitor Godhead.

Pita: Prabhupada saw the *Gandharvas* we had made and said, "What is this?" We said, "These are *Gandharvas.*" Prabhupada says, "*Gandharvas* don't have wings. Only Garuda has wings. He is unique." We thought, "Angels don't have wings." With Srila Prabhupada we would learn that some things were not the way we thought they were. Prabhupada would say, "No, it's not like that."

Sukadev: Once Hari Sauri's alarm clock went off and Prabhupada said, "What is that sound?" Hari Sauri said, "That's the alarm clock, Srila Prabhupada." Prabhupada said, "Oh? Who is in danger?" I looked at Hari Sauri and thought, "Wow! My spiritual master has a sense of humor!" I couldn't believe it because I had never heard Prabhupada use puns or sarcasm. Prabhupada didn't make a habit of it, but it was there. We laughed.

Candramauli Swami: Prabhupada said that out of the four bodily activities—eating, sleeping, mating and defending—the most dangerous one for a devotee is oversleeping because it leads to the others. He said, "First of all, if you sleep too much you're wasting time that should be used for Krishna's service. And secondly, too much sleep enhances the attraction for eating and for mating." That shocked me. I thought another one of the bodily activities was the most dangerous.

Sarvabhavana: Once, in the Calcutta temple in '76, the evening *arati* had just ended and I was supposed to call Srila Prabhupada from his room so he could come and give the lecture. Before I entered his room, which was near the temple room, I slightly pulled his

Venetian blinds and peeked in. Prabhupada was sitting with his back to me. The little garlands from small Radha-Govindaji—the Deities worshiped in the Calcutta temple—were around his ears. Devotees in the temple room were singing the Nrisimha prayers, Prabhupada was swaying his head in time and those garlands were also swinging. He was totally absorbed in his transcendental world but, although I don't think I made any noise, he immediately said, "Yes, please come in." That's Srila Prabhupada. It's incredible that he was here and at the same time he was totally absorbed in Krishna.

Jagajivan: We stopped near a concrete tank that had two crocodiles in it. I don't know how but Prabhupada was able to distinguish which was the male and which was the female. Just as Prabhupada said, "This is the male," that crocodile opened his huge mouth. Prabhupada said, "Ohhh, no food." The timing was just right. Then Prabhupada said, "He is inviting us." That was Srila Prabhupada's humor.

Pita: In Vrindavan Prabhupada commented about the atmosphere and the birds and when he heard the *arati* ceremony he said, "The highest service that a human being can perform is to be a *pujari* because, although the *pujari* has a material body, the *pujari* serves the Supreme Personality of Godhead. The *pujari* wakes the Lord up, bathes, dresses and feeds Him. These are activities of the spiritual world, but the *pujari* does them in this world. This is the perfection of human life. There is nothing higher than being a *pujari*." My godbrothers had always told me that the highest service was distributing books but Prabhupada said that on the absolute platform the highest service is to serve Krishna eternally and being a *pujari* is a way to do that. If you are a *pujari*, you have attained your constitutional position even within *samsara*. Prabhupada said, "This person is liberated."

Prajapati: Once Prabhupada told us how he stays Krishna conscious. He said, "In my room I have a *mridanga* so I play it for a while. When I get tired of that, I do some translation. When I finish with that, I sing a song on the harmonium. Then I have correspondence to do. I have one activity after another, all connected to Krishna."

Sumati: Once a week, Satsvarupa, Suhotra and I did a radio show at Northeastern University in Boston. It was a big radio station and a lot of people listened. We would pick a story from *Krsna Book,* Satsvarupa would write a script and we would do an hour-long dramatization on the show. When Prabhupada was in New York, Satsvarupa took him tapes of three or four shows. Satsvarupa played Krishna, Suhotra played the demon and I played Mother Yasoda. One story was Krishna subduing the Kaliya serpent. When Mother Yasoda saw Krishna wrapped in Kaliya's coils she cried Krishna's name with the utmost desperation and I really cried Krishna's name. Srila Prabhupada said to Satsvarupa, "Stop the tape." Prabhupada said, "Who is that?" Satsvarupa said, "That's Sumati." Prabhupada said, "Tell her to always cry for Krishna like that." That's my favorite story and I try to keep it in my heart, even though I don't cry for Krishna like that.

Jagajivan: In Caracas an Indian man was babbling on a lot of nonsense to Prabhupada. Prabhupada said, "One thing I want to tell you is that while you are speaking I am chanting Hare Krishna." And you could see that Prabhupada was in fact chanting—his Adam's apple was moving. *Kirtaniyah sada hari*, Prabhupada was constantly chanting Hare Krishna. Someone may say, "Did Prabhupada chant a fixed number of rounds?" But at that time I understood that Prabhupada was always chanting Krishna's glories. He also may have been indirectly telling the man, "You are speaking nonsense and therefore I am chanting Hare Krishna." Anyway, I understood that Prabhupada always chanted Hare Krishna.

Sukadev: Pusta Krsna said, "Prabhupada, what should I do with this bug?" I thought, "In this city—or state or country—who else can we ask, 'What to do with this bug?'" If you go to the mayor or the governor or the president of the United States and say, "What should I do with this bug?" he would look at you like you're crazy. "Why's he asking me? You squish it or do whatever you want with it." But a devotee was asking Prabhupada this question and Prabhupada didn't look at him as if he was crazy or asking something bizarre. Prabhupada said, "Take him to the window." Pusta Krsna let the bug out the window. Prabhupada said, "This is Vaishnava. A Vaishnava is kind to every living entity. Not this squishing business." We were amazed that Prabhupada made a question about a bug into a Krishna conscious event.

Jagajivan: Prabhupada stopped walking in front of some stool and said, "They think that dry stool is better than wet stool. Similarly, they say that dying a violent death is not good, but dying a quiet death is very good."

Pita: Although it was devastating when you first saw Prabhupada's deteriorated physical condition, after you were with him for a while you got used to it. When devotees saw him in that condition for the first time they'd cry and we'd all start crying seeing these devotees crying. At one point Prabhupada said, "Why are you all crying?" We said, "Srila Prabhupada, we're crying because you're so sick and we are afraid that you may leave." Prabhupada said, "I will never leave you. I live forever in my books so there's no reason to cry. Old people die, that is natural. When a young person dies there's some mistake because a young person should live until he's old. When he's old he should die. For me it's a natural thing, so don't cry."

One devotee said, "But Srila Prabhupada, we are crying because we can't be without you and when you leave, we won't know how to communicate with you." Prabhupada said, "I will communicate with you through your heart. I will come to you in your dreams. I will communicate with you through dreams as *caitya-guru*." I found that controversial because I thought my god-brothers wouldn't have approved, but Prabhupada said it, that he would communicate with us through dreams.

At times Prabhupada would say, "You all have very good mothers. Yes, all you boys have very good mothers." We said, "But our mothers, are meat-eaters." Prabhupada said, "The qualities of the son come from the mother. You are all good devotees, so I know you have good mothers." Prabhupada complimented us.

Prabhupada also said, "My Guru Maharaj left his body out of disgust—his disciples had not followed his order. But I'm not disgusted with you. I'm very satisfied and pleased with my disciples. Never think that I'm not happy with you. And I'm happy to have your association. You are good association." Because Prabhupada trained us in Krishna consciousness he saw us as good association.

Sumati: I heard the maha-mantra on the radio as part of the musical "Hair," and as soon as I heard it I loved it. It was my favorite song and I sang it all the time. I chanted for two years but I still didn't know there was such a thing as a devotee. I didn't even know that Krishna was a name of God.

When I finally went to New Vrindavan I was brand new to Krishna consciousness. I didn't know anyone there and felt lost. But in a *Bhagavad-gita* class I heard Ishan say, "If you don't have any service and you're not sure what to do, pray to Prabhupada and he'll send you some." Later that day I was sitting under a tree trying to read *Bhagavad-gita*. I couldn't understand it but I suddenly remembered what Ishan had said. I thought, "Srila Prabhupada, could you please send me some service?" Instantly a woman walked up to me and said, "There's going to be three weddings tonight. Could you go to that field and pick flowers?" I said, "Yeah, I'd love to." I honestly felt that Srila Prabhupada was walking beside me. I felt his presence so strongly that it was almost as if I could see him. It was mystical and miraculous because at that time I had no sense of Prabhupada but I knew that he was with me. It was powerful and loving and wonderful.

Prajapati: The day after Prabhupada saw one of the *Bhagavad-gita* dance programs that I had narrated he went on a tour of the BBT warehouse. I wasn't there but I heard that one of the devotees running a forklift ran into the ceiling lights and other devotees apologized to Prabhupada for his mistake. Everybody was nervous around Prabhupada. At that time Prabhupada talked about our dance performance and said, "Let them dance only, let them paint only. Whatever they love to do, let them do that for Krishna. That is the most important thing."

Prabhupada liked having the drama or dance narrated so that we could perform it in any language. The actors or dancers wouldn't have to learn Spanish or Russian or whatever, because a narrator told the story while the others performed. We did the *Bhagavad-gita* dance twice for Prabhupada and after the first time he saw it he said there should be rear projections. If the narration was about a sage in the forest, then we should show a picture of that. A year or two later we did the same performance again but we still didn't have the projections and Prabhupada mentioned the same point again. He thought it important that, instead of just seeing Krishna and Arjuna in a *Bhagavad-gita* performance, the audience should also see what the narrator was talking about.

Sukadev: Prabhupada was sitting on the stage in the temple on La Cienega Boulevard and to his right was Lord Jagannatha. At the end of the class some Christian spoke some nonsense philosophy but Prabhupada didn't even look at him. He simply sat there and occasionally looked at Lord Jagannatha, as if the person speaking didn't exist. But Prabhupada listened to everything that man said. Then Prabhupada looked at him and screamed, "Christ said, 'Thou shall not kill!' Why are you killing?" At that time I was a new devotee and a meat-eater but when Prabhupada said that, it scared the meat-eating right out of me. Everyone in that temple room was frozen and the Christian had nothing to say, although he had plenty of time to respond. Prabhupada's potency was immediate. There was no philosophy that you had to learn, there was nothing that you had to retain or absorb. Prabhupada was so powerful that your realization was immediate. In front of Srila Prabhupada you would never again think of eating meat. His speaking was like a cold wind blowing off a tree's last few leaves. Prabhupada blew all the nonsense out of that person and anyone else there was convinced to never eat meat.

Prajapati: One day when I went to see Prabhupada, he talked about the principles of dance and drama and he asked me to come back the next day to talk about theology. That day he said, "Call all the *sannyasis* in here." The *sannyasis* were wondering, "What's going on?" and crowded into Prabhupada's room. Prabhupada talked about Christianity and Krishna consciousness. He said, "If Christians want to worship Jesus, all they have to do is have two altars – one altar where Jesus is worshiped and one altar where Radha and Krishna are worshiped." I said, "Prabhupada, it would be better if they had an altar for Lord Jesus and then one for you." Prabhupada modestly motioned "no" with hand but I thought, "Prabhupada's in the same category as Lord Jesus Christ. He is the guru for the world."

Jagajivan: I filmed Prabhupada speaking with two lawyers in Caracas. He preached to them about responsibility, about the differences between state law and the laws of nature, and about how in the state law sometimes you will not be convicted after you've done something wrong. But in the natural law, the law of nature, "If you kill an ant you will be prosecuted."

Pita: Prabhupada's god-brother, Akincana Krishna das Babaji, was a great devotee, always jovial and laughing. Prabhupada spoke Bengali with him a lot of the time, but when he first came in Prabhupada said, "Babaji Maharaj, just look at my disciples. See how advanced they are. See how much they love me. See how attentive they are to me and to my every word. They are here to listen to every word I say. They are so obedient and so devoted to me." Babaji Maharaj said, "Yes, they are advanced." At that time I couldn't understand what Prabhupada meant by "advanced."

For many years I remembered the different things that happened in Prabhupada's room, and I kept thinking of that part, how these two *paramahamsas* said we were advanced. But I'm full of material desires and in those days my mind was filled with all kinds of nonsense, even worse than it is now. Then I remembered that Prabhupada said why were advanced: "They are so attentive to me, they love me so much, they are so devoted to me, they want to please me so much, they are listening to my every word." I realized, "An advanced devotee is the one who is attentive to Srila Prabhupada, who is devoted to Prabhupada, who listens to his every word—this is an advanced devotee." It took many years for me to understand this, but that is what Prabhupada was teaching me and teaching all of us.

Candramauli Swami: In New Vrindavan a devotee asked, "Prabhupada, what happens if we have no determination?" Prabhupada said, "Then you are an animal. An animal cannot be determined. As soon as they hear a little sound, they run in fear. So no determination means animal life. You must have determination otherwise you can't execute Krishna consciousness." He made a strong and clear statement: "You are an animal if you can't become determined."

Pita: I never heard Prabhupada refer to the eleven disciples that he was going to ask to initiate as "gurus," but Prabhupada called them "*ritvik acharyas* transparent to the previous *acharya*." For a long time Srila Prabhupada talked to Tamal Krishna Goswami, Bhavananda Maharaj, Satsvarupa Maharaj and others about what he wanted them to do, about how they were to initiate and carry on. Everyone understood that the new people these devotees initiated would be their disciples. In that letter of July 9, 1977, I was surprised to see that the names of the new initiates were entered into Prabhupada's book of disciples because while I was in the room, it seemed that the new people were going to be our god-brothers' disciples and Srila Prabhupada would be their grandfather guru. Prabhupada actually used that phrase, "grandfather guru".

There were tape recordings made all the time. As soon as Prabhupada spoke, someone would turn the recorder on and when he stopped then they'd turn it off. It's not that Prabhupada spoke as he did when he was in good health. Prabhupada mostly just lay quietly and appeared to be resting. But as soon as Prabhupada spoke, they'd hit the "On" switch on the recorder, which was by his head. That's why, when you hear those tapes, there's so much on-off clicking.

Sumati: I was most struck and I'm still always struck by Srila Prabhupada's absolute faith in and his surrender to and his love for Krishna. When he spoke of Krishna, in his voice I could hear his love for Krishna. On one level, I was afraid of Prabhupada because he was also very stern and the devotees were strict about the rules and regulations. But at the same time, whenever Prabhupada would specifically talk about Krishna, there was so much love in his voice that it gave me faith in Krishna—that Krishna is real—and that faith continues to increase. I feel so grateful to Prabhupada. I'm not a good disciple anymore, but every day I thank him that Krishna is in my life and that all of my most intimate friends are devotees of Krishna. I hope that someday I'll again be a good disciple, a good daughter.

Pita: Prabhupada said, "I want to go to Govardhan." Everyone else said, "Srila Prabhupada, we don't think that's a good idea." Prabhupada said, "In the Ramayana, Marici was given a choice: If he didn't become a deer and tempt Rama away from Sita, Ravana would kill him. And if he became a deer, Rama would kill him. So Marici told Ravana, 'Better to be killed by Rama.'" Prabhupada said, "Better to be killed by Rama, better to go to Govardhan. If I stay in this room, it's like being killed by Ravana."

The devotees said, "But Prabhupada, you can't go. The doctor said that if we carry you, you won't even make it to the gate." There was a 15-minute discussion about this around Prabhupada's bed and Prabhupada said, "You have to talk outside. It is too exhausting for me to hear this going on." The devotees went to Prabhupada's garden and discussed his request for a long time. Hansadutta and Lokanath, who went to get the bullock cart to carry Prabhupada, wanted to fulfill Prabhupada's desire. Tamal Krishna Maharaj did not want to take Prabhupada to Govardhan. The talk went on and on and on until the bullock cart came to the gate of the Krishna-Balaram Temple. It was dusk when we heard, "The cart's here. It's time to move Prabhupada from the bed to the cart." Not only were we going to put Prabhupada on the cart, which would probably kill him, but also it was to be at night—even worse. We feared that Prabhupada would leave his body somewhere along the way.

We all went into Prabhupada's room, myself included, went around his bed and said, "Srila Prabhupada, please, please, don't make us put you on this cart." Prabhupada didn't say anything. We begged and begged him—we were crying. Prabhupada said, "If it worries you so much, I don't need to go." The whole anxiety level went from fifty thousand back to zero. We felt, "Oh, now we can relax," and the devotees started leaving Prabhupada's room. When there weren't many people in the room, Tamal Krishna Goswami, who was very intimate with Prabhupada and who had gotten fried in this situation, went to Prabhupada and said, "Prabhupada, we can't understand why you insist on us taking you to Govardhan. We got so upset and worked up. We got this cart and brought it here and were so worried that if we put you on the cart you would die. The way you deal with us simply deepens our attachment every moment. Prabhupada said, "It is my duty." Tamal Krishna said, "What?" Prabhupada said, "It is my duty to make you love me more."

When Prabhupada said, "To make you love me more," whatever love I had for Prabhupada multiplied a thousand times. Prabhupada made us love him so much. If we were with Prabhupada, he increased whatever love we had for him—we became more and more loving toward him. His duty, he said, was to make us love him more. What a wonderful duty. We already loved Prabhupada, but he was getting us to love him more.

Candramauli Swami: The qualities in Srila Prabhupada that stand out in my mind are assuredness, certainty and conviction. Prabhupada didn't hypothesize or theorize. He spoke the truth with such conviction that you could understand that what he said was true. His purity came through with his message and his message could not be argued. I was convinced by Srila Prabhupada's conviction and purity. When he said something with that conviction and that purity, there was nothing else to say. You were convinced. That's the outstanding quality that attracted me to Prabhupada.

Generally when philosophers speak, there's a sense of uncertainty. Or if they're not uncertain, then they're trying to convince themselves while they try to convince you. Prabhupada wasn't like that. When he spoke it was, "This is the way it is. This is it." I liked that. I'm impressed and attracted when someone speaks like that. And when Prabhupada spoke, it was powerful. Therefore I had no problem with anything he did or said. I never questioned anything because I could see that he was a unique personality.

Pita: At one point, all the devotees were with Srila Prabhupada in his room. Bhavananda, Giriraj, Jayapataka Maharaj, Satsvarupa Maharaj, Jayadvaita, Panca Dravida, they were all there. Prabhupada said, "Of my disciples, I see no one who has my qualities. But if I look at this or that disciple, I see some qualities. And if I look at a group of them, some percentage of my qualities is certainly there. So I have some hope that this movement can continue. The test of your love for me will be shown in how well you work together."

I felt Prabhupada was saying that no one person was going to be our leader but that a group of devotees together would have a percentage of Srila Prabhupada's qualities. Even all the devotees on the GBC taken together have only a percentage of Srila Prabhupada's qualities. I heard this from Prabhupada himself that within the GBC there is a percentage of his qualities, so we have some hope that this society will go on. It has gone on for thirty years and it will continue to go on. Of his *sannyasa* disciples Prabhupada said that if they fall down after he leaves they can never be given *sannyasa* again. He said, "If you do give them *sannyasa* again, their fall down will go on forever. So if a *sannyasi* falls down, they can never enter the *sannyasa* ashram again. Only I can do this. Only I can reinstate them. You cannot reinstate." That was his order.

I think all this happened in the same day in the order that I'm saying it. Prabhupada then said, "I want one million dollars put in a fixed account, and I want that money never to be withdrawn. And the interest on this money will go to renovate the holy places of Lord Chaitanya's pastimes, those that are *gupta* or *lupta*, hidden or lost. We want them revealed and brought back." A devotee said, "Srila Prabhupada, which holy places, the ones in Bengal, Bangladesh or in Orissa?" Prabhupada said, "The ones in Bengal first. But before we do any renovation of these holy places, I want my god-brother Sridhar Maharaj's Sri Chaitanya Saraswati Math finished because he's worked his whole life to establish this *math*. I want him to see that finished before he dies."

Sarvabhavana: After the Gaur Purnima festival in March-April of '77, Prabhupada came to Juhu. At that time the Juhu temple had opened but work was still going on in the adjoining twin towers guesthouse. Prabhupada's quarters were on the top floor of one of the towers. We greeted Srila Prabhupada at the front gate and I took the opportunity to hop into the one little place left in the front seat of the car. Srila Prabhupada was in the back seat, and Gopal Krishna Maharaj, Surabhi Maharaj (the architect), and Hari Sauri prabhu were also in the car. Srila Prabhupada was looking straight ahead and his features were a little drawn because he was not well. When we passed the twin towers, Prabhupada looked to the right, saw it pass, didn't say anything and again looked straight ahead. We stopped in front of his old quarters in one of those two-story buildings in the back of the property, where the BBT was housed, and we all hopped out, opened the trunk and took out the luggage while Prabhupada sat in the car. There was a flurry of activity as we took Prabhupada's luggage and everything else upstairs. Then a devotee informed Prabhupada, "All your luggage is upstairs, you may come now." Prabhupada said, "This is not my house. My quarters are there in the twin tower. Why did you bring me here?" It was embarrassing for Surabhi Maharaj because Prabhupada's quarters in the tower were not complete. Surabhi Maharaj hedged and hawed and wrung his hands, and Prabhupada said, "I'm not staying here. You promised to take me to my quarters so take me there," and remained seated in the car. He didn't raise his voice—he was very calm. Everybody put all the things back in the car and we returned to the guesthouse.

Since the guesthouse elevator wasn't complete, it didn't reach the ground level yet, so two of us carried Prabhupada on a palanquin to the first floor and from there Prabhupada took the elevator to the top floor. We all went up also. His marble floor needed to be polished, there was muck everywhere, and his windows were not in place so a strong breeze was blowing in from the sea about fifty meters away. Prabhupada sat in a chair as we washed his lotus feet and then Surabhi Maharaj offered him *gurupuja*. Surabhi Maharaj wanted to make amends for what he had done but the flame in the ghee lamp he was offering kept blowing out and he was fumbling.

In the meanwhile Surabhi Maharaj arranged to have Prabhupada's reception area cleansed and he also arranged for a little carpet, a small table and a sitting *asana* for Prabhupada there. After the *gurupuja*, Prabhupada quietly came and sat in his reception area. Most of the devotees were asked to leave and about ten of us remained—Gopal Krsna Maharaj, Surabhi Maharaj, Giriraj and some others—and we all sat down with our heads hanging down. We expected a thunderstorm from Prabhupada because his quarters were so messy and noisy. Prabhupada had his head hanging down also. We sat like this for several minutes in pin drop silence. Time lost its meaning. Finally Prabhupada raised his head and spoke in a soft and tender voice. He said, "All of you are trying so hard to please this old man who gets irritated so fast. I am old and on top of that I am unwell so little things irritate me, but all of you are so tolerant." He went on like that for about ten minutes. I thought I was the only one who was crying but when I looked around I saw that everyone had tears in their eyes, including Prabhupada. It was so sweet, so wonderful. How can you not love such a person? That was one of the most beautiful experiences I had with Srila Prabhupada.

Pita: When he was in his room, Srila Prabhupada talked about his god-brothers. He said, "I am the only son of my Guru Maharaj. The son inherits the father's business and of my god-brothers, I'm the only one who has inherited my father's business. The rest of my god-brothers are like daughters because the daughters stay within the house of the father. They don't inherit the business. My Guru Maharaj had only one son and that is me. The Gaudiya Math deviated so much from our spiritual master. But next to me they're still the best representatives of Lord Chaitanya on this planet." So first is Prabhupada, then the Gaudiya Math. That's how Prabhupada saw it.

At this time, Prabhupada told Swarup Damodar that there are four kinds of birth. There is birth from the egg, birth from sweat, birth from the womb and birth from the seed. He said, "So there's four kinds of birth, but scientists say that life comes from a combination of chemicals. Life comes in four ways—through seeds, through sweat, through the womb and through eggs. Life comes from life. The scientists cannot understand the verse from *Bhagavad-gita, brahma-bhuta prasannatma, na socati na kanksati*. They cannot understand that the *brahma-bhuta* person is self-realized and experiences happiness within. Even if his body is completely destroyed, he is in ecstasy." Then he said, "I am that *brahma-bhuta* person." Those were Prabhupada's last words when he was speaking to us. "I am that *brahma-bhuta* person."

Candramauli Swami: Prabhupada talked about his eternal bodily color. He said, "My color is golden with a tinge of red." If we search the scriptures we will find that Lord Nityananda is gold with a red tint. I don't want to say anything beyond that, but Prabhupada said that was his color. It was one of those moments.

Pita: At one point Prabhupada said that he had prayed his whole life to give up eating, sleeping, mating and defending. Can you imagine praying to Krishna, "Dear Krishna, please let me give up eating, sleeping, mating and defending?" Prabhupada said, "I already gave up the defending and the mating and by this disease I have also given up the eating and the sleeping. So Krishna has finally answered my prayer. Now my sense of smell is gone. When you cannot smell anymore, that means death will come soon." Prabhupada was revealing his true nature to us. He is completely free from eating, sleeping, mating and defending. The eating and the sleeping part are a little hard to give up, but he did it.

GLOSSARY

abhishek—the ceremony of bathing the Deity of the Lord or the feet of a great devotee.

Accha—a mild exclamation: "I see!" or "Oh, good!"

acharya—a spiritual master who teaches by example.

advaita—nonduality; that is, there is no difference between the form of the Lord and the Lord Himself.

Advaita Acharya—the associate of Lord Caitanya Mahaprabhu who invoked the Lord's appearance by his prayers.

antya-lila—the final pastimes on earth, including one's passing away.

arati—a ceremony of worship to the Deity form of the Lord or His pure devotee.

Arya-samaj—a recent sect whose teachings are based exclusively on the four *Vedas,* rejecting all other Vedic scriptures.

asana—seat.

ashram—(1) one of the four spiritual orders of life; (2) a residence for those in spiritual practice.

Back to Godhead—the periodical founded by Srila Prabhupada in 1944 to explain the science of Krishna consciousness and its applicability to our life; it continues to this day.

babaji—a renounced devotee who practices chanting Hare Krishna in solitude.

badi—spicy, dried *dahl* (bean) cakes used as an ingredient in many Indian dishes.

BBT—Bhaktivedanta Book Trust, the publishing entity founded by Srila Prabhupada to publish his books and treatises on Krishna consciousness.

Bhagavad-gita—"Song of God," the essential summary of spiritual knowledge spoken to Arjuna by the Supreme Lord, Sri Krishna.

Bhagavat—that related to Bhagavan, the Supreme Lord, especially the Lord's devotee and the scripture *Srimad-Bhagavatam.*

Bhagavat sabdas—recitations of devotional hymns about the Supreme Lord, especially *Srimad Bhagavatam.*

Bhagavatam—See: *Srimad-Bhagavatam.*

bhajan—devotional music and song performed in worship of God or His pure devotee.

bhajan-kutir—a small hut in which a renounced devotee lives and practices his worship of the Lord.

bhakta—a devotee, one who practices devotion (to God).

bhakti—devotion and love, especially for the Supreme Lord.

Bhaktisiddhanta—Srila Bhaktisiddhanta Sarasvati, the spiritual master of A.C. Bhaktivedanta Swami Prabhupada.

Bhaktivedanta Swami—A.C. Bhaktivedanta Swami Prabhupada, the subject of this book.

Bharat-natyam—a classical, devotional Indian dance form.

bhava—ecstasy; the stage of *bhakti* just prior to pure love for God.

bhoga—unoffered foodstuff.

brahma-bhuta—the transcendentally blissful state of freedom from material contamination.

brahmachari—a male celibate student of the spiritual master.

brahmacharini—a female celibate student of the spiritual master.

brahmajyoti—the impersonal effulgence of Krishna's form.

brahmana—one in the intelligent class; a second spiritual initiation.

Brahma-samhita—a scriptural text, prayers to Lord Krishna by Lord Brahma.

brahminical—related to the *brahmanas* and their principles, especially cleanliness, truthfulness, mercy, and austerity.

brijbasis—the residents of Vrindavan (Vraja, or Braja).

BTG—*Back to Godhead* magazine, the official publication of ISKCON, founded by Srila Bhaktivedanta Swami Prabhupada.

burfi—a sweet similar to a milk fudge.

Caitanya Bhagavat—Vrndavan das Thakur's account of Lord Caitanya Mahaprabhu's early life.

caitya-guru—Krishna, as the spiritual master within the heart of the living being.

chadar—a shawl.

Chaitanya-caritamrita—the authoritative scripture by Krishnadas Kaviraj, which describes Lord Chaitanya's teachings and pastimes.

Chaitanya Mahaprabhu, Lord—the avatar of Lord Krishna in this age whose mission is to teach love of God through the chanting of His holy names.

Caitanya Siksamrta—Srila Bhaktivinoda Thakur's work about the life and glories of Lord Chaitanya Mahaprabhu.

chamara—a yak-tail fan.

champak—an especially fragrant orange-yellow flower of an evergreen tree native to India.

chapati—a whole-wheat flatbread.

charanamrita—water remnants from bathing the Deity or a saintly person.

chokidar—watchman.

dab—a green coconut, still filled with a quantity of drinkable coconut "milk."

dahl—a spicy bean or pea soup.

dakshin—a gift offering to one's spiritual master.

danda—the staff of a sannyasi.

dandavats—prostrate obeisances.

darshan—audience with the Deity or a saintly person.

Deities—the authorized forms of the Lord worshiped in temples.

dham—a holy place.

dharma—the intrinsic service nature of the living entity; the particular service or duty according to one's nature.
dhoti—the standard Indian men's garment, a simple piece of cloth wrapped around the lower body.
diksa—formal initiation into devotional life.

Ekadasi—twice-monthly days of fasting and remembering the Lord.

Gaudiya Math—the spiritual organization and missions founded by Srila Bhaktisiddhanta Sarasvati, the spiritual master of A.C. Bhaktivedanta Swami Prabhupada.
Gaudiya Vaishnav—a follower of Lord Krishna (Vishnu) in the line from Lord Chaitanya Mahaprabhu.
Gaura-Nitai—Lord Chaitanya (Gaura) and Lord Nityananda (Nitai) together, especially in Their Deity forms.
Gaur-purnima—the appearance day anniversary of Lord Caitanya.
gayatri—a transcendental vibration chanted by *brahmans* for spiritual realization.
GBC—the Governing Body Commission of ISKCON, the International Society for Krishna Consciousness.
ghee—clarified butter.
Gita—See: *Bhagavad-gita.*
gopis—the cowherd girls and women of Vrindavan, who are the most advanced and intimate devotees of Lord Krishna.
Grantha—the principal sacred text of Sikhism.
grihamedhi—a materialistic householder.
grihastha—the stage, or one in that stage, of householder life according to the Vedic social system.
gulabjamons—cake-like fried milk balls in scented syrup.
guna—material mode, or quality.
guru—spiritual master.
gurudeva—an affectionate reference to guru.

gurukula—the school of the spiritual master.
gurupuja—the ceremony of worship to the spiritual master.
guru-tattva—the knowledge of the true nature of the *guru*, or spiritual master.
Gurvastakam—the standard prayer to the Vaisnav spiritual master by Visvanatha Cakravarti Thakur.

halava—a dessert made from toasted grains, sugar, and butter.
Haribol—a greeting or exclamation meaning "Chant the holy names of Lord Hari (Krishna)."
harinam [*sankirtan*]—congregational, public chanting of the holy names of Hari, or Krishna.
harmonium—an organlike keyboard instrument with reeds actuated by air from a bellows.

ISKCON—International Society for Krishna Consciousness, whose Founder-Acarya is A.C. Bhaktivedanta Swami Prabhupada.
Isopanishad—See: *Sri Isopanishad.*
istagosthi—a meeting of devotees to discuss the instructions of their spiritual master.

Jagannatha—the Lord of the Universe; a special Deity of Lord Krishna, first appearing in Puri, India.
jagat guru—the guru, or spiritual master, for the entire world.
Janmastami—the day of celebration of the "birthday," or appearance day, of Lord Krishna.
japa—soft, measured chanting of the holy names of God, performed with the aid of 108 prayer beads.
Jaya—an expression of acclaim.
Jaya om prayers—the *prema-dhvani* prayers of obeisances and respects recited following *arati.*
jiva / *jivatma*—the soul, or atomic living entity.
jiva-tattva—the living entities, atomic parts of the Supreme Lord.

kachori—a deep-fried stuffed savory pastry.
Kali-yuga—the present age of confusion and quarrel, which began 5,000 years ago.
karma—action; results of fruitive actions.
karmi—one engaged in karma (fruitive activity); a materialist.
kartals—small hand cymbals used to accompany chanting during *kirtans*.
kartik—a lunar month in autumn.
katha—recitations.
kaviraj—an Ayurvedic doctor.
kichari—a cooked preparation made from spiced rice and lentils.
ki jaya—an expression of acclaim.
kirtan—chanting of the Lord's names and glories.
kirtaniya—a leader of congregational chanting.
kripa-siddha—one liberated via the mercy of the Lord.
Krishna—the all-attractive Supreme Lord, God, in his original, eternal form.
Krishna-katha—topics about or by Krishna or His devotees.
Krishnaloka—the topmost spiritual abode of Lord Krishna.
krishna-tattva—in truth the Supreme Lord, Sri Krishna, or His direct, personal expansion.
Krsna book—the summary study of the Tenth Canto of *Srimad-Bhagavatam,* detailing Krishna's pastimes, by A.C. Bhaktivedanta Swami Prabhupada.
ksatriya—the administrative or protective occupational classification according to the *varnashram* system; one of that occupation or nature.
kurta—the long, loose-fitting, Indian men's shirt.

lakh—100,000.
laxmi—money meant for the Lord's use. (Informal derivative from "Laksmi," the goddess of fortune.)
lila—transcendental pastimes of the Lord; a type of relationship with the Lord.

Lilamrta—the ISKCON-authorized, multivolume biography of Srila Prabhupada.
lota—a small pot for water used for personal cleaning.
lugdoo, lugloo—a sweet of fried batter pearls, nuts, and dried fruit.

madhyama-adhikari—one in the intermediate stage of God realization.
maha—See *maha prasadam*.
mahabhagavata—a great personality who sees all in relation to God.
maha-mantra—the great chanting for deliverance: Hare Krishna, Hare Krishna, Krishna Krishna, Hare Hare / Hare Rama, Hare Rama, Rama Rama, Hare Hare.
maha prasadam—*prasadam* remnants directly from the plate or the person of the Deity or the pure devotee.
mala—a string of prayer beads, as *japa* beads.
mandala—district.
mandap—a shelter.
mandir—a temple.
mangal arati—pre-dawn worship ceremony in temples of the Lord.
mangalacharanam—the standard prayers of glorification to the spiritual master.
mantra—a sound vibration, a phrase or prayer, that liberates the mind.
mata-guru—the mother as *guru,* or guide.
mataji—"mother," a respectful appellation for women; a respected woman.
maya—illusion, accepting as true what is not; forgetfulness of Krishna, or God, and our own spiritual nature.
Mayapur—the holy birthplace of Lord Caitanya Mahaprabhu, in Bengal, India.
mayavadi—impersonalist or voidist, who adheres to the mistaken belief that God is ultimately formless and without personality; pertaining to such a philosophy.

mleccha—a low-class person; meat-eater.
mleccha-desh—the land of *mlecchas.*
mridanga—a two-headed drum used to accompany chanting in *kirtan.*
muchi—dirty.
mudhas— foolish, asslike persons.
mudras—specialized symbolic hand gestures.
murti—a bona fide form of the Lord, wherein He appears to accept service.

nagar sankirtan—the congregational chanting of the Lord's names in moving line.
nama-hatta—"marketplace of the holy name," a home-to-home preaching program.
Nanda—Lord Krishna's foster father, who raised Him in Vrindavan.
Narada Muni—a great devotee of the Lord, who is empowered to travel anywhere in the material or spiritual worlds.
Navadvipa—the holy birthplace of Lord Caitanya Mahaprabhu in Bengal, India.
neem—the *nima* tree, whose wood and leaves have antiseptic properties.
nirvana—the blissful state at the of end of materialistic life and material consciousness.
nitya-siddha—eternally perfected or liberated.
Nrisimha(deva)—the incarnation of Lord Krishna in the form of half-lion, half man, who is especially dedicated to protecting the Lord's devotees.

om—*Omkara,* the sacred sound that is the beginning of many Vedic *mantras* and which represents the Supreme Lord.

paisa—1/100 of a rupee.
pakoras—vegetable pieces fried in a spiced chick-pea-flour batter.

Panchatattva—Lord Chaitanya with His associates.
pandal—a large tent covering.
pandit—a scholar.
papita—a tree cultivated for its edible fruits and medicinal qualities.
paramahamsa—a topmost, God-realized devotee.
parampara—the line of disciplic succession; also, that in accordance with their teachings.
parikram—circumambulation of a holy place.
Pishima—Bengali for "Aunty," Prabhupada's affectionate name for his sister.
pita-guru—the father as *guru,* or guide.
prabhu—respected devotee.
Prabhupada—"the spiritual master at whose feet all others take shelter"; here, His Divine Grace A.C. Bhaktivedanta Swami.
prakriti—material nature, the energy of the Supreme; the enjoyed.
pranams—obeisances with folded hands.
prasadam—"mercy," vegetarian foodstuffs and other items that are sanctified by being first offered to Lord Krishna for His enjoyment.
puja—worship service.
pujari—the priest who cares for and performs worship service for the Lord.
puri—a fried, puffed, white-flour flatbread.
purusha—the enjoyer, or male; the living entity or the Supreme Lord.

Radha, Radharani—the eternal consort of Lord Krishna, a manifestation of His internal pleasure potency.
raga—a traditional melodic type in spiritually-themed music.
Rama(chandra)—Krishna's incarnation as the ideal king.
rasa—the relationship between the Lord and the living entities, which is in different categories.

rasa lila—Krishna's pastime, or *lila,* of dancing with the *gopis.*
rasagulla—a milk sweet made from curd soaked in sweetened water.
Rathayatra—a large *sankirtan* festival wherein Deities of the Lord ride in parade.
regulative principles—the four prohibitions for human life, which disciples accept by vow: no illicit sex, no gambling, no intoxication, and no meat-eating.
Rig Veda—the first of the four *Vedas,* the original scriptures spoken by the Lord Himself.
ritvik—priest.
rupee—the money unit of India.

sabdas—recitations of devotional hymns such as *Srimad-Bhagavatam.*
sadhana—disciplined spiritual practice.
sadhana-siddha—one liberated via regulated practice.
sadhu—a saint, holy man, or Krishna conscious devotee.
sahajiya—a pretender who imitates the outward mood and ecstasies of the Lord's devotee, but who is without any real devotion or internal realization.
samadhi—(1) a spiritual trance, complete absorption in God consciousness; (2) a tomb memorial of a saintly person.
samosa— a fried pastry, stuffed with spiced vegetables.
sampradaya—disciplic succession.
samsara—the cycle of repeated birth and death.
Samsara prayers—"Sri Sri Gurv-astaka" by Srila Visvanatha Cakravarti Thakura, a song in eight verses glorifying the spiritual master.
sanatana-dharma—the eternal duty, or religion, of devotional service to God.
sandesh—a sweet prepared from milk curd.
sandhya arati—the evening worship ceremony to the Deities of the Lord.

sangam—association.

sankirtan—congregational glorification of God, especially through chanting of His holy name, the recommended process of yoga for this age.

sannyasa—the renounced order of spiritual life.

sannyasi—one in the renounced order of spiritual life.

sarat season—the autumn season, when Lord Krishna danced his *rasa* dance with the *gopis*.

sari—the standard woman's garment in Indian society, a long piece of (usually decorative) cloth wrapped around the lower and upper body and often also covering the head.

sastra—scripture.

sat-sanga—the company of the highest knowledge and truth, esp. as embodied in the Lord's pure devotees.

seva—service.

shakti—spiritual energy or potency.

shalagram shila—a small stone form of the Lord.

siddhanta—the fundamental truth or scriptural conclusion on a subject.

siksa guru—the guru who gives spiritual guidance.

Siksastaka(m)—the eight and only verses written personally by Lord Caitanya Mahaprabhu.

Siva—the great devotee demigod in charge of the mode of ignorance and destruction of the material universe.

sloka—a verse.

Sri Isopanishad—an ancient, 19-verse, Upanishadic scripture providing insight into God's nature.

Srimad-Bhagavatam—the scriptural *Purana,* or history, written by Vyasadeva specifically to give an understanding of Lord Sri Krishna.

subji—a cooked vegetable preparation.

suchi—clean.

sudras—the laborer occupational classification according to the *varnashram* system; one of that occupation or nature.

Sumati Morarji—a wealthy Indian industrialist; she provided Srila Prabhupada passage to America.
sutra—a philosophical aphorism.
swami—one who has mastered his senses.

tapasya—austerity.
Teachings of Lord Chaitanya—the summary study, by A.C. Bhaktivedanta Swami Prabhupada, of the life and teachings of Lord Chaitanya Mahaprabhu.(See also: Chaitanya Mahaprabhu.)
The Nectar of Devotion—the summary study, by A.C. Bhaktivedanta Swami Prabhupada, of Srila Rupa Goswami's *Bhaktirasamrita Sindhu*, which explains the science of *bhakti*-yoga.
tiffin—lunch box, typically in a stacked container set.
tilak—sacred clay marking the body of a devotee as a temple of God.
tulasi(-devi)—a great devotee of Krishna, in the form of a plant.

ugra-karma—horrible, or sinful, works that bring concomitant karmic reactions.
Upadesamrta—The Nectar of Instruction, by Srila Rupa Gosvami.
urad dahl—a soup made from the *urad* bean.
uttama-adhikari—one in the highest stage of God-realization.
uttariya—an upper garment of wrapped and draped cloth.

Vaikuntha—the spiritual world, where there is no anxiety.
Vaishnav—a devotee of the Supreme Lord Vishnu, or Krishna.
vaisya—the class of persons involved in business and farming according to the *varnasrama* system of four social and four spiritual orders.
vanaprastha—one retired from householder life to cultivate greater renunciation, according to the Vedic social system.
Vandeham prayers—The *Mangalacharana* prayer for offering respects to one's spiritual master, other Vaishnavs in disciplic succession, and the Supreme Lord.

varnashram—the four divisions of society and four divisions of spiritual life according to one's individual nature.

varnashram-dharma—*varnashram,* especially the rules and duties of *varnashram.*

Vedanta—related to the *Vedas,* the "end of all knowledge."

Vedanta Sutra—the philosophical summary of all Vedic conclusions, written in short aphorisms by Srila Vyasadeva.

Vedas—the original four revealed scriptures, first spoken by the Lord Himself, and their supplements.

vina—a stringed musical instrument favored by the devotee Narada Muni.

Vishakhapatnam—a city of eastern India on the Bay of Bengal northeast of Chennai (Madras), in Andhra Pradesh.

Vishnu—the all-pervading Personality of Godhead, a plenary expansion of Krishna.

Vrindavan—Krishna's eternal abode, where He fully manifests His quality of sweetness; the village on this earth where He enacted His childhood pastimes 5,000 years ago.

vyakarana—grammar education.

Vyasa-puja—the observance of the appearance day of one's spiritual master, the representative of Vyasadeva.

vyasasana—the seat of honor offered to the spiritual master.

wala—a merchant, tradesperson.

yajna—sacrifice; sacrificial ceremony.

Yasoda—Krishna's foster mother, who raised Him in Vrindavan.

yavana—one who does not follow the Vedic principles of life; meat-eater.

yogi—one who practices spiritual discipline to link with the Supreme.

yogini—a female yogi.